Walking the Parables of Jesus

A Journey into the Words, Life and Times of Jesus Christ

Deacon Robert E. Evans

En Route Books & Media, LLC
St. Louis, MO

Nihil obstat:
Rev. Michael L. Diskin
Censor Deputatus

Imprimatur:
Most Rev Thomas J. Olmsted
Bishop, Diocese of Phoenix

June 27, 2018

Unless otherwise stated, the Scripture citations used in this work are taken from the *New American Bible, revised edition* © 2010, 1991, 1986, 1970 by the Confraternity of Christian Doctrine. Excerpts are from the United States Conference of Catholic Bishops website, www.usccb.org.

Excerpts from the *Catechism of the Catholic Church* are from the second edition for use in the United States of America, © 1994 and 1997, Libreria Editrice Vaticana. Excerpts from Vatican documents are from the Vatican website, www.vatican.va.

Every reasonable effort has been made to determine copyright holders and to give proper credit to those sources of materials used. If any copyrighted materials have been inadvertently used without proper credit being given, in one manner or another, please notify the author so that correction may be made in any future editions.

cover design by TJ Burdick
asyouwishmedia.com

ISBN: 978-1-950108-26-8

Library of Congress Control Number: 2019947135

Subject: REL006710

Copyright © 2019 by Deacon Robert E Evans

If anyone wishes to use any of the material in this work, just indicate where it came from.

Dedication

To my wife, Rose, whose love is my greatest
treasure as we walk together with Jesus Christ,
in this life and into eternity.

Preface

There is a wonderful movement going on among Catholics in recent years, a growing desire to better understand Scripture, and particularly the teachings of Jesus in the Gospels, and most especially in His parables.

For a very long time, if there was a Bible in the Catholic household, it was often just the place for keeping the records of the children's baptisms and marriages. Rarely did the family read from the Bible, letting "Father interpret it for us at mass." Our Protestant friends and neighbors (and more recently, family members) have been much more "fluent' in biblical verses. Bible Study classes were provided, almost exclusively by Protestant denominations. But all that is changing. More and more Catholic parishes are offering Bible Study sessions.

Vatican II sought to invigorate Catholic, as well as non-Catholic, engagement in reading the Bible. In doing so, the Council's Dogmatic Constitution on Divine Revelation (*Dei Verbum*, which means "Word of God") stated that for the correct understanding of what was intended in Sacred Scripture attention must be paid to the culture and characteristic styles of speaking and narrating which prevailed at the time of the writer.[1]

Catholics, and indeed most Christians, understand that God did not literally dictate biblical passages. And, biblical passages were not intended to teach history. They are faith lessons taught through prophetic and story forms. God's "message" is conveyed through the lesson taught by the original author, using that author's manner of expression, imagery and cultural terminologies which would have been understandable to the original author's listeners. While God's "message" is timeless, the original author's lesson is rooted in the times and life circumstances of the text's author.

This book expands on a series of "Bible Study" sessions which I led at Blessed Sacrament Roman Catholic parish in Scottsdale, Arizona from September 28, 2016 through February 8, 2017. Unlike many Bible Study series, these sessions did not cover individual Bible books, cover to cover, but rather addressed the broader subject of Jesus' Parables, which come from the Gospels of Matthew, Mark and Luke.

In keeping with the spirit of *Dei Verbum*, article 12, the sessions particularly focused on "hearing" the parables in their original context (at least as best as a number of biblical scholars have placed them), taking into account the culture and traditions of those who were likely Jesus' first listeners. Catholic teaching stresses that there is no one method for Biblical Study. Instead, Catholics remain open to a wide variety of approaches and these sessions were one such approach.

I am an ordained deacon in the Roman Catholic Church. As such, I sought in these sessions, and in this book, to adhere to the principles of Bible Study set out in the *Catechism of the Catholic Church,* particularly in articles 112 thru 114.

There is a unity to the whole of Scripture. All are part of God's mysterious and unfolding revelation of Himself and His plan of salvation. [cf. *Catechism of the Catholic Church* #112]. Jesus' parables, and how they were interpreted, made Old Testament passages and events more fully understood, in His time, and in our own.

Recognizing the role of the Holy Spirit in guiding the process of interpretation throughout history, interpretations were consistent with "the living Tradition of the whole Church." [cf. *Catechism of the Catholic Church,* #113]. Also, there is a mutual consistency to the whole of Scripture. Though we may not comprehend every detail of God's plan of salvation, there is a "coherence of truths" embedded in the Scriptures. [cf. *Catechism of the Catholic Church* #114]. God's revelation does not contradict itself.

My training as a deacon, from 2000 through 2006, included a number of courses in Biblical Studies at the Kino Institute, which is operated by the Roman Catholic Diocese of Phoenix. Since then, through self-directed study, I have focused on gaining a deeper understanding of the cultural and social aspects of life in Jesus' time and the works of biblical scholars who have studied and taught in the Middle East; this with the intent of being able to proclaim the Gospels more meaningfully and to teach their lesson more clearly. So, I am not a biblical scholar, rather I draw heavily from the works of many others. (See the **Bibliography** section of this book for a complete list of the sources and references for the material presented in the class sessions and in this book.)

I welcome you to the pages of this book on Jesus' Parables. More than 36 hours of recording were made of the class sessions held at Blessed Sacrament, from which the text of this book was derived. I have edited the material to remove some of the banter that is typical of a classroom setting, and I tried to avoid giving too much of a "textbook tone" to the result. I have applied my best efforts to making this book accurate and true to the Gospel texts. But, it is not intended to be a scholarly treatise but, truly, a journey into the words, life and times of Our Lord, Jesus Christ that we might draw closer to Him in our own lives.

As we journey, we can offer some educated guesses as to why Jesus did or said certain things. But, we recognize that much of the "why" about Jesus lies in that impenetrable area He called *"my Father's will"* [Jn 6:40]. This is an area forever beyond the reach of our full understanding. There will be those who may disagree with some of the conclusions or interpretations offered in this book; that's to be expected. Biblical Study is not an exacting science; and people come to Scriptures from many different perspectives. We do the best we can with what we have in our times. We are fortunate in that we benefit from the exegetic efforts of many others to gain deeper insights into the word of God, in our day, than were available to our parents. And, as the Holy Spirit continues to work in our midst, our children and grandchildren will have even deeper insights than we've been blessed with.

I thank the many who attended the sessions, week after week. They were deeply investing in hearing the Word of God more clearly and many of their questions, along with the handouts, have been blended into the material covered in this book. My special thanks go to our recently retired pastor, Fr Patrick Robinson, whose long support for Bible Studies at the parish level fostered a number of Bible Study series that are on-going each year at Blessed Sacrament. I personally owe much to Fr. Pat for his encouragement, support and friendship in my diaconate service.

The prophet Jeremiah once wrote: *"When I found your words, Lord, I devoured them; and they became the joy and happiness of my heart"* [Jer 15:16]. My hope is that your time with the pages of this book will help you hear His Word more clearly, expressed in Jesus' Parables, and that it will become the joy and happiness of your heart.

Dcn. Bob Evans
May 2018

Contents

1. Preparing for the Journey	1
1.1 What is a Parable?	2
1.2 Why did Jesus Teach in Parables?	4
1.3 Ancient Middle Eastern Storytelling	5
1.3.1 Details Convey the Message	5
1.3.2 Honor, the Highest Virtue	10
1.3.3 Public Honor Challenges	13
1.3.4 Chiasms, the Point is in the Middle	16
1.3.5 Dialog is more "Telling"	19
1.3.6 Emphasis through Exaggeration	22
1.4 Knowing the Land	22
1.5 The Synoptic Gospels	28
1.5.1 Mark	30
1.5.2 Matthew	31
1.5.3 Luke	32
1.6 The Benefit of Chronology	33
1.6.1 Estimated Dates in Jesus' Life	34
1.6.2 Estimated Dates of the Events in Holy Week	37
1.7 A Brief Look-ahead	39
2. Jesus' First Journey	42
2.1 Joseph: Jesus' Earthly Father	42
2.2 Nazareth: Jesus' Hometown	44
2.3 Crossing the Jordan	49
2.4 The Judean Wilderness	54
2.5 Ancient Jewish Wedding Customs	56
2.6 The Town of Capernaum	59
3. Jesus' Second Journey	61
3.1 The Samaritans	62
3.2 Shechem (Sychar) and Jacob's Well	64
3.3 The Roots of Hometown Expectations	67
4. Jesus' Third Journey	70
4.1 The Day of Atonement or Yom Kippur	72
4.2 Parable of the New vs. the Old	74
4.2.1 In Matthew's Gospel [Matthew 9:10-17]	75
4.2.2 In Mark' Gospel [Mark 2:15-22]	76
4.2.3 In Luke's Gospel [Luke 5:29-39]	76

4.3 The Spiritual Lesson in the Parable	77
5. Jesus' Fourth Journey	**81**
5.1 Fishing on the Sea of Galilee	81
5.2 Agriculture in Ancient Israel	85
5.3 His Family Came to Get Him	91
6. Jesus' Fifth Journey	**93**
6.1 The Jewish Expectation of the Kingdom of God	94
6.2 Parable of the Two Foundations	95
6.2.1 In Matthew's Gospel [Matthew 7:24-29]	96
6.2.2 In Luke's Gospel [Luke 6:46-49]	96
6.3 The Spiritual Lesson in the Parable	96
6.4 Acting for Beelzebub	99
7. Jesus' Sixth Journey	**102**
7.1 Ancient Jewish Burial Practices	102
7.2 Parable of the Lender [Luke 7:36-50]	106
7.3 Debtors, Servants and Slaves in Ancient Israel	107
7.4 The Spiritual Lesson in the Parable	108
7.5 Parable of the Sower	111
7.5.1 In Matthew's Gospel [Matthew 13:1-23]	111
7.5.2 In Mark's Gospel [Mark 4:1-20]	113
7.5.3 In Luke's Gospel [Luke 8:4-15]	114
7.6 The Spiritual Lesson in the Parable	115
7.7 Discourse Following the Parable of the Sower	116
7.8 The Weeds and the Wheat [Matthew 13:24-43]	121
7.9 The Spiritual Lesson in the Parable	122
7.10 Discourse Following the Parable	124
7.11 Parable of the Lamp	126
7.11.1 In Matthew's Gospel [Matthew 5:14-16]	126
7.11.2 In Mark's Gospel [Mark 4:21-23]	127
7.11.3 In Luke's Gospel [Luke 8:16-17]	127
7.12 The Spiritual Lesson in the Parable	127
7.13 Parable of the Growing Seed [Mark 4:26-29]	128
7.14 The Spiritual Lesson in the Parable	128
7.15 Land "Ownership" in Ancient Israel	131
7.16 Parable of the Joy of Finding [Matthew 13:44-46]	132
7.17 The Spiritual Lesson in the Parable	132
7.18 Parable of the Fishing Net [Matthew 13:47-50]	133
7.19 The Spiritual Lesson in the Parable	133
7.20 Parable of the Head of Household [Mt 13:51-52]	134

7.21 The Spiritual Lesson in the Parable	135
8. Jesus' Seventh Journey	**137**
8.1 Rejected, Again	137
8.2 Bethsaida, Childhood Home of Jesus' 1st Disciples	140
8.3 The Bread of Life Discourse	146
8.4 The Ancient City of Tyre	150
8.5 A Closer Walk with Thee	153
8.6 Parable of Unforgiving Servant [Matthew 18:21-35]	163
8.7 The Spiritual Lesson in the Parable	164
9. Jesus' Eighth Journey	**168**
9.1 Leaving Galilee for the Last Time	168
9.2 Hospitality in Ancient Israel	171
9.3 Parable of the Good Samaritan [Luke 10:25-37]	173
9.4 Role of Lawyers in Ancient Israel	173
9.5 The Hebrew System of Ritual Purity	174
9.6 The Spiritual Lesson in the Parable	176
9.7 The Light of the World	180
9.8 Parable of the Friend in Need [Luke 11:1-13]	182
9.9 The Spiritual Lesson in the Parable	183
10. Jesus' Ninth Journey	**186**
10.1 Perea, Judea across the Jordan	187
10.2 Parable of the Rich Fool [Luke 12:13-22]	192
10.3 The Spiritual Lesson in the Parable	192
10.4 Rabbah, Jewel of the Levant	194
10.5 Parable of the Vigilant Servants	197
10.5.1 In Luke's Gospel [Luke 12:35-41]	197
10.5.2 In Mark's Gospel [Mark 13:33-37]	198
10.6 The Spiritual Lesson in the Parable	198
10.7 Parable of the Prudent and Wicked Servants	201
10.7.1 In Luke's Gospel [Luke 12:42-48]	201
10.7.2 In Matthew's Gospel [Matthew 24:45-51]	202
10.8 The Spiritual Lesson in the Parable	202
10.9 Parable of the Barren Fig Tree [Luke 13:6-9]	210
10.10 The Cultural Position of Fig Trees	210
10.11 The Spiritual Lesson in the Parable	211
10.12 Grace and how it Works in Our Lives	213
10.13 Parable of the Mustard Seed	217
10.13.1 In Matthew's Gospel [Matthew 13:31-32]	217
10.13.2 In Mark's Gospel [Mark 4:30-32]	218

10.13.3 In Luke's Gospel [Luke 13:18-19]	218
10.14 The Spiritual Lesson in the Parable	218
10.15 Parable of the Yeast	219
10.15 1 In Matthew's Gospel [Matthew 13:33]	219
10.15.2 In Luke's Gospel [Luke 13:20-21]	219
10.16 The Spiritual Lesson in the Parable	220
10.17 Parable of the Invitations [Luke 14:7-14]	221
10.18 The Spiritual Lesson in the Parable	222
10.19 Parable of Costs of Discipleship [Luke 14:25-33]	226
10.20 The Spiritual Lesson in the Parable	227
10.21 Parable about being like a Child	229
10.21.1 In Matthew's Gospel [Matthew 18:1-5]	229
10.21.2 In Mark's Gospel [Mark 9:33-37]	229
10.22 The Spiritual Lesson in the Parable	230
10.23 Parable of the Lost Sheep	234
10.23 1 In Luke's Gospel [Luke 15:1-7]	234
10.23.2 In Matthew's Gospel [Matthew 18:12-14]	235
10.24 The Spiritual Lesson in the Parable	235
10.25 Parable of the Lost Coin [Luke 15:8-10]	239
10.26 The Spiritual Lesson in the Parable	239
10.27 "The Man Who Had Two Sons"	241
10.28 Parable of the Prodigal Son [Luke 15:11-32]	243
10.29 The Spiritual Lesson in the Parable	244
10.30 The Encounter with Zacchaeus	253
10.31 Parable of the Shrewd Steward [Luke 16:1-8]	256
10.32 The Spiritual Lesson in the Parable	257
10.33 The "Bosom of Abraham"	257
10.34 Parable of Rich Man and Lazarus [Lk 16:19-31]	258
10.35 The Spiritual Lesson in the Parable	259
10.36 "Whoever believes in me will never die"	264
11. Jesus' Final Mission Journey	267
11.1 Parable of the Attitude of a Servant [Lk 17:7-10]	267
11.2 The Spiritual Lesson in the Parable	268
11.3 Parable of the Persistent Widow [Luke 18:1-7]	273
11.4 The Spiritual Lesson in the Parable	273
11.5 Parable of Pharisee and Tax Collector [Lk 18:9-14]	277
11.6 The Spiritual Lesson in the Parable	278
11.7 Jerusalem and the Temple in the Time of Jesus	282
11.8 Parable of the Workers [Matthew 20:1-16]	292
11.9 The Spiritual Lesson in the Parable	293
11.10 Parable of the Two Sons [Matthew 21:28-32]	299

11.11 The Spiritual Lesson in the Parable	299
11.12 Parable of the Wicked Tenants	302
11.12.1 In Matthew's Gospel [Matthew 21:33-46]	302
11.12.2 In Mark's Gospel [Mark 12:1-12]	303
11.12.3 In Luke's Gospel [Luke 20:9-19]	304
11.13 The Spiritual Lesson in the Parable	305
11.14 Parable of the Feast	309
11.14.1 In Matthew's Gospel [Matthew 22:1-14]	310
11.14.2 The Spiritual Lesson in the Parable	311
11.14.3 In Luke's Gospel [Luke 14:15-24]	314
11.14.4 The Spiritual Lesson in the Parable	314
11.15 Parable of the Fig Tree	327
11.15.1 In Matthew's Gospel [Matthew 24:32-34]	327
11.15.2 In Mark's Gospel [Mark 13:28-30]	327
11.15.3 In Luke's Gospel [Luke 21:29-32]	327
11.16 The Spiritual Lesson in the Parable	328
11.17 The Role of Virgins in Ancient Israel	329
11.18 Parable of the Ten Virgins [Matthew 25:1-13]	331
11.19 The Spiritual Lesson in the Parable	331
11.20 Parable of the Talents	333
11.20.1 In Matthew's Gospel [Matthew 25:14-30]	333
11.20.2 The Spiritual Lesson in the Parable	335
11.20.3 In Luke's Gospel [Luke 19:11-28]	339
11.20.4 The Spiritual Lesson in the Parable	340
11.21 Parable of the Final Judgment [Mt 25:31-46]	346
11.22 The Spiritual Lesson in the Parable	348
12. Closing Thoughts	352
Notes	353
Bibliography	366
Credits	376
Glossary	380
Index of the Parables	420
Index of Names & Subjects	422
Appendix 1: Map of Israel in the Time of Jesus	440

Tables
1. Parables in the Old Testam	3
2. Chiasmic Structure of Parable of the Good Samaritan	18
3. Principal Jewish Holidays	36
4. Estimated Dates of the Events in Holy Week	38

5. Chiasmic Structure of the Parable of the Lost Sheep   237
6. Chiasmic Structure of the Parable of the Lost Coin   240
7. Numbering of the Psalms   356
8. Moral Principles Underlying the Ten Commandments   362

<u>Figures</u>
1. Remains of paved section of Via Maris in Galilee   23
2. Looking South into Samaria   24
3. Looking East from Jerusalem   25
4. Topographical View of Israel   27
5. The Town Well in Nazareth (1894 photo)   44
6. The Jordan River south of the Sea of Galilee   50
7. Al-Maghtas: The Traditional Site of Jesus' Baptism   53
8. David's Falls at Ein-Gedi   55
9. Jacob's Well (1920 photo)   66
10. The Caves of Arbela   71
11. A Musht Fish from the Sea of Galilee   82
12. View from Mt Eremos   93
13. First Interment Caves near Nain   104
14. The Remains of Magdala (colorized 1900 photo)   126
15. The Shoreline near Gergesa   130
16. Ruins of Roman Pools at Bethsaida   142
17. Aerial View of Tyre (1934 French Army photo)   151
18. The Leonites River in the Mount Lebanon Foothills   153
19. Mount Tabor (colorized 1890 photo)   161
20. Samarian foothills (colorized 1895 photo)   177
21. *Biq'ah Yitro* (Valley of Jethro) in Perea   190
22. Ruins of Castle of the Servant   197
23. The upper Jabbok River Valley   208
24. Bedouin Tents at Site of Ancient Penuel   233
25: Topography of Jerusalem in the First Century   284
26: New Testament Jerusalem map   286
27: Map of the Temple in the First Century   289

1. Preparing for the Journey

We're going on a journey. We will "walk along" with Jesus' disciples hearing Him proclaim His parables. We will follow them, from one town to another. In each place, we will consider the social mix Jesus encountered there and the history of the place. We will consider how that might have influenced the 'storyline' of His parable, as well as how they might have understood His message - that we might gain greater insight into the lesson Jesus intended for them, and for us.

I know we are anxious to begin hearing Jesus' parables, but there are several things we need to be more familiar with in order for us to get the most benefit from what we will be hearing. At first, they may seem like a lot to take in at the start, but if you bear with me, these things will prove to be very useful, if not enlightening:

1. We need a better understanding of just what a parable is. There are widely varying views on what a parable is, resulting in considerably different lists of "Jesus' Parables;"
2. We need an appropriate answer to why Jesus taught in parables because that will influence how we interpret what He meant for His listeners;
3. We need to recognize that all of Scripture, including Jesus' Parables, is Middle Eastern stories, by Middle Eastern authors, to Middle Eastern listeners. From Middle Eastern Biblical Anthropology, we learn that ancient Middle Easterners told stories much differently than do people in Western cultures. From knowing the principal features of ancient Middle Eastern storytelling, we can get a better idea of what Jesus intended at the time He was speaking, and what the evangelists, writing decades later, intended in recounting the story of Jesus sharing the parable;
4. We need to "know the land" of first-century Israel. The geography and the cultural norms of the times shaped how the people of that time got from one place to another, where they went and where they did not go; and how they understood one another. And, in particular, how a listener's location might have influenced how they interpreted what they were hearing;

5. Since the accounts of Jesus' Parables come to us from the gospels of Matthew, Mark and Luke (there are no parables recounted in John), we need to have some idea of who these evangelists were writing to, the life circumstances of those first listeners, and how that might have shaped which stories from the life of Christ each evangelist chose to recount and the details each used in telling the story;
6. We also need to know the role chronology plays in forming a framework for understanding history. God's intervention in the life of man, Jesus' coming as a man, His teachings, and how His lessons were carried on and interpreted by the Apostles and evangelists are all rooted in history. This is why we seek to hear Jesus' parables in as close to their chronological order as we are able to discern.

So, let us begin.

1.1 What is a Parable?

The English word, parable, comes from the Greek word, *parabolé*, which means to place alongside for comparison purposes. The Greek word *parabolé* is used in the Bible as a direct substitute for the Hebrew word, *mashal*, which means a wisdom-saying. Both *mashal* and *parabolé* are translated into English as "parable."

However, in recent years, the word "parable" has taken on a more specific meaning:

A parable uses some well-recognized life situation to illustrate a deeper spiritual truth or lesson. A parable is intended to stir curiosity and calls for intelligent discerning by the listener. It often involves a deliberately "made up" story in which some lesson is taught but which the listener must discern, which is what Jesus meant by His statement "*He who has ears ought to hear*" [Mt 13:9]. The meaning of a parable is not intended to be obvious. In fact, it was considered an insult to the listeners to make the lesson too obvious.[2]

But, in the context of the word's use in the Bible, "parable" has meant anything from simply a wisdom saying to a story-based comparison. The Old Testament has a dozen wisdom sayings (or *mashalim*) which we would call today "parables:"

Walking the Parables of Jesus

Table 1: Parables in the Old Testament

Old Testament Parable	Bible Reference
"Jews and Moabites" by Balaam	Numbers 23:24
"Trees make a King" by Jotham	Judges 9:7-15
"Strong brings forth sweetness" by Samson	Judges 14:14, 18
"Poor man's ewe lamb" by Nathan	2 Samuel 12:1-4
"Two sons fighting" by Woman of Tekoah	2 Samuel 14:5-20
"Escaped prisoner" by Son of a prophet	1 Kings 20:35-43
"Thistle and cedar" Jehoash, King of Israel	2 Kings 14:9, and 2 Chronicles 25:18
"Vineyard and wild grapes" by Isaiah	Isaiah 5:1-6
"Farmer prepares his fields" by Isaiah	Isaiah 28:24-28
"Lion's whelps" by Ezekiel	Ezekiel 14:2-9
"Boiling pot" by Ezekiel	Ezekiel 24:3-5
"Great eagles and wine" by Ezekiel	Ezekiel 17:3-10

In Jesus' day, parables were regularly used by the Temple priests and scholars. Back then, the characters in most of their parables were well-to-do people. The theme of their parables was usually some principle of Mosaic Law, and the "hero" of the story was *almost always* a Temple priest or scholar of the law. It was culturally necessary in Jesus' time to tell the parable in a way that the listener had to figure out the theme that was being taught. In fact, it was considered a grave insult to the listeners to make the theme too obvious. Jesus' parables were quite different than others of His time. He used characters from all walks of life. His parables had little to do with a principle of Mosaic Law; and, the "hero," if there was any, was *never* a Temple priest or scholar of the law.

In early centuries, it was common to treat parables as allegories. An allegory is a story in which each person, event and detail stands for something or someone else. The most famous allegorical treatment of a parable was by St Augustine in his explanation of the Good Samaritan. In St Augustine's version, the man who went down to Jericho was Adam, the robbers were the devil's agents, and the Good Samaritan was Christ who saved him, and so on.[3] While this approach led to some very interesting and in many cases useful interpretations, there has been no evidence found that parables were intended as allegorical. Rather, they were metaphoric, that is, the life situation described in the parable illustrates some greater spiritual truth or lesson, not each individual part of the parable standing for something else. We will encounter the subject of allegorical interpretation of parables when we later hear the Parable of the Sower.

1.2 Why Did Jesus Teach in Parables?

Over the centuries, a wide range of answers have been offered to this question. Most of the answers suggested reflect the theology of the one offering the answer. I am a deacon in the Catholic Church. I approach this question from the standpoint that Jesus' parables are the word of God articulated in an especially challenging manner intended to draw the listeners into a deeper understanding of themselves, of God and of their relationship with one another.

Actually, Jesus disciples asked Him that very question [cf. Mt 13:10]. And Jesus answered them; but His answer "sailed over their heads", so to speak. It wasn't until well after the decent of the Holy Spirit on Pentecost that His disciples were able to begin understanding why Jesus taught in parables.

As noted earlier, in Jesus' day, parables were a common form of religious teaching by the Temple priests and scholars of the law. But, Jesus' parables were quite different than others of His time. There was a higher purpose to Jesus' parables: they were to lead to a fuller understanding of the Kingdom of God (or the "Kingdom of Heaven" as Matthew termed it). Jesus opened a dozen parables with the phrase, "The Kingdom of Heaven may be likened to...."

During the nearly one thousand years between God's promise to David and the birth of Christ, the Israelites' vision of the Kingdom their Messiah was to inaugurate evolved into something quite different than what God had intended. By Jesus' time, they were expecting a kingdom that would rule forever over the world as they knew it, much as they had in David's day. Oppression by the Romans or any other power would be gone forever, in a sudden flash of God's power. The Israelites anticipated doing little more than watching the splendor of the event.

So, Jesus knew that before Israel could embrace the *true* Kingdom of God, which He came to inaugurate, there would have to be a major change in how they saw themselves and others in the world. In the true Kingdom, liberation would be from the domination by sin - not domination by the Romans. Vindication would be for *tsedaqah* (righteousness) - not for Temple rule. They were to lead the world by their example, not by royal edicts. A profound change of heart, called a *metanoia* in Greek, was necessary before the true Kingdom would be embraced by Jesus' listeners.

In time, Jesus' disciples saw that enabling a grass-roots *metanoia* was His purpose in telling parables that required the listeners to see themselves and others in the world differently. Parables are intended to engage each listener's imagination. Imagination is that creative faculty in us that enables us to form mental images, ideas or concepts of persons and things that are not present to our senses. It is only in our imaginations that we can see ourselves differently, free of our limitations and failures, able to be more than we currently are. Imagination is the essential resource of hope[4] and, from ancient times, the basic training for imagination has been listening to storytelling.

1.3 Ancient Middle Eastern Storytelling

1.3.1 Details Convey the Message

Ancient Middle Eastern storytelling was a partnership exchange; the speaker/writer was responsible for conveying the lesson; it was the responsibility of the listeners to discern the lesson. If the speaker/writer made the lesson too obvious it was a grave insult to the listener. The "message" was not primarily in the plot but in the details used to tell the story. Details were omitted if they did not relate to the lesson, or they could be altered to support the lesson. A person's name was often a hint on how to interpret what they said or did.[5]

One of the most difficult adjustments people in a Western culture are faced with in hearing Scripture is the role of the listener is much different in ancient Middle Eastern storytelling. We expect the speaker/writer to clearly state the "message" or lesson they are seeking to convey. We then judge whether we accept or agree with the speaker / writer's point.

Among ancient Middle Easterners, the storyteller does not directly state the "message" or lesson. Rather, it is the role of the listener to discern the lesson by using the hints given by the storyteller and following the details used in telling the story. In ancient Middle Eastern stories, the details are not there for color-commentary or to lend authenticity to the story; rather they convey the lesson. But, to pick up on the hints and details, one needs to be familiar with the culture and traditions of those times.

This means that Westerners must listen much more closely than they are accustomed to and listen with a discerning ear rather than a judging ear. This takes a learning period and some getting used to.

It is essential for those listening to / reading Scripture to recognize that, in ancient Middle Eastern storytelling, historic details were omitted if they did not relate to the lesson, or they may be altered to support the lesson.

Example of omitted historical details that don't contribute to the lesson: The Infancy Narratives by Luke vs. Matthew

Most anyone who has listened to the Infancy Narratives in the Gospels has noted that the versions differ, in some ways considerably, in their details. Those who look to the Gospels as a history of the life and ministry of Jesus are troubled by these "discrepancies." It isn't until we recognize that the evangelists were not teaching history; they were teaching faith and encouragement lessons using stories from the life and ministry of Jesus.

This does not mean that Jesus was not an historical figure or that the Gospel accounts of Him are unreliable. Matthew's lesson for his faith community was that Jesus was the "king" in the line of David, foretold by prophecy, long awaited by the Jewish people (Matthew's listeners were mostly Jews). So, Matthew, following the well-established Middle Eastern convention of using details from the actual events that support his lesson, related those stories; and. he left out any details that did not contribute to the lesson. So, in Matthew's Infancy Narrative, Mary and Joseph start out already in Bethlehem; there's no census, no shepherds, no visit to Elizabeth, and no angel visiting Mary.

But Luke's lesson for his faith community was that Jesus came from poor, obedient working-class people "like us" (most of Luke's listeners were working class Gentiles). So, Luke used details from the actual events that supported his lesson and he left out the rest. In Luke's infancy narrative, Mary and Joseph start out in Nazareth and journey to Bethlehem, there's no Magi, no flight into Egypt, no Holy Innocents.

As I said, neither Matthew nor Luke was teaching the "*Life and Ministry of Jesus Christ*." They were teaching faith and encouragement lessons to their communities using stories from the life and ministry of Jesus Christ as "vehicles" to convey the lesson. Matthew was not claiming there was no Annunciation; Luke was not claiming there was no flight into Egypt. For each of them, these were details that did not relate to their lesson and so these details were omitted from their telling of the story.

This point is essential to the issue of the historicity of the Bible. None of the biblical authors were teaching history. Attention to the actual details of the historical events only had meaning to them to the extent that the details supported each author's lesson. In ancient Middle Eastern storytelling, one omitted any details that might lead the listeners away from the author's "message" or lesson.

God did not dictate biblical passages. Rather, God's "message" is conveyed through the original author's lesson, using that author's manner of expression, images and cultural terminologies which would have been understandable to the original author's listeners. While God's "message" is timeless, the original author's lesson is rooted in the times and life circumstances of the author. This is why identifying, as best we can, who the original author was writing to is so important in interpreting biblical passages. See *Dei Verbum* ("the Word of God"), article 12.

Before leaving this very important point, let's look at an example of biblical authors changing the details to fit their intended lesson: *The First Sending*, Mark's account [Mk 6:7-13] vs. Luke's account [Lk 9:1-6].

Mark 6:7-13
Jesus summoned the Twelve and began to send them out two by two and gave them authority over unclean spirits.
He instructed them to take nothing for the journey but a walking stick— no food, no sack, no money in their belts.
They were, however, to wear sandals but not a second tunic.
He said to them, "Wherever you enter a house,
stay there until you leave from there.
Whatever place does not welcome you or listen to you, leave there and shake the dust off your feet in testimony against them."
So, they went off and preached repentance.
They drove out many demons, and they anointed with oil many who were sick and cured them.

Luke 9:1-6
Jesus summoned the Twelve and gave them power and authority over all demons and to cure diseases, and he sent them to proclaim the Kingdom of God and to heal the sick. He said to them, "Take nothing for the journey, neither walking stick, nor sack, nor food, nor money; and let no one take a second tunic.
Whatever house you enter, stay there and leave from there.
And as for those who do not welcome you, when you leave that town, shake the dust from your feet in testimony against them."
Then they set out and went from village to village proclaiming the Good News and curing diseases everywhere.

Note from these passages that some of details have been changed to fit each evangelist's lesson:

- In Luke's account, the Twelve were sent to "proclaim the Kingdom of God," but that detail is not in Mark's account. To Gentiles, the proclamation of the Kingdom of God was "good news." But to Jews, Jesus' proclamation of the Kingdom of God was much different than what they were expecting. So, to avoid leading his listeners "off on a tangent," Mark omits any mention of proclaiming the Kingdom of God in his account of The First Sending.

- In Mark's account, the Twelve were to take a walking stick, but in Luke's account, they are not to take a walking stick. To Jews, one carrying a walking stick conjured up images of Moses coming to speak a message from God to His chosen people. But, Luke's lesson was that Christ came for all mankind, not just Jews. So, in his account, the Twelve are not to go out "looking like Moses going to the chosen people."

- In Mark's account, the Twelve went about preaching repentance but in Luke's account, it's all about proclaiming the Good News. At that point in history, Gentiles were only just beginning to grasp the concept of sin, so preaching repentance wouldn't have had much impact on them, but they would readily grasp the Good News that "Jesus came to save us all."

Again, these two accounts of The First Sending were not intended as history lessons; the actual historical details of the event were secondary to the lesson each evangelist was trying to convey in using the event to illustrate some point of faith or encouragement for his community. Consequently, when more than one evangelist provided an account of one of Jesus' parables, we should expect that the details in each account are likely to be different. This is not a matter of one or more of them making an error in recounting the parable. It's that each evangelist only used those details that conveyed the lesson he intended for his listeners.

Western listeners look to details to convey authenticity, but to Middle Easterners, details convey message or lesson; authenticity lies in the speaker. To cement this understanding that details have an entirely different meaning and purpose in Middle Eastern storytelling than in Western storytelling, let's consider one last example, which many fundamentalists find troubling.

Matthew 2:23
> "He went and dwelt in a town called Nazareth, so that what had been spoken through the prophets might be fulfilled, 'He shall be called a Nazorean.'"

There was no prophet anywhere in the Old Testament who made that statement. The nearest was: Isaiah 11:1 "*a shoot shall sprout from the stump of Jesse.*" A small shoot was called, in Hebrew, a "netzer," the root word for the place name: Nazareth. Through this typically Middle Eastern 'play on words,' Matthew presented Jesus' living in Nazareth as prophecy-fulfilling. Matthew was not falsifying history here; he was employing the standard Middle Eastern storytelling practice of adapting the details in his account to fit the intended lesson.

This does not mean that we can't learn about historical events from the Bible. There are a number of historical events for which the Bible is our only source. But we should not look upon the Bible as primarily a history book and become concerned when different accounts of the same event do not "agree" in their details.

1.3.2 Honor, the Highest Virtue

Honor was regarded as the highest virtue in the Middle East, it is held above all else.[6] This is one of the most difficult concepts of Middle Eastern culture for Westerners to grasp. "Honor" in the Middle East does not have to do with one's personal integrity; it's the esteem others hold you in. In the Middle East, personal identity is group-centered; one's worth was defined by the "witness" of those around them, not by one's character or deeds. The Parable of the Shrewd Steward gives an excellent example of the role honor played in Middle Eastern life, which we must discern by following the details used in the telling of the story in Luke's Gospel. [Note: the text of the parable is in gray type].

Luke 16:1-8
Then Jesus said to his disciples, "A rich man had a steward who was reported to him for squandering his property.

Detail: A steward was an employee; this is not an indentured slave; this is a paid employee. He is the manager of the master's household and possessions; and, he's been reported to the master for "squandering his property."

Detail: "squandering his property" – an important phrase. Jesus did not say the steward was stealing; He did not say he was cheating; the man was *squandering his master's property*. So, this is telling us that this master is a wealthy landowner; he has tenants who are using his land as sharecroppers. This steward is not collecting the full value of what the land use is worth. That's the "squandering of the property" he is charged with.

Detail: the land owner has heard first about the misconduct of his steward *from his tenants*. So, this is a story about honor and shame. We need to figure out who's the one who is being shamed or suffering dishonor.

He summoned him and said, "What is this I hear about you?" Prepare a full account of your stewardship because you can no longer be my Steward.

Detail: if the man was stealing, he would have been immediately jailed or worse. But, he's being asked for an accounting instead, suggesting that the master is expecting the steward to take some action concerning the situation he's in.

You're no longer going to be my Steward. The Steward said to himself "What shall I do now that my master is taking the position of steward away from me. I am not strong enough to dig; I'm ashamed to beg? I know what I shall do so that when I am removed from the stewardship they may welcome me into their homes.

So, he called in his master's debtors one by one. To the first he said "how much do you owe my master? And, he replied "100 measures of olive oil."

Detail: Notice the specifics. It is not just a huge amount owed but a specific amount. And it is owed in olive oil. In their world, olive oil was the symbol of safety. Recall on Noah's Ark, when the water was receding, and he sent the dove out - the dove come back with an olive branch, the symbol of safety. Olive trees and olive oil has been the symbol of safety ever since. And, he owed a "hundred measures." One measure equaled 39 liters, liquid.[7] In their culture, numbers had symbolic meaning. The number 100 symbolized: fullest of full.[134] This debtor owed the master the "fullest of full" in safety. While this might seem an odd statement, remember that there is a deeper spiritual lesson being illustrated via the life situation depicted in the parable.

He said to him, "here is your promissory note, sit down and quickly write one for 50."

<u>Detail</u>: The Steward didn't doctor the books, he didn't amend the original note; he literally gave the original note back to the debtor and said, "*give me back one for half of the debt.*" What does the debtor who's writing the new note for 50 measures think? He thinks the master is being enormously generous; after all, a steward acts on behalf of his master.

In the first century, a hundred measures of olive oil were worth about 1560 denarius, or 1560 days wages. That's what it would take for this man to pay off his debt. Since a denarius was a subsistence level pay, one could just about feed a small family on that. So, it will be essentially impossible for the man to save 1560 denarius.

Then he says to another "how much do you owe?" He replied "100 kors of wheat." Here is your promissory note, write one for 80.

<u>Detail:</u> The second man's debt was in wheat; why? In Hebrew the word for wheat, *hittah*, also means sustenance. It is estimated that 50% to 70% of the calorie intake in those days came from wheat. That's why they would call it "sustenance." One kor equaled 935 liters, dry wgt.[8] So, this man owed the "fullest of full" in sustenance. The number 80 symbolized "fullness of life," therefore this debt would not be passed on to the debtor's descendants – extraordinary generosity!

When we encounter this parable later in our journey, we will look at agriculture in ancient Israel and how tenants could amass debts that were almost impossible to pay off. For now, we are addressing the importance of honor in the Middle East, how one loses honor by being shamed and the lengths people in that culture would go to restore honor.

The parable abruptly ends by Jesus saying: and the master commended that dishonest steward for acting prudently.

So, it's the master who has been dishonored by learning first from his tenants that his trusted steward has been squandering his property. In that culture, the one being deceived is the one dishonored, not the one doing the deceiving.

Jesus was not praising the steward for being dishonest. Restoring the honor of his master is what mattered most in that man's life circumstances. The steward was praised for applying himself to what mattered most.

When all seemed lost, the steward turned to what matters most. By drastically reducing the accounts of the master's debtors, the steward greatly enhanced the esteem in which the master would be held by them. Of course, it was through dishonesty. But, in the Middle East, honor matters most – and, consequently the praise.

Later, when we encounter the circumstances under which Jesus shared this parable, we can get a better idea of "what is the lesson in this story for us?"

1.3.3 Public Honor Challenges

A question posed in public is always, initially, regarded as a challenge to one's honor which must be defended in the culturally-appropriate way.[9] One of the most difficult Gospel passages for Westerners to understand is Matthew's account of Jesus' Encounter with the Woman in Tyre. It starts to make sense to us when we understand the dynamics of a public honor challenge, particularly an honor challenge initiated by a woman.

<u>Matthew 15:21-28</u>
Then Jesus went from that place and withdrew to the region of Tyre and Sidon.
And behold, a Canaanite woman of that district came and called out, "Have pity on me, Lord, Son of David! My daughter is tormented by a demon."
But he did not say a word in answer to her.
His disciples came and asked him,

"Send her away, for she keeps calling out after us."
He said in reply, "I was sent only to the lost sheep of the house of Israel."
But the woman came and did him homage, saying, "Lord, help me." He said in reply, "It is not right to take the food of the children and throw it to the dogs."
She said, "Please, Lord, for even the dogs eat the scraps that fall from the table of their masters."
Then Jesus said to her in reply,
"O woman, great is your faith! Let it be done for you as you wish." And her daughter was healed from that hour.

Western listeners are stunned by the seemingly callous way in which Jesus responds to the woman's plea, even at one point referring to her as a dog. But, in Jesus' day a woman was never to address a male over the age of twelve in public, unless she was his mother. Her plea addressing Him as *"Son of David"* would have been interpreted in that culture as, "Are you going to live up to the obligation you have as the son of a king?" This had all the trappings of an honor challenge. The culturally-appropriate response to a public challenge to honor, from a woman, was to <u>ignore her</u>. And, that's exactly what Jesus did.

But, the woman presses, and He's forced to pushback, speaking to her indirectly through the Apostles, stating the well-known Jewish understanding that the Messiah *"was sent only to the lost sheep of the house of Israel."*

She will not back off but instead blocks Jesus' way by prostrating herself in front of Him. <u>As seen by the crowd</u>, she is publically shaming Him. Jesus must pushback even harder, He says: *"It is not right to take the food of the children and throw it to the dogs."* Her response is astounding: in essence she said, "Your people are treating you like scraps from the table while we, the dogs out here, plead for your mercy."

At this point, Jesus sees that an honor challenge was not intended; it was a true plea for help and He responded accordingly. To Matthew, this was the turning point in Jesus' public ministry. Prior to this, in Matthew's Gospel, Jesus has been ministering only to Jews. From this point on, Jesus openly ministered to Gentiles as well – a powerful message to the Jews in Matthew's community.

Now, let's compare this passage with Mark's account of the same event.

Mark 7:24-30
From that place, he went off to the district of Tyre.
He entered a house and wanted no one to know about it, but he could not escape notice.
Soon a woman whose daughter had an unclean spirit heard about him. She came and fell at his feet.
The woman was a Greek, a Syrophoenician by birth,
and she begged him to drive the demon out of her daughter.
He said to her, "Let the children be fed first.
For it is not right to take the food of the children and throw it to the dogs."
She replied and said to him,
"Lord, even the dogs under the table eat the children's scraps."
Then he said to her, "For saying this, you may go.
The demon has gone out of your daughter."
When the woman went home, she found the child lying in bed and the demon gone.

There is a critical difference between these two accounts. In Mark's account, the encounter takes place in a house – therefore there is no public challenge to honor, in his telling of the event. Mark's message is much different from Matthew's. Mark casts the event as a test of faith; whereas, Matthew presented the encounter as one involving, what seemed initially, as an honor challenge. In Matthew's account, the focus is on the effect the encounter had on Jesus' subsequent ministry; in Mark's account, the focus is on the immediate effect the encounter had on the woman pleading for help.

1.3.4 Chiasms, the Point is in the Middle

Chiasmic constructs were often used to convey the principal message.[10] A "chiasm" is a repetition of similar ideas, first presented in a forward sequence then repeated in the reverse sequence. The objective of the chiasmic construct is to point to a central idea, which is in the center between the two sequences.

Chiasmic constructs in storytelling are largely unknown in Western cultures but they are quite common in Middle Eastern storytelling. In 1742, German scholar, J.A. Begel, after studying in the Middle East, first identified that there were a number of Biblical textual constructs he called "chiasms."[11] The objective of these constructs seemed to be to point to a central idea or message that lies at the center of the construct. But, because this form of storytelling was so "foreign" to western minds, it was not until 1929 that the chiasmic structure of many passages in Scripture was first described in detail for scholars outside the Middle East. [12] Luke's account of the Parable of the Good Samaritan provides an excellent example of a parable told in chiasmic form.

Luke 10:25-37
There was a scholar of the law, who stood up to test Jesus and said,
"Teacher, what must I do to inherit eternal life?"
Jesus said to him, "What is written in the law?
How do you read it?" He said in reply,
"You shall love the Lord, your God, with all your heart, with all your being, with all your strength, and with all your mind, and your neighbor as yourself."
He replied to him, "You have answered correctly; do this and you will live."
But because he wished to justify himself, he said to Jesus, "And who is my neighbor?"

Jesus replied,
    "A man fell victim to robbers as he went down from Jerusalem to Jericho.
    They stripped and beat him and went off leaving him half-dead.
    A priest happened to be going down that road,
    but when he saw him, he passed by on the opposite side.
    Likewise, a Levite came to the place,
    and when he saw him, he passed by on the opposite side.

    But a Samaritan traveler who came upon him

was moved with compassion at the sight.
He approached the victim, poured oil and wine over his wounds and bandaged them.
Then he lifted him up on his own animal,
took him to an inn and cared for him.
The next day he took out two silver coins
and gave them to the innkeeper with the instruction,
'Take care of him.
If you spend more than what I have given you,
I shall repay you on my way back.'

Which of these three, in your opinion, was neighbor to the robbers' victim?" He answered, "The one who treated him with mercy." Jesus said to him, "Go and do likewise."

At first, this sounds like a lesson in how we are to treat our neighbors. But, we need to recognize that the encounter began with a "scholar of the law" posing a question to Jesus in public. This was an honor challenge disguised as an intellectual exchange over God's commandments. It starts with a member of the priestly class addressing a lay person, Jesus, with the title: "Teacher." The scholars of the law saw themselves as the only authoritative teachers. The challenge becomes even more apparent when he poses the question; "And, who is my neighbor?"

The culturally proper response to a public honor challenge from a male was to pushback with an even more challenging question. And, the more subtly the question was posed the more effective the pushback. So, there was a very challenging question posed in the parable, and it's not the question at the conclusion.

Detail: Jesus said that the man was "half-dead," therefore there was no danger of defilement for someone who touched him. It was touching the dead that defiled. Later, on in our journey we will address the Hebrew System of Ritual Purity in some detail.

The hint that we are hearing a chiasm is that the specificity of the details is beyond what the storyline needs. For example,

Detail: the victim is "robbed" of his dignity by being stripped; Why not just take what he has and go?

<u>Detail</u>: first a priest then a Levite; Why not just say that some people passed the victim by? Why specifically say it was a Priest and then a Levite?

<u>Detail</u>: oil and wine; Why not just say that the Samaritan treated the man's wounds? Why specifically that he poured oil and wine on the wounds?

<u>Detail</u>: lifted him up on his own animal. Why not say that he transported the man to an inn?

<u>Detail</u>: he gave to the innkeeper two silver coins (typical fee for a 7 day stay). In Hebrew, the number 7 was the divine number of completion signifying a covenant promise.

There are more specifics here than the storyline needs. The speaker, Jesus, was using them to construct parallels that led to a central point. The chiasmic construct of the parable is illustrated below:

Table 2: Chiasmic Structure of Parable of the Good Samaritan[12]

A   <u>Robbers steal</u> money and take his dignity by stripping and beating man (10:30)

B   Priest [a] sees, but <u>does nothing</u> (10:31)

C   Levite [b] sees, but <u>does nothing</u> (10:32)

D   **Samaritan sees/acts out of compassion** (10:33)

C'   Pours oil and wine on wounds, <u>compensating for</u> the Levite's failure (10:34a)

B'   Places man on his animal, <u>compensating for</u> Priest's failure (10:34b)

A'   <u>Spends money for him</u>, compensating for robbers and restores dignity (10:35)

(a) Priests always traveled on a horse or donkey to avoid stepping on something that might defile them.

(b) Levites carried oil and wine with them in route to the Temple to be ready for any ceremonial task asked of them.

Note that line A' compensates for what happened in A; and B' compensates for what happened in B; and C' compensates for what happened in C. The chiasmic construct of the parable points to D, the Samaritan responding compassionately, when those who the listeners would think might did not. So, in response to the public honor challenge, Jesus pushed back with an even deeper question: Why did the Samaritan stop?

Be careful not to be too hasty in offering an answer to that question. Remember that many of Jesus' parables were very subtle and this one is particularly so. Your answer to this question will tell you a lot about how you "see" God. That's why Jesus posed the question to His challenger that day.

1.3.5 Dialog is more "Telling"

What is conveyed in dialog is more "telling" than what is conveyed in narrative.[13] In our culture and literature, we treat quotation marks as identifying the speaker's actual words. Ancient Middle Eastern authors had no quotation marks, indeed, no punctuation marks at all. Nor were they interested in a speaker's actual words. They sought the essence of what was said, not the precise wording. For example, the wording of the beatitudes in Luke's Gospel is different from Matthew's; Luke portrayed a different essence to Jesus' words than did Matthew because the life circumstances of Luke's listeners were quite different from those of Matthew's listeners.

Modern translations of ancient works use quotation marks to distinguish dialog from narrative because, in ancient writings, what was conveyed in dialog was regarded as more "telling' than what was conveyed in narrative. Luke's account of the Presentation of Jesus in the Temple is an excellent example.

<u>Luke 2:22-38</u>
When the days were completed for their purification
according to the law of Moses,
[they took him] [a] up to Jerusalem to present him to the Lord,
just as it is written in the law of the Lord,
> *Every male that opens the womb shall be consecrated to the Lord,*

and to offer the sacrifice of a pair of turtledoves or two young pigeons, in accordance with the dictate in the law of the Lord.

Now there was a man in Jerusalem whose name was Simeon.

Dcn. Bob Evans

This man was righteous and devout, awaiting the consolation of Israel, and the holy Spirit was upon him.

It had been revealed to him by the Holy Spirit that
he should not see death before he had seen the Messiah of the Lord.
He came in the Spirit into the temple; and when the parents brought in the child Jesus to perform the custom of the law,
in regard to him, he took him into his arms and blessed God, saying:
"Now, Master, you may let your servant go in peace, according to your word, for my eyes have seen your salvation, which you prepared in sight of all the peoples, a light for revelation to the Gentiles, and glory for your people Israel."

The child's father and mother were amazed at what was said about him; and Simeon blessed them and said to Mary his mother, "Behold, this child is destined for the fall and rise of many in Israel, and to be a sign that will be contradicted and you yourself a sword will pierce so that the thoughts of many hearts may be revealed."

There was also a prophetess, Anna, the daughter of Phanuel, of the tribe of Asher. She was advanced in years, having lived seven years with her husband after her marriage, and then as a widow until she was eighty-four.
She never left the temple, but worshiped night and day with fasting and prayer. And coming forward at that very time, she gave thanks to God and spoke about the child to all who were awaiting the redemption of Jerusalem.

(a) When read from the Lectionary at Mass, the phrase "Mary and Joseph took Jesus" is often substituted for "they took him."

At first, this passage seems to be about the Holy Family obediently observing the strictures of Judaism. And, indeed they were, but there is an important detail Luke uses in telling the story that indicates that the lesson he is conveying is not about obedient Jews but about "good news" for Gentiles. In Middle Eastern storytelling, every detail is there for a reason, they relate to the lesson.

<u>Detail:</u> Simeon is the only one with dialog in this passage. So, Luke's lesson principally lies in the words of Simeon.

Simeon's first statement was a proclamation:
> "Now, Master, you may let your servant go in peace, according to your word, for my eyes have seen your salvation, which you prepared in sight of all the peoples, a light for revelation to the Gentiles, and glory for your people Israel."

Simeon's words capsulated three well-known Old Testament verses that now had great significance to Luke's Gentile listeners:

[Psalm 128:1] *Blessed are those who fear the Lord and walk in his ways.*
[Malachi 3:1] *The Lord you are seeking will come to his temple.*
[Isaiah 49:6] *I will make my servant a light for the Gentiles that my salvation may reach to the ends of the earth.*

Simeon's second statement was directed to Mary:
> "Behold, this child is destined for the fall and rise of many in Israel, and to be a sign that will be contradicted and you yourself a sword will pierce so that the thoughts of many hearts may be revealed."

The "falling and rising of many in Israel" began almost immediately in Mary's lifetime, from the house of Herod, to the Jewish Temple; all of which benefited Gentiles. As a sign of contradiction, crucifixion was seen as a sign of shame, but Mary, and all Christians, Jews and Gentiles, would come to see it as a sign of triumph. As Mary would be pierced in the soul by the agonies of her Son, so she will continue to stand by the side of her Son in His Heavenly Kingdom, interceding for all, Jews and Gentiles alike.

1.3.6 Emphasis through Exaggeration

Emphasis was often made through exaggeration; the more extreme the exaggeration, the stronger the emphasis.[14] Exaggeration to make a point was common in Middle Eastern speech; it was cultural. They considered it insulting to speak loudly or in a very animated way to make a point. So, speakers used exaggeration instead. And, there are some clear examples of Jesus doing just that. For example, in Matthew's account of the Sermon on the Mount, Jesus said:

> "If your right eye causes you to sin, tear it out and throw it away. ... And, if your right hand causes you to sin, cut it off and throw it away"
> [Mt 5:29-30].

Certainly, He didn't mean that we're to mutilate ourselves to avoid sin. But, we also can't dismiss as exaggeration every statement Jesus made that we find uncomfortable, or "unworkable."

1.4 Knowing the Land
(see Appendix 1 for a map of Israel in the Time of Jesus)

The most important influence on the history of the greater Israel region was the trade routes. The trade routes were the lifeline of the ancient world. For nearly 5000 years, Egypt was the "breadbasket" of the world. While other countries had famines and drought, Egypt rarely did. The regular flooding of the Nile produced reliable crops year after year. Food and grain from Egypt headed east along the trade routes and goods that could be traded for food, i.e. dyes, fabrics and wool went west into Egypt.

The main trade route began in the Persian Gulf at the eastern end and came up the Euphrates River in what is now known as Iraq. It then cut across into the Syrian foothills. Just before Damascus, the trade route split for strategic reasons. In those days, if you controlled the trade routes, you controlled the world. One leg went over and down the Mediterranean coast and the other went through the mountainous regions to the east and down to Aqaba. From there ships carried the goods and eventually rejoined the Mediterranean leg in Memphis, Egypt.

The route that headed south was known as the King's Highway. There were times when Jesus was on the King's Highway. The Bible doesn't explicitly tell us that, but we can tell from where they were at. For example, at one point they were passing through the Province of Perea. The biggest city in Perea was Philadelphia. The only main road through Perea passed through Philadelphia, which was where the King's Highway also passed. The branch that went along the Mediterranean coast was called the Via Maris, which means "way to the sea" [on some maps, it's labeled as the Great Truck Road].

Figure 1: Remains of paved section of Via Maris in Galilee

In Syria, the Via Maris trade route went into the region of Caesarea Philippi. It then followed the Upper Jordon River, down to the town of Capernaum, then around the shoreline of the Sea of Galilee to Gennesaret and to the town of Magdala. The trade route then headed west through the town of Garis and went just north of Nazareth.

It should be evident from the map (see Appendix 1) that the only practical route Mary could have taken to visit Elizabeth, in the town of Ein Karem, was to travel on the Via Maris, a journey of 120 miles (taking at least ten days). She would not have gone unescorted down the path through Samaria because, while shorter (only 75 miles), it went through enemy territory. The other possible path was down the Jordon River, but then she would have had to wade across the Jordon River twice on that route. Being pregnant, she would have avoided wading through dirty water.

Figure 2: Looking South into Samaria

So, she would have needed to meet up with a caravan that was traveling along the Via Maris and passing near Nazareth. Traveling with the caravan, which would have had other women and children among them, would have taken her all the way south to the western leg of David's Highway. There, she would join up with a caravan headed to Jerusalem, passing by Ein Karem.

It was the trade routes that made Palestine "desirable" land. Because the trade routes passed through Palestine, they were regularly overrun by larger powers. Around the year 1000 BC, King David established his capital in Jerusalem because he was trying to connect the Via Maris with the Kings Highway through Jerusalem, so he could "control the world." God didn't like the idea, so it didn't happen. But they did manage to build a road (western leg of David's Highway) from the Via Maris on the

Mediterranean coast to Jerusalem, and on the other side of the river opposite Jericho all the way up to Philadelphia, which was where the Kings Highway was. However, they could not complete the leg between Jerusalem and Jericho because the terrain there was so difficult, and the rock so hard.

Figure 4, below, is a topological view of Israel. Note from the topological view the large trench that runs all the way from the Syrian Mountains through the Sea of Galilee, through the Dead Sea, all the way to the Gulf of Aqaba. This is known as the Rift Valley. The Rift Valley was formed by the Arabian section of the Asian Continental Shelf sliding against the African Continental Shelf, pulling the land apart along their line of contact and causing the collapse of the Rift Valley. There are places where the trench is nearly a half mile deep. So, to get from Jerusalem to Jericho, one had to go downhill some 1700 feet in a distance of 17 miles.

Figure 3: Looking East from Jerusalem

In those days, and in that area, people could typically walk about 13 miles (or 20 km) in a day.[15] In addition, one always traveled in a group or caravan because the biggest law-and-order problem those in the Roman Empire faced was the robbing of travelers. Roman soldiers did not protect the citizens, they protected tax collecting operations.

Dcn. Bob Evans

The Sea of Galilee is 700 feet below sea level. For many centuries, it was the most dangerous place in the world to fish, and it's only 14 miles north-south and 8 miles east-west. During the day, the sun heats the air over the land and the breezes are all toward the Mediterranean. As soon as the sun sets, all the heated air that has gathered moisture from the Mediterranean rushes back onto the land and down into the Rift Valley trench. Frequently, violent storms hit the Sea of Galilee. There are many thousands of shipwrecked vessels at the bottom of the Sea of Galilee.

The usual route for Galileans traveling to Jerusalem was by going around the west shore of the Sea of Galilee, hiking down the edge of the Rift Valley trench near Beisan, wading across the Jordan River there (which is just south of the Yarmouk River). They would hike back up the other side of the Rift Valley and continue south on the east bank of the Jordan River, wade back again at Jericho, and then "climb" from Jericho to Jerusalem - a strenuous 106-mile journey.

South of Jericho, the Jordan flowed into the Dead Sea. The Dead Sea is a salt-lake which is more than 1400 feet below sea level, the lowest point on the earth's surface. This salinity makes for a very harsh environment in which plants and animals cannot flourish, hence its name. The Dead Sea is 47 miles long and 10 miles at its widest point. The Jordan River is the only inflow to the Dead Sea and there are no outlets. In the northeastern section the water is more than 1250 feet deep, whereas in the southern section it is only 10 to 15 feet deep. The air above the sea is very humid because nearly 7 million tons of water is evaporated into the air each day.

Walking the Parables of Jesus

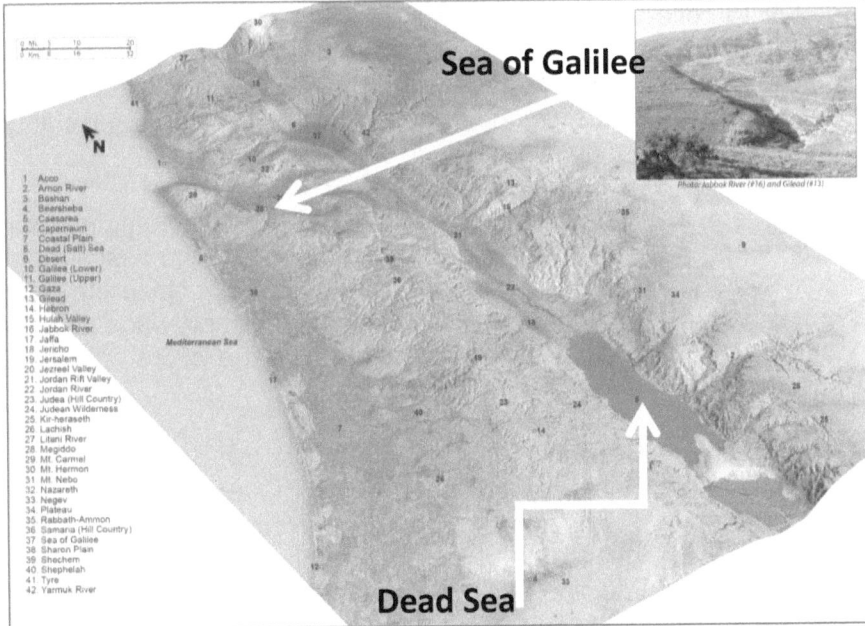

Figure 4: Topographical View of Israel

An important consideration in traveling in the greater Israel region was that each time one crossed a border between one political unit and another (called "Roman tetrarchies") they had to pay an import-export tax (called *"portoria"*) on everything they were carrying - other than the clothes they wore.

The Roman tax system was based on transactions, not income. Taxes were collected by professionals, called *publicani* (Greek: *telones*), who had to buy via auction a Roman license, every five years. Everything bought, everything sold, and everything carried across a border was subject to the transaction tax. In addition, everything bought and sold had to involve a tax collector who served as broker. One could not sell anything to another individual; one had to work through a broker.

If one rendered a service, one had to use a broker also. These brokers were paid for the work, took their cut and then paid the tradesmen. Tradesmen were the most "taken advantage of" occupation in the Roman Empire. The Roman license allowed the broker to collect transaction taxes in a particular location; but he could charge any amount he wanted to for the taxes. The Roman treasury did not concern itself with how the taxes were collected because they got their money up front in the licenses. That's why tax collectors were so despised.

So, Joseph and Jesus, who were "tektons" or tradesmen, in order to do work, had to deal through a broker. Joseph and Jesus most likely worked in the town of Sapporis, 4 miles from Nazareth. The broker found them work there and negotiated their wages. They then did the work and took home what little the broker cared to give them.

Sapporis means "place of the birds.' Prior to the death of Herod, the Great, there was an uprising in Sapporis, and they seized all the arms that were stored there. The Roman army not only defeated them, but they also destroyed the whole city. Following the death of Herod, the land of Palestine was divided up among his sons. Herod Antipas received Galilee ("the outback") and Perea. Herod Antipas decided to rebuild Sapporis as his capital city, which he did, from 10 AD into the late 20's AD. That is why there were many tektons, or tradesmen, living in nearby Nazareth during Jesus' childhood and young adult years.

1.5 The Synoptic Gospels

Because of their striking similarity, the Gospels of Matthew, Mark, and Luke are referred to as the "Synoptic Gospels" (synoptic" means: view together). They include many of the same stories, often in a similar sequence and with generally similar wording. Yet, they are distinctly different in form and style from John's Gospel.

For example, in each of the Synoptic Gospels, Jesus begins His public ministry and healing in Galilee; He travels with His disciples on a series of missionary journeys from a "home base," eventually concluding His mission in Jerusalem, where He experiences final rejection, death and resurrection. In the Synoptic Gospels, Jesus' preaching was mostly concise lessons, and He made frequent use of parables. A major theme of His teaching was the Kingdom of God (or, Kingdom of Heaven, as Matthew called it).

In John's Gospel, the overarching story is the same however, there are no recognizable missionary journeys, few healings, no exorcisms, and the Kingdom of God is only referred to indirectly. His preaching is more in the form of long discourses and there were no parables used. Yet, it appears to be the closest to being in chronological order.

But, it would be a mistake to regard the Synoptic Gospels as approximate copies of each other. Each has a distinctive character and view of Jesus' mission; and, each was clearly written for different faith communities.

In the late 19th and early 20th centuries, a considerable effort was expended by Western scholars in trying to "harmonize" the Gospels into a single text to compile a mutually consistent "history" of Jesus' life and teachings. Also, observing that there were a number of times in the Synoptic Gospels with identical wording of some of Jesus' sayings led, in 1900, to the theory that there was a text of Jesus' sayings from which the evangelists (principally Matthew and Luke) worked. The scholar, B.H. Streeter, called this text *Quelle* (German for "source").

No remnants of Quelle have ever been found. In the early 20th century, more than a dozen attempts at reconstruction of Quelle (or "Q") were made. But these reconstructions differed so much from each other that not a single verse of Matthew was present in all of them. As a result, interest in the Quelle theory subsided and it was neglected for many decades.

But, as the study of Middle Eastern Biblical Anthropology advanced in the 20th century, it was realized that while the "harmonizing" effort has given us much insight in the flow of events in Jesus' life, obscuring the differences between the Gospel versions would do much harm. It was increasingly evident that each evangelist had been addressing faith communities with quite different needs and concerns, which prompted them to select different stories as their teaching "vehicles" and to use different details in telling those stories. A deep richness of insights into the Christian message would be lost in a fully "harmonized" Gospel.

Dcn. Bob Evans

1.5.1 Mark

By the mid-20th century, most biblical scholars had concluded that Mark's Gospel was the first; written shortly after the death of Paul in Rome in 67 AD. A violent war between Rome and Judea had broken out in the previous year. That war would result in more than a million people being killed upon the destruction of the Temple in 70 AD. Most of the inhabitants of Jerusalem were scattered throughout the eastern Mediterranean. Shortly after, the Romans renamed Jerusalem, Aelia Capitolina.

Christians saw this all as the "beginning of the end times," the Great Tribulation (see Matthew 24, Mark 13, and Luke 21) which Jesus spoke of on Mount Olivet ("mount of olives") There was an urgency to getting the "good news" out to as many as they could as fast as they could; and, the Gospel Era began.

Paul had arrived in Rome around the year 60 AD and many of Mark's faith community were fairly recent converts to Christianity. Over several years, Mark became very close to the Christian community in Rome and he was most likely writing his Gospel to the Jews in and around Rome. Many of them were several generations removed from living in Palestine.

In the summer of 64 AD, Rome suffered a terrible fire that burned for six days and seven nights consuming almost three quarters of the city. The Roman citizens accused the Emperor Nero for the devastation, claiming he set the fire for his own amusement. In order to deflect these accusations and placate the people, Nero laid blame for the fire on the Christians and began a brutal persecution of them for the next four years.

Mark was a disciple of Peter and he relied on Peter's teachings in Rome, as attested to by Papias, a 3rd generation Christian. Similar testimony was given by Irenaeus, a disciple of Polycarp (who personally knew the apostle John).
Mark is also regarded as the same John Mark, a cousin of Barnabas, who first traveled with Paul and is mentioned in both *Acts of the Apostles* and in three of Paul's letters. John Mark's mother owned a large house in Jerusalem which was one of the earliest meetings places for Christians. Later tradition holds that,

following the deaths of Peter and Paul in Rome, Mark went to Alexandria where he became the first "bishop" there. The Coptic community in Alexandria put Mark's death by martyrdom in the spring of 68 AD. The feast day of St Mark is April 25th.

1.5.2 Matthew

There is wide-spread agreement that the author of the Gospel According to Matthew is the apostle and former tax collector, Matthew. This was attested to by Irenaeus and Clement of Alexandria, as well as Papias who served as one of the earliest bishops in Hierapolis (in modern-day Turkey). Papias contended that Matthew preached for a time in Hierapolis.

Tradition has it that Matthew mostly preached throughout Judea and the region around Antioch in Syria. It is to this area that thousands of people from Jerusalem fled upon the outbreak of the First Jewish-Roman War (66 AD – 73 AD). It was during that war, in September of 70 AD, that the Temple and much of Jerusalem were destroyed with more than a million casualties. It is to this community around Antioch that most scholars believe Matthew wrote his gospel, probably around 71 AD.

In the 40s and 50s AD, Antioch in Syria had been the center of Christian missionary fervor. It was from that community that Paul and Barnabas were first sent. Matthew's Gospel concludes with Jesus' instruction:
> "*Go therefore, and make disciples of all nations, baptizing them in the name of the Father, and of the Son, and of the Holy Spirit, teaching them to observe all that I have commanded you. And behold, I am with you always, until the end of the age*" [Mt 28:19-20]

This sums up the principal theme that runs throughout Matthew's Gospel. Matthew sought to reawaken the missionary zeal that had animated that region previously. But, of course, following the destruction of the Temple, life circumstances there were radically different than in previous years.

The Christian community in Ethiopia, Africa, has long contended that Matthew was martyred in the city of Nadabah, Ethiopia in 74

AD. In 954, in the face of advancing Muslim armies, his relics were moved to Salerno, Italy, where a large cathedral was completed in 1084. St Matthew's feast day is September 21st.

In ancient writings, the names Matthew and Matthias were often confused. Matthias was the one chosen to replace Judas as an apostle. Matthias preached in the region of Persia; known as Colchis, on the coast of the Black Sea. Some ancient writers, beginning with Herodotus, referred to Colchis as "Ethiopia" contending that the area had been settled by black Africans. [16] Matthias was martyred in Colchis (Ethiopia) around 80 AD. This led some to the impression that Matthew preached in Persia but was martyred in Ethiopia, in Africa. St. Helena had Matthias' relics moved to Trier in Germany around 325 AD.

1.5.3 Luke

It is generally accepted that Luke, the "physician" companion of Paul mentioned in several of Paul's letters and with Paul in his final days in Rome [2 Timothy 4:11], is the author of the Gospel According to Luke. In the first century, most physicians were indentured servants of large wealthy families. The physician's training was arranged and financed by an extended family and the physician-servant served the needs of that family almost exclusively.

At some point, Luke converted to Christianity, possibly when the family he served converted. It was standard practice then that when the head of household was baptized, the entire family infants on up including all the household servants were baptized.

Luke joined Paul and his companions in Antioch's port city of Troas [Acts 16:9-11], probably in 52 AD, as Paul's physician. This suggests that Luke was a "gift" to Paul or Luke had been released to Paul by the family he was serving, much like the indentured servant, Onesimus, had been released to Paul by Philemon. [See section 7.3 for more on this].

Luke was with Paul during the period of their missionary journeys based out of Ephesus (43 – 57 AD) and this is most likely the time when Luke met and talked at length with Mary, whom John the Apostle had taken there to be with him.

Most scholars agree that Luke wrote Acts of the Apostles in Rome during the period of Paul's house arrest (64-67 AD). Luke most likely wrote his Gospel to the largely Gentile community in Antioch, shortly after the destruction of the Temple and the arrival there of thousands of refugees from Jerusalem. Luke returned to the community in Antioch; it's not clear whether that was before or after he finished his Gospel around 72 AD.

Tradition has it that Luke then traveled to preach in Galatia, Dalmatia, and Macedonia, ending up in Thebes, Greece where he was martyred in 84 AD. The subsequent transfer of Luke's remains to Constantinople is well-documented, having taken place in the year 357 during the reign of the Emperor Constantius. Later, during the struggles with the Iconoclasts (711-843 AD), a priest named Urio fled Constantinople with the relics of St. Luke and brought them to Padua, Italy. They reside there, in the Basilica of St. Justina, to this day. St Luke's feast day is October 18th.

1.6 The Benefit of Chronology

The Life of Christ has an historical basis. God intervened in the lives of mankind by sending His Son at a particular time and in a particular place.

History is a systematic account of events, in the order in which they occurred, thus conveying possible cause-effect connections, the evolution of thought and tradition through experience and placing events in the context of other circumstances and events taking place elsewhere. So, chronology is the backbone of history; it serves as the framework for understanding our past.

Our intent here is not to study the history of Jesus' parables, but to place each parable in the context of the likely location and the approximate time when Jesus first shared the parable. To this we bring an understanding of the culture, the traditions and major prior events in that area which would have shaped how His first listeners would have interpreted what He was saying. From this, we hope to gain a better understanding of Jesus' message to His listeners, the evangelist's message in recounting the story and what message God has expressed to us in the process.

After many years of effort, biblical historians have been able to arrive at general conscientious on estimated dates in Jesus' life. While there is not universal agreement on those dates, they are generally accepted and they "fit well" with most of the evidence available.

Actually, the Bible gives us a great deal of information about the "When" of Jesus' life. It took matching it up with historical, archeological and cultural knowledge of those times for us to recognize it.

1.6.1 Estimated Dates in Jesus' Life

The date of the birth of Jesus has been estimated from the following:

a) Matthew tells us that Jesus was born "in the days of King Herod" [Mt 2:1]. Josephus tells us that an eclipse of the moon occurred not long before Herod's death. [17] Recent astronomy studies have established that such an eclipse occurred on 12/13 March, 750 a.u.c. (*) or 4 BC. Herod died before the Passover of that year which fell on April 11.[18] Since Herod killed the Bethlehem children up to two years old [Mt 2:16-18], in order to destroy the new born King of the Jews, Jesus was born some two years earlier in 748 a.u.c. [which on the Gregorian calendar would have been 6 BC to 5 BC].

b) In addition, recent astronomy studies have established that a remarkable astronomical conjunction of Mars, Jupiter, and Saturn in Pisces, occurred in the spring of 748 a.u.c. or 6 BC. This was quite probably the "great star in the east" seen by the Magi [Mt 2:1-12].

c) Roman historical records show that the Census of Quirinius, in Herod's domain, mentioned by Luke [Lk 2:1-5] in connection with the nativity of Jesus began in 6 BC, which would put Jesus' birth shortly after, likely in 5 BC.

Consequently, with some confidence, albeit 2000 years later, we can place the birth of Jesus in 749 a.u.c. or 5 BC.

(*) a.u.c. Roman Calendar year, literally *ab urbe condita* "from the founding of the city (Rome)."

The date of the beginning of Jesus' ministry has been estimated from:

a) Luke reported that "in the fifteenth year of the reign of Tiberius" John the Baptist began his ministry in the wilderness. The sole reign of Tiberius began in August, 14 AD, which would put his fifteenth year at 28 AD and John's ministry beginning in late 28 AD or early 29 AD. John likely baptized Jesus some months later in late 29 AD.

b) When, shortly before the first Passover of His public life, Jesus had cast the buyers and sellers out of the Temple, the Jews said: "Six and forty years was this temple in building" [Jn 2:20]. Josephus reported that the building of the Temple began in the eighteenth year of Herod's reign, i.e. 17 BC. [19] Hence, adding the forty-six years of building, the Passover of Jesus' first year of public life must have been in the spring of 30 AD. [Note: 1 BC transitioned to 1 AD with no year 0 in between]. So, he would have left Nazareth in late 29 AD. His first public Passover observance was Nisan 15 (or April 3/4) 30 AD.

c) From Luke we read: "Now Jesus himself was about the age of thirty years old when he began his ministry" [Lk 3:23]. The year, 29 AD, is 32-33 years after 5 BC.

The date of Jesus' crucifixion has been estimated as follows:

John's Gospel explicitly mentions three Passovers during Jesus' public life, [Jn 2:13; 6:4; 11:55]. Following the Passover in 2:13, John speaks of Jesus going up to Jerusalem for "the feast" in John 5:1. This "feast" almost certainly refers to the Feast of Tabernacles in Sept/Oct. [Passover was referred to as "Passover." "Feast" referred to the lesser holidays]. So, many scholars have concluded that there was a Passover between John 2:13 and

John 6:4, making for four Passovers in Jesus' public life. Since it has been estimated that the first was in 30 AD; then the Passover of Passion Week was in 33 AD.

Jews in that period did not have names for the days of the week, only, the first day, the second day, and so on. It is clear from all four Gospels that the Resurrection was on the "first day of the week." Passover was the previous day (the "seventh day of the week"), and the crucifixion the day before that (the "sixth day of the week"). From astronomical calculations, the Passover occurred on the "seventh day of the week" in years 30 AD and 33 AD. If the death and resurrection of Jesus was in 30 AD, that would mean He had only one year of public ministry (since He began in 29 AD). Consequently, the 33 AD dating is accepted because it meant that Jesus had a public ministry of a little over three years, which is in keeping with the position of early church fathers. In addition, throughout the Gospels, we are told that Jesus observed the Jewish holidays:

Table 3: Principal Jewish Holidays

Holiday	Date	Time of Year
Yom Kippur (Day of Atonement)	Tishri 10	5 days before Sukkot
Sukkot (*) (Festival of Booths or Tabernacles)	Tishri 15	late Sept to late Oct
Hanukkah (Feast of Dedication or Lights)	Kislev 25	early Dec to late Dec
Purim (Festival of Lots)	Adar 26	early Mar to late Mar
Passover (*) (Pesach)	Nisan 15	late Mar to late Apr
Shavuoth (*) (Festival of Weeks or Pentecost)	Silvan 6	50 days after Pesach

----

(*) the three Jewish festivals ("*Shalosh Regalim*") on which all able-bodied men were required to pilgrimage to Jerusalem.

From these, we can tell the approximate time of year the holidays were observed. We know the date of Nisan 15 (Passover) in the year 33 AD. Also, John tells us that "Six days before the Passover," (which would be Nisan 9), Jesus returned to Bethany [Jn 12:1] as the guest of Simon the Leper.

1.6.2 Estimated Dates of the Events in Holy Week

The other dates of the events in Holy Week have been estimated below, based on astronomical observations. All of these dates are, of course, just estimates drawn from certain evidence. But, the evidence is not as precise as it may seem. For example, when Luke reports that

> "*In the fifteenth year of the reign of Tiberius, John the Baptist began his ministry in the wilderness*" [Lk 3:1]

did Luke mean: from the year Tiberius reigned as co-regent with Augustus (11 AD) or from when his sole reign began in 14 AD? Also, when the Jews said: "*Six and forty years was this temple in building*" [Jn 2:20], did they mean the Temple building itself or the whole area collectively called the "Temple?"

In the Jewish calendar, the "day" begins at sundown and extends to the next sundown, whereas in the Gregorian calendar, the "day" begins at midnight and extends to the next midnight. Consequently, each Jewish calendar date has a corresponding double-date in the Gregorian calendar. For example, Nisan 15, in Jewish year 3794, corresponds to April 3/4 in 33 AD.

Dcn. Bob Evans

Table 4: Estimated Dates of the Events in Holy Week

Jewish Dates in year 3794	Gregorian Dates in 33 AD (a)	
Nisan 9 1st Day	March 28 Saturday	Sundown to midnight
	March 29 Sunday	Midnight to sundown return to Bethany
Nisan 10 2nd Day		Sundown to midnight
	March 30 Monday	Midnight to sundown entry into Jerusalem
Nisan 11 3rd Day		Sundown to midnight
	March 31 Tuesday	Midnight to sundown cleanses the Temple
Nisan 12 4th Day		Sundown to midnight on Mount Olivet
	April 1 Wednesday	Midnight to sundown confrontations in Temple
Nisan 13 5th Day		Sundown to midnight Olivet Discourse
	April 2 Thursday	Midnight to sundown Judas meets Temple officials; Jesus sends 2 to prepare meal
Nisan 14 6th Day		Sundown to midnight Last Supper
	April 3 Friday	Midnight to sundown Crucifixion
Nisan 15 7th Day PASSOVER		Sundown to midnight
	April 4 Saturday	Midnight to sundown
Nisan 16 1st Day		Sundown to midnight
	April 5 Sunday	Midnight to sundown Resurrection met on road to Emmaus
Nisan 17 2nd Day		Sundown to midnight

(a) equivalent Gregorian Dates from Steffen Thorsen, *Time and Date AS*, 1998, at timeanddate.com.

There is much to be gained from some knowledge of the chronology and the interpretations that led to the above date estimates. They are generally, but not universally, accepted; and, the Catholic Church takes no official position on the matter of specific dates.

1.7 A Brief Look-ahead

So far, we've come to an understanding of what a parable is and why Jesus taught in parables. We've learned a bit about Middle Eastern storytelling and how it would have shaped the parables and how they were understood in Jesus' day. We've learned some about the land of Israel; and how a listener's location would have influenced how they interpreted what they were hearing.

We've also reflected on the Gospel writers, Matthew, Mark and Luke and the communities they were probably writing to. And, lastly, we have considered the role chronology plays in serving as a framework for understanding history, as well as the basis for the estimated dates of key events in the life of Jesus.

Many presentations and books about Jesus' parables focus, in depth, on interpreting the parable's words, phrases and imagery in the world of the modern-day listener. Little attention is given to what was likely going on in Jesus' public life or the lives of His listeners at the time the parable was first spoken. There are also many texts that examine the "Life of Christ," but most of them touch on the parables only in passing. By addressing each parable in the context of the moment in Jesus' public ministry when the parable was likely first spoken, this text is not going to read like a typical treatise on the parables. Neither will it read like a typical "Life of Christ." Instead, this text is a journey into the words, life and times of Jesus Christ that you may not have encountered before.

Over the course of our journey, we will delve deeply into the culture of ancient Israel, not because it's intellectually interesting (although many may find it intellectually interesting) but because Jesus grew up in that cultural setting. Virtually everyone He spoke to grew up in that cultural setting. To better understand Jesus' words and actions we must be more familiar with their world, their daily concerns, their history, their traditions, their typical manners of communicating and their expectations of God and one another.

The conclusions drawn in section 1.6 concerning the likely dates of Jesus' public ministry are, at best, educated guesses. But, they have been carefully researched by many and they are generally regarded as fairly reliable; at least to the extent of giving a good timeline context to Jesus' public ministry. And, therefore they provide an approximate timeline setting for the parables.

One thing we will notice is that early in Jesus' public ministry He shared very few parables. Indeed, we don't hear Jesus' first parable until late in His Third Journey, nearly a year after He was baptized in the Jordan by John. But, over time, parables become the almost exclusive form of Jesus' public teaching [see for example Mt 13:34, Mk 4:34]. So, some patience in the early phases of this journey will be needed.

In some respects, this slow build-up in parables is to our advantage. Along the way, we will be able to reflect on a number of subjects, such as: Jewish wedding customs, fishing, meals, clothing, agriculture, slavery, land ownership and many more. When reading these, they may seem like mental detours on our journey, but they will prepare us for the parables we will hear later. Adequately understanding them will rely on that background and insight.

So, this journey will quite likely be different than what you may have encountered before. And, it offers to be an engaging, and hopefully informative, time for your contemplating Jesus' words and actions, the reactions of those around Him, what they likely understood and what it means to you in your life. But, ultimately you must confront your level of willingness to do more than just "observe" Jesus from a comfortable distance. I urge you to draw closer to Him as you journey, for He seeks to draw closer to you. He desires that you come to know Him as well as He already knows you.

Something to bear in mind is that, as we listen with a "Middle Eastern ear," we must be much more attentive and discerning than we might be accustomed to as Westerners. Please guard against your journey being largely an intellectual exercise. Let the insights take you deeper. But, also guard against being disappointed that you do not quickly experience some profound awakening of your spiritual life. Gestation takes its time.

Before we set out on our journey seeking to know Jesus better, there is one more point we need to reflect on. There is no way of proving, with any kind of logic or philosophical argument, that Scripture is in fact the Word of God, yet it is what we believe.

Indeed, it is something we must believe, or we will be unable to "hear" God speaking to us through Scripture. Therefore, we read and "hear" Jesus' Parables with a different mindset than we would approach a novel (to be entertained) or a work of non-fiction (to be informed). We must do more than just "hear" Jesus' words; we must "enter into" them, trusting that it is God who is speaking through them, as recounted in the inspired author's words. If we come to the Parables seeking an onlooker's knowledge of Jesus, we will never truly know Him. If we stand back, hearing His words, coolly analyzing, trying to force His words to prove themselves in our lives, we will never know their power to change our lives.

Ultimately, we can only truly know someone whom we love. At some point, we must make a leap of faith and "enter into" Jesus' words before they will fully speak to us. Without that leap of faith, we will remain just another curious onlooker in the crowd who walked away, scratching his/her head a bit over what they had just heard, and sank back into the consuming world around them. Just like so many of them, we too will have missed an opportunity of a lifetime; God was *that close* to us, yet we missed Him, perhaps never to come that close again, in this life.

And so, we are now prepared to begin our journey. We will meet up with Jesus just as He is leaving His hometown of Nazareth, heading for Jerusalem, and His public ministry.

2. Jesus' First Journey

We meet up with Jesus in Nazareth as He prepares to head for Jerusalem. If the estimated dates of Jesus' public life are reliable, then it's likely to be late in the year, 29 AD and He's probably going to Jerusalem to celebrate Hanukkah (Feast of Dedication). In that year, Kislev 25 occurred on what we would call December 8/9. Although the Feast of Dedication was not one of the "high holidays," on which all males over the age of 12 were required to attend Temple, we know from John's Gospel [Jn 10:22] that Jesus would go to the Temple in Jerusalem for the Feast of Dedication.

There's an old Middle Eastern saying: "If you tell me your father's name and where you are from, I will know who you are." The human Jesus was certainly a product of His upbringing: a poor, hard-working devout Jewish family in a rural Galilean village.

2.1 Joseph: Jesus' Earthly Father

We know from the Gospels, that Jesus' earthly father was named Joseph. But, we don't know Joseph's full name in the sense of the Middle Eastern expression: "your father's name." Joseph's full name would have been: *Josef bin* _____, where _____ would have been <u>his</u> father's given name. This was their way of conveying one's extended family identity.

Unfortunately, we don't know Joseph's father's name, and therefore his extended family; only that Joseph was of the house of David. In Matthew 1:20, he was addressed by an angel as "Joseph, Son of David." This was a salutation and not Joseph's full name. And, Luke tells us that Joseph *"was of the house and family of David"* [Lk 2:4]. Neither of these tells us that Joseph's father's name was David. In both Matthew's and Luke's Gospels, we hear the genealogy of Jesus. In Matthew: *"Jacob the father of Joseph, the husband of Mary"* [Mt 1:16]. In Luke: *"Jesus was the son, as was thought, of Joseph, the son of Heli"* [Lk 3:23]. In Middle Eastern writing, a genealogy was intended to confirm the physical existence and present the pedigree of an important figure who was being introduced to the readers; it was not a recitation of the person's family tree. So, these are not telling us that Joseph's father's name was Jacob or Heli.

We simple don't know Joseph's full name, only that he was of the house of David and was probably born in Bethlehem; because that is where his ancestral home was, forcing him to go there for the Census of Quirinius, in Herod's domain, mentioned by Luke [Lk 2:1-5]. Although we don't know his full name, Matthew paid Joseph the highest compliment a Jew could give another, he called him a *tsedeq,* "a righteous person" [Mt 1:19]. A righteous person was one who keeps mercy and justice in right balance as God does. That alone tells us volumes about Jesus' earthly father.

In ancient Judaism (and among Orthodox Jews today), a child was a Jew if the mother was a Jew. This was the rabbinic interpretation of Leviticus 24:10. In Jesus' day, the mother was responsible for the religious, as well as the social training, of the children up to the age of 12 years old. Consequently, Jesus would have learned Hebrew Scripture, forms of prayer, Jewish traditions, social norms and expectations, etc. from His mother, Mary. They would have recited the psalms together each day, until He was twelve. It was the responsibility of the father to train his son in his trade. Every male was expected to continue the trade of his father, in the support of his mother upon his father's death, as well as the support of his own family and sustaining the community where he lived. [20]

We know from Matthew 13:55 and Luke 6:3 that Joseph was a "tekton" (or tradesman, sometimes translated as carpenter}. As noted earlier, because of the Roman taxation system, tektons had to obtain work and be paid through brokers. Sadly, tektons sustained many work-related injuries, some of them fatal. And, they were among the most exploited workers in the Roman Empire. So, Jesus certainly learned from Joseph humility, perseverance, "making do with what you're given" and enduring insults and suffering in silence. Fortunately, for several decades there was plenty of work for tektons near Nazareth, with the rebuilding of the city of Sapporis only four miles away. Such were the expectations of the Nazareth community for Jesus. Jesus would have worked, along with his father, as a tekton, or tradesman.

2.2 Nazareth: Jesus' Hometown

The village of Nazareth, occupying only about ten acres in the first century, extended mostly north-south on a hilltop about 1150 feet above sea level, near the valley where the trade route, the Via Maris, passed a few miles to the north. Steep ravines and terraces on the northern slope confined the oval-shaped community. Archaeological finds show that the first signs of life in the Nazareth area date back to the Middle Bronze Age (2000-1550 B.C.).

Throughout most of the first century, the population was not more than about 300 people, made up of only a few extended families. The peasant families who lived there eked out a living, paid their taxes, and tried their best to live in peace. In those days, an important factor in sustaining a small village community was to avoid notice by the ruling powers. The people of Nazareth had done that quite successfully for centuries before the time of Jesus. Indeed, Nazareth did not appear in any census list of the communities in Galilee before 300 AD.[21] Its quite likely the community wanted to keep it that way. The less attention they got from the powers that be the more likely they would be left in peace. It is little wonder that the future apostle, Nathanael, exclaimed: *"Can anything good come out of Nazareth?"* [Jn 1:46].

Figure 5: The Town Well in Nazareth (1894 photo)

The well is the only feature in the present-day town of Nazareth that can be linked directly to Jesus' time, although the structure may have been upgraded since then due to earthquake damage.

The hub of the village was the central marketplace. And, the synagogue was the town meeting place as well as the seat of the community council of elders. Most of the houses were 1 or 2 room squares arranged in clusters of 6 to 8 houses around a central shared courtyard. The houses had dirt floors, flat roofs, low and narrow doorways, and front wooden doors. People slept on mats; and would often sleep on the flat roofs during hot nights. Cooking and eating were done in the courtyard where extended-family members also performed daily chores (like laundry, etc.) in each other's company. People ate reclining on mats and lighting in the houses and courtyard was provided by earthenware oil lamps. Water was carried from the town well and stored in courtyard cisterns for use.

Typically, peasant families ate two meals: one at sunrise, only light or small amounts of food; and one at sundown – a large meal usually with cheese, wine, vegetables and fruits, and sometimes eggs. Bread was an essential, being the utensil used in eating. As for meat, fish was most common in the villages of Galilee, followed by chicken or other fowl. Red meat (beef and lamb) was served only on special occasions, and pork and crustaceans were absolutely forbidden. Most foods were boiled or stewed in a large pot and seasoned with salt, onions, garlic, cumin, coriander, mint and dill. Food was sweetened with wild honey or syrup from dates. Food was generally served in a large common bowl and eaten by dipping in with the fingers. Each diner had a *mapeet*, a small cloth towel, or napkin.

The land around Nazareth was quite rocky with small patches of fair to poor soil, only suitable for family gardens. There were only a few scattered trees. The grazing of animals was the principal form of agriculture in the Nazareth area. However, the very fertile Jezreel Valley (also known in Scripture as the Plain of Esdraelon) was less than a day's journey to the east where many food stuffs could be obtained through bartering. Also, fish could be obtained from Magdala on the Sea of Galilee within another day's journey to the northeast.

Dcn. Bob Evans

We don't know the physical size or appearance of Jesus, Mary or Joseph but we are told that most inhabitants of Israel then were fairly small in stature, physically robust and darkly tanned from the sun. Their average daily caloric intake was about 1400 calories and their average life expectancy was only about 40 years, principally due to infections from injuries.[22]

Most Israelites had black or brown hair worn long; and all married men wore beards. Their undergarment was called a *kethōneth* or "tunic." It was a fairly tight-fitting garment, sometimes reaching only to the knee, but most often to the ankle. Women also wore a *sadin*, a finer linen underdress. The outer garment was called a *simlāh* ("mantle" of "cloak"); it was loose fitting with fringes, often made of wool or flax. The Torah[23] commanded that Israelites wear tassels or fringes, called *tẓiẓit*, attached to the corners of their outer garments [Deuteronomy 22:12, Numbers 15:38-39]. These were to serve as reminders to keep the Lord's commandments. A *tekhelet* (or blue-purple colored) thread was in each tassel. The quality, style and markings on one's outer garment conveyed one's social status. To strip one of their outer garment rendered the person "naked" and without personal identity.

Also, when in prayer, their head and shoulders were covered by a *tallit*, or "prayer shawl." During weekday morning prayers, all males wore, on their forehead and left arm, *tefillin* or phylacteries, which were small black leather boxes containing scrolls of parchment inscribed with verses from the Torah.

Just like other men of his day, Jesus would have worn a girdle-style belt, called an *ezohr*, wound several times around the waist to bind the clothing tightly to the body. All adults, except slaves, wore *na'alayim* or sandals, on their feet. No footwear was worn in the house. Only slaves and small children were barefoot in public. In the summer, adults wore a white cloth, called a *keffiyeh*, over their head hanging to their shoulders and held in place by a sweatband around the forehead. This cloth protected them from the sun. Women also wore a *miṭpaḥaṭh*, a neck-cloth that covered their hair when they were in public. These have been mistakenly referred to as a "veil" by some writers. Among ancient Jews, women did not cover their faces with a veil; indeed, to do so was regarded as flirtatious [see Genesis 24:65 and Genesis 38:15]. Only a bride or bride-to-be wore a veil. The present custom in the Middle East to veil the face originates with Islam.[24]

Those adults who were Roman citizens wore an additional outer garment called a *toga*. This was a one-piece woolen garment that draped loosely around the shoulders and down the body. Roman citizens were required to wear these rather uncomfortable garments because the manner of wrapping of one's *toga* conveyed their social status. It's quite likely that few if any in Nazareth were Roman citizens but many would be encountered in Sapporis and Tiberias.

There are only two seasons in Israel, wet and dry. Prevailing westerly winds from the Mediterranean bring rainy weather; prevailing easterlies from the desert bring hot, dry weather. The rainy season begins in mid-September to mid-October. Planting begins then, immediately after Yom Kippur, or the Day of Atonement. Main harvesting occurs in the 50 days in March-April, between Passover and Pentecost. So, in late 29 AD, the rainy season would have been well underway. The rainy season bought mild temperatures to Galilee and the little village of Nazareth.

Since Jesus had a full day's travel ahead, it was likely just a little after their sunrise meal that Mary gave Jesus her blessing, or *berakhah*. And, as a devout Jew of His day, Jesus would have recited the *Tefilat HaDerekh*, or "Traveler's Prayer," before leaving her side. The Gospels don't tell us why Jesus chose this time to leave, only that "*Jesus came from Galilee to John at the Jordan to be baptized by him*" [Mt 3:13]. So, we don't know what was shared by Mother and Son that day; it will be forever held in their hearts.

Indeed, the Gospels don't explicitly say that Jesus traveled from Nazareth to Jerusalem, only that He was baptized by John in the Jordan. But, then only those details that relate to conveying the author's message were included in each evangelist's account. John the Baptist was baptizing on the Jordan River at Bethabara (which means "across the river"). It was also known as Bethany-across-the-Jordan [Mt 3:13; Mk 1:9]. It's highly unlikely that Jesus would travel down the Jorden River valley to Bethabara and not go to Jerusalem for the Feast of Dedication. That would not be in keeping with what we know of Jesus (for example, see John 10:22).

So, we are left to bring to those details given by the evangelists, bits of information from non-scripture sources of those times; some knowledge of the people, culture, and life circumstances in first century Israel; to piece together "what most likely happened," recognizing that what we might infer about "what most likely happened" must be consistent with what we know from the whole of Scripture. Our objective is not to reconstruct history for history's sake. Rather, we seek to draw closer to the people around Jesus; the land in which He lived on earth; and the person of Jesus Himself in order to gain a deeper insight into the lessons He intended for His first listeners, and for us. Our faith is often fed by hearing the word of God in settings that are conducive to deeper insight and understanding.

In that spirit, then, we set out with Jesus as He heads north the few miles to the Via Maris trade route. Since robbery of travelers was the biggest law-and-order problem in the Roman Empire, one never traveled the roads of the Middle East alone. The Via Maris was a main thoroughfare of the Middle East and Jesus would not have to wait long for a small group traveling east together to come along. Travel in ancient Israel was very arduous and most often on foot. So, food, water and shelter were freely given by people along the way, and travelers relied on that. Hospitality and its associated protocol were central to their culture. And, almost anywhere they went, they were "walking the pages of their history."

The first substantive community they would come to would be the town of Garis. Garis was a fairly affluent community in the Jezreel Valley and the Shechem Road through Samaria heads south from Garis. But, Jews did not travel through Samaria unless they were with a sizable group capable of fighting off potential foes. The "standard" route for Galileans back and forth to Jerusalem was the Jordan River valley, and that is almost certainly the route Jesus took – continue east on the Via Maris to Magdala, then south along the Sea of Galilee, descending to Beisan, and crossing the Jordan there. It was about an 8-day journey from Nazareth to Jerusalem via the Jordan River valley route.

2.3 Crossing the Jordan

The Jordan River flows north to south through the Sea of Galilee and on to the Dead Sea. Over its upper course, the river drops rapidly in a 47-mile run to a swampy area, known as Lake Hula also spelled Huleh), which is slightly above sea level. Exiting the lake, the river goes through an even steeper drop of over a distance of 16 miles down to the Sea of Galilee, where it enters at its northern end.

The Jordan (meaning "descender") leaves the Sea of Galilee near its southern tip. The lower course is some 75 miles-straight-line distance; but due to its many twists and turns, it is 165 miles long. It follows what is commonly called the "Jordan Valley," which has less gradient (dropping about 700 feet), so that the river meanders most of the way to the Dead Sea.

Throughout its length, the Jordan River is at the bottom of the Rift Valley trench. There are places where the trench is nearly a half-mile deep. There are only a few points along the lower course of the river where the sides of the trench are sufficiently sloped for it to be practical for people to cross the Jordan there. One such place, only a few miles south of the Sea of Galilee, is the town of Beisan. Archeological findings show that the town, which is 360 feet below sea level, has been occupied ever since the latter part of the Early Bronze Age (3200 BC-3000 BC). Today, it is known as Beit She'an.

Beisan (also known by its Greek name: Scythopolis) has been a principal crossing point on the Jordan River since at least 1500 BC. The place is steeped in history. For example, during a battle between the Philistines and the Jewish King Saul at nearby Mount Gilboa in 1004 BC, the Philistines prevailed. 1 Samuel 31:10 states that *"the victorious Philistines hung the body of King Saul on the walls of Beisan."*

East of Beisan, there is a winding slope, called a *ma'aleh* (which means "ascent") in the Rift Valley rim to a spot on the river, called an *abarah* (which means "crossing"). At this point, during the wet season, the river flowed quite heavily, amounting to nearly 3,000 acre-feet per day.[25] So, the water level was likely at chest height on an adult, and wading across the river was quite an effort, requiring group cooperation among those crossing. On the east bank, they would all air-dry before heading up the slope to the rim of the Rift Valley trench.

Figure 6: The Jordan River south of the Sea of Galilee

Arriving at the town of Pella, Jesus and His fellow travelers would have ended their day with food, lodging and replenishment of water. Devout Jews of that time did not carry food with them during the day out of concern for inadvertently violating one or more of the Jewish ritual purity strictures. Adhering to ritual purity was seen as so important that to become "unclean" not only affected the individual but threatened the whole nation's relationship with God.

The town of Pella was about 20 miles south of the Sea of Galilee. For many centuries, Pella was a very prosperous city, named Pihilum. But, by Jesus's day, it was little more than a town, although it continued to hold the status of a "City of the Decapolis." Following the destruction of the Temple by the

Romans in 70 AD, Pella was a major center for Christian refugees from Jerusalem.

The east rim of the Rift Valley trench consists largely of limestone, sandstone and chalk with intermittent patches of soil. Occasionally, the land is cut east-west by a wadi. A wadi is a seasonal stream, or "wash," that flows only after snow melt off or a heavy rainfall. Since it's the rainy season, Jesus and His fellow travelers will encounter some wadis they have to wade across. But, there is little shade or vegetation due to increasing salinity in the soil as one progresses south. The walk would be very demanding; and, Jesus and His fellow travelers would encounter only a few communities along their way; there were almost no houses or farms in between.

The next community they would come to would be Penuel. This is where the Jabbok River flows into the Jordan, the place where Jacob wrestled with God [Gen 32:22-32]. We will learn more about Penuel when Jesus and His disciples make their mission journey through Perea. Then, He will be the center of attention in Penuel; but, today He is just another traveler passing through.

As they continued their journey south, about 9 miles north of Jericho, they would have come to Damia (also known as A'dam), believed to be the site where the Israelites first crossed into the Promised Land for the Battle of Jericho [cf. Joshua 3:1-17].

Several miles beyond Damia, Jesus and His fellow travelers would have come to a point where the trench rim slopes down to a point on the river enabling crossing. At this point, the river is much wider but flows much slower than further north at Beisan. A more precise location where they would have crossed is not known. Archeological findings show that the crossing point at Jericho was moved several times. The Jordan carries a lot of silt downstream and deposits of it can make wading through it very difficult. Also, the riverbed shifts in this area as it slowly makes its way to the Dead Sea. In this area, the Rift Valley trench is nearly 14 miles wide. During the rainy season, the river is more than 500 feet across, while in the dry season it is only about 75 feet across.

Dcn. Bob Evans

After wading across the river, Jesus and His fellow travelers would have air dried and then continued south on the west bank to the entrance of the oasis city of Jericho. Jericho is on the Wadi Qelt which intermittently flows into the Jordan River from the mountains around Jerusalem. Jericho is 846 feet below sea level, which makes it the lowest city in the world. Natural springs in and around Jericho have drawn people for many centuries. It has a hot desert climate and rich alluvial soil.

The name, Jericho, means "fragrant" and the area has been regularly inhabited since around 9500 BC. It is believed to be the oldest continuously inhabited city in the world. In the time of Jesus, many of Israel's ruling and priestly classes lived there.

The final leg of their journey, Jericho to Jerusalem, would have been quite a hike. It rose 1700 feet up, over 17 miles, along the Wadi Qelt to Jerusalem. They would find much needed rest and refreshment in Jericho before setting out the next day.

In Jerusalem, Jesus and His fellow travelers would have no trouble finding food and lodging. Pilgrims to the city for celebrations in the Temple were readily welcomed into people's homes. The Feast of Dedication (Hanukkah) was observed for eight days beginning on the 25th of Kislev. It was instituted in the year 165 B.C., in commemoration of the re-consecration of the Temple, after it had been desecrated during the persecution under the Greek king Antiochus Epiphanes in 168 BC. The holiday was referred to by some as the Feast of Lights.

Again, we are not certain that Jesus attended the Feast of Dedication in the year 29 AD, but we do know that at some point He headed for Bethabara [Jn 1:28]. The Wadi Gharrar flows into the Jorden at Bethabara from the east. It was at, or near, Bethabara that Jesus was baptized by John the Baptist [Mt 3:13-17; Mk 1:9-11; Lk 3:21-23; Jn 1:29-33].

We have no way of knowing the specific location of Jesus' Baptism and several spots in the Jordan and in the Wadi Gharrar have been claimed over the centuries. The traditional spot, known today as Al-Maghtas (which is Arabic for "baptism"), is about 5 miles north of where the Jordan flows into the Dead Sea.

The Baptism of Jesus is one of the five major milestones in the gospel narrative of the life of Jesus, the others being the Transfiguration, Crucifixion, Resurrection, and Ascension. From Scripture, it's the first occasion since the days of Creation that the three persons of the Blessed Trinity were physically manifested at the same time: the Father (as the voice from heaven), the Son (in the person of Jesus), and the Holy Spirit (as the descending dove).

Figure 7: Al-Maghtas: The Traditional Site of Jesus' Baptism

The Synoptic Gospels tell us that immediately after His baptism; Jesus went into the Judean Wilderness to face the devil's temptation. He spent 40 days and nights in this desert without food. [Mt 4:1; Mk 1:12; Lk 4:1]. As Luke put it: *"Filled with the Holy Spirit, Jesus returned from the Jordan and was led by the Spirit into the desert for forty days,· to be tempted by the devil. He ate nothing during those days"* [Lk 4:1-2].

2.4 The Judean Wilderness

The Judean Wilderness is a vast desert region, which lies east of Jerusalem, which descends in the direction of the Dead Sea. Because of its lack of water, the Judean Wilderness has been essentially uninhabited throughout history. It has very little vegetation and is marked by many natural terraces and deep ravines. On its eastern side is the Dead Sea Fault Escarpment, a cliff that falls more than 2500 feet to the Dead Sea. East of the sea, the Plateau of Moab rises nearly 3000 feet above the water.

There is very little rainfall in the Judean Wilderness, but it has a large aquifer beneath it which is fed from rains in the mountains around Jerusalem. The aquifer flows underground in a northeasterly direction into the Dead Sea. The aquifer comes to ground level in only four known locations, the most famous of which is Ein Gedi, close to the Dead Sea Fault Escarpment.

Ein Gedi (which means "spring of the kid goat") is where David hid when fleeing from King Saul who was trying to kill him [1 Samuel 23:29 and 24:1-2]. We have no way of knowing where Jesus went in the Judean Wilderness. The human Jesus could have survived having no food for 40 days and nights, but He could not have survived without water. So, He had to have gone to a site where the waters of the aquifer surfaced. Perhaps it was Ein Gedi.

It's fairly certain that Jesus went to the Judean Wilderness during the rainy season because, during the dry season, the waters in the aquifer springs become brackish (salty) and sulfurous and unfit for drinking. This is why there had been no established settlements at any of the springs in the Judean Wilderness.[26]

The Judean Wilderness is hot, dry and silent, very silent. There are essentially no birds in the air, no creatures scurrying about the ground; silence prevails there. God speaks in silence. In the heart of every man there is innate silence for God abides in silence. [27] And so, into the silence the human Jesus went to find the strength in God to fight off the devil's efforts to dissuade Him from the mission He sensed He was being called to.

Figure 8: David's Falls at Ein-Gedi

Later, back in Bethabara [Jn 1:28], Jesus called his first six disciples [Jn 1:35-51]. These were John, James, Andrew, Simon Peter, Philip and Nathanael all of whom were from the city of Bethsaida in Galilee [Jn 1:44]. It was likely very early spring of 30 AD, when Jesus returned north to Galilee with his disciples [Jn 1:43]. There, He and his first disciples were invited to a wedding in the village of Cana.

The village of Cana in Galilee was north of the Via Maris, in the hill country of Upper Galilee, while Nazareth was south of the Via Maris. This is important. In the time of the Assyrians, they invaded northern Israel and took away the ten tribes of Israel that lived there. These are the "10 Lost Tribes of Israel" spoken of in Jesus' day. Thus, this region was without Jews for centuries. The Assyrians, Babylonians and Greeks, who ruled Israel, gave free land in this region to their retiring military officers. This whole region, therefore, was populated by Gentiles for many centuries. Jews all lived south of Samaria in the province of Judea.

In 165 BC, the Maccabees overthrew the Greeks and started opening up Galilee to Jews. So, Jews began to populate the region south of the Via Maris, but the region north of it remained largely Gentile. Matthew tells us in his Gospel that Jesus went to "Galilee of the Gentiles" [Mt 4:15] that was the region north of the Via Maris where Capernaum is located.

So, Jesus, His family and His disciples were invited to a Jewish wedding in Cana, which was in a predominately Gentile area. When a Jewish wedding was held in those days, one invited all the neighbors. However, in this case, the groom's neighbors in Cana were mostly Gentiles. Jews and Gentiles never associated with one another. Jews from Nazareth were invited to attend the wedding in Cana, which was quite some distance away. It's likely that Jesus and Mary were related to either the bride or the groom, or both.

2.5 Ancient Jewish Wedding Customs

Ancient Jewish weddings were quite different from those we have today. In those days, marriage was not only a union between two individuals, but between two extended families. Essentially all marriages were arranged by the families. Such arrangements were called the *shiddukhin*. A family sometimes employed the services of a *shadkhan*, or one who arranged a marriage on their behalf. An example of a *shadkhan* was Abraham's servant, Abarbanel. Because of Abraham's advanced age, Abarbanel traveled to Haran to arrange the marriage of Isaac to Rebekah [cf. Genesis, chap 24].

An important part of the *shiddukhin* was the amount and form of the *mohar*, or "bride price." The suitor, together with his father (if he was still alive), went to the home of the prospective bride's father. The suitor would begin by offering *matan*, or "bride gifts," to the prospective bride. He would then cast his cloak over her. The act of placing a cloak or mantle over another was a commitment to care for the one covered [cf. 1 Kings 19:19].

If the prospective bride tossed the cloak off, she was rejecting marriage to this suitor and the process ended there. If she let the cloak rest upon her, she was accepting marriage to him and the *ketubah*, or wedding contract, was drawn up. The woman was now a *kallah*, or bride, and the man a *chatan*, or groom. When the bride took a cup of wine, called the Cup of Acceptance, offered to her by the groom, they became legally married and they entered the *erusin*, or betrothal period.

The bride would then receive the *mohar* as her "social security" in the event of her husband's death or their divorce. Also, if the bride was from a wealthy family, she would receive from her father several maidservants who would remain with her throughout her marriage.

During the *erusin* period, the couple was legally married, but the bride remained in her father's house while the groom prepared a place for her in his father's house. This often took several months to a year. Before leaving the house of the bride's father, the groom would speak the *Tenaim*, or Groom's Promise: "I go to prepare a place for you in my father's house that where I am you also may be" [cf. Jn 14:2-3]. Later, when the groom's father declared that "all is ready," the groom's father called together both extended families and threw a wedding feast, called the *nisuin*, which means "the lifting up," referring to the custom of the groom lifting the bride up and carrying her to the wedding feast.

Prior to carrying the bride to the feast, both the bride and the groom underwent separate ritual immersion baths, or *mikvot*. They then consummated their marriage in a tent-like marriage chamber, called the *chuppah*. Beneath the couple was placed the *betulim* ("proof cloth"), a white linen cloth on which the new bride bled providing proof of her virginity. The *chuppah* was surrounded with "witnesses" who would let out a loud cheer upon seeing the evidence on the proof cloth. The proof cloth was retained by the bride's father to counter any later claims that his daughter was not a virgin at the time of her marriage. The father's servants or family members would then escort the couple to the wedding feast.

The wedding feast joined the extended family of the bride with the extended family of the groom. The feast would begin with the groom greeting each guest, one by one. Each guest would receive a *kittel*, or wedding garment, from the groom. Typically, the *kittel* was a robe or scarf. Everyone at the feast wearing identical wedding garments symbolized the union of the two families. [Note: today, the *kittel* is a white robe worn only by the groom; it no longer symbolizes the union of the families but rather the purity of the groom]. The groom would bring each guest to be formally presented to his father, before he went to greet the next guest. John's Gospel often used the Jewish wedding motif; recall Jesus saying: *"no one comes to the father except through me"* [Jn 14:6].

When all the guests had been properly presented to the groom's father, the couple would share a cup of wine, called the Cup of Blessing. The couple would then leave for the marriage chamber and the guests partied on, uninterrupted, eating and drinking for seven days.

On the seventh day, the groom would return with his bride, and all present shared the last cup of wine, called the Cup of Joy. It was essential to the wedding that the full extended families share in the Cup of Joy. This was the act that officially joined the two families into one larger family, committing them to the mutual support of the couple. This is why Mary's words that day to Jesus *"They have no more wine."* [Jn 2:3] were such a powerful intercession calling on the mercy of Christ to perform His first recorded miracle.

Running out of wine was far more than an embarrassing situation. Without all sharing in the Cup of Joy, that day, the couple would suddenly be without connection to either family or the larger community around them. And, there was no means in ancient Jewish wedding customs to rectify that situation.

Following the miracle at Cana, Jesus went to Capernaum (also spelled Capharnaum), on the northern shore of the Sea of Galilee *"with his mother, brothers* [male family members of Jesus' generation] *and disciples and stayed there a short time"* [Jn 2:12].

2.6 The Town of Capernaum

Capernaum was a "crossroads" location. And, missionaries go to "crossroads" where people are coming and going. There, people are more open to new ideas than those in an established community like Nazareth. Capernaum was a strategic import-export site, situated where the Upper Jordan River enters the Sea of Galilee. Everything and everyone that moved along the Via Maris, in the area, passed through Capernaum. Everything and everyone who crossed the Jordan between Galilee and the tetrarchy of Philip to the east passed through Capernaum. River traffic from the province of Abilene to the north passed through Capernaum. That's why there was a customs house in Capernaum where Matthew worked [cf. Mk 2:14].

In addition, the fishing docks and fish brokers in northern Galilee were located in Capernaum. During the period of Roman rule, there was no private fishing on the Sea of Galilee. Everyone had to have a Roman license to fish there.[28] So, Peter and Andrew together with their father must have run a commercial fishing vessel out of Capernaum. Consequently, they would take their catch into Capernaum, sell it to their broker who would pay them, and withhold his fees and taxes. The broker in turn sold the fish to others.

A very common action for the broker was to sell the fish to other brokers from the city of Magdala. Magdala was where they made the fish sauce known as *garum*. Garum was like the caviar of the ancient world. It was a very pungent fish sauce which was cured in the afternoon sun. Garum was packed in clay pots, put into wooden boxes, loaded on mules and taken along the Via Maris to Ptolemais, which was the shipping port of Galilee. Revenue from the exporting of garum was how Herod Antipas gathered enough money each year to pay his taxes to Rome.

It was more than a 20-mile journey along the Via Maris from Cana to Capernaum. Since His family and disciples were with Jesus, it was likely at least a two-day walk. We don't know why the family went with Him to Capernaum, or at what point the family returned to Nazareth. But, it's clear that Capernaum and the company of His new disciples was now Jesus' new "home base."

Dcn. Bob Evans

Jesus' first journey has ended. Since He encountered no opposition in His first journey, or any teaching situations that we know of, there were no parables.

3. Jesus' Second Journey

In mid-March 30 AD, Jesus and His disciples traveled south from Capernaum to Jerusalem for the Passover - the first one mentioned in the Gospels [Jn 2:13]. As was noted earlier, Nisan 15 occurred that year on April 3/4. While in Jerusalem, Jesus drove the moneychangers out of the Temple [Jn 2:14]. This was a provocative act sure to draw the ire of the Sadducees. They were the sect of Judaism that controlled the Temple and the Great Sanhedrin, the ruling religious assembly of 72 men in Jerusalem.

John tells us that Jesus also met with *"a Pharisee, named Nicodemus, a ruler of the Jews; he came to Jesus at night"* [Jn 3:1-2a]. John gave us several important details in that brief statement.

Detail: The man's name was Nicodemus (which means "the people's victory.") This may not be his actual name. Middle Eastern authors often gave characters names that helped their listeners interpret what the character said or did. Since this man may represent in some way the people's victory, this could be a way of John telling his listeners that this man will play some later role in the life of Christ, (which he did.)

Detail: The man was a member of the Great Sanhedrin; yet he was a Pharisee. The Great Sanhedrin was dominated by Sadducees. So, we should expect this man to act "out of character" from others in that ruling body. Sure enough, he is a seeker of truth.

Detail: He came to Jesus at night. Under Jewish law, all "public" activities had to take place in the daylight. By approaching Jesus at night, this man could pose questions to Jesus without them being interpreted as public honor challenges.

After the festival days, Jesus remained in the countryside of Judea well into the summer during which time He received the final testimony from John the Baptist, *"who was also baptizing at Aenon near Salin"* [Jn 3:22a]. Aenon means "spring;" this is the spring that feeds the Wadi Gharrar. This detail which John gives tells us that baptism is not to be linked to a particular place, such as the Jordan River. This detail is there for a purpose, but we're not sure why. There may have been an issue in John's community over the validity of baptisms not performed in the Jordan.

Around mid-summer 30 AD, Jesus and his disciples traveled northwards from Judea heading to Galilee. This time, Jesus passed through the territory of Samaria [Jn 4:3-4]. The only north-south road through the region was the Shechem Road. This route was much less strenuous than the Jordan River valley route. It was also much shorter, only about 75 miles, principally through rolling hills.

But, it was quite unusual for Galileans to pass through the "enemy territory" of Samaria. Jesus may have felt prompted to do so; and there may have been a large enough group of them that they felt safe in passing through that region.

3.1 The Samaritans

The name *Samaritan* means "guardian" (of the Torah). The Samaritans claim descent from the tribe of Ephraim and tribe of Manasseh (two sons of Joseph). In 458 BC, work in reestablishing a functioning people and nation in Israel, following the Babylonian Captivity, was progressing so slowly that the Persian king, Artaxerxes I, sent Ezra the Scribe (also known as "Esdras") to Jerusalem to organize efforts there. Ezra took it as his mandate to renew and enforce observance of the Torah.

Through the Edict of Ezra, in 457 BC, he sought to "purify the community" by enforcing the dissolution of marriages between those who had returned from Babylon and those who had remained in Israel during the captivity period. Thousands of women, children and only a few men were "deported" from the Jerusalem area to the lands further north that had been apportioned to Ephraim and Manasseh after the Exodus. Great bitterness and hostility arose out of this action.

In time, the "deportees" built a temple on Mount Gerizim and began referring to themselves as the true guardians of the Torah. The Temple on Gerizim rivaled the Temple in Jerusalem. The bitterness turned to warfare in 113 BC when a Jewish army under

Hyrcanus destroyed the Samaritan temple and put the inhabitants of Samaria in slavery until 104 BC.

Later, the Samaritan temple complex was rebuilt. The hostility between Jews and Samaritans persisted. Josephus reported that, in the year 9 AD, a band of Samaritans scattered human bones throughout the Temple in Jerusalem just before Passover, preventing the "proper" observance of Passover that year.[29]

In the time of Jesus, Jews referred to Samaritans as the *Kuthim*, which means the "Idiots." [30] And, the Samaritans resented that intensely. So, it's easy to see why Jews would avoid passing through the "enemy territory" of Samaria. Yet, Samaritans were staunch observers of Judaism, and hospitality to strangers was a cardinal rule of Judaism. So, while the Samaritans were very hostile to Jews, Jewish travelers could find enough people in Samaria willing to provide some food, shelter and water for the passage through Samaria to at least be possible, sometimes.

To head north on the Shechem Road, Jesus and His disciples would have begun at the town of Bethphage on Mount Olivet in Judea. The name, Bethphage means the "house of green figs." It was a walled village that served as a meeting place for the Great Sanhedrin for decisions about what was holy and what was not holy. It was to Bethphage on Mount Olivet that the Messiah was expected to first appear. It's ironic that Jesus would pass right through Bethphage and no one would recognize Him.

Preceding north from Bethphage a day's journey on the Shechem Road, they would again be "walking the pages of their history." They would have passed the town of Bethel (which means "house of God") near the border between Judea and Samaria. It was here that Jacob, fleeing from the wrath of his brother Esau, fell asleep on a stone and dreamed of a ladder stretching between Heaven and Earth. He named the site, Bethel [Genesis 28:10-22]. Later, following the Exodus, the Ark of the Covenant was kept in Bethel, under the care of Phinehas, the grandson of Aaron [Judges 20:27]. Over the centuries, Bethel figured prominently in the ministries of the prophets: Samuel, Elijah, Elisha, Hosea and Jeremiah.

By the first century AD, the *"wickedness of Bethel"* [Hosea 10:15] was legendary, so it's unlikely that Jesus and His disciples stayed in Bethel. It's more likely that they pressed on another four miles to the village of Ephraim (also known as Ophrah). The village is perched on a prominent hilltop with an extensive view of the Samarian countryside. (The name of this village was changed from Ephraim to Taybeh around 1187. Today, Taybeh is reported to be the last all-Christian village left in the Holy Land [31]).

Another day's walk from Ephraim would have taken them to Sychar (formally known as Shechem); where they stopped at Jacob's Well [Jn 4:5].

3.2 Shechem (Sychar) and Jacob's Well

Shechem (which means "saddle" because of the shape of the land around it) is located between Mt. Gerizim and Mt. Ebal. In Jesus' time, the city was known as Sychar; today it is known as Nablus. Shechem had long been a Canaanite settlement and was the place where Abraham first stopped on entering Palestine [Genesis 12:6-8]. It was here that God confirmed the first covenant He made with Abraham and it was here that Jacob settled after his meeting with his brother, Esau, at Penuel [Genesis 33:18]. Also, it was the first capital of the northern kingdom established by Jeroboam I, following the breakup of Solomon's domain in 932 BC. [1 Kings 12:25].

For centuries, Shechem had been a place for Jews to avoid, and the first listeners to John's Gospel would have been distressed, initially, to hear that Jesus stopped there. Shechem was not very hospitable to Abraham and he promptly continued south, eventually settling in Hebron [Genesis 12:8-9] in the region known during the Exodus as the Land of Kadesh (meaning "holy"). It was in Shechem that Jacob's oldest sons, Simeon and Levi, avenged the rape of their sister Dinah by killing every adult male in the city. Jacob abruptly left Shechem in fear and disgrace [Gen 34:1-31]. The rapist was also named Shechem.

At Shechem (Sychar) is Jacob's Well. The Book of Joshua tells us that the remains of Jacob's son, Joseph, were taken out of Egypt during the Exodus and buried at Shechem [Joshua 24:32].

Shechemites insisted that Joseph and his two sons, Ephraim and Manasseh, were buried in a tomb that was less than 1000 feet from Jacob's Well.

Jacob's Well was dug with great effort through solid limestone before water was found. The well has a narrow neck at the top which then opens to a shaft more than 7 feet wide. The shaft descends 135 feet through the rock. There, instead of opening into the water table, it opens into an underground river that flows easterly from Mt. Gerizim to the Jordan River. In the rainy season, the river water rises into the well shaft such that water can be fetched with a bucket and winch within as little as 15 feet. But, in the dry season, it can require as much as a 200 feet line to reach the water. It was likely a community winch and each family brought their own bucket.

The flowing of the subterranean river and the shape of the well shaft results in considerable gurgling noise that can be heard at ground level near the well. This is where the phrase "living water" came from. For many centuries, the well was known as the Well of Living Water. It was at this well that Jesus met a Samaritan woman [Jn 4:5]. So, when Jesus initially talked about "living water," the woman thought He was referring to the water in the well. [In Christian terminology, "living water" refers to grace which we get from the sacraments.]

His encounter and conversion of the woman lead to many in Sychar believing in Him [Jn 4:39]. Today, the woman is venerated by the Eastern Church as a saint, St Photina. She is credited with the later conversion of Domnina, the Roman Emperor Nero's daughter, and is believed to have been martyred in Rome around 60 AD.

From Sychar, Jesus and His disciples continued on to Galilee [Jn 4:43], crossing the shallow Kishon River (the border between Samaria and Galilee) at the village of En-gannim ("spring of gardens"). We will learn much more about En-gannim and its history later when we hear the Parable of the Good Samaritan.

Figure 9: Jacob's Well (1920 photo)

At this point in their journey, they've reached the fertile Jezreel Valley with its abundant produce and water. They probably spent some time there before, as all four Gospels report, they went on further north to the village of Cana [Mt 4:12; Mk 1:14; Lk 4:14; Jn 4:45]. In Cana, Jesus healed the son of a Roman official from Capernaum who traveled to Cana to personally plead for his son with Jesus [Jn 4:46]. Clearly, news of Jesus and growing belief in Him was spreading throughout Galilee.

From Cana, Jesus returned to his home-town of Nazareth, and preached in their synagogue [Lk 4:16]. He was violently rejected by the town-folk and they took Him to the cliff edge to throw Him off, but He walked away through their midst [Lk 4:28-30]. Many of us find the intensity of the reaction to Jesus by His neighbors in Nazareth puzzling.

3.3 The Roots of Hometown Expectations

In the ancient Middle East and in many areas there today, life was very much community centered. So much so, that one was not judged on their personal accomplishments but on what others had to say about them. This is the foundation of the Middle Eastern concept of honor.

Further, the long-term sustainability of the community, rather than the individual's survival, was paramount in the Middle East. Everyday life was very labor-intensive, and everyone had their part. And, everyone doing their part was essential in their subsistence economy world.

Every pair of hands was needed by all, and this had been the case ever since villages first appeared in the Middle East near the end of the late Bronze Age (1500-1250 BC). Archeological evidence shows that in that period more than 60 percent of the nomadic peoples of that area died of starvation. Famine then led to regional wars and the population declined even more. A cooperative community-based way of life was essential to human survival in that area of the world. In time, small villages grew into towns, towns into cities, but the basic mutual dependence persisted.

God's providence often works in unexpected and unrecognized ways. Biblical historians estimate that Jacob and his extended family entered Egypt around 1750 BC. In subsequent times, they were subjected to slavery in Egypt. It's estimated that when Moses led them out of Egypt, and they entered the Promised Land it was around 1280 BC. Despite the harshness of being in slavery, the people of God had been "sheltered" in Egypt from the most traumatic and sweeping events of the late Bronze Age. They entered Egypt as nomadic herders; they came out a people who had to adapt quickly to village-based life, principally founded on agriculture.

The complexity of life and the range of skills and tasks to be performed in this new life-setting were much broader than when they lived as nomads. A community strategy for survival evolved: each young man was to carry on the trade of his father so that there would not be too many doing one type of task and too few doing another.

In Nazareth, there would be those who cared for the community water supply and in droughts knew where to find water; there would be those who made and repaired knives, plows, and other agriculture tools; those who maintained the roads in and around the community; those who built and maintained masonry works, tables, benches, etc.; those who dug and regularly moved the community latrines, and so on. Many, many things had to be done and the community needed to have a dependable way to ensure that these things went on generation after generation - thus, the strategy for survival that prevailed in the time of Jesus.

Jesus was expected, indeed required, to carry on in Nazareth the trade of Joseph, His (apparent) father. This was seen as imperative; and, its harsh enforcement was their *community duty* to prevent other young men from "going off and doing what they pleased." Of course, we find their attempt to kill Jesus as beyond extreme. But, we do not live the life circumstances these people did. It was not excusable, but it's a little more understandable when we see the situation through their eyes.

The Synoptic Gospels tell us that Jesus left Nazareth and returned to His new home base of Capernaum [Mt 4:13; Mk 1:21; Lk 4:31]. But, Matthew and Mark tell us that, later in His public life, Jesus would make a second attempt to gain the acceptance of His Nazareth neighbors [Mt 13:54-58; Mk 6:1-6].

We've come to the end of Jesus' second missionary journey; there were great "highs" and great "lows." Along the way, we didn't hear any parables. But, we did gain a lot of insights into the people around Him, their life struggles and circumstances, their history, culture and traditions, and their expectations. All of these will shape both the stories Jesus will tell in subsequent journeys and how they will interpret those stories.

Dcn. Bob Evans

4. Jesus' Third Journey

In Capernaum, as Jesus walked along the shore of the Sea of Galilee, He called His disciples (now including James, brother of John) to a fuller discipleship with Him [Mt 4:18; Mk 1:16; Lk 5:1]. It wasn't long before miraculous healings were a principal part of Jesus' ministry. In Capernaum, he healed a demoniac in the synagogue [Mk 1:23; Lk 4:33]. And, a short while later, He healed Peter's mother-in-law of her fever [Mt 8:14-15; Mk 1:29-31; Lk 4:38-41].

In their culture, they saw someone ailing as being punished by God for some wrongdoing, either on their part or on the part of their parents. But, in the words of St Augustine, Jesus' healing miracles were both deeds and words. They were deeds done in testimony of His power and His Divine mission; they were words "spoken" to both the one who was healed and those who observed that this child of God had his/her full human dignity restored.[32]

It was probably late autumn of 30 AD when Jesus set out with His disciples on a missionary journey throughout Lower Galilee, preaching and healing [Mt 4:23; Mk 1:39]. Lower Galilee was the area south of the Via Maris, which was almost exclusively Jewish. The evangelists did not give us any indication of which communities they visited beyond the fact that all three of the Synoptic Gospels tell us that while in Lower Galilee Jesus healed a leper [Mt 8:2; Mk 1:40; Lk 5:12].

Sadly, one of the most tragic consequences of the Hebrew ritual purity system was that those with mental illness were seen as being possessed by "unclean" spirits. And, any form of physical deformity was seen as the mark of one who was permanently defiled. These people were banished from the community indefinitely. Also, any skin ailment that gave one the appearance of dying, was termed, "leprosy," and it made the person "unclean" [see Leviticus chs.11-15 and Numbers ch.19]. Those banished from the community were literally cut off from the people and access to God; they were reduced to being non-persons. The Caves of Arbela at the foot of Mount Arbel, just west of Magdala, were the first-century dwelling place in Galilee of those who were banished as being "permanently unclean." So, this is the most likely location where Jesus encountered this leper. [33]

Figure 10: The Caves of Arbela

At some point, Peter's house in Capernaum became "home" for Jesus. The house was located on the town square only 84 feet from the synagogue. Although slightly larger than most, the house was simple; like others of those times. It would have coarse walls, likely made of black rock, called basalt, which is common to the area. The roofs were made of crisscrossed tree branches covered by a mixture of earth and straw. Recent archeological findings have established that the house consisted of several small rooms and it opened onto two separate courtyards. This would suggest that two extended families dwelled in the house. [34] That would be Andrew's family, as reported by Mark [Mk 1.29].

After Jesus' Ascension, the house was transformed into a Christian meeting place. Sometime later, a church was built over it. In 1968, the remains of Peter's house were unearthed beneath the ruins of that church.

When Jesus and His disciples returned to Capernaum such large crowds gathered around the door of Peter's house that some men lowered a paralyzed man down through the roof [Mt 9:2; Mk 2:3; Lk 5:18]. Jesus responded by saying, "*Child, your sins are forgiven*" [Mt 9:2; Mk 2:5; Lk 5:20]. Some scribes who were present exclaimed, "*He is blaspheming; who but God alone can forgive sins?*" [Mt 9:3; Mk 2:7; Lk 5:21].

In ancient Israel, the *soferim* ("lawyers," also known as "scribes" and "scholars of the law") were Jewish officials whose role was to serve as the interpreters and copyists of God's law. Central to their understanding of sin and forgiveness was their point: "only God can forgive sins," and at that, only on one day of the year, Yom Kipper (Day of Atonement).

4.1 The Day of Atonement or Yom Kippur

The Day of Atonement, or Yom Kippur, was, and still is, the holiest day in the Jewish calendar. From the days of the Exodus until the destruction of the Temple in 70 AD, a period of more than 1300 years, the High Priest was to perform elaborate rituals in the tabernacle area known as the "Holy of Holies" to atone for the sins of the people [cf. Leviticus 23:27-28].

This atonement ritual began with Aaron. Before entering the tabernacle, Aaron, and in later years the High Priest, was to bathe and put on special garments, and then sacrifice a bull as a sin offering for himself and his family. The blood of the bull was to be sprinkled on the altar in the Holy of Holies. Then he was to bring two goats, one to be sacrificed "because of the uncleanness and rebellion of the people" and its blood was also sprinkled on the altar. The other goat was used as a "scapegoat."

The High Priest placed his hands on the scapegoat's head, confessed over it the rebellion and wickedness of the people, and sent the goat out with an appointed man who released it into the wilderness. The goat carried on itself all the sins of the people, which were forgiven for another year, hence the name "scapegoat." While the High Priest performed these functions, all the people fasted.

Yom Kippur occurs each year on Tishri 10 (in late Sept to late Oct) and it ends with a great feast. Their planting season would begin at the next sunrise. The name, "Yom Kippur," means "a day like Purim." Purim was their great day of deliverance described in the Book of Ester. Yom Kippur is preceded by a ten-day period of repentance, called the Days of Awe. Rosh Hashanah (which means "the new beginning") starts the Days of Awe. In Jesus' day, Rosh Hashanah was known as the "Festival of the Trumpets."

Since the destruction of the Temple in 70 AD, each individual Jew is expected to privately focus on his/her own personal repentance and refrain from all pleasures of life during the day of Yom Kippur. The Yom Kippur fast lasts for 25 hours during which time Jews are to "live as though they are dead." Some men even wear white burial robes on Yom Kippur. In the post-Temple era, some ultra-orthodox Jewish families perform the *Kapparot* ceremony in which a rooster is used as the "scapegoat." The rooster is "sacrificed" by their kosher butcher and the bird is given to the poor for their evening meal, which concludes Yom Kippur.

Jesus responded to the scribes' objection by saying: *"Which is easier to say* (to the paralytic), *'your sins are forgiven,' or to say, 'Rise and walk'? But that you may know that the Son of Man has authority on earth to forgive sins"* he said to the man who was paralyzed, *"I say to you, rise, pick up your stretcher, and go home." He stood up immediately before them, picked up what he had been lying on, and went home, glorifying God"* [Mt 9.5-7; Mk 2:9-12a; Lk 5:23-25]. This was the first occasion Jesus asserted that He was divine, consequently the charge that He was blaspheming. The penalty for that offence was stoning to death [cf. Leviticus 24:10-23]. Open opposition to Jesus was starting to surface.

Shortly after this event, Jesus was walking by the customs house in Capernaum and, there, called Matthew (also known as Levi) the tax-collector to be His disciple [Mt 9:9; Mk 2:14; Lk 5:27]. Later, Matthew invited Jesus to dine at his home.

As noted earlier, cooking and eating were done in the courtyard, not in their houses. The dinner would begin at sunset and the people ate reclining on mats. Lighting in the courtyard was provided by earthenware oil lamps. When one held a dinner party for an honored guest, all the neighbors and fellow villagers would gather around the sides of the courtyard to hear the honored guest speak as well as listen to the table-talk. In the Middle East, everyone knew everyone else's business, so eavesdropping was just a part of the culture.

While not as formal as a banquet, these fellowship dinners had some elements of protocol. Those invited had their feet washed by the host's slaves. Having slaves was quite common in the Roman Empire. [We will look more deeply at the subject of slaves and indentured servants when we hear the Parable of the Lender]. If the host had no slaves, the task fell to his youngest sons. The honored guest would be welcomed by having oil poured over his head, signifying the outpouring of God's blessings upon him. And, it was common for the host to serve the meal.

For Jews, such dinners were the most intimate form of socializing, and it was the norm for those invited to pose questions to the honored guest, the host and/or one another; these were not regarded as honor-challenges. Arguing during a meal, sometimes just for the sake of it, to needle, to provoke and push, is a time-honored trait of Jews. It was regarded as an expression of friendship. But, it was not at all appropriate for someone who was not invited to question anyone at the dinner, let alone the guest.

Among the on-lookers that evening was some Pharisees who openly questioned what Jesus was doing. Also, some disciples of John the Baptist approached Jesus with a question. Both of these would readily have been considered "public" honor challenges. The culturally appropriate response to such an honor-challenge was to pushback at the questioner(s) with an even more challenging question or thought. For the first of many times, Jesus responded with a parable as a pushback to an honor challenge.

4.2 The Parable of the New vs. the Old

The Parable of the New vs. the Old appears in Matthew, Mark and Luke - three different versions of the same parable. We should expect that the wording will be a little different because each evangelist was writing to a different community. Each was trying to teach a little different lesson using the same story from the life and times of Jesus

The first thing to notice is that the wording of each version is remarkably similar, yet it is not identical. As noted earlier, most biblical historians have concluded that Mark wrote his gospel first. Matthew and Luke likely had a copy of Mark's gospel. They most likely also had a copy of what has come to be called: Quelle. Quelle is German for "source," referring to Jesus' sayings. No parts or fragments of Quelle have ever been found.

Let's first hear each of the three versions and then reflect on what Jesus' first listeners might have concluded was the point or lesson in the parable.

4.2.1 The Version in Matthew's Gospel [Matthew 9:10-17]

While he was at table in his [Matthew's] house, many
tax collectors and sinners came and sat with Jesus and
his disciples. The Pharisees saw this and said to his
disciples, "Why does your teacher eat with tax
collectors and sinners?" He heard this and said,
"Those who are well do not need a physician, but the
sick do. Go and learn the meaning of the words, 'I
desire mercy, not sacrifice.' I did not come to call the
righteous but sinners."

Then the disciples of John approached him and said,
"Why do we and the Pharisees fast [much], but your
disciples do not fast?" Jesus answered them, "Can the
wedding guests mourn as long as the bridegroom is
with them? The days will come when the bridegroom is
taken away from them, and then they will fast.
> "No one patches an old cloak with a piece of unshrunken
> cloth, for its fullness pulls away from the cloak and the tear
> gets worse.
> Likewise, people do not put new wine into old wineskins.
> Otherwise the skins burst, the wine spills out, and the skins
> are ruined.
> Rather, they pour new wine into fresh wineskins, and both
> are preserved."

4.2.2 The Version in Mark's Gospel [Mark 2:15-22]

While he was at table in his [Matthew's] house, many tax collectors and sinners sat with Jesus and his disciples; for there were many who followed him. Some scribes, who were Pharisees, saw that he was eating with sinners and tax collectors and said to his disciples, "Why does he eat with tax collectors and sinners?" Jesus heard this and said to them [that], "Those who are well do not need a physician, but the sick do. I did not come to call the righteous but sinners."

The disciples of John and of the Pharisees were accustomed to fast. People came to him and objected, "Why do the disciples of John and the disciples of the Pharisees fast, but your disciples do not fast?" Jesus answered them, "Can the wedding guests fast* while the bridegroom is with them? As long as they have the bridegroom with them they cannot fast.

But the days will come when the bridegroom is taken away from them, and then they will fast on that day."
> "No one sews a piece of unshrunken cloth on an old cloak.
> If he does, its fullness pulls away, the new from the old,
> and the tear gets worse.
> Likewise, no one pours new wine into old wineskins.
> Otherwise, the wine will burst the skins,
> and both the wine and the skins are ruined.
> Rather, new wine is poured into fresh wineskins."

4.2.3 The Version in Luke's Gospel [Luke 5:29-39]

Then Levi gave a great banquet for him in his house, and a large crowd of tax collectors and others were at table with them. The Pharisees and the scribes complained to his disciples, saying, "Why do you eat and drink with tax collectors and sinners?" Jesus said to them in reply, "Those who are healthy do not need a physician, but the sick do. I have not come to call the righteous to repentance but sinners."

And they said to him, "The disciples of John fast often and offer prayers, and the disciples of the Pharisees do the same; but yours eat and drink." Jesus answered them, "Can you make the wedding guests fast while the bridegroom is with them? But the days will come, and when the bridegroom is taken away from them, then they will fast in those days." And he also told them a parable.
> "No one tears a piece from a new cloak to patch an old one.
> Otherwise, he will tear the new and
> the piece from it will not match the old cloak.
> Likewise, no one pours new wine into old wineskins.
> Otherwise, the new wine will burst the skins, and it will be spilled, and the skins will be ruined.
> Rather, new wine must be poured into fresh wineskins.
> And, no one who has been drinking old wine desires new, for he says, 'The old is good.'"

4.3 The Spiritual Lesson in the Parable

When challenged by the Pharisees with "what is this teacher doing dining with sinners (we are the teachers and we do not dine with sinners), Jesus pushed back with a verse from Hosea: "*I desire mercy, not sacrifice*" [Hosea 6:6]. Their word for mercy was, *hesed*, literally meaning to "hold close to the heart." Far from being judgmental, God holds them close to His heart. But, what is really startling, initially unbelievable to them, was that God holds all peoples, including sinners, and Gentiles, close to His heart. Jesus brought mercy; He did not come to call the righteous to repentance, but sinners.

Then, the disciples of John the Baptist challenged Jesus with "why are your disciples not fasting (like we do)?" One of the basic practices of Jewish piety was fasting. Jesus pushed back with a wedding metaphor: "*wedding guests do not fast when the bridegroom is present.*" But, the disciples of John had gone too far by asserting that Jesus' disciples lacked sincerity in their behavior. Jesus was very protective of His followers, so He pushed back with a more penetrating question through the use of a parable. And, the more subtly the question is posed the more effective the pushback.

Recall that a parable uses a well-recognized life situation to illustrate a deeper spiritual truth or lesson. Just like Jesus' first listeners, we as discerning listeners must first identify the life situation described in the parable and then try to determine the spiritual lesson being illustrated.

The titles of the parables, such as Parable of the New vs. the Old, along with numbering the chapters and verses, originated in 1551 as a way of identifying the particular passages in Scripture. Such titles reflected the interpretation of the parables in the mid-1500s. Unfortunately, these titles can be very misleading. This parable is not necessarily about "new vs. old." We have to follow the details used in telling the story.

Detail: in the life situation, a cloak was being repaired. One's cloak (or mantle) conveyed one's social status; one's personal identity.

Detail: in the life situation, wine was being preserved. To Jews, wine was the essence of God's goodness to His people. It was a *mitzvah* (precept of Mosaic Law) for them to drink wine on the Sabbath and Festivals. And, it's *tirosh* (or "new wine") that was to be preserved. *Tirosh* also means "still fermenting or developing"

Detail: Luke's version has the additional phrase," And, no one who has been drinking old wine desires new, for he says, 'The old is good.'" Their word for "old wine" was *shekar* which also means "intoxicating."

Detail: all three evangelists tell us that it was disciples of John the Baptist who had challenged Jesus. Why were John's disciples in Capernaum?

The lesson in this parable was a penetrating question Jesus was posing to His challengers, the disciple of John the Baptist, who challenged Him at Matthew's dinner party. However, His pushback was not hostile but inviting.

Discerning the lesson taught by Jesus is not a task that's primarily "piecing together clues." Rather, it's one of faith-guided synthesis. We are hearing the word of God spoken by the Word of God.

Before moving on, we should pause a moment here and remind ourselves that this journey we are on is not about hearing Jesus' parables yet another time; but to hear them differently than ever before that we might draw closer to Jesus to "be in His company;" and, hear Him speak to us in a manner different than we have ever heard before. From that perspective, we conclude that His lesson for them, and for us, might well have been:

> "Why are your minds so closed?
> Why are you, who have received what these
> Pharisees have not, so intoxicated with matters of
> form and ceremony, but lack substance?
> I bring a new path to salvation whose full
> revelation is still developing or fermenting (*).
> Repair and protect the identity of who you were
> called to be. Preserve what is new in ways that
> will not fail."

(*) The "new wine" that was to be preserved will ultimately be Christ's Precious Blood, but His listeners that evening had no way of making that connection.

Some may content that we have "read into" Jesus' parable more than is there. In a Western culture context, that's probably true. But, reading into what they heard was the norm for Middle Eastern listeners. They brought to their task of discerning the speaker/writer's "message" knowledge of their culture, history, traditions and social expectations. And, that was the context in which Jesus was speaking to them and ultimately to us.

It's difficult for us to discern the point of the fourth detail concerning why the disciples of John were in Capernaum. Was it because John was already imprisoned by Herod Antipas? Matthew speaks of the imprisonment well after this dinner [in Mt 14:1-12]. Mark also speaks of it well after the dinner [in Mk 6:17-19].

But, Luke speaks of it before this dinner [in Lk 3:19-20]. So, did these disciples resent the followers of Jesus who had left John to follow Him? We don't know; but its point was important enough for all three evangelists to include it in their accounts of that evening.

We should expect that we will encounter some details in scripture passages whose purpose we cannot figure out. They refer to events and circumstances that are "lost to history" now. We do the best we can with what we have.

Jesus' third journey has concluded. We heard our first parable and applied some of the insights we've learned about parables and, in particular, about Middle Eastern culture and storytelling. How well we've done will depend on how much we take the lesson in the parable to heart. Are we, who have received so much, also intoxicated with matters of form and ceremony but lacking substance? Are we preserving who we have been called to be?

Finally, the challenge-pushback behavior of ancient Middle Easterners may still puzzle us a bit, but we need to see how socially functional it was. In their world, words were responded to with words; weapons were responded to with weapons, and they did not confuse the two. How wonderful it would be if, in our world, we did not confuse the two either.

5. Jesus' Fourth Journey

Each year, around mid-September to mid-October, the rainy season begins in Israel. And, the rainy season brings the peak fishing season on the Sea of Galilee. At this time, in the fall of 30 AD, most of Jesus' disciples were fishermen. Jesus has not yet called the Twelve to full-time ministry, so their attention for the next few months was likely directed to fishing and support of their families.

5.1 Fishing on the Sea of Galilee

Originally known as the Sea of Kinneret in the Old Testament [Numbers 34:11; Joshua 13:27], evidence of fishing on the Sea of Galilee (also known as Lake of Gennesaret [Lk 5:1] and Sea of Tiberias [Jn 21:1]) dates from at least 3500 BC. The "sea," which is actually a fresh-water lake, is about 14 miles north-south and 8 miles east-west. It is fairly shallow (typically 35 to 65 feet) with a maximum depth of only 141 feet. As a result of its shallowness, the water is fairly warm, conducive to supporting a large number and variety of fish. Some 37-different species of fish have been identified so far.

Because of its position at the bottom of the Rift Valley trench, the Sea of Galilee is among the stormiest locations on earth for fishermen. The bottom of the Sea of Galilee is littered with thousands of shipwrecks. This posed a constant concern over getting fishing nets snagged on underwater wreckage. It was further complicated by the fact that fishing was normally done at night when the fish came up from the cooler waters. They attracted the fish by waving light torches.

In the first century, most of the edible fish used in commerce were of three kinds: *musht* (sometimes called Tilapia Galilea); Biny Carp (sometimes called Barbels); and, Kinneret Sardines. Biny Carp were used by Jews for Sabbath meals, Kinneret Sardines were pickled in Magdala.

Dcn. Bob Evans

Figure 11: A Musht Fish from the Sea of Galilee
(sometimes called "St Peter's Fish")

One of the oldest methods of fishing on the Sea of Galilee was the use of the dragnet. Dragnets were typically shaped like a long wall, as much as 900 feet long, 10 feet high at its "wings" and 25 feet high at the center. The dragnet started from shore and it was dragged out by boat. Then, it was pulled parallel with the shore for some ways and, finally, dragged back to the shore by boat.

On shore, they separated out the fish to keep and discarded, as "unclean," anything which had no fins or scales (in accordance with Deu 14:9 and Lev 11:19). The dragnet had a weighted foot-rope and cork floats for the head-rope. A large dragnet could take 15 to 18 men to haul and control it. This method of fishing required the use of at least two large boats. Some Biblical references to dragnets are found in: Hab. 1:14-15, Ezek. 26:5; 26:14; 47:10, and Matthew. 13:47-48.

The cast-net was the most common method of fishing in the first century. The cast-net was circular in shape, measuring from 18 to 25 feet in diameter. There was no head-rope on this net; however, it had a foot-rope that was attached to the outside diameter of this net. And, attached to the foot-rope were weights to allow the net to sink quickly.

This net was cast or thrown by a single person either from a shallow area near shore or from the side of a boat. As the net was cast, it spread out and landed on the water like a parachute, descending quickly trapping any fish that were underneath it. After the net was on the bottom they had to retrieve the fish from the net. So, a fisherman would dive to the bottom and gather the foot-rope and bring it up at once so that others on-board could haul up the net.

It was common for the fisherman who was doing the diving to be naked because their garments were very heavy when wet and they were vulnerable to getting caught on underwater wreckage. In John's account of the Apostles' meeting with the Risen Jesus at the Sea of Galilee, he wrote: *"When Simon Peter heard that it was the Lord, he tucked in his garment, for he was naked, and he jumped into the sea"* [Jn 21:7]. It's clear that Peter was the diver whose task was to retrieve the footrope on their cast-net.

One of the most important fishermen skills was making and mending nets. Their nets were made of linen, a common fabric used in the ancient Middle East. Their nets had to be carefully cleaned and dried each day or they would quickly rot and wear out. Much time in a fisherman's life was spent mending nets [cf. Lk 5:2]. They had to regularly replace the weights for the nets, which were stones with holes drilled in them.

Recent archeological finds of well-preserved fishing boats from the bottom of the Sea of Galilee, show that the fishing boats in the first century were made of cedar planks with pegged joints and flat bottoms. One such boat measured about 27 feet long and 7.5 feet wide. It could hold a crew of 15 men and carry a half ton of fish. During the rainy season, fish were plentiful; but in the dry season, they often toiled for hours with little results.

Just like the other fishermen of their times, the Apostles were, of necessity, strong, hardy and accustomed to working cooperatively for both success and safety. In those days, commercial fishing was the most dangerous occupation in the world. A crew-chief, like Peter, had to be decisive and quick-acting, even with little or no information to go on. Hands and feet, arms and legs were often severed in net-lines; crewmen were swept overboard each year; and whole ships were lost at sea never to be seen again.

Jesus did not choose pious learned men, but simple hardworking men who could endure for the long haul – a life they couldn't have imagined in their wildest dreams.

The peak fishing season would be largely past by mid-March of 31 AD and thoughts and plans would naturally turn to Passover. Since all able-bodied men were required to celebrate Passover in Jerusalem, Jesus and His disciples began preparing for the long journey. In Judaism, each man was required to bring with him to the celebration his *ma'aser sheni*, or "second tithe." This was grain, wine or oil representing 1/10th of the produce of their land from the 1st, 2nd, 4th and 5th years of each 7-year cycle. Those who did not have agricultural produce, had to bring the monetary equivalent. [35]

The *ma'aser sheni* was to be consumed in Jerusalem and shared with the poor there [Deu 14:22-27]. They also had to bring sufficient money to buy an unblemished lamb for sacrifice in the Temple and the Passover meal. Consequently, pilgrims to Jerusalem for Passover were prime targets for bandits. So, part of preparing for the journey was arranging who you would be traveling with.

While the Gospels don't explicitly say that Jesus and His disciples attended the Passover that year, all three Synoptic evangelists give an indirect indication of it. Matthew wrote: *"At that time, Jesus was going through a field of grain on the Sabbath. His disciples were hungry and began to pick the heads of grain and eat them. When the Pharisees saw this, they said to him, 'See, your disciples are doing what is unlawful to do on the Sabbath'"* [Mt 12:1-2; see also Mk 2:23-24 and Lk 6:1-2].

Grain is ripe enough to eat off the plant just a few weeks before harvest (main harvest began the day after Passover). So, it was only a few weeks before Passover. In addition, it was a Sabbath. On the Sabbath, devout Jews are forbidden to travel outside the boundary of their community a distance greater than 2000 cubits (about 3000 ft.) [Joshua 3:4-5] <u>except</u> when traveling to Jerusalem for one of the High Holy Feasts. In Galilee, the main grain growing area was the Plain of Gennesaret which extended from a few miles southwest of Capernaum around the west side of the Sea of Galilee to the town of Magdala. This was also the way to Jerusalem via the Jordan River valley route. Many biblical scholars have concluded that the setting of this confrontation with the Pharisees over plucking grain on the Sabbath indicates that they were all headed to Jerusalem for the Passover. [36]

So, the confrontation was over observance of the Sabbath, not what Jesus' disciples were doing. Passing through a farmer's field eating some of the crops as one went was a time-honored agriculture practice in ancient Israel. As we move forward, we will encounter more and more agricultural practices in their times, many of which differ considerably from our times. So, we should take a few minutes to become more familiar with their world of agriculture.

5.2 Agriculture in Ancient Israel

The basic economy of the biblical world relied on two main resources, land and children [cf. Gen 12:1-8]. Having land and children distinguished free households from what were known as "strangers in the land," those who did not share in God's promise of land. The Bible explains very little about agriculture in ancient Israel; it was so much a part of the first listeners' lives that it needed no explanation, then.

The land area the Bible initially called "Canaan" and later "Israel" was only a little over 90 miles east-west and about 200 miles north-south. It is a little larger than the US state of Vermont, yet it has six distinct climate zones. There are patches of good soil, large regions of fair to poor soil and even larger regions of rock, sand and little to no soil. In all, less than 1/5th of the land had arable soil.

The first climate zone is the narrow moderate coastal area along the Mediterranean with fairly good soil. The second zone is the foothills zone, known as Cisjordan, where there is considerable outcropping of chalk and limestone rock with patches of fairly good soil, particularly in the Jezreel Valley. Moving eastward, there is the Jordan River valley (the Rift Valley trench) with an oasis here and there, like Jericho. The fourth zone is the plateau region east of the Jordan, known as Transjordan, with patches of good soil and some forests north of the Jabbok (or "blue") River. South of the foothills is the fifth zone, the mountains around Jerusalem with intermittent soil and rock. The sixth zone is the large deep desert of the Negev ("dry land") where there is virtually no vegetation at all.

As noted earlier, there are only two seasons in Israel, wet and dry. This is because prevailing westerly winds bring rainy weather; prevailing easterlies bring hot, dry weather. The rainy season begins in mid Sept to mid-October. Planting begins then, immediately after Yom Kippur, or the Day of Atonement. Main harvesting occurs in March-April, between Passover and Pentecost. This is followed by some six months of almost no rain, when the land is left fallow. Typically, crops failed in ancient Israel about 3 out of 10 years, because there was either too little rain, too much rain or rains that came at "the wrong time."

Initially, the Hebrews were herders. During the period of their enslavement in Egypt, about 400 years, they served as forced labor on the Pharaoh's construction projects. So, upon arriving in the Promised Land from Egypt, they had little experience in agriculture. As their population grew with limited grazing lands, herding alone could not sustain them and, little by little, they were forced to learn how to farm. We know a good deal about their early farming experiences from a recently found text, known as the *Gezer Almanac*, which dates from around 925 BC, or shortly after the time of King Solomon.

In time, the Hebrews formed villages that collectively relied on barley, wheat, grapes, figs, nuts, olives, pomegranates, and a variety of vegetables (such as leeks, onions, cucumbers, and rue) along with meat from their herds. Together they cleared the land, terraced the hillsides for vineyards and orchards, planted their fields and harvested their crops. They obtained metal implements for farming by trading with the passing caravans on the trade routes, who regularly needed to replenish their food and water as they journeyed. In times of drought, the Hebrews traded livestock for food and grain coming along the trade routes from Egypt.

In Palestine, the level of the rivers was well below the level of the farmland and there is no archeological evidence of any irrigation measures; instead they had to rely on God's providence to provide rains. Also, they were not very advanced in their planting practices. Following the adage that "just as the wind scatters the seeds, so should man scatter," they hand-scattered seeds across their property, then cultivated where they could with ox-drawn plows followed by a man with a hoe to break up the soil [cf. Isa 28:24]. Then, they had their livestock trample the ground forcing the seeds into the soil [cf. Isa 32:20]. They were essentially emulating nature. To our way of thinking this is very inefficient and even wasteful, but then most of us don't have the deep-rooted reliance on God's providence these people had.

The main harvesting season was the 50 days between Passover and Pentecost; wheat was harvested after Pentecost. The volume of harvested crops typically was about 10 to 15-fold over the volume of seeds scattered. While there may have been some very good harvests, perhaps 30 to 40-fold, a 100-fold harvest was largely unheard of. Over centuries, they learned that rotating their crops was essential to avoiding depletion of the soil nutrients. Families always tried to store a portion of each harvest as insurance against a short fall in the next season.

Mosaic Law required that portions of the fields, especially the corner areas, were to be left for travelers, the poor, the less fortunate and the "strangers in the land" so that they could glean those crops for themselves and their families [Lev 19:9]. This is described in some detail in the Book of Ruth. [Ruth would later become the paternal grandmother of King David]. Also, every harvest barn had an area reserved for storing the family's "second tithes" (mentioned earlier) along with their "Temple tithes." The Temple priests would go around to each barn to "collect" the Temple tithes. Since the priests had no way to transport or store large amounts of crops, they auctioned off the tithed crops at the farmer's barn and took the proceeds back to the Temple.

Sources of water were few and far between. What is commonly translated as "well" in the Bible were often cisterns or rock formations into which rainwater was stored for later use. While cisterns date back to pre-historic times, it was the Hebrews who perfected cutting cisterns in chalk rock and lining them with slake lime that made them both watertight and less prone to contamination.

Unlike fields for grain, which once planted were largely left to nature to mature, vineyards were very labor intensive. Vines require regular and extensive pruning to obtain "good fruit' and this is often alluded to in Scripture. Also, the terrace areas needed regular repair from rain erosion. Hedges and walls around the vineyard kept livestock from trampling the vines. These walls often had a tower in which one of the children of the family served as watchman for predators. Many villages, of a few hundred people or more, had a wine press carved out of the bedrock. In a large vat, the children trampled the grapes into pulp which was then left to ferment. While the fish sauce, *garum*, was the principal export crop of Galilee, wine was the principal export of Judea.

Many villages also had a threshing barn for separating wheat grain from the chaff. Wheat was harvested by pulling the plant up or by cutting the plant stack with a sickle. The plants were bundled into sheaves and carried to the threshing barn, laid out on the floor and trampled by the villagers to break the grain-bearing parts from the stalks.

Threshing barns were long buildings with a unique shape. They were very wide on the western end; the sides and roof narrowed to produce a much smaller eastern end. This resulted in an overall funnel shape to the building. During the day, prevailing breezes were from the east. Following sunset, the breezes would shift to coming from the west into the west end of the threshing barn; the funnel shape of the building caused the air flow to accelerate in order to exit out the smaller eastern end of the building. Men would take turns, using a large pitchfork-shaped fan, called a winnowing fan, scooping up material from the floor and throwing it into the breeze passing through the building. There was a large hole in the floor just ahead of the winnower. The heavier grain would fall through the hole into a grain bin below while the lighter chaff was carried by the breeze out the east end of the building where it was gathered into bundles for fuel. This process of separating wheat from the chaff in their threshing barns was spoken of many times in Scripture. The threshing barn was also the village meeting place for community decision-making.

Children have been mentioned several times in connection with farming. Having many children was essential to the survival of most Hebrew families. They were the principal unpaid labor force in the villages. There were also men who hired themselves out as day laborers; they were called "hirelings." Hirelings appear in several of Jesus' parables. From 14 AD to 37 AD, the standard daily wage for hirelings throughout the Roman Empire was one denarius. [37] Since this wage was so minimal, it was impractical for Rome to collect a transaction tax on it, so there were no brokers involved in retaining hirelings. Generally, it was the large landowners who hired these men; most households could not afford to hire workers. They had to rely on neighbors, their extended family and most of all on their children.

Continuing on their way to Jerusalem, Jesus and His disciples would have had plenty of company along the way. Several Biblical scholars have attempted to estimate how many Galileans made the journey to Jerusalem for Passover each year, counting wives and children as well. It was probably about 20,000 to 25,000 people. Since the rainy season had ended, the crossing at Beisan was not as treacherous as during the winter months.

The Roman historian, Josephus estimated that the population of Jerusalem swelled to nearly 2.5 million people for Passover. This was nearly 5 times the normal population of Jerusalem. [38] All those celebrating Passover were required to spend Passover night in Jerusalem. Over the centuries, the crowds grew to the point that Temple authorities had to expand the boundaries of "in Jerusalem" to include Mount Olivet and the towns of Bethphage and Bethany. For reasons of family ties and language, Galilean pilgrims favored staying east of the city, around Bethany. At some point in His journeys, Jesus formed a friendship with Lazarus and his sisters Martha and Mary. They had a large house in Bethany where Jesus often stayed [Mk 11:11; Mt 21:17]. That may be where they stayed this Passover.

Returning north to Galilee, Jesus healed a man with a withered hand [Mt 12:9-14; Mk 3:1-6; Lk 6:6-11]. Matthew tells us that the Pharisees were watching Jesus in the synagogue "*looking for a reason to bring charges against him*" [Mt 12:10]. This was most likely in Tiberias, the political and religious center of Galilee.

The Caves of Arbela are only a few miles north of Tiberias. The penalty for anyone considered "permanently unclean" to enter the city, let alone enter the synagogue was a flogging of 40 lashes. So, the man with the withered hand took a great personal risk. "*But, the Pharisees went out and took counsel against Jesus to put him to death*" [Mt 12:14; Mk 3:6]. Opposition to Jesus is rising rapidly in Galilee now. So, "*Jesus withdrew toward the sea with his disciples and a large number of people followed them*" [Mk 3:7].

Back in Capernaum, Jesus continued to teach and to cure many. Opposition to Jesus was mounting rapidly. The time had come; it was clear to Jesus that His God-given mission would not be completed during his earthly lifetime. There would be a need for others to carry on His mission in the world and so after a night in prayer, "*He appointed twelve, whom he also named apostles, that they might be with him and he might send them forth to preach*" [Mk 3:14]. There were the initial seven: Peter, Andrew, James, John, Philip, Nathanael (also known as Bartholomew) and Matthew; to which Jesus added: Thomas, James (son of Alphaeus), Thaddeus (also known as Jude or Judas [Jn 14:22]), Simon the Zealot and Judas Iscariot [Mt 10:1-4; Mk 3:13-19; Lk 6:12-16].

They were now Apostles ("those who are sent"). Their days as fishermen have ended; they were now to be fishers of men, and they willingly accepted that. We are struck by the significance of all this. They had little comprehension of what He was calling them to. Yet, they willingly accepted. They had come to know Him well enough to have that level of trust in Jesus. Oh, that out of this journey we might come to have that same level of trust in Him.

5.3 His Family Came to Get Him

In the spring of 31 AD, shortly after naming the Twelve Apostles, an incident occurred in Capernaum that has confused and troubled many modern-day listeners to the Gospels. Mark said that when Jesus' relatives heard that the crowds in Capernaum were so large that He was not even taking time to eat, *"they set out to seize him, for they said, 'He is out of his mind'"* [Mk 3:21].

"Then, his mother and his brothers⁎ came to him but were unable to join him because of the crowd. He was told, "Your mother and your brothers are standing outside, and they wish to see you." He said to them in reply, "My mother and my brothers are those who hear the word of God and act on it" [Lk 8:19-21].

At first this sounds like considerable disrespect to His mother and brothers. But, to understand this exchange, we need to become familiar with the ancient principle of *pietas*. Pietas is a Latin word meaning "loyalty." To Romans, pietas was a solemn duty "to the gods, to country and to family." It was even touted on some of their coins.

But to Middle Easterners, pietas had a much deeper more personal meaning. It did not relate to "the gods" or to "country" but rather it was the profound responsibility each person had for the guidance and care of each member of their extended family. In the ancient Middle East, family came before all else. In their communities, there was no police force. Each extended family was responsible for the proper conduct of its members and the larger community relied on them to meet that responsibility. There was also no social security system; each extended family was responsible for caring for its members, even those who no longer lived at home.

In their culture, Jesus' extended family in Nazareth saw themselves, and was perceived by their neighbors, as being responsible for bringing him back to right reasoning. Mary's presence in the group indicates that she was now the matriarch of Jesus' extended family. Their word *adelphoi*, which is translated as "brothers," meant male kinsmen of the same generation.

By His family saying of Jesus that *"He is out of his mind,"* they were expressing their concern that His thinking was disturbed; that He was unmindful of what was proper conduct for a man in His station in life; and that He was not taking proper care of His health (which would put a future burden on them).

In addressing those around Him, "who hear the word of God and act on it," as "His mother and brothers," Jesus was pointing out to them that, as His new "extended family" in faith, they owed each other the same level of pietas ("loyalty") as His Nazareth family was exhibiting to Him. Rather that disrespecting them, He was holding them up as an example to be followed.

The Gospel accounts are silent on what Jesus' Nazareth family had to say to Him, privately; or if they got to speak with Him at all. We just don't know. His family had come to fulfill what they had understood was their responsibility to Him and their neighbors. And, they left "empty handed." They likely had very troubled minds and heavy hearts on their journey back home without Him.

Jesus could count on the love and support of His mother, Mary. But the rest of the family, especially His brothers just *"did not believe in him"* [Jn 7:5]. One of many painful realities Jesus would face in the months ahead. (Luke tells us later that the disbelief of His brothers would change drastically following Jesus' Resurrection and Ascension [cf. Acts 1:14]).

6. Jesus' Fifth Journey

In 31 AD, as it does each year, the harvesting season ended with Pentecost, the first day of a six-day festival known as Shavuot. Shavuot is one of the three Jewish festivals on which all able-bodied men were required to make a pilgrimage to Jerusalem. So, we conclude that Jesus and His disciples were among them that year.

Shortly after returning to Galilee, Jesus and His disciples, along with a large crowd, were on a hillside outside Capernaum. Theologians have made a "guess" as to which hillside in Galilee. There just isn't enough information for us to know for certain. Most theologians postulate that the hillside was Mount Eremos, between Gennesaret and Capernaum. And there is where the Sermon on the Mount was delivered [Mt 5:1]. (NOTE: In Luke's account, Jesus comes down from a hillside to give the Sermon [Lk 6:20]). Mount Eremos overlooks both the Plain of Gennesaret and the Sea of Galilee. On Mount Eremos, the slope of the hillside facing the Sea of Galilee forms a natural amphitheater; it's been estimated that as many as 7,000 people could easily hear a person speaking from a point near the base of the hillside.

Figure 12: View from Mt Eremos,
Traditional Site of Sermon on the Mount

In the Sermon on the Mount, Jesus explained what it means to live in the reign of God. But the expectations of His Jewish listeners concerning the time when God will reign on the earth, the "Kingdom of God" (or 'Kingdom of Heaven" as Matthew called it), was quite different from what Jesus was portraying.

6.1 The Jewish Expectation of the Kingdom of God

In the ancient Jewish view of time there was no end to time, it was anticipated to go on indefinitely. There was a beginning of time, when God created the world, but there was no end foreseen.

In the Jewish way of thinking, the period up to the coming of the Messiah was known as the "Present Age." For them, it was in the "Present Age" that poverty, affliction and oppression existed. Following the Messiah's coming was known as the "Age to come," or "Kingdom of God," which would go on forever.

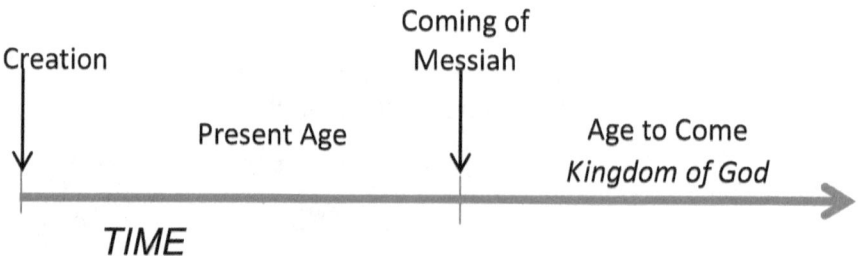

The roots of their expectation are in Isaiah 25:6-9, which underwent centuries of rabbinic interpretation. Out of that came the vison that when the Messiah came a big cataclysmic event would happen. And, the Messiah would host The Great Eschatological Feast spoken of by Isaiah.

There are no creeds or dogmas in Judaism. Jewish beliefs evolved over time and their scripture passages were greatly expanded upon through rabbinic interpretations, called *Midrash*. Thousands of midrashic writings or commentaries, from the period 536 BC to around 220 AD, were codified in a 63-volume text called the *Mishnah* (which means "the review"). From around 200 BC to about 500 AD, the *Talmud* (which means "the instructions") was formulated as commentaries on the commentaries. It follows the same 63 volume organization as the *Mishnah*. In Jesus' day, their scriptures were read in Aramaic from the *Targumim* (which means "the explanations") which also contained extensive commentaries. So, we can tell from these writings what the generally understood beliefs were at different times in their history.

Initially, the Great Eschatological Feast was for "all the people, Jews and Gentiles" and there would be endless peace. But, over many centuries of oppression by Gentile rulers, the expected feast morphed into a "feast for the righteous" only, as was evident in several of the recently translated Dead Sea Scrolls at Qumran in Jesus' day.[39]

For most of Jesus' listeners, it was only faithful Jews who would be invited by the Messiah to the banquet. And, while the banquet was going on, God was going to descend on the world, "level the mountains," "fill in the valleys" and eliminate all non-believers so that when the banquet was over, the faithful would walk out into the Kingdom of God devoid of all poverty, oppression and hatred. Then, God would reign; and there would be endless peace in the world. The arrival of that Kingdom of God would be the cataclysmic event in which only the believers remained.

But, Jesus was proclaiming that "*the Kingdom of God (*Kingdom of Heaven*) is at hand*" [Mk 1:15; Mt 3:2, 4:17] and He was now explaining the reign of God on earth in terms totally new to His listeners. While it was wonderful news that the poor, the hungry, the oppressed were "blessed," it would have been very difficult for Jesus' first listeners to imagine how that was possible. The Synoptic Gospels recount a dozen parables that Jesus subsequently shared with His listeners, each intended to give them greater insight into the true Kingdom of God.

6.2 Parable of the Two Foundations

Following the Sermon, as they headed to Capernaum, Jesus continued to expand on the Sermon using the Parable of the Two Foundations. There is a version of the parable in Matthew and a version in Luke.

6.2.1 The Version in Matthew's Gospel [Matthew 7:24-29]

Jesus said to them,
> "Everyone who listens to these words of mine and acts on
> them will be like a wise man who built his house on rock.
> The rain fell, the floods came, and the winds blew and buffeted
> the house. But it did not collapse; it had been set solidly on
> rock.
>
> And everyone who listens to these words of mine
> but does not act on them will be like a fool who built his house
> on sand. The rain fell, the floods came, and the winds blew
> and buffeted the house. And it collapsed and was completely
> ruined."

When Jesus finished these words, the crowds were astonished at his teaching, for he taught them as one having authority, and not as their scribes.

6.2.2 The Version in Luke's Gospel [Luke 6:46-49]

Jesus said to them, "Why do you call me,
'Lord, Lord,' but not do what I command?

> I will show you what someone is like who comes to me,
> listens to my words, and acts on them.
> That one is like a person building a house, who dug deeply
> and laid the foundation on rock; when the flood came, the river
> burst against that house but could not shake it because it had
> been well built.
>
> But the one who listens, and does not act is like a person
> who built a house on the ground without a foundation.
> When the river burst against it, it collapsed at once and was
> completely destroyed."

6.3 The Spiritual Lesson in the Parable

We begin by looking for the life situation that is being used to illustrate a deeper spiritual truth or lesson. To do this, we follow the details used in telling the story.

Detail: the first building effort is taking place on rock. Jesus did not say, "solid ground," but "rock." To Jews, there's an important cultural connotation when referring to "rock."

Detail: In Matthew's version, the second building effort is on sand.

Detail: In Matthew's version, it's torrential rains that challenge the buildings.

Detail: In Luke's version, the effort involved digging deeply to reach the rock.

Detail: In Luke's version, the second building effort is on "ground without a foundation" – essentially a short-cut building effort.

Detail: In Luke's version, it's a swollen river that challenges the buildings.

In Hebrew Scriptures, God was often referred to as being "rock" [e.g. 2 Sam 22:3; Ps 18:2; Isa 30:29]. Sometimes the Hebrew word, *tsuri*, was used, meaning that God was imposing or strong. Sometimes *sali* was used, "God gives me a safe hiding place." But quite often *ovna* was used, meaning God was like a birthing stone.

In the ancient Middle East, all birth deliveries were done with the woman squatting above a large rock (*ovna*) that she had spent months polishing and getting just right for her child. These *ovnalym* (pl. of *ovna*) were family heirlooms, passed down from generation to generation. At delivery, the midwife would catch the child and place the child on the birthing rock while the umbilical cord was severed. So, the first foundation they were set on at the moment of their birth was the *ovna* or birthing stone. The reference to "rock" in the parable brings to mind God as their birthing rock, their first solid foundation in life.

Many of Jesus' first listeners grew up with the concept that as long as they were Jews and diligently performed *mitsvot* (met the requirements of Mosaic Law); they were "entitled" to be included in the Kingdom of God. But, this parable reminded them that their first solid foundation in life was "the rock" - an up-close and personal contact with God. Their fastidious religious practices were no substitute for that close personal relationship with God. Their sense of entitlement stood on nothing more than sand.

For many centuries, Mosaic Law had prescribed almost every aspect of their lives. Now Jesus was essentially turning all this on its head. He was not negating Mosaic Law, He was not replacing it either; He was casting a totally new light on its interpretation and its role in their lives. Matthew's closing comment that they *"were astonished at his teaching, for he taught them as one having authority"* [Mt 7:29] is certainly an understatement.

As for us, we need to recognize that many of us grew up with the concept that as long as we went to Mass and received the sacraments, kept the Commandments; we were "in." We had a mistaken sense of entitlement as well. It's a personal relationship with Jesus Christ on which we must build the foundation of our life's "house."

This does not mean that the commandments or the sacraments are unimportant for us, nor does it mean that performing *mitsvot* are unimportant for Jews. It means that we, just as they, need to be sure that God is the foundation of our life, not the rituals and practices of our faith. Jesus would make this point again and again in His public ministry. On this occasion, He used a parable.

Let's now consider Luke's version of the same parable. Luke speaks about putting in a great effort to achieve a foundation that's on rock. Also, it was a "river" that challenged the buildings. And, Luke says that the other house had "no foundation at all."

Luke did not employ parallelism in his wording as Matthew did. Luke focused on the effort required in forming the foundation. He stressed to his faith community that forming and building the relationship takes effort.

Luke's Gentile listeners had seen, only a short while before Luke's gospel was written, that the Jews' whole world collapsed when the Temple was destroyed. Luke may have been signaling to his community that there was persecution ahead for all of them, Jew and Gentile. They would need the solid foundation to take them through the trials that were ahead.

Jesus and His disciples returned to Capernaum. And there, Jesus healed the Roman centurion's servant [Mt 8:5-13; Lk 7:1-10]. On this occasion, Jesus experienced a profound expression of faith from a Gentile, when the centurion said to Him, "*Lord, I am not worthy to have you enter under my roof; only say the word and my servant will be healed*" [Mt 8:8].

About a year and a half has passed since Jesus left Nazareth for Jerusalem on His first missionary journey. In that time, we have heard only two parables. Yet, in the next year and a half we will hear 36 parables. Why this change? Biblical scholars have puzzled over this; no broadly held conclusion has been reached. However, some contend that Jesus' decision to change the genre of His speaking came after the following event, which is recounted in all three Synoptic Gospels.

Likely it was in the summer of 31 AD, a crowd brought to Jesus a demoniac who was blind and mute. Jesus cured the person but then a number of Pharisees leveled a charge against him saying "*This man drives out demons only by the power of Beelzebub, the prince of demons*" [Mt 12:24; Mk 3:22b; Lk 11:15]. Mark referred to them as scribes who had come from Jerusalem [Mk 3:22a]. This was more than a nasty comment from some detractors; it was one of the vilest and hateful things one could say about a Jew.

6.4 Acting for Beelzebub

Beelzebub was the most derogatory name Jews could give to Satan. Beelzebub literally means "lord of the flies." To them, Satan was like dung and those around him like filth-ladened flies.

Today, Christians see Satan as the ultimate opponent of God, whereas the Israelites saw Satan as the ultimate opponent of the people of God. The word, *satan*, means the "accuser" or "adversary" [e.g. Job 1:6; Num 22:2; Zech 3:1-2; Psalm 109:6; 1 Chron. 21:1]. To them, Satan was the one who was constantly disparaging them before God; and this view echoed by Jews into the early Christian era [e.g. 1 Tim 4:13; Rev 12:10].
So, to be acting by the power of Beelzebub (Satan) was to be an enemy of the people in the worst possible way. This was worse than treason, punishable by death. But, in 30 BC, the power to

exact the death penalty was removed from the Great Sanhedrin by the Romans. Thus, the worst the Pharisees could do was to stir up hated of Jesus. And, they meant to do just that. They would seek to undermine everything Jesus said and did.

Since the meaning of a parable is not intended to be obvious, speaking in parables would provide a way for Jesus to "speak to the hearts" of those who were willing to discern His message while "speaking over the heads" of those who opposed Him. His narrow-minded opponents would be frustrated and unable to undermine His teachings.

While this argument makes sense, and has been advanced by several biblical scholars,[40] we need to recognize that we are really not sure whether this charge of *"driving out demons by the power of Beelzebub"* was the incident that convinced Jesus to make much greater use of parables than previously.

In the fall of 31 AD, Jesus traveled with His disciples from Capernaum south to Jerusalem for "a Jewish festival" [Jn 5:1]. This is regarded as being Sukkot, or the Feast of Tabernacles, which was celebrated from October 21 through Oct 28 that year. Even though this was the beginning of the peak fishing season in Galilee, we assume that His closest disciples were with Jesus on this trip because the Feast of Tabernacles is one of the three Jewish festivals on which all able-bodied men were required to pilgrimage to Jerusalem. And, His Apostles were no longer *"fishermen but fishers of men"* [Mt 4:19].

In Jerusalem, on the Sabbath, Jesus went to the pool of Bethesda [Jn 5:2]. Bethesda means 'house of healing'. Bethesda was an unusual pool. It had a portico around it; and people would gather around and wait for the water to stir, thinking that an angel was there stirring up the water. In fact, it was probably due to an underground geyser. If they hurried and entered the pool while the water was moving, they believed that they would be healed.
Sadly, a poor crippled man Jesus encountered there could never get to the water in time, while the water was still moving. Years went by yet every day he'd be there [Jn 5:5].

Detail: John tells us that it was 38 years; the number 38 had the symbolic meaning: time of great labor.[134]

But on this day, Jesus happened along. Jesus did not bring the man to the water; rather he touched and healed him where he was. This was on the Sabbath and John tells us that *"the Jews began to persecute Jesus because he did this on a Sabbath. But Jesus answered them, "My Father is at work until now, so I am at work." For this reason, the Jews tried all the more to kill him, because he not only broke the Sabbath, but he also called God his own father, making himself equal to God"* [Jn 5:16-18].

Following this, Jesus and His disciples returned north to Galilee, thus ending His fifth missionary journey. The "highs" were higher, but the "lows" were much lower. We heard Jesus begin to open the eyes and hearts of many of His listeners to a deeper understanding of the Kingdom of God. He called to mind for those willing to discern what our true foundation in life must be. But, we also heard some very ominous things: In Capernaum, Jesus was charged with a crime worse than treason: acting by the power of Beelzebub. And, later the Jewish authorities in Jerusalem plot to kill Jesus for healing a crippled man on the Sabbath.

We have the benefit of hindsight; we know that in the end Jesus triumphed over death itself. But, at the end of His fifth missionary journey, the Apostles were likely wondering just what they had gotten themselves into.

Dcn. Bob Evans

7. Jesus' Sixth Journey

In was probably late in 31 AD when Jesus and His disciples set out on another missionary journey through Lower Galilee. [Recall that Lower Galilee was predominantly Jewish, while Upper Galilee was still largely Gentile in Jesus' day]. Luke tells us that as Jesus and His disciples traveled in Lower Galilee they came to the town of Nain. Quite likely they were returning from Jerusalem having celebrated the Feast of Dedication (Hanukkah) which was observed on December 28/29 that year.

Nain (sometimes spelled Nein) was located on the northwestern slope of the Hill of Moreh. The hill is between Mount Tabor and Mount Gilboa, two mountains that had great historical importance to Jews. Not far from Nain, on the southwest slope of the Hill, was the town of Shunem, which also had great historical importance.

The name, Nain, means "green pastures," and, Shunem means "second resting place." To understand the significance of these names, we need to know a little more about ancient Jewish burial practices.

7.1 Ancient Jewish Burial Practices

Judaism, like all religious traditions, regarded death and the treatment of the dead with great reverence. Jewish burial practices had very comforting as well as very practical elements. Yet, they also regarded death with great fear, as we will see later when we address the Hebrew System of Ritual Purity.

Since God *"breathed into the man's (Adam's) nostrils the breath of life"* [Gen 2:7], death was seen by Jews as the breath of life, or *nephesh*, leaving the body. Their Scriptures often used the word, *va'yigvah*, which is usually translated "expired," to indicate that someone had died. There was no concept of soul in early Judaism. Rather, death was seen as the progressive loss of the *nephesh* which was thought to take place over a period of three days. So, one was not dead-dead until the third day.

Jews regarded it as a religious duty to properly bury the dead, including Gentiles. The body of the deceased was normally prepared for burial by an immediate family member (usually the eldest who was physically able to do so). After washing the body, it was bound, heavily perfumed and covered with a white burial shroud, or *tachrichin*, which was made of linen (if the family could afford it). Burial was to take place promptly, on that same day if possible [Deuteronomy 21:23]. Recall that in the Jewish calendar, a new day begins at sundown.

The body of the deceased was carried on a bier in procession, by the family, accompanied by a great deal of wailing. In biblical times, the family was expected to hire "professional" dirge-singers and flute players for this procession [e.g., Mt 9:23]. In addition to wailing, a mourning practice that is mentioned many times in the Bible was *keriah*, the ritual tearing of one's outer garment as an expression of great grief.

Ancient Jews followed the practice of *ossilegium*, or double burial, which was common throughout the Middle East, except in Egypt (where very elaborate corpse preservation measures were undertaken). For Jews, the first interment took place in a limestone cave in which an array of shelves had been cut into three sides of the cave. Families used the same set of shelves generation after generation, giving rise to the expression that one "*went to sleep with his fathers*" [cf. 1 Kings 11:23]. This was done so that deceased loved ones could easily enter "*the realm of their ancestors*" [see for example: Genesis 49:33]. Following the closing of the cave entrance, the immediate family remained in seclusion for a seven-day period, known as *shiva* – a mourning practice that dates from the time of the death of Jacob [Genesis 50:7].

One year after the first interment, the family would return to the cave and recover their loved one's bones and place them in a limestone box, called an ossuary. The ossuary was then buried in the ground, usually not far from the cave of first interment. There were, generally, no grave markers. The fact that there were no grave markers in Israel posed a very practical problem for Jews. One was regarded as "defiled" or ritually impure if he/she stepped, even accidently, on a spot where someone had been buried.

He/she was then required to perform an extensive sacrifice ceremony, known as the *he'tot*, to regain ritual purity.

The only time grave markers were used was in the case of one who could not be buried in the "family plot." Then, a stone marker, called a *matzevah*, was placed there to indicate "*one who died away from their ancestors*" [see for example: Jerimiah 31:14]. This was patterned after what Jacob had done for his wife Rachel [Gen 35:19-20], who was buried near Bethlehem after dying in childbirth. (Rachel is the only member of the extended family of Abraham-Isaac-Jacob who is not buried in the "family plot" of Machpelah near the city of Hebron.)

The name, Nain ("green pastures") does not refer to the local terrain but was a reference to Psalm 23:2, [41] "*In green pastures the Lord makes me lie down.*" Nain was a site of first interments for many families in Lower Galilee, and Shunem ("second resting place") was a site of second interments.

Figure 13: First Interment Caves near Nain

Upon arriving in Nain, Jesus and His disciples encountered a burial procession for the only son of a widow. By just touching the bier on which the dead man was being carried, Jesus raised the man from the dead and returned him to his mother [Lk 7:11-17]. This was the first of three miracles of Jesus, recounted in the canonical gospels, in which Jesus raised the dead.

Many of Luke's first listeners in the Antioch area were Gentiles who would most likely have seen this event as Jesus mercifully responding to a situation that was before Him. But, the fact that Luke included the name of the town, Nain, makes it's clear that he was also addressing many of the Jews who were recent refugees to his community in Antioch.

For Jews, everything that happens in the present is connected with the past. Nain was "next door" to Shunem and the parallels between Jesus raising from the dead the son of a widow in Nain and Elisha raising the dead son of a widow in nearby Shunem [2 Kings 4:8-37] would not have gone unnoticed by Jews.

Jesus' act was a pure expression of kindness. The widow of Nain never asked for His help; she may not have even known who He was; whereas, the widow of Shunem had to send for Elisha, begging for his help. The crowd at Nain and the crowd at Shunem, upon seeing the dead men raised, reacted in great fear. In that culture, one who had such power over death was to be feared. Jesus and His disciples immediately left the area and headed north a half-day's journey to the city of Garis, where the Shechem Road meets the Via Maris.

Arriving in Garis, which was a fairly affluent community in the Jezreel Valley, a Pharisee invited Jesus to dine at his house. As we've learned earlier, they would have actually dined in a common courtyard area where all meals were served. And, consequently, the neighbors would have gathered around the perimeter to observe and "listen in." Here Jesus shared with them the Parable of the Lender.

Dcn. Bob Evans

7.2 Parable of the Lender [Luke 7:36-50]

A Pharisee invited him to dine with him,
and he entered the Pharisee's house and reclined at table.
Now there was a sinful woman in the city who learned
that he was at table in the house of the Pharisee.
Bringing an alabaster flask of ointment,
she stood behind him at his feet weeping
and began to bathe his feet with her tears.
Then she wiped them with her hair, kissed them,
and anointed them with the ointment.

When the Pharisee who had invited him saw this, he said to himself, "If this man were a prophet, he would know who and what sort of woman this is who is touching him, that she is a sinner."

Jesus said to him in reply, "Simon, I have something to say to you."
"Tell me, teacher," he said.
    "Two people were in debt to a certain creditor;
    one owed five hundred days' wages and the other owed fifty.
    Since they were unable to repay the debt, he forgave it for
    both. Which of them will love him more?"

Simon said in reply, "The one, I suppose, whose larger debt was forgiven." He said to him, "You have judged rightly."

Then he turned to the woman and said to Simon,
"Do you see this woman? When I entered your house,
you did not give me water for my feet,
but she has bathed them with her tears and wiped them with her hair. You did not give me a kiss, but she has not ceased kissing my feet since the time I entered.
You did not anoint my head with oil, but she anointed my feet with ointment. So, I tell you, her many sins have been forgiven; hence, she has shown great love. **But the one to whom little is forgiven, loves little.**"

He said to her, "Your sins are forgiven."

The others at table said to themselves, "Who is this who even forgives sins?" But he said to the woman, "Your faith has saved you; go in peace."

Before we attempt to discern the spiritual lesson in this parable, we need to better understand the life circumstances of debtors, servants and slaves in ancient Israel.

7.3 Debtors, Servants and Slaves in Ancient Israel

Under Mosaic Law, every Hebrew household was entitled to a plot of land in fulfillment of God's promise: *"to you and your descendants I will give this land"* [Gen 12:7]. In principle, land in Israel could not be sold, but, in practice, land was frequently lost through foreclosure on a debt.

The most common reasons for debt were crop failure and inability to pay taxes, which were an enormous economic burden then. A wealthy neighbor would loan a poorer neighbor the money, but the loan was secured by the debtor's land and the labor of the members of the debtor's household.

When a household defaulted, which was very common, the Creditor foreclosed on the land and those in the debtor's household became "indentured," or debt-slaves to the Creditor. [In Israel, there were also forced-labor slaves who were prisoners of war, but these people were the property of the king, not individual households].

Because it was unlawful for a Hebrew to enslave another Hebrew, debt-slaves were referred to as "servants" [Lev 25:35]. Since these people were racially identical to their "masters," these servants were marked by a symbol of shame: large earrings or "tags of ownership" [cf. Ex 21:6]. These servants were slaves in every sense of the word, except they could not be physically abused [cf. Deu 24:14-15] and they were allowed to celebrate the Hebrew holidays with the master's household [cf. Deu 12:18].

A debt could be paid-off or forgiven prior to foreclosure, but unfortunately, this rarely happened, and foreclosure usually led to indentured servitude, or debt-slavery, for generations to come. It is estimated that, in the time of Jesus, every 1 in 5 persons in the Roman Empire was an indentured servant, or debt-slave.[42]

Under Hebrew law, debt-slaves were to be released every Sabbatical Year (each seventh year on the Hebrew calendar). However, any children born during their servitude, as well as a wife who might have been provided by the Creditor, "belonged" to the Creditor. Members of a debt-slave's family who "belonged" to the Creditor were known as *vernae*. In addition, the debt-slave no longer owned any land and therefore no longer "shared in the promise" and was termed a "stranger in the land."

Upon their release, former debtors often had no means of support and frequently exercised their "right" [cf. Ex 21:1-6] to remain as a servant in the master's household. All debt-slaves ("servants") were property and passed from father to sons via inheritance. Thus, debt was a pit into which a whole household might fall and remain for generations, until being freed as part of a Creditor's will or magnanimous gesture.

In Mosaic Law, a Jubilee year was to be celebrated every 50 years (the year following a set of seven Sabbatical year cycles). In a Jubilee year, all land was to revert back to its "original owner" as a way of preventing "endless" indentured servitude. But, Jubilee years were outlawed by both the Greek and Roman Empires because it undermined their imperial power structure which was built on indebtedness. The historian, Josephus, reported that the last Jubilee year observed in ancient Palestine was the "177th Seleucid Year" or 135-134 BC.[43] Consequently, Jubilee Years were a "thing of the past" in Jesus' day.

7.4 The Spiritual Lesson in the Parable

Again, we begin by looking for the life situation that is being used to illustrate a deeper spiritual truth or lesson. To do this, we follow the details used in telling the story.

Detail: a Pharisee invited Jesus to dine with him. The standard practice on such occasions was for the host to provide the traditional gestures of hospitality: having the guest's feet washed on arrival, greeting the guest with a kiss and anointing the guest's head with oil (a symbolism of the outpouring of God's blessings on the guest).

Detail: there was a "sinful" woman in the city – an indirect way of saying that she was a local prostitute.

Detail: it was the "sinful" woman who provided the traditional gestures of hospitality, not the host – something for which the host reviled her.

Detail: Jesus used the Pharisee's name, Simon, in addressing him. Simon is the English version of *Shema'on*, which means 'one who has heard'. What's indicated here was that the Pharisee has heard God's command: "do not judge," which is what the Pharisee had just done to the woman. Luke included the man's name in his narrative because there was information about the lesson in the man's name.

Detail: The Pharisee initially answered Jesus in a very arrogant way, to which Jesus replied with a parable about the forgiving of debts. He did this before He admonished the Pharisee for how he had treated Him, the guest.

Detail: Jesus asked His host, "which debtor will love more?" The one who had the larger debt forgiven may have involved having his whole family in indentured servitude; so, he had much more at stake.

Detail: in admonishing Simon, Jesus stated: "*I tell you, her many sins have been forgiven; hence, she has shown great love; but the one to whom little is forgiven, loves little*" [Lk 7:49]. The word, hence, is an insert that is not in very early texts of Luke's Gospel. Without the word "hence" it had long been interpreted that she was forgiven because she loved much. "Hence" makes it clearer to modern day listeners that she loved much because she had been forgiven much – indicating that there had been some previous encounter between Jesus and the woman at which time she had been forgiven of her sins. This was what prompted her very public expression of love. [44]

Jesus used this parable to make the case that great love is not the cause of forgiveness, but the proof of it. And, this is confirmed by Jesus' words to the woman: "*Your faith has saved you; go in peace*" [Lk 7:50]. So, we also are to forgive even what we regard as inexcusable because God has forgiven the inexcusable in us.

It was at this point, upon their leaving Garis, that Luke mentioned that Jesus "*journeyed from one town and village to another, preaching and proclaiming the good news of the kingdom of God. Accompanying him were the Twelve and some women who had been cured of evil spirits and infirmities, Mary, called Magdalene, from whom seven demons had gone out, Joanna, the wife of Herod's steward Chuza, Susanna, and many others who provided for them out of their resources*" [Lk 8:1-3]. The most striking thing about the role of women in the ministry of Jesus is the fact that they were there. This was without precedent in then contemporary Judaism. [45] Although women are not explicitly mentioned in Jesus' company again until the accounts of Passion Week, it's clear that there were women among the disciples who accompanied Him during his travels and ministry; and, their support "out of their resources" of Jesus and His closest followers was essential.[46]

After about a day's journey from Garis, they arrived at the city of Tiberias on the Sea of Galilee. Tiberias was on the eastern edge of the Jezreel Valley, the "bread basket" of Lower Galilee. Tiberias was also the political and religious center of Galilee, founded in 20 AD, by King Herod Antipas to honor the Roman Emperor Tiberius. It was built on the ruins of the ancient Hebrew city of Rakkath [Joshua 19:35]. The city was a resort destination for the well-off; the city had several hot spring health spas and a very large Roman amphitheater.

The hot springs were a result of geothermal activity along the west coast of the Sea of Galilee; and, Tiberias had experienced an earthquake the year before, in 30 AD.[47] So, there would have been considerable reconstruction work going on requiring many tradesmen to be in town. Some of them might have been present in the large crowd that gathered around Jesus. Perhaps there were some there who Joseph and Jesus had worked with years earlier in the rebuilding of Sapporis.

Along the shore at Tiberias, Jesus shared with the crowd the Parable of the Sower and the Parable of the Weeds among the Wheat. Later, away from the crowd, Jesus' disciples questioned Him about the Parable of the Sower and the Parable of the Weeds among the Wheat. However, that discourse appears in the Gospel texts immediately after each of these parables, rather than in a later section. So, we will address the discourse in the order in which it appears in the Gospel texts, recognizing that it actually took place privately between Jesus and His disciples, not before the large crowd that had gathered to see and hear Him by the shore of the Sea of Galilee. Recall that questioning someone in public was interpreted as an honor challenge. Therefore, this discourse would have had to be in private, and most likely in the evening.

7.5 Parable of the Sower

This parable involves agriculture in a way that is quite unlike the way we plant. The parable was recounted in Matthew, Mark and Luke. Matthew began his account with the statement: "Jesus went out of the house and sat down by the sea." It's not clear what house Matthew was referring to; perhaps it was the home of an affluent disciple who was providing lodging for Jesus during His brief stay in Tiberias.

7.5.1 The Version in Matthew's Gospel [Matthew 13:1-23]

On that day, Jesus went out of the house and sat down by the sea. Such large crowds gathered around him that he got into a boat and sat down, and the whole crowd stood along the shore.

And he spoke to them at length in parables, saying:
"A sower went out to sow.
And as he sowed, some seed fell on the path, and birds came and ate it up.

Some fell on rocky ground, where it had little soil.
It sprang up at once because the soil was not deep,

and when the sun rose it was scorched, and it withered for lack of roots.

Some seed fell among thorns, and the thorns grew up and choked it. But some seed fell on rich soil, and produced fruit, a hundred or sixty or thirtyfold.
Whoever has ears ought to hear."

The disciples approached him and said,
"Why do you speak to them in parables?"

He said to them in reply,
"Because knowledge of the mysteries of the kingdom of heaven has been granted to you, but to them it has not been granted. To anyone who has, more will be given, and he will grow rich; from anyone who has not, even what he has will be taken away.

This is why I speak to them in parables, because 'they look but do not see and hear but do not listen or understand.

Isaiah's prophecy is fulfilled in them, which says:

'You shall indeed hear but not understand, you shall indeed look but never see. Gross is the heart of this people, they will hardly hear with their ears, they have closed their eyes, lest they see with their eyes and hear with their ears and understand with their heart and be converted, and I heal them."

"But blessed are your eyes, because they see, and your ears, because they hear.

Amen, I say to you, many prophets and righteous people longed to see what you see but did not see it, and to hear what you hear but did not hear it."

"Hear then the parable of the sower.
The seed sown on the path is the one who hears the word of the kingdom without understanding it, and the evil one comes and steals away what was sown in his heart.

The seed sown on rocky ground is the one who hears the word
and receives it at once with joy. But he has no root and lasts only
for a time. When some tribulation or persecution comes because
of the word, he immediately falls away.

The seed sown among thorns is the one who hears the word,
but then worldly anxiety and the lure of riches choke the word and
it bears no fruit.

But the seed sown on rich soil is the one who hears the word and
understands it, who indeed bears fruit and yields a hundred or
sixty or thirtyfold."

7.5.2 The Version in Mark's Gospel [Mark 4:1-20]

On another occasion, Jesus began to teach by the sea.
A very large crowd gathered around him
so that he got into a boat on the sea and sat down.
And the whole crowd was beside the sea on land.

And he taught them at length in parables,
and in the course of his instruction he said to them,

> "Hear this!
> A sower went out to sow.
> And as he sowed, some seed fell on the path, and the birds
> came and ate it up.
>
> Other seed fell on rocky ground where it had little soil.
> It sprang up at once because the soil was not deep.
> And when the sun rose, it was scorched, and it withered for
> lack of roots.
>
> Some seed fell among thorns, and the thorns grew up and
> choked it and it produced no grain.
>
> And some seed fell on rich soil and produced fruit.
> It came up and grew and yielded thirty, sixty, and a
> hundredfold."

He added, "Whoever has ears to hear ought to hear."

And when he was alone, those present along
with the Twelve questioned him about the parables.
He answered them,
"The mystery of the kingdom of God has been granted to you.
But to those outside everything comes in parables, so that
'they may look and see but not perceive,
and hear and listen but not understand,
in order that they may not be converted and be forgiven.'

Jesus said to them, "Do you not understand this parable?
Then how will you understand any of the parables? The sower sows the word.
These are the ones on the path where the word is sown.
As soon as they hear, Satan comes at once and takes away the word sown in them.
And these are the ones sown on rocky ground who,
when they hear the word, receive it at once with joy.
But they have no root; they last only for a time.
Then when tribulation or persecution comes because of the word,
they quickly fall away.

Those sown among thorns are another sort. They are the people who hear the word, but worldly anxiety, the lure of riches, and the craving for other things intrude and choke the word, and it bears no fruit.

But those sown on rich soil are the ones who hear the word and accept it and bear fruit thirty and sixty and a hundredfold."

7.5.3 The Version in Luke's Gospel [Luke 8:4-15]

When a large crowd gathered,
with people from one town after another journeying to him,
Jesus spoke in a parable:

> "A sower went out to sow his seed.
> And as he sowed, some seed fell on the path and was trampled,
> and the birds of the sky ate it up.
>
> Some seed fell on rocky ground, and when it grew,

> it withered for lack of moisture.
>
> Some seed fell among thorns, and the thorns grew with it and choked it.
>
> And some seed fell on good soil, and when it grew, it produced fruit a hundredfold."

After saying this, he called out, "Whoever has ears to hear ought to hear."

Then his disciples asked him what the meaning of this parable might be. He answered,
 "Knowledge of the mysteries of the kingdom of God has been granted to you; but to the rest, they are made known through parables so that 'they may look but not see and hear but not understand.'

"This is the meaning of the parable. The seed is the word of God. Those on the path are the ones who have heard, but the devil comes and takes away the word from their hearts that they may not believe and be saved.

Those on rocky ground are the ones who, when they hear, receive the word with joy, but they have no root; they believe only for a time and fall away in time of trial.

As for the seed that fell among thorns, they are the ones who have heard, but as they go along, they are choked by the anxieties and riches and pleasures of life, and they fail to produce mature fruit. But as for the seed that fell on rich soil, they are the ones who, when they have heard the word, embrace it with a generous and good heart, and bear fruit through perseverance.

7.6 The Spiritual Lesson in the Parable

Detail: The sower sowed seeds by merely scattering them about. We would regard this as a very inefficient way of planting. But, in their minds, they were trying to emulate nature: "*just as the wind blows the seeds about, man should also sow*" [cf. Ecc 11:4]. So, you can imagine that there would be quite a few seeds that fell on land which was not productive, just as the parable states.

Detail: three examples are given of effort that yielded failure. The number three had the symbolic meaning: full circle or spiritual perfection.[134] It's not clear why Jesus used three examples; He could have been using three to indicate that throughout the full cycle of life there will be efforts that will yield failure.

Detail: "But some fell on rich soil and produced fruit a hundred or sixty or thirtyfold" (in both Matthew and Mark); "it produced fruit a hundredfold" (in Luke's version). In those days, their yields were typically about 10 to15 fold. [The volume of what one harvested was about 10-15 times the volume of what one planted.] For them that was a good yield. So, a 30-fold yield was extraordinary; a 100-fold was unbelievable. And yet, the parable speaks about a 100-fold harvest. This was clearly emphasis through exaggeration.

Following the details, it appears that the parable is more about the promised harvest, rather than the act of sowing of seeds. There is a promise in the parable of a harvest yield of 100 or 60 or 30-fold; yet the sower need only scatter the seeds and wait. They did not try to cultivate the field; they didn't irrigate, they didn't water the fields at all. They relied entirely upon God's providence to provide rain. There was a promise here of an almost unbelievable harvest. And, that promise is based on the providence of God.

To many of the inhabitants of Tiberias, who were accustomed to easy living, this was a radical idea. To them, wealth and comfort was the indication of God's favor. The poorer you were the more God was punishing you. But, here Jesus was saying, "No, that's not it at all; relying on God will yield you an unbelievable benefit." On the spiritual level, that promise is eternal life, not necessarily abundance in this life.

7.7 Discourse Following the Parable of the Sower

In all three Synoptic Gospels, there's an extensive discourse following the Parable of the Sower. There is an important difference between metaphor and allegory. A "metaphor" contrasts some activity or situation with some other activity or situation. In an "allegory," individual concepts or elements of one story are symbolic of some other concept or element. Generally speaking, Middle Eastern parables were intended to be metaphoric, not allegoric. That is generally speaking. What we find in the discourse following this parable was that it's all about allegory. Different kinds of soil were "interpreted" as symbolic of different kinds of people. That seems out of place for a Middle Eastern parable. It's not that allegory was entirely unknown; indeed, it was quite common among Greeks. It's that it was uncommon among Hebrews.

Further, the question: "Why did you speak to them in parables?" was certainly a reasonable question for Jesus' disciples. They had been on several journeys with Him when there were no parables. But, recently they are hearing parables. Recall that parables were often 'pushbacks' against opposition, a means for Jesus to separate those who were willing to invest the effort to discern His message from those who were not. Unfortunately, the discourse following this parable blurs that answer somewhat, and that discourse is found in all three Synoptic Gospels.

Jesus replied to this question with: "*Because knowledge of the mysteries of the Kingdom of Heaven has been granted to you, but to them it has not been granted.*" That sounded to many like Jesus was sharing 'secrets' or secret knowledge with His followers but not with other people. This gave rise to the Logos position that Christianity is about "knowing the secrets." "If you know the secrets, you are part of the 'in' crowd, and if you don't, you are part of the 'damned.'" This response seems to support that kind of thinking. So, that must be an interpretation that is incorrect, because it is inconsistent with what we know about Jesus Christ. For, God's revelation does not contradict itself.[48]

But, Jesus cited for them a passage from Isaiah [Isa 6:9-10] in which the prophet condemned those who did not embrace what was being said about God's will. And, Jesus noted that they were seeing the same thing in His day. Jesus' disciples were "blessed" because they were willing to put in the effort to discern what they were hearing. When something challenged them, they did not abandon Him like, so many others had.

Then, something even more puzzling: Jesus proceeded to explain the Parable of the Sower. In their culture, one who told a parable did not normally explain the parable; the listeners were expected to discern the message or lesson. In the Gospel accounts, Jesus proceeded to give an allegorical interpretation of the parable in which the various types of soil symbolized various receivers of the word. Referring to the footnote to this passage in the New American Bible translation (which is the one used in the Catholic lectionary): "Many theologians hold that the explanation may come basically from Jesus, even though it was developed in the late Christian experience."

To understand this "late Christian experience," we need to look at when the Synoptic Gospels were written. As we saw earlier, they were written in the period of about 68-72 A.D; the destruction of the Jewish Temple was in 70 AD. The impression at the time was that the destruction of the Temple was the beginning of the end times. The impetus was to get the good news of Jesus out to as many people as possible, as fast as possible. This prompted the writing of the gospels ('good news'). At the time, it was expected that Jesus would return "any day now."

But the Roman Reign of Terror occurred in 90-96 A.D. Emperor Domitian was paranoid, believing that everyone was a threat to him. So, he labeled Christianity an "outlawed superstition." All those who held to that "superstition" were to be executed immediately. Christians were rounded up by the thousands. What followed were crucifixions, burnings, and being fed to the lions, etc. In situations like that, there were many who, when faced with the loss of their family, their children, loved ones, denied their faith. That is called "apostasy." Those who denied the faith were called "apostates."

During the period of the Reign of Terror, there were thousands of apostates. When Domitian was finally assassinated by the Roman Senate, the Reign of Terror ended. After a while, many apostates wanted to come back into the Church. The Church was faced with a new problem: "Are we to accept apostates back; and if so, how do we do that?" The Church struggled for decades trying to resolve this. The theory concerning the allegorical explanation of the parable was that the "soil groups" who did not hold to the faith were the groups of apostates.

Some have speculated that the allegorical explanations originated with the evangelists. However, since there was no widespread apostasy prior to the severe persecutions of the late first century, many theologians conjecture that this discourse following the parable is a later addition to the gospels. Their theory is that the addition was intended to deal with the apostate crisis in the Church. And that idea was held for a very long time until it was noted that while giving an allegorical explanation to a parable may have been inconsistent with the norms of teaching by use of parables, Jesus certainly did a number of things that were inconsistent with their expectations for Him as Messiah. So, it's reasonable although unlikely that Jesus might have intended an allegorical parable.

Going back into Biblical archives looking for the oldest copies of the gospels, they found the oldest existing copy of Matthew dates from about 150 A.D. We have no surviving versions older than that. That's well after the struggle with the apostates. So, the fact that we find the explanation text in the oldest version available doesn't answer the question: "was it in the original?" So, they turned to Mark's Gospel. The oldest version available of Mark dates from about 250 A.D. And the oldest version of Luke dates from around 175 A.D. The text of the explanation is in those versions as well. Jesus may have actually given an allegorical explanation of his parable.

Mark's wording of the parable is almost identical to Matthew's. In addition, the wording of Jesus' answer to "Why do you teach them in parables" is also almost verbatim to Matthew's. In Mark, Jesus proceeded to explain the parable, even though no one asked about it. This of course tended to fuel the argument that the explanation was a later addition to the gospel. And, the allegorical explanation is almost identical to Matthew's.

In Luke, there is no boat by the sea where Jesus sits down. Jews were accustomed to their rabbis being seated when teaching, so they would recognize the inference of Jesus being seated before teaching, But Gentiles had no such experience, so Luke (who was writing principally to Gentiles) leaves that detail out. In Luke, the seed that fell on rocky ground withered for lack of moisture, not lack of roots (as in the two Jewish versions - Matthew and Mark). Jewish listeners at the time had their "roots" in an understanding of God that went back nearly 1500 years. At the time, those Jews who lacked the sense of rootedness, even those who converted to Christianity, were in serious risk of losing their faith. Gentiles did not have those roots to start with, so they relied on "moisture" - God's provision of rain, namely grace.

Luke states that Jesus' disciples asked what the parable meant. Also, in Luke meaning is given to the seed by indicating that "the seed is the word of God." "Word of God" was a new concept to Gentiles, but not to Jews.

Gentiles were also new to the concept of sin and the role of the Devil, so Luke casts the allegorical explanation in "devil temptation" terminology. This has a very Lukan character to it and suggests that it was actually in Luke's original, thus undermining the argument that the allegorical explanation was a later addition.

Further, in Luke, the good soil did not yield a promised 100-fold harvest; rather it empowered them to perseverance. Many of Luke's listeners were working class people in a large metropolitan city, Antioch. They were not farmers; a promise of a 100-fold harvest had little significance to them. But, they did need perseverance in the face of persecution.

So, we've gone full circle in trying to fathom the allegorical explanation of the parable, even though the idea that it was a later addition prevailed for centuries.

For many centuries, people sought to determine the 'right' interpretations of parables. What was concluded however was that parables are often so deep in meaning that there's more than one suitable interpretation. There are many interpretations that are wrong, but there is not necessarily a single interpretation that's the only "right" one. There are faith lessons in the parables that will be more meaningful to some than to others, or more meaningful to you at one point in your life than at another. So, what Jesus was asking His listeners to do was to discern meaning that resonated in their hearts and was consistent with their understanding of God's will; and we seek to do the same.

Also, at the Sea of Galilee at Tiberias, Jesus shared with the crowd the Parable of the Weeds Among the Wheat. This parable and the discourse that followed only appear in Matthew's Gospel. Jesus began publicly teaching about the Kingdom of Heaven (or Kingdom of God as Mark and Luke referred to it) in the Sermon on the Mount. We don't know at what point He began teaching His disciples in private about it, but we encounter here the first parable on the Kingdom He shared in public.

7.8 Parable of the Weeds Among the Wheat [Matthew 13:24-30, 34-43]

He proposed another parable to them.
> "The kingdom of heaven may be likened to a man
> who sowed good seed in his field. While everyone was asleep his enemy came and sowed weeds all through the wheat, and then went off.
>
> When the crop grew and bore fruit, the weeds appeared as well. The slaves of the householder came to him and said, 'Master, did you not sow good seed in your field?
> Where have the weeds come from?'
>
> He answered,
> 'An enemy has done this.' His slaves said to him,
> 'Do you want us to go and pull them up?'
>
> He replied, 'No, if you pull up the weeds you might uproot the wheat along with them.
> Let them grow together until harvest; then at harvest time I will say to the harvesters,
> "First collect the weeds and tie them in bundles for burning; but gather the wheat into my barn."

All these things Jesus spoke to the crowds in parables.
He spoke to them only in parables,
to fulfill what had been said through the prophet:
"I will open my mouth in parables,

I will announce what has lain hidden from the foundation [of the world]."

Then, dismissing the crowds,* he went into the house.
His disciples approached him and said,
"Explain to us the parable of the weeds in the field."
He said in reply, "He who sows good seed is the Son of Man, the field is the world,*
the good seed the children of the kingdom. The weeds are the children of the evil one, and the enemy who sows them is the devil. The harvest is the end of the age,* and the harvesters are angels. Just as weeds are collected and burned up with fire, so will it be at the end of the age.

The Son of Man will send his angels, and they will collect out of his kingdom all who cause others to sin and all evildoers.
They will throw them into the fiery furnace, where there will be wailing and grinding of teeth. Then the righteous will shine like the sun in the kingdom of their Father.

Whoever has ears ought to hear.

7.9 The Spiritual Lesson in the Parable

Detail: *"The kingdom of heaven may be likened to ..."* Jesus had to move His listeners, most of whom where Jews, from their initial understanding of the Kingdom of God to something much different. Instead of stating on a single occasion "what you previously understood is wrong, the Kingdom will really be like this ...." He decided to use a very incremental approach. Over a period of months, Jesus shared many parables; a dozen is recounted in the Synoptic Gospels, which basically began with this same line: "The Kingdom of Heaven (Kingdom of God) may be likened to ...."

Detail: *"sowed weeds all through the wheat."* The weed, darnel, looks almost identical to wheat but it is not edible.

Detail: "*While everyone was asleep.*" Evil acts were often referred to as "things done in the darkness."

Detail: it was the master of the household who personally sowed the seeds; it was the slaves who observed the problem; an unexpected role reversal.

Detail: "*Let them grow together until harvest,*" then separate them. The good will co-exist with the bad until the end.

Detail: "*Whoever has ears ought to hear.*" If you are capable of listening, you are capable of discerning.

The details used in telling the parable convey an image of the Kingdom of Heaven that is quite different from the long-held Jewish expectation. In Jesus' version, good and evil co-exist in the Kingdom until the end, when they are separated. But, in the Jewish expectation, the separation of good (righteous Jews) from the bad (Gentiles) was to take place at the commencement of the Kingdom, the coming of the Messiah; and, only the righteous would experience the Kingdom, which would have no end.

We also get from the parable that in the master's holding off until harvest, weeds (bad) might be able to change into wheat (something good). Yet, there was no prospect of changing in the old expectation; non-believers (Gentiles) would always remain Gentiles.

We can almost hear the murmuring spread throughout the crowd: "What could he possibly mean by this parable?" This was certainly not the only occasion when most, if not all, of Jesus' listeners were left to discern a parable that might take years to unpack its message. We have the benefit of centuries of Church teachings; it would be a very long time before Jewish Christians would grasp the full meaning of Jesus' teaching about the Kingdom of God.

In Matthew's account of the Parable of the Sower, just ahead of this parable, Jesus replied to His disciples' question: "Why do you speak to them in parables?" Following this parable, Matthew offers his own answer: "to fulfill what had been said through the prophet:

"'I will open my mouth in parables, I will announce what has lain hidden from the foundation [of the world].'"

Actually, Matthew was quoting from Psalm 78:2, not from one of the prophets. Matthew did not err here. His theme was that Jesus is the Messiah because He fulfilled biblical prophesies (which would have included the Psalms, in their minds).

7.10 Discourse Following the Parable of the Weed among the Wheat

The dialogue that followed this parable continued the same pattern which followed the previous parable. As noted in the discourse following the Parable of the Sower, while explaining a parable may have been out of character for first century Jews, it's reasonable that Jesus may have intended an allegorical parable here as well.

In the explanation of this parable, emphasis lies on the fearful end of the wicked; whereas the parable itself concentrates on patience with them until judgment time. Being thrown into "the fiery furnace" would have brought to mind for Jesus' listeners the Valley of Hinnom (also known as *Gahenna*) just west of Jerusalem, where the early Canaanites, and later idolatrous Jews, sacrificed children by burning them. So, the Jews envisioned fire, or being burned, as the worst possible treatment one could receive (which is why the original description of Hell involves fire).

Also, in this dialogue we encounter the word 'righteous'. The Hebrew word for righteous was *tsedaq*. A righteous person was one who kept mercy and justice in right balance. So, this dialogue is saying that those who are saved are those who hold mercy and justice in proper balance; it's not based on entitlement, which was the Jewish expectation. In the Kingdom of Heaven, the door to being saved is open to all who keep mercy and justice in right balance.

Clearly, Jesus was now using parables as His principal means of teaching. He expected those who were willing to listen to do so with their whole being: mind, heart, and life experiences in discerning what they've heard. We must do the same.

The more we journey with Jesus, the more we feel blessed to have this chance to know Him better. We saw His great compassion as He went, without ever being asked, to where a grieving mother was on the verge of becoming destitute. There He mercifully restored her dignity by raising her son from the dead. And, when the locals responded with fear, He showed His great humility by just withdrawing from the area and continuing on His way to encounter others in their life circumstances.

Then in Tiberias, the most cosmopolitan city in Galilee, He gently taught those who would listen that their future, indeed our future, lies not in prosperity but in the Providence of God. His vision of the Kingdom of God was certainly startling for them, but, He did not begin with the premise that "you've got it all wrong." Rather, He used a simple agricultural story to begin laying out God's plan for His kingdom on earth where evil will be allowed to exist with the good until they are separated at the final "harvest."

Accompanied by the twelve apostles and some women, Jesus headed some 5 miles north to the city of Magdala (also known as Magadan) near the base of Mount Arbel on the Via Maris trade route. Located on the western shore of the Sea of Galilee in the ancient area known as Dalmanutha, Magdala (which means "tower") was a center of shipbuilding and fish processing for many centuries. The Greek name for the town was Taricheac ("place of salted fish"). As noted earlier, Magdala was where they made the fish sauce known as *garum*, the principal export crop of Galilee.

In a distance of only 5 miles, Jesus and His disciples had entered a much different world from that in Tiberias. Magdala was a working-class city. The marketplace was the center of the community which was a hotbed of Roman resistance. To avoid skirmishes, there was no Roman garrison in Magdala despite all the tax revenue collected there from the fish trade. In 67 AD, during the Great Jewish Revolt, the Romans killed every inhabitant of the town of Magdala, estimated to be about 40,000 people. [49]

The residents of Magdala that day were virtually all Jews, and Jesus shared the Parable of the Lamp with a large crowd that had gathered.

Figure 14: The Remains of Magdala (1900 colorized photo)

7.11 Parable of the Lamp

7.11.1 *The Version in Matthew's Gospel* [Matthew 5:14-16]

Jesus said to them,
> "You are the light of the world. A city set on a mountain cannot be hidden.
> Nor do they light a lamp and then put it under a bushel basket;
> it is set on a lampstand, where it gives light to all in the house. Just so, your light must shine before others,

that they may see your good deeds and glorify your heavenly Father."

7.11.2 The Version in Mark's Gospel [Mark 4:21-23]

In the course of his instruction he said to them,
> "Is a lamp brought in to be placed under a bushel basket or under a bed, and not to be placed on a lampstand?
> For there is nothing hidden except to be made visible; nothing is secret except to come to light.
> Anyone who has ears to hear ought to hear."

7.11.3 The Version in Luke's Gospel [Luke 8:16-17]

When a large crowd gathered, with people from one town after another journeying to him, he spoke in a parable,
> "No one who lights a lamp conceals it with a vessel or sets it under a bed; rather, he places it on a lampstand so that those who enter may see the light.
> For there is nothing hidden that will not become visible, and nothing secret that will not be known and come to light."

7.12 The Spiritual Lesson in the Parable

Detail: (in Matthew's version) "*You are the light of the world.*" The very first verses of Genesis read: "*In the beginning.... darkness covered the abyss; and then God said, 'Let there be light.'*" So, the very first thing God created was light. We know from science that light emanates from agitated electrons. We need to have matter first in order to have light. So, this verse is not intended to be taken literally.

Detail: (in Mark's and Luke's versions) "*there is nothing hidden except to be made visible.*" What was hidden that would become known was God's plan of salvation through Jesus Christ.

The expectation that God, Himself, would become man and die at the hands of man, then to rise from the dead on the third day, was inconceivable prior to it actually happening. In the primordial darkness, God was present but there was no perceivable indication of His presence – until there was light. Jesus was calling all who believe to be a visible indication of the presence of God in the world.

His Jewish listeners would have readily recognized the reference to light, but how they would be the visible indication of God's presence in the world would take some serious pondering. Yet, it was those who had to labor each day, depending out of necessity on the Providence of God, who would invest themselves in discerning Jesus' words.

And so, Jesus proceeded to share with them a parable, the Parable of the Growing Seed. This parable only appears in Mark's Gospel.

7.13 Parable of the Growing Seed [Mark 4:26-29]

Jesus said,
> "This is how it is with the kingdom of God;
> it is as if a man were to scatter seed on the land
> and would sleep and rise night and day
> and the seed would sprout and grow, he knows not how.
> Of its own accord the land yields fruit, first the blade,
> then the ear, then the full grain in the ear.
> And when the grain is ripe, he wields the sickle at once,
> for the harvest has come."

7.14 The Spiritual Lesson in the Parable

Detail: *"This is how it is with the kingdom of God."* The people of Magdala now get to hear Jesus describe the Kingdom of God.

Detail: *"Of its own accord the land yields fruit."* The Kingdom will provide all that you need if you persevere and trust in God.

Today, Jesus spoke this parable in Magdala. The day before, they were in Tiberias. The people in Tiberias did not hear "today's" parable. The only group of listeners who will hear all of the parables about the Kingdom is the Apostles. That's why He told them they were "blessed." "*You get to hear what others longed to hear and did not hear. You get to see what others longed to see and did not*" [Mt 13:7; Lk 10:24]. The apostles stayed with Jesus even when they were totally puzzled by what He was saying. And because they stayed, they were the continuity; and later went on to evangelize others. But, it was not until after Pentecost that they "put it all together." And, it's only because they "put it all together" that we know of the Kingdom of God today.

From Magdala, Jesus had anyone who would follow sail across the Sea of Galilee to the eastern shore [Mt 8:18; Mk 4:35; Lk 8:22]. On the way, Jesus calmed a storm [Mt 8:24; Mk 4:37; Lk 8:23]. After sailing through the night, they arrived at the city of Gergesa in the region of the Joulan, originally known as Bashan ("light soil") and known today as the Golan Heights.

The city of Gergesa ("place of fighters") was located on a cliff overlooking the Sea of Galilee, in the area known then by the Greek name: *Decapolis* ("ten cities"). It was also referred to as "the region of the Gerasenes" [Mk 5:1; Lk 8:26] or "the Gadarenes" [Mt 8:28]. In the first century, Gergesa was almost exclusively pagan (Gentile).

Upon arriving, Jesus was confronted by demoniacs (possessed men) and He drove the demons into a herd of swine. All three Synoptic Gospels [Mt 8:28-34; Mk 5:1-20; Lk 8:26-39] describe this miracle, but only Matthew writes about two possessed men instead of one. On seeing what happened, the locals "*began to beg Jesus to leave their neighborhood*" [Mt 8:34, Mk 5:17, Lk 8:37]. And, so Jesus and his disciple withdrew to another area, probably near the shore at Gergesa where their boats were anchored. Jesus's first missionary venture into pagan territory did not seem to go well.

We don't know how many people in Magdala accepted Jesus' call to "*Let us cross to the other side*" [Mk 4:35] but there were several boatloads [Mk 4:36]. Recognizing that, to sail due east, they had to set sail at night because the prevailing winds were from the Mediterranean Sea toward the west at night. Also, it was the rainy season, and they all knew that the violent storms on the Sea of

Galilee were usually at night. It took great courage for many of them to head for pagan territory in the first place, let alone sail across the Sea of Galilee at its widest point at night during the stormiest time of the year. So, these were *true* disciples, intentional listeners (which is what the word disciple means).

In Gergesa, they could get food and water but there would be little hospitality shown them. The Gerasenes were very hostile to Jews. Consequently, it's likely that Jesus and His disciples spent the night on the shore near Gergesa to await prevailing winds to the west in the morning.

Figure 15: The Shoreline near Gergesa

And so, to these true disciples alone Jesus shared the Parable of the Joy of Finding, the Parable of the Fishing Net and the Parable of the Head of Household. All three parables are only recounted in Matthew.

To understand the point of the Parable of the Joy of Finding we need to first have some background on land ownership in ancient Israel.

7.15 Land "Ownership" in Ancient Israel

In modern terminology, "ownership" means the right to possess, use and/or dispose of something. In Ancient Israel, "ownership" did not have that broad a meaning. The ownership rights observed in ancient Israel were patterned after those in the neighboring kingdoms of Egypt and Mesopotamia, with one important exception. In Egypt and Mesopotamia, the land was owned by the pharaoh or king, who allocated it to his subjects to be its custodians. In Israel, the land was owned by God who allocated it to His people to be its custodians: *"the land is mine and you are but aliens and my tenants"* [Leviticus 25:23]. As such, one of the constant issues mentioned by the prophets was warnings against *"adding house to house and joining field to field"* [Isiah. 5:8], that is, amassing large property holdings.

So sacred to the Israelites was land that there was a complete absence of any land or property taxes in biblical times. God clearly intended that the land laws should give stability to society, thus he protected the land from any, and all, taxation.

Throughout, Egypt, Israel and Mesopotamia only the landowner (pharaoh, king, God) was free to dispose of land in the way they saw fit. The custodians of the land had three basic rights:
- Right to exclude trespassers, including livestock
  (In Israel, this did not include the poor, the alien or the widow)
- Right to decide the land's use
- Right against expropriation of the land by others.

In ancient times, there was no police force, so these three rights were enforced by the elders of the local community who sat in judgment of disputes while convened on the floor of the local threshing barn. If the community had no threshing barn, the elders convened at the main village gate. By Jesus' day, the role of adjudicator of land disputes had been taken over by the Temple priests, which led to many cases of great injustice.

Most "land sales" in those days did not involve actual ownership change but rather a transfer of custodian rights. And, such "land sales" could be modified or vetoed by one's extended family or by the local community. In modern terminology, something is part of the land (i.e. "real property") if it is affixed to or connected to the land in some way. In ancient times, if something was resting on the land, it was part of the land. So, something that was found on the land belonged to the owner of that land.

7.16 The Parable of the Joy of Finding [Matthew 13:44-46]

Jesus said to them,
> "The kingdom of heaven is like a treasure buried in a field,
> which a person finds and hides again, and out of joy goes and sells all that he has and buys that field.
>
> Again, the kingdom of heaven is like a merchant searching for fine pearls. When he finds a pearl of great price,
> he goes and sells all that he has and buys it.

7.17 The Spiritual Lesson in the Parable

Detail: "*The kingdom of heaven is like*," Jesus seeks to deepen His disciples' understanding of the Kingdom of heaven with another parable about the Kingdom.

Detail: "*treasure buried in a field*," - something of great value hidden in a secure place during a time of danger, but never retrieved. To find it would have required diligent effort.

Detail: "*finds and hides ... then buys*," the treasure belongs by right to the owner of the field, so the finder must buy the field to take rightful possession.

Jesus' disciples' sense of entitlement is challenged. The Kingdom of Heaven is a priceless find which one must seek and on finding it one must take rightful possession of it. The parable suggests that the way one takes rightful possession is by committing oneself totally: "*sells all that he has and buys it*" [Mt 13:46].

Jesus then shared with them another parable about the Kingdom of Heaven, the Parable of the Fishing Net.

7.18 The Parable of the Fishing Net [Matthew 13:47-50]

Then Jesus said,
"Again, the kingdom of heaven is like a net thrown into the sea, which collects fish of every kind.

When it is full they haul it ashore and sit down to put what is good into buckets. What is bad they throw away.

Thus, it will be at the end of the age.
The angels will go out and separate the wicked from the righteous and throw them into the fiery furnace,
where there will be wailing and grinding of teeth."

7.19 The Spiritual Lesson in the Parable

Detail: *"haul it ashore."* The type of net that is hauled ashore rather than onboard was a dragnet.

Detail: *"put what is good into buckets; what is bad they throw away."* After hauling a dragnet to shore they would discarded, as "unclean," anything which had no fins or scales.

Detail: *"at the end of the age."* To most Jews, that would've meant the end of the Present Age when the Messiah comes, but Jesus knows that the Messiah is already here. So, He must be referring to the end of the Age to Come. He's telling them, indirectly, that there is an end to time; it doesn't go on indefinitely. He doesn't refer to any 'second coming,' at this point, but He's indicating that there will be an end and that's when the separating of good and bad takes place.

Detail: *"The angels will go out and separate the wicked from the righteous."* Again, the separation of the good from the bad will take place at the conclusion of the Kingdom of Heaven, not at its commencement, as they had expected.

<u>Detail:</u> *"fiery furnace."* Again, a reference to fire, or being burned; to Jews the worst possible treatment one could receive.

Dragnet fishing was normally done during the day when the fish were near the bottom. From Gergesa, one could easily see people fishing on the Sea of Galilee. There, the water depth falls off quite slowly from the eastern shore. So, one could observe fishermen out quite some distance from shore doing the very thing Jesus was speaking of in this parable. The deepest part of the Sea of Galilee is about 140 feet in the west central area. But, on the eastern side it is much shallower. So, dragnet fishing was more common on the east side. Unfortunately, one of the drawbacks to dragnet fishing is that the nets picked up a lot of weeds, parts from sunken vessels and just plain junk from the bottom, which all must be removed onshore.

Jesus said that the Kingdom of Heaven is like dragnet fishing which pulls in all, good and bad. And He made the point again that the good will be separated from bad at the end of the age. So, what is emerging is that the Kingdom of Heaven is a period of progression; there's an unfolding that goes on, perhaps for a very long time, but an end comes. And, while it's going on, as in dragnetting, there's a whole collection of people in the world, good and bad, coexisting, who are going to live and die and come to judgment; and, all that will be taking place during this Kingdom of Heaven.

Jesus concluded His teaching of them, at least as recounted by Matthew, with the Parable of the Head of Household.

7.20 Parable of the Head of Household [Matthew 13:51-52]

Jesus said to them,

"Do you understand all these things?"
They answered, "Yes."
And he replied,
> "Then every scribe who has been instructed in the kingdom of heaven is like the head of a household who brings from his storeroom both the new and the old."

7.21 The Spiritual Lesson in the Parable

Detail: *"Do you understand all these things?"* They answered, *"Yes."* Did they, really; do we?

Detail: *"scribe"* – one who ponders the meaning of Scripture.

Detail: the *"new and the old"* – the very subject of Jesus' first parable which he shared at Matthew's house.

A principal duty of the scribes was to meticulously copy scrolls. The copying process was so laborious that as they worked, they pondered over what the Scripture was saying. They struggled with the question: "What does this Scripture passage mean?" During the time of Jesus, the Jewish people were very dependent upon the scribes because the language of the Jews had passed into the Aramaic dialect, and most of the people were unable to understand the language of their own Torah,

Jesus was, in a sense, saying "You, who have been instructed in the Kingdom, will be like the scribes; you will ponder what it is I have said, and you will have the task of relaying it on to others. Furthermore, you will be like the head of the household who brings from his storeroom both the "new and the old." Just as He had taught them in the first parable He shared: what is "new" is the path to salvation whose full revelation is developing right before them. What is "old" is the identity of who they were, chosen children of God, which must be restored and protected.

It was probably a restless night for many of them. They had witnessed what had to be acts of divine power. They had heard several lessons about the Kingdom of Heaven which were quite unlike what they had been expecting for centuries. Accepting Jesus' call to "get in the boat and go where He goes" was life-changing. Many likely pondered, "Am I ready for this?"
The next morning, they all sailed back across the Sea of Galilee [Mk 5:21] to Jesus' "own town" of Capernaum [Mt 9:1]. Those who lived and worked in Magdala likely continued on to their homes,

although some may have decided, at this point, to stay with Jesus; their future lay in following Him.

Shortly after returning to Capernaum, Jesus raised from the dead the daughter of the synagogue official [Mt 9:18-26; Mk 5:22-43; Lk 8:41-56]. Both Mark and Luke tell us the official's name: Jairus, which means "enlightened." Jairus was almost certainly a leading Pharisee in the community, perhaps one of the few who had been "enlightened" to see who Jesus really was.

At this point in His public ministry, Jesus envisioned that He was there for the Jews; he was the Messiah of the Jews. So, it's possible that He didn't know, at the beginning, what his full mission was about, since He was fully human and grew in age and wisdom [cf. Lk 2:52].

It's early in 32 AD; Jesus' sixth missionary journey has come to an end. This was truly a remarkable journey we've been blessed to take in His company, with His disciples. Along with them, we've seen power beyond their wildest imagination; courage in the face of demons who called themselves: "Legion" (a regiment of 6,000) [Mk 5:9; Lk 8:30]; mercy to the violently insane; calm acceptance of rejection and an intense desire to have those who were willing to listen take to heart His "good news" that their lives might be transformed.

And, there is far more to come.

8. Jesus' Seventh Journey

A short while later, in early 32 AD, Jesus traveled from Capernaum to "his own native town" of Nazareth. We don't know how many of his disciples went with Him, although it's most likely that at least the Twelve were with Him. Jesus again entered the synagogue in Nazareth, but He was sternly rejected for a second time [Mt 13:54-58; Mk 6:1-6].

8.1 Rejected, Again

In those days, it was a full two-day's walk from Nazareth back to Capernaum. It must have been a somber journey; the Apostles not knowing quite what to say to comfort Jesus after such a disheartening rejection by His extended family and former neighbors. Jesus could always count on His ever-faithful mother, Mary, but as for the rest of His family, he was *persona-non-grata*.

Nazareth was where He had grown up [Mt 4:12; Mk 1:14; Lk 4:14]. It's where He had played with the neighbors' kids, celebrated with them their births and marriages, mourned with them as they laid loved ones to rest. And surely, they had mourned with Mary and Him as they laid Joseph to rest. These were "His people;" or so He thought, for He was a Nazorean [Mt 2:23].

It was about a year since His family had come to get Him in Capernaum to bring Him home and admonish Him. He probably thought that their disappointment that He didn't return with them had eased up somewhat. He felt sure that His mother, Mary, had been striving to get His extended family to see Him differently. If they could just accept that He has a calling that's much different from what they want for him; then, maybe the rest of the community would come around. Because Jesus came back to Nazareth a second time, we conclude that He wanted very much to be one with them, but He just could not turn His back on what He was being called to.

We're seeing a very human side of Jesus here that we all too often forget. His formative years were spent with these simple hard-working people in the little town they shared together. Along with many of them, He too had suffered the humiliation of daily laboring as lowly tradesmen in the opulence of nearby Sapporis. But, He had also experienced with them the great satisfaction of being able to share in providing for His extended family and community through honest, hard work.

The major portion of Jesus' life was spent in the common, everyday activities of this small town in the Galilean foothills. Surely, He was hopeful that at some point they would get beyond their anger that He was not living the expectations they had of Him.

He had gone to the small synagogue in town where He had prayed with that community countless times [Lk 4:16] and had spent many hours there engaged in *machloket* ("Torah debate") with the men of the community. That's how relationships were built among those who called themselves: *am ha'sefer* ("people of the book"). And. Jesus certainly knew the "book" well. But, where were those relationships now?

His mother, Mary, would have been there in the *ezrat nashim* ("women's court"), the small room at the back of the synagogue, where the women were separated from the men based on a long-standing rabbinic interpretation of Zechariah 12:12-14: "*And the land shall mourn, each family apart: the family of the house of David, and their women; the family of the house of Nathan, and their women; the family of the house of Levi, and their women; the family of Shimei, and their women; and all the rest of the families, each family apart, and the women apart.*"

A commotion was brewing in the men's section, but she could not see. As in all synagogues of those times, the men and women's side were separate by a large opaque *mechitzah* ("partition"). All she could do was close her eyes and pray.

Soon mocking laughter would be heard; they were astonished and said: "*'Are not his sisters all with us? Where did this man get all this?" And they took offense at him*" [Mt 13:56-57a; Mk 6:3b].

And, many of His own relatives dishonored him by openly trying to shame Him in public. He loved His extended family, His neighbors, and His town; but, they vehemently rejected Him, again.

In time, Jesus would be rejected by the whole nation, but on that day, it was His extended family and neighbors, and it hurt very much. Jesus wanted so much to bring His message of salvation to them; but they would have none of it. With their mocking ringing in His ears, He and His disciples left Nazareth. But, Jesus did not give up on them; He never gives up on anyone.

Upon returning to Capernaum [Mk 6:6], Jesus prayed and discerned that it was time for some of His disciples to become Apostles ("those who are sent") because He sent out the Twelve *"two by two"* [Mk 6:7], giving them *"authority over unclean spirits to drive them out and to cure every disease and every illness"* [Mt 10:5-15; Mk 6:7-13; Lk 9:1-6]. He sent them only to *"the lost sheep of the house of Israel"* [Mt 10:6] to proclaim: *"the Kingdom of Heaven is at hand"* [Mt 10:7]. These were the same ministries that Jesus was doing, with one important exception. At this time, they were not instructed to teach. That would come later after His resurrection [Mt 28:20].

None of the evangelists recounted for us anything about what happened on the Apostles' first mission; where they went or what they experienced. Since they were to go only to "the lost sheep of the house of Israel," they would have concentrated on Lower Galilee which was predominantly Jewish. It was a full three-day's walk from Capernaum on the east to the western boundary of Lower Galilee where the Via Maris entered the province of Phoenicia. So, the mission must have been for at least a week or more. Mark tells us only briefly that *"They drove out many demons, and they anointed with oil many who were sick and cured them"* [Mk 6:13]. This new experience must have had quite an effect on them.

Sadly, during the time the Apostles were away, Jesus received word about the beheading of His cousin, John the Baptist [Mt 14:1-12; Mk 6:14-27; Lk 9:9]. Herod Antipas had been holding John in the prison at Herod's palace at Machaerus, overlooking the Dead Sea. How tragic that, because of an oath from an intoxicated king to a young girl who performed a salacious dance, the world and Jesus personally would lose the one of whom Jesus would later say: "*I tell you, among those born of woman none is greater than John*" [Mt 11:11; Lk 7:28].

Sometime later, the Twelve returned from their mission and reported all they had done [Mk 6:30]. Then, in a mix of both great joy at the return of His Apostles and great sorrow at the loss of His cousin, Jesus went off by boat with them to a "*deserted place*" [Mt 14:13; Mk 6:32] "*near Bethsaida*" [Lk 9:10].

8.2 Bethsaida, Childhood Home of Jesus' First Disciples

As noted earlier, Jesus' first six disciples, John, James, Andrew, Simon Peter, Philip and Nathanael grew up in Bethsaida. The name, Bethsaida, means "house of fishing." It was situated on a large mound of Jordan River silt just east of where the river enters the Sea of Galilee. It began as a fishing village well before the 10th century BC. In the period following the Exodus, the area northeast of the Sea of Galilee, where Bethsaida was located, was known as the Land of the Arameans. Later in the Old Testament period, it became the kingdom of Geshur with Bethsaida as its capital city. King David married Maacha, daughter of the King of Geshur; she was the mother of Absalom, David's third son.

Recent archeological findings at Bethsaida show that the city was divided into two parts: a lower city, extending over most of the mound; and an upper city, the "acropolis," on the higher northeastern part of the mound. The acropolis was surrounded by a massive, fortified wall with a gate, constructed of large black basalt stones. Inside the gate was a broad, paved plaza; on its northern side, stood the palace of the kings. The palace at Bethsaida was typical of the palaces during the early biblical period; it included a central hall which served as the throne room, surrounded by eight very large rooms.

The city of Bethsaida was conquered and destroyed by the Assyrian king Tiglath Pileser III during his campaign in the region in 734 BC [2 Kings 15:29-30; 16:7-9] From that time on, the site was only sparsely inhabited, up until the Hellenistic period shortly after the death of Alexander the Great in 323 BC. Then, the city was greatly expanded by his Greek generals until it was the leading city in the area by the time of its conquest by the Romans in 63 BC.

Upon the death of King Herod in 4 BC, the area once known as the Land of the Arameans was inherited by his son, Philip. The area was then known as Gaulanitis and the tetrarch Philip greatly expanded Bethsaida and made it his capital. Herod's oldest son, Herod Antipas, inherited the Galilee and the region south of the tetrarchy of Philip and east of the Jordan, known as Perea. Capernaum was in the tetrarchy of Herod Antipas. King Herod's other son, Herod Archelaus, inherited Samaria, Judea (where Jerusalem was located), and the region south of Perea, known as Edom. [Although Herod was named "king of the Jews" by the Romans, he was not a Jew but an Edomite].

Upon the division of Herod's territory, the Romans established Capernaum as the center for the fish trade on the Sea of Galilee because Capernaum was located on the main trade route, the Via Maris. This prompted many of the families in Bethsaida, who relied on fishing for their livelihood, including the families of Jesus' first disciples, to relocate to Capernaum.

During the formative years of Jesus' first disciples in Bethsaida, the tetrarch Philp gave the city a distinctly Roman character with massive buildings and paved roads, an amphitheater, large houses with internal dining rooms (known as *triclinia*) as well as large public baths. Jews would never use a public bath; for a Jew to be without clothing was to be without one's identity.

In 30 AD, the tetrarch Philip renamed the city, Julias, after Julia Livia, the Roman emperor Augustus's wife and mother of Tiberius, the reigning emperor at the time.[50] However, New Testament writers continued to refer to the city as Bethsaida. Although Philip kept up the designation of the area as a Roman *polis* ("city"), in the first century the population had declined to that of little more than a large village [cf. Mk 8:23, 26]. By Jesus' day, there were few Jews left in Bethsaida although there were enough to sustain a small synagogue there.

Bethsaida was largely abandoned between 250 AD and 350 AD, likely because of increasing seismic activity in the area. Over the centuries since, the land around the northeast shore of the Sea of Galilee has been pushed up by tectonic action. Together with recent use of the Sea of Galilee water for irrigation, these have caused the shoreline to recede from the ancient site of Bethsaida by more than a mile. This resulted in making the quest for the exact location of Bethsaida to be one of the most difficult biblical archeology mysteries to solve in the past century or so.

Figure 16: Ruins of Roman Pools at Bethsaida

It's not a coincidence that Jesus' first disciples grew up in Bethsaida, not in Nazareth. To sustain the faith in a predominantly pagan place like Bethsaida would have taken people with perseverance who could hang on to their beliefs and values in the face of pressure and ridicule. Yet, they were also open to adapting to new life situations. In Nazareth, essentially everyone was a Jew sharing similar values, traditions and attitudes. Life remained the same, generation after generation. In such a setting, self-righteousness can easily set in that closes minds and hearts to seeing things anew.

East and north of Bethsaida the land slopes upward from 700 feet below sea level at the Sea of Galilee shoreline to several thousand feet above sea level in the region known today as the Golan Heights. There is less rainfall in this area than further west such that the area is better suited for grazing than for agriculture. Many biblical scholars have concluded that this was, most likely, the *"quiet place"* [Mk 6:32] Jesus had sought to get away from the crowds.

But, He and His Apostles did not get much time of retreat before a large crowd gathered around them. As recounted in all four gospels, it was then that Jesus miraculously fed the crowd of about five thousand men, not counting women and children [Mt 14:15-21; Mk 6:34-44; Lk 9:12-17; Jn 6:1-15] in a location that both Mark [Mk 6:39] and John [Jn 6:10] described as having "much green grass." So, it was early springtime there. As John said, *"The Jewish feast of Passover was near"* [Jn 6:4].

Detail: (location) Matthew and Mark say that they went to a "deserted place" but gave no further location information. John says only that they went *"across the sea of Galilee"* [Jn 6:1]. It was Luke alone who indicated that the location was "near Bethsaida." It appears to have been important to Luke, who was writing to a largely Gentile community that Jesus had sought a place of quiet in a predominately Gentile place. Yet, the "traditional" site, since the 4th century, of the Feeding of the 5000 is west of Capernaum, near the springs of Tabgha; not northeast of the city of Bethsaida. This doesn't fit the New Testament accounts very well. It is unlikely one would have referred to the fairly populated region around Tabgha as a "deserted place."

In recent times, some scholars have speculated that there was a small community, also called Bethsaida, near Tabgha that might account for the event taking place in the Plain of Gennesaret rather than in the Golan Heights. This speculation was fueled by the fact that elsewhere in John's Gospel, John says that Phillip was from *"Bethsaida in Galilee"* [Jn 12:21]. Since John grew up in Bethsaida, he certainly would have known that the city of Bethsaida was not in Galilee. Was John identifying Phillip as a Galilean although he grew up in Bethsaida, or were there two places known as Bethsaida? Unfortunately, we don't know for sure.

Following the Feeding of the 5000, Jesus "*made His disciples get into the boat and precede him to the other side*" [Mt 14:22; Mk 6:45a; Jn 6:17a], while he dismissed the crowd and went up the mountain to pray [Mt 14:23; Mk 6:46; Jn 6:15].

Detail: Jesus prayed in solitude. Prayer among Jews had long been something that was done in public. Prayer, fasting and almsgiving were the ways in which a Jew manifested his/her faith. But, Jesus practiced, and would soon introduce to His followers, praying in solitude.

Detail: (direction of travel) Mark added that they went "*toward Bethsaida*" [Mk 6:45b] and John said, "*to Capernaum*" [Jn 6:17b]. Since they went to a "deserted place" they would not have docked at Bethsaida but most likely come ashore at some spot further east where there was no community. So, to head from such as spot "toward Bethsaida" or "to Capernaum," is the same direction of travel – west.

During the night, a severe storm arose, but Jesus, "*walking on the water toward them calmed the sea*" [Mt 14:22-23; Mk 6:45-51; Lk 8:22-25, Jn 6:16-21]. Then," they *came to land at Gennesaret*" [Mt 14:34; Mk 6:53]. At Gennesaret, another crowd came to Jesus and He healed many who were ailing [Mt 14:34-36; Mk 6:53-56].

Detail: (destination) Sailing at night, they were traveling west against the prevailing winds. The storm likely blew them off course causing them to land at Gennesaret, west of Capernaum. Since John did not include in his Gospel their brief stay in Gennesaret, before heading on to Capernaum, John recounted them going directly to Capernaum following Jesus' walking on the water. Again, biblical accounts were not intended as history lessons.

Detail: (large crowds forming quickly) Passover was near, consequently many Jews from Galilee and those in the diaspora to the north and east would have been heading through the area, many of them going to Jerusalem via the Jordan River valley route.

The next day, they made their way back to Capernaum where they entered the synagogue. A large crowd, many of whom were among "the 5000" fed from the few loaves and fish, gathered in and around the synagogue [Jn 6:22-24]. There, *"Jesus said to them, "I am the bread of life; whoever comes to me will never hunger, and whoever believes in me will never thirst"* [Jn 6:35] ... *"Amen, amen, I say to you, unless you eat the flesh of the Son of Man and drink his blood, you do not have life within you""* [Jn 6.53].

There must have been a moment when it seemed like time was suspended. Then it started: some murmuring here, harsh voices there, a burst of laughter in the back – then, full scale uproar. "What did he say?" "He can't mean that!" *"Eat my flesh and drink my blood"* ... *"How can this man give us his flesh to eat?"* ... *"This is too hard; who can accept this"* [Jn 6:52, 54, 60]. And, those in the synagogue stormed out in disgust leaving Jesus and the Apostles behind.

Soon the commotion must have filled the main plaza outside where the larger crowd had gathered. In the plaza, the sense of expectation quickly turned to ridicule as that short-lived band of 'followers' made their way noisily down the hill to the docks and the marketplace. After a while it was quiet again in the synagogue. Jesus and His twelve stood there, alone.

We know that for several of them, this was their hometown. They'd been coming to *this* synagogue since they were young boys. Today, they were stunned, humiliated, mortified. And, they had felt so proud only a short while earlier. They were in the company of the most captivating figure of their time ... but, now what? They were feeling intense ridicule and rejection from neighbors, just like Jesus had less than a month earlier. They had recently "walked in his shoes" healing and driving out demons; now they were "walking in his shoes" suffering ridicule and rejection.

Finally, Jesus turned to His twelve and quietly asked the most haunting question in the Gospels: *"Do you also want to leave me?*" [Jn 6:67]. To this, Peter replied, "*Master, to whom shall we go? You have the words of eternal life*" [Jn 6:68].

Jesus' ministry in Galilee changed radically that day. As John put it, "*As a result of this, many of his disciples returned to their former way of life and no longer accompanied him*" [Jn 6:66]. Jesus' Father in heaven had called Him to something very profound, something that would change the whole course of the history of mankind. Yet at this point in Jesus' public ministry, it might not have been clear yet what the scale of that mission was. But, He must have sensed that He needed to know who was really open to Him and what might lie ahead; and who were merely curious onlookers.

8.3 The Bread of Life Discourse

Jesus' words that day in the synagogue at Capernaum, as recounted by John in his Gospel [Jn 6:22-66] have come to be known as the Bread of Life Discourse. On that day, the Apostles would have had no idea of the mystery of the Eucharist that we know now; it would be another year before they would experience the Last Supper. And even then, they didn't fully get it.

But, as incomprehensible, even demoralizing, as things seemed that day, not one of the Twelve, not even Judas, headed for the door. They didn't know where it was all going but, they felt in their hearts that He was the one who would give their lives full purpose. "*…we are convinced that you are the Holy One of God*" [Jn 6:69], Peter said.

Detail: The Bread of Life Discourse only appears in John's Gospel. John's community was situated in an area where Greek culture, language and ways of thinking still prevailed. In Greek mythology, it was not uncommon for the gods to bestow divinity on an extraordinary human.

There were some who preached that Jesus was made Son of God as a reward for His willingness to undergo crucifixion, death and then be raised from the dead. This heresy came to be known later as Adoptionism. It was important for John to establish in the minds of his listeners that Jesus was, and always had been, the Son of

God. So, John used the occasion of Jesus' words in the synagogue that day to convey that message.

To the crowd there, Jesus said:
> "I came down from heaven not to do my own will but the will of the one who sent me. And this is the will of the one who sent me, that I should not lose anything of what he gave me, but that I should raise it on the last day. For this is the will of my Father, that everyone who sees the Son and believes in him may have eternal life, and I shall raise him on the last day" [Jn 6:38-40]

Right then and there, this was clearly a direct statement by Jesus that He was the Son of God; it was not something that came about much later. This spoke directly to the Greek thinkers in John's community. They were very familiar with the practice in Greek literature of the *anagnorisis* – the scene in popular Greek writings of that time where the hero made known his true identity. This, for John's listeners, was Jesus' *anagnorisis*. [51] But, this was not grasped by Jesus' listeners at all. They fixated on "eat my flesh, drink my blood" [cf. Jn 6:53] and missed His proclamation of divinity.

It was important to John to establish, early and often in his Gospel, that Jesus was divine from the very beginning, for the heresy of Adoptionism was circulating in his community. This does not appear to have been as big an issue a few decades earlier when the Synoptic Gospels were written. There is evidence in the subsequent letters from St. John to his community that another heresy was also circulating in that area. Docetism denied the humanity of Christ. Some former members of the Church of Ephesus were contending that Christ only "looked human" so that he would be accepted by those around him.

To this day, many people struggle with the directness of Jesus' words: "eat my flesh and drink my blood." They contend that He was only speaking metaphorically, and not literally. While such directness was most uncharacteristic of Middle Eastern speakers, Jesus needed to be clear and direct and not open to differing interpretations by His listeners, even if they were offended by such directness.

In the Bread of Life Discourse, Jesus proclaimed a new reality to the world: God humbled Himself to become man and began a totally new relationship with mankind. He would dwell amongst His people, not in a building, but literally within them, by their consuming God Himself. How that would be accomplished would later be revealed at the Last Supper. On that day in the synagogue, it was simply stated: "Trust in what I say." Only the Apostles, and perhaps a few others, were willing to trust in what He said.

Passover was at hand [Jn 6:4] and it was time for them to head to Jerusalem. Passover was celebrated on April 13/14 in 32 AD, so it would have been around early April when they set out. We don't know what route they took to Jerusalem but considering the uproar they confronted in Capernaum, they probably avoided the Jordan River valley route and took the Shechem Road through Samaria instead.

Following Passover, Jesus had them return via the Mediterranean coast route through the region of Tyre [Mt 15:21; Mk 7:24]. Tyre (which means "strength") originated as an island about a mile off the shoreline, in what is modern day Lebanon.

Detail: Why go to Tyre? Matthew said that they *"withdrew to the region of Tyre"* [Mt 15:21]. Mark said that they *"went off to the district of Tyre"* {Mk 7:24]. It's not clear from the narrative why Jesus had them go to Tyre or why have them take such a long round-about route home to Capernaum. Many biblical scholars assume that Jesus was seeking respite by distancing them from crowds and people who might recognize them by going into predominantly Gentile territory. But, both Matthew and Mark included this detail, and other details to follow, so that the purpose of this route and its consequences might unfold as the story progresses.

(See Appendix 1 for a map of Israel in the Time of Jesus to follow their journey.)

To reach Tyre, Jesus, His Apostles and a few close followers, would have traveled from Jerusalem along the western leg of

David's Highway to the port city of Joppa (also known as Jaffa, which is now surrounded by the modern city of Tel Aviv). West of Jerusalem they would have traveled through the Pass of Beth-Horon and entered the Valley of Ajalon where many ancient battles were fought. After about a four-day walk they would have reached Joppa. In the Book of Jonah, Joppa is where Jonah sailed from attempting to flee the Lord [Jonah 1:3]. Joppa sat on a rocky hill surrounded by yellow sand dunes overlooking the Mediterranean. In Joppa they would meet up with the Via Maris trade route for the journey north along the Mediterranean coast. With caravans coming and going along the Via Maris they could easily obtain food and fresh water from them and so they could have avoided entering Joppa.

Heading north from Joppa, they would wade across the Yarkon ("greenish") River and after two full days walk would arrive at the coastal town of Caesarea. In 22 BC, Herod the Great began this site as a Roman seaside resort in honor of Caesar Augustus. It was in Caesarea, that Pontius Pilate lived and operated the administrative center of Judea during Jesus' day. It's quite likely Jesus and His companions also avoided entering Caesarea.

At Caesarea, the road headed northeast inland through the *Shephelah* ("lowlands") to go around Mount Carmel (which means "God's vineyard"). Mount Carmel is a 40-mile long mountain range on the Mediterranean coast, whose highest point is 1700 feet above sea level. It was on Mount Carmel that Elijah confronted the prophets of Baal [cf. 1 Kings 18:16-45]. Later, the prophet Elisha lived on Mount Carmel at the time he raised the widow's son in Shunem from the dead [cf. 2 Kings 4:8-37] (which we addressed earlier in Chapter 7).

On the southeastern side of Mount Carmel, the road must pass through a narrow canyon known as Megiddo. Controlling this narrow canyon controls the entire trade route and land passage into Egypt from the north and east. It was so strategic that it has been a place of military battles from as long ago as 4500 BC to as recent as World War I. It was at Megiddo that the Jewish King Josiah (known as the "Last Father of Israel") was ambushed in 609 BC by Egyptian archers [2 Chronicles 35:20-27]. And, this is the location of *Armageddon*, referred to in Revelation 16:16, where the end-times battle is to take place.

In ancient times, there was a small city at Megiddo, but it was destroyed in 586 BC by the Babylonians; and it was never re-built. Considering the number of men who perished in the battles fought in this narrow canyon over the centuries, it must have felt eerily quiet as they passed through it and out into the Jezreel Valley.

At Megiddo, the Via Maris entered Galilee, so they would have taken the Ptolemais Road northwest back to the coast. They probably stayed on the outskirts of the Jezreel Valley, for they would need all the daylight they could get the next day to make it as far as the port city of Ptolemais in Phoenicia by sundown. Jews, indeed most travelers, didn't walk the roads at night. During the Roman Empire, Ptolemais (previously known as Acre) was a retirement location for Roman military leaders and the principal seaport serving Galilee and the surrounding area. Jesus and His companions probably avoided entering Ptolemais as well.

They would have been walking for days, in predominantly Gentile lands. The evangelists did not share anything about what was said; whether there were any parables shared along the way; nothing. They only told us where they were headed: Tyre. At this point, we are left to wonder and trust right along with Jesus' companions that there's a purpose to this. It would have been another full two-day walk, along the Coast Road, from Ptolemais to Tyre. Along the way, they would have had to go through a narrow passageway, known as the Ladder of Tyre, where the road between the mountains and sea was a series of steps cut in the white rock.

8.4 The Ancient City of Tyre

The city of Tyre (today known as Sur) was well-known in ancient times for the production of a rare and extraordinarily expensive blue-purple dye, called *tekhelet*, extracted from Murex snails. The strategic location of the island enabled the Phoenicians to dominate the Eastern Mediterranean seaways for centuries. Their capital, Tyre, could not be attacked by a land-based army. This so infuriated the Greek conqueror, Alexander the Great, who lacked his own navy, that he had his army spend seven months progressively piling rocks from the shoreline out to create a land bridge, or causeway, to the island. In 332 BC, when Alexander reached the city, the Greeks largely destroyed it. He sold nearly 30,000 of its inhabitants into slavery. Following the sacking of Tyre by the Greeks, the elegance of the city was slowly restored over the centuries, and a permanent causeway was constructed; but Tyre never regained its seafaring prominence.

Figure 17: Aerial View of Tyre (1934 French Army photo)

Tyre would have seemed an ideal place for them to get away from crowds and not be recognized. So, they crossed the causeway to enter the city. But, a local woman, a Gentile, recognized Jesus and called out: *"Have pity on me, Lord, Son of David! My daughter is tormented by a demon"* [Mt 15:22].

We looked at this encounter earlier in section 1.3.3. As Matthew recounted it, this was the turning point in Jesus' public ministry. Prior to this, Jesus had been ministering only to Jews, except for their brief excursion to Gergesa. As we will see, from this point on, Jesus openly ministered in Gentile lands.

As they left Tyre, Jesus' companions must have been startled when He had them continue north to Sidon. To get from Tyre to Capernaum, the normally-traveled route would have been back south to the Ptolemais Road to meet the Via Maris in Galilee and on eastward to Capernaum. But, Sidon was in the opposite direction. Why go that way? Again, the evangelists didn't answer our question.

The encounter with the woman in Tyre, and her profound faith in the face of what would have seemed almost insurmountable discouragement, seems to have brought about deep contemplation over the full scale of Jesus' mission and the vital role His closest followers would have to play in the future. What may have begun as a respite walk was to turn into an extended period of much needed one-on-one time for them with Jesus.

As Mark put it, they *"left the district of Tyre and went by way of Sidon to the Sea of Galilee, into the district of the Decapolis"* [Mk 7:31]. This was going deep into lands that had been Gentile ever since the invasion by the Assyrians. They were about to take a very infrequently traveled route along which there were virtually no roads, and in some places not even foot paths. The evangelist, Mark, was telling his listeners, indirectly, that this was not a nature walk or a long recreational hike Jesus was taking them on. Rather, it was a time of training of the Apostles and surely a time for introspection on Jesus' part on ministering to Gentiles.

North of Tyre, about halfway to Sidon, near the town of Zarephath, the Leonites River (known today as the Letani) flows into the Mediterranean. It was to Zarephath that the prophet Elijah fled from a drought and there he later raised from the dead the son of a widow [1 Kings 17:7-16]. It seems that everywhere they went; they were walking the pages of their history.

The narrow valley cut by the Leonites provides a pleasant walking route into the interior of Lebanon. The river descends to sea level near Zarephath from about 3600 feet above sea level, over a distance of nearly 20 miles, from the base of Mount Lebanon where the river turns abruptly from the north.

Walking upstream along the footpaths on the banks of the Leonites would have taken at least three days, at a steady pace. But it was likely much longer. Because the group would have been spread out along the riverbanks, there would have been many opportunities for Jesus to speak one-in-one with each of His followers. He likely spoke with each of them along the way for He knew there would be days ahead that would challenge them to the breaking point.

Figure 18: The Leonites River in the Mount Lebanon Foothills

8.5 A Closer Walk with Thee

It was late April in 32 AD, in the middle of the main harvesting season, the 50-day period between Passover and Pentecost. Snowmelt from Mount Lebanon would still be making its way to the sea via the Leonites. Mount Lebanon is actually a mountain range running about 140 miles north-south. A number of peaks in the range are 8,000 to 10,000 feet in height; many are snow-covered most of the year.

In early centuries, the banks of the lower Leonites were lined mostly by oak trees. Further upstream, pine trees were encountered until one reached the elevation where there were the towering cedar trees for which Lebanon was famous. Many Lebanon cedars grew as high as 150 feet tall. For centuries, the Phoenicians used these trees in their ship building. Solomon also used them in building the Temple in Jerusalem.

So much had happened in recent months for them, exhilarating highs and crushing lows. Their faith in Jesus was both raised up and dashed down, almost in rapid successions. They were seeing no evidence that His Messiahship was anything like what they had expected. They needed His assurance that there was purpose in all this.

The river would provide plenty of fresh water and small farms and orchards along the way would provide them with food. And, they could spearfish in the river shallows. Since it was harvest time, at some farms along the way, they may have traded labor for food, a very common practice on small farms that could not afford to pay workers. If they did, it must have been quite a sight seeing a bunch of fishermen trying to wield sickles to harvest barley. Perhaps on a rainy day, a farmer offered them his barn for shelter. But for the most part, they would "sleep out under the stars."

Progress along the footpaths would be slow and unhurried; time to talk, time to think. The evangelists tell nothing of what was said, they didn't need to. Their telling us the route alone painted the picture of a time of active friendships, long chats and time alone with one's thoughts.

And we are on this journey too. We started out expecting to hear many of Jesus' parables, and we've heard a few, so far! But, each of us has this time to talk with Jesus one-on-one in a way we never had before. Here we sit on a fallen tree on the side of the river, next to Jesus Christ, fully divine, fully human. And, with our tired feet bobbing up and down in the cool water, He speaks with us about our trust in Him like a friend from our childhood. What will we share with Him at this moment? We can only imagine.

The forestation would become denser, and the river flow swifter, as they progressed upward in elevation toward Mount Lebanon. At the base of Mount Lebanon, the river passes within 4 miles of a southeast bound river, the Snir Stream (known today as the Hasbani). The Snir joins the flow from the Dan Spring and the Banias River to form the Upper Jordan River.

Following the Snir, as it descends the western ridge of the Rift Valley trench, would take them to the site of the ancient city of Dan. But, along the way, there would be areas where the only passable path was walking in the streambed itself. Snowmelt from Mount Lebanon feeds two springs that form the Snir, and it was still April. So, the strongly flowing stream would be very cold water indeed, numbing the toes within minutes. It would have been slow going along the Snir the ten miles or so to Dan, with frequent pauses along the stream banks in order to warm their feet.

Recent archaeological excavations at the site of Dan, situated on the floor of the Rift Valley trench, show that the area was originally occupied as long ago as 4500 BC; it was then abandoned for almost 1,000 years, but it was later resettled. The earliest mention we have of Dan in the Bible was when Abraham traveled there to rescue his nephew Lot [cf. Gen 14:14]. At the time of the Exodus, the place was known as Laish.

Originally, the Tribe of Dan was given the land west of what was later Jerusalem. But the Philistines drove them out, so they migrated north to take over the city of Laish around 1200 BC. They rename it Dan (which means "judge"). Dan was the birthplace of Samson, the strongman who valiantly fought against the Philistines around 1100 BC. Sadly, Dan was destroyed by the Assyrian king, Tiglath Pileser III, in 732 BC, and it was never rebuilt.

In the first century, Dan was in ruins surrounded by small farms and orchards because of the very fertile soil fed by the snowmelt from Mount Hermon. Although these farms and orchards were in a remote area, they could float their produce on rafts down the Upper Jordan River to the marketplace at Capernaum. And, it was the main harvest time when Jesus and His companions arrived. There would have been plenty of activity there. Again, they may have worked for food on one or more of the farms around Dan. Typically, small farms could use every hand they could get.

It was at this point that Jesus' companions received another surprise. It would have been a very easy journey from Dan to Capernaum, either working as "raft sweeps" (those who steered the rafts using long poles) headed down the Upper Jordan or by following the Via Maris on the eastern side of the river. It would have been so easy. But, easy was not what Jesus was after. He wanted them to head instead into the Province of the Decapolis [Mk 7:31]. The Decapolis was staunchly Gentile; clearly Jesus intended to try ministry again among the Gentiles. Was this the result of His encounter with the woman in Tyre? Matthew thought so.

In this area, the Rift Valley trench narrows to about 5 miles across, passing between the Mount Lebanon range on the west and the Mount Hermon range on the east. In this area, the sides of the trench are nearly 2000 feet high. Snowmelt from both ranges converges on the floor of the trench to form the Upper Jordan River. Dan was on the east side of the trench floor and the Roman mountain resort town of Caesarea Philippi was north and east at the headwaters of the Banias River.

The Via Maris trade route passed very near to Caesarea Philippi. So, Jesus and His companions most likely followed one of the farmers' paths along the river to where they could climb up the steep east ridge of the trench. They probably avoided Caesarea Philippi and opted instead to get food and water from caravans on the trade route as they made a full two days walk along the Via Maris in the direction of Damascus before they would leave the trade route to go south into the Province of the Decapolis.

It is more arid on the east side of the Rift Valley trench than on the west. To continue their journey into the Decapolis they would need water and food. It was late April; the rainy season had ended but snowmelt from Mount Hermon would still have been flowing in the Wadi Ruqqad (which means "lazy"). Recall that a wadi is a seasonal river that only has water in the rainy season or after a heavy rain (which were very infrequent during the dry season). The Wadi Ruqqad crosses the Via Maris roughly 30 miles east of

Caesarea Philippi. A number of biblical scholars have concluded that this was the most likely path that Jesus and His companions took south into the Decapolis. [52] The Wadi Ruqqad forms the eastern edge of the region known as the Golan Heights.

It was a full five-day walk from the Via Maris, along the Wadi Ruqqad, to the first town, Gamala. In the mountainous region in the north they would have encountered a few farms where they could obtain food, but further south they would encounter mostly grazing land. So, there would have been days when they had fish at dinner around a campfire.

Gamala was situated on a steep hill shaped like the back of a camel (Hebrew word: *gamla*), from which the town derived its name. Although the town was Roman in character, the inhabitants sided with the Jews in the Great Jewish Revolt. Following its destruction by the Roman army in 71 AD, the town was lost to history until the site was excavated in 1968.

As Jesus entered Gamala, "*people brought to him a deaf man who had a speech impediment and begged him to lay his hand on him*" [Mk 7:32]. It was then that Jesus uttered the word that is voiced to this day in Catholic baptisms: "*Ephphatha!*" (that is, "Be opened!") [Mk 7:34]. Remarkable! Even in this remote Gentile town, people recognized and sought Him out. He was right, He had interpreted correctly; His mission was not just for Jews but for all mankind.

It wasn't long before a large crowd gathered around Him, and He taught them at length. When it was late, Jesus again fed a multitude. Both Matthew and Mark say there were about 4000 people fed from a few loaves and fish [Mt 15:32-39; Mk 8:1-10]. The traditional site of the Feeding of the 4000 is at Gamala in the Golan Heights.

We note that the first feeding of a multitude was largely of Jews headed through the Golan Heights to Jerusalem for Passover; the second feeding was largely of Gentiles in the Golan Heights drawn to Jesus where they lived. They were not headed somewhere else, they headed to see and hear Him.

We have no idea how long Jesus and His companions stayed in Gamala, teaching, curing and enjoying their hospitality. What a remarkable contrast to what they encountered in their homeland and from their countrymen. But, at some point, they headed west to Gergesa where they crossed the Sea of Galilee by boat to the Magadan/Dalmanutha region around Magdala [Mt 15:39; Mk 8:10].

We might reasonably ask, "How could they cross the Sea of Galilee by boat if their boats were still in Capernaum?" Trading labor for free passage by boat dates back thousands of years and is still used today. Fishermen relied on hirelings (day laborers) just as farmers relied on hirelings during harvest time. On fishing vessels, hirelings earned their passage by doing the rowing while the crew maned the nets. So, they may have earned their passage across the Sea of Galilee by doing the rowing on several fishing vessels out of Gergesa. We note the acceptance they now received in Gergesa, a community they were rejected from a few months earlier.

Detail: they sailed to Magdala, not Capernaum; this very personal time with Jesus was not to end yet. Evidently, this was the destination of the Gerasenes and there were brokers also in Magdala who could purchase their catch for processing in Magdala.

One of the women we hear about in all four Gospels as being a faithful follower of Jesus was Mary Magdalene (which means "of Magdala"). Indeed, she is specifically named 12 times in the Gospels. Both Mark and Luke say of her that Jesus cast seven [53] demons out of her [Mk 16:9; Lk 8:2]. Yet, in all the mentions of her, the evangelists did not indicate when this event occurred or when she joined Jesus' band of disciples. On the basis of what is recounted in the Gospels; this was the last occasion Jesus was in Magdala, although there were later occasions when He passed by Magdala on the Via Maris. So, this occasion appears to be the time when Mary of Magdala first encountered Jesus and joined Him as a disciple. It was also in Magdala that *"the Pharisees and Sadducees came and, to test him, asked him to show them a sign from heaven"* [Mt 16:1-4; Mk 8:11-21]. Confrontation again!

Leaving Magdala, they backtracked across the Sea of Galilee to Bethsaida, most likely using the same means that got them to Magdala. *"When they arrived at Bethsaida, they brought to him a blind man and begged him to touch him"* [Mk 8:22]. Graciously taking the man away from public view, He cured him. Again, Gentiles seeking out Jesus; they recognize Him as the one they need. There is an obvious and growing split between how Jesus was received among Jews and among Gentiles. And, we're learning this from two Jewish evangelists, Matthew and Mark.

From there, they headed back north to Caesarea Philippi. A few weeks earlier, they had passed by Caesarea Philippi, most likely avoiding the place. Now, they were heading directly there, a full three days walk on the Via Maris (they were traveling upstream along the Upper Jordan River). We don't know why they went there; we don't know what took place there. We only know of a profound exchange that took place on their return. All three Synoptic Gospels recount the exchange [Mt 16:13-20; Mk 8:27-30; Lk 9:18-21].

Jesus asked them: "Who do people say that I am? - a very typical Middle Eastern question. In their culture, you are who others say you are. But, then He made the question very personal, He needed to know: "But who do you say that I am?" Peter immediately replied: "You are the Messiah ("anointed one") of God." At that point, Jesus shared with them, for the very first time, what had been weighing on Him for some time: *"Son of Man must suffer greatly and be rejected by the elders, the chief priests, and the scribes, and be killed and on the third day be raised"* [Mt 16:21; Mk 8:31; Lk 9:22].

This was an astounding statement; their long-awaited Messiah would not be the conquering one who would drive the Roman oppressors out; rather he would go the way of the Son of Man, the one who would sacrifice himself for his people. That was how He would be the Anointed One of God, here to conquer death. Clearly, they didn't get it; this was too much. Even Peter took Jesus aside to rebuke him for making such a frightening statement. We heard the response he got from Jesus: *"Get behind me, Satan! You are an obstacle to me. You are thinking not as God does, but as human beings do"* [Mt 16:23; Mk 8:33]. Jesus then went on to say something that they would have found mystifying at the time:

> "Whoever wishes to come after me must deny himself,* take up his cross and follow me. For whoever wishes to save his life will lose it, but whoever loses his life for my sake will find it. What profit would there be for one to gain the whole world and forfeit his life? Or what can one give in exchange for his life? For the Son of Man will come with his angels in his Father's glory, and then he will repay everyone according to his conduct. Amen, I say to you, there are some standing here who will not taste death until they see the Son of Man coming in his kingdom." [Mt 16:24-28].

The evangelists have made sure that we observed the striking difference between the Jewish and the Gentile responses to Jesus. Jews, including the Apostles, were seeing and hearing in Jesus something much different than the expectations that had evolved over generations. But, Gentiles had no such expectations; they were "free" to take Jesus for what they saw and heard, without any ancestral baggage.

To most Jews, Jesus couldn't possibly be their Messiah; to the Apostles He was definitely their Messiah. But now, the outcome for their Messiah, as foretold by the Messiah Himself, was so frightening it was unthinkable. Things had moved from exhilarating at times, to bewildering at times, to downright terrifying. Trusting in Jesus would keep coming up over and over. They would need to recall the one-on-one time they had with Jesus, over the previous few weeks, much more than they could have imagined.

Jesus knew that His closest companions would need something to reassure them. Returning south from Caesarea Philippi on the Via Maris, Jesus had them continue on by Capernaum, by Magdala, by Garis to a place where *"he took Peter, James, and John, and led them up a high mountain by themselves"* '[Mt 17:1; Mk 9:2; Lk 9:28].

There, He was transfigured in the presence of Elijah and Moses [Mt 17:1-9; Mk 9:2-10; Lk 9:28-36]. At Jesus' baptism, the Father's voice was heard saying: *"This is my beloved Son."* But at the Transfiguration, there was something more; the Father added: *"Listen to him"* [Lk 9:35b]. For the word translated into English as "listen," all three evangelists used the Greek word, *akouete*. *Akouete* means more than to just "hear" or "pay attention to" but to "listen with a submissive heart." Yes, they were to listen to Jesus with a submissive heart. His total divinity was manifested to them in a brilliant, astounding event, so powerful that He *"charged them not to relate what they had seen to anyone, except when the Son of Man had risen from the dead"* [Mt 17:9; Mk 9:9; Lk 9:36].

The traditional site of the Transfiguration is Mount Tabor, located on the eastern end of the Jezreel Valley. It is shaped almost like a half-sphere, suddenly rising from the flat surroundings and reaching a height of 1,900 feet. It was from Mount Tabor that very bright beacons were lit to inform the northern villages of the beginning of Jewish holy days and of new months.

Figure 19: Mount Tabor (colorized 1890 photo)

Upon descending from the mountain, Jesus healed a boy with epilepsy, at the pleading of the boy's father [Mt 17:14; Mk 9:14; Lk 9:37] in the small town of Galileearea at the foot of Mt Tabor.

Then, they headed back to Capernaum along the Sea of Galilee; and on the way Jesus shared with them, the second time, that *"The Son of Man is to be handed over to men, and they will kill him, and he will be raised on the third day"* [Mt 17:22-23; Mk 9:31]. Mark said that *"they were afraid to ask Him about it"* [Mk 9:32], and Matthew said that *"they were overwhelmed with grief"* [Mt 17:23].

No sooner had they arrived in Capernaum [Mk 9:33] then they were confronted at Peter's house by the collectors of the Temple Tax. Every male Jew above nineteen years of age was required to pay a tax equivalent to a half shekel of silver that went towards the upkeep of the Temple, following a rabbinic interpretation of Exodus 30:13. Only the *kohanim* (Jewish priests) were exempt from this tax.

It was to Peter, head of the household, that the tax collectors posed the question: *"Doesn't your teacher pay the temple tax?"* [Mt 17:24]. To which Peter replied: *"'Yes;' when he came into the house, before he had time to speak, Jesus asked him, 'What is your opinion, Simon? From whom do the kings of the earth take tolls or census tax? From their subjects or from foreigners?' When he said, 'From foreigners,' Jesus said to him, 'Then the subjects are exempt'"* [Mt 17:25-26].

Detail: Jesus' question to Peter was about tolls or census tax, not about Temple Tax. This exchange appears to address an issue in Matthew's community about a tax to support the local church, because the Temple and its tax were gone by the time Matthew's Gospel was written.

However, the lesson is clear: those who are subjects of the Kingdom of Heaven are exempt from taxes that support the corrupt Temple system. But, Jesus instructed Peter: *"that we may not offend them, go to the sea, drop in a hook, and take the first fish that comes up. Open its mouth and you will find a coin worth twice the temple tax. Give that to them for me and for you."* [Mt 17:27]. We must forgive them and pay the tax anyway.

Subsequently, Peter asked: "Lord, if my brother sins against me, how often must I forgive him? As many as seven times?" Jesus answered, "I say to you, not seven times but seventy-seven times. Then Jesus went on to share the Parable of the Unforgiving Servant.

8.6 The Parable of the Unforgiving Servant [Matthew 18:21-35]

Then Peter approaching asked him,
"Lord, if my brother sins against me, how often must I forgive him?
As many as seven times?"

Jesus answered, "I say to you,
not seven times but seventy-seven times. That is why

> the kingdom of heaven may be likened to a king
> who decided to settle accounts with his servants.
> When he began the accounting,
> a debtor was brought before him who owed him a huge
> amount.
> Since he had no way of paying it back, his master ordered
> him to be sold, along with his wife, his children,
> and all his property, in payment of the debt.
>
> At that, the servant fell down, did him homage, and said,
> 'Be patient with me, and I will pay you back in full.'
> Moved with compassion the master of that servant let him go
> and forgave him the loan.
>
> When that servant had left, he found one of his fellow
> servants who owed him a much smaller amount.
> He seized him and started to choke him, demanding,
> 'Pay back what you owe.' Falling to his knees, his fellow
> servant begged him,
> 'Be patient with me, and I will pay you back.'
> But he refused. Instead, he had him put in prison until he paid
> back the debt.
>
> Now when his fellow servants saw what had happened,
> they were deeply disturbed and went to their master and
> reported the whole affair.

> His master summoned him and said to him,
> 'You wicked servant! I forgave you your entire debt because you begged me to. Should you not have had pity on your fellow servant, as I had pity on you?'
>
> Then in anger his master handed him over to the torturers until he should pay back the whole debt.

So, will my heavenly Father do to you,
unless each of you forgives his brother from his heart."

8.7 Spiritual Lesson in the Parable

Sometimes, to understand a parable we need to look to the larger context in which the parable was told. This is one of those times. We're given four hints that this parable addresses something bigger than just responding to Peter's question about forgiving his brother.

<u>Hint</u>: This parable is only recounted in Matthew's Gospel and the encounter with the Temple Tax collectors just ahead of it is also only recounted in Matthew. There appears to be some thematic connection between that encounter and the parable which Matthew wanted his listeners to discern.

<u>Hint:</u> Peter's question was asked in his house, not in public. Therefore, there was no honor challenge to respond to. Jesus and Peter had just come from weeks of walking and talking together in several different settings. Perhaps they had several long one-on-one talks on the way. Responding to Peter's question with a parable was probably out of place, <u>unless</u> Jesus intended the parable to speak to a larger matter.

<u>Hint:</u> Jesus' direct response to Peter's question was: "*I say to you, not seven times but seventy-seven times*" [Mt 18:22]. Why 77 times? If Jesus meant unlimited or the "fullest of full," He would have used the number 100. However, using the number 77 made a direct reference to the words of Cain's descendent, Lamech, who boasted to his wives: "*I have killed a man for wounding me, a young man for bruising me. If Cain is avenged seven times, then Lamech seventy-seven times*" [Genesis 4:23-24]. Extreme vengeance in response to hurts had been the norm in the Middle East ever

since. Jesus was telling Peter that extreme vengeance must be replaced by extreme forgiveness. This more than adequately answered Peter's question.

Hint: Jesus began the parable with: "the kingdom of heaven may be likened to ...." Clearly, He was addressing something much bigger that just Peter's question. But what?

Looking back over our journey with Jesus and His companions, they had completed traveling nearly 300 miles together and, on the way, encountered seven situations where forgiving others for harms done was an issue. Yet, they likely missed that point, but Jesus did not.

1. The rejection by the people of Nazareth hurt deeply. Yet, Jesus could see that His extended family and former neighbors didn't mean Him harm; they had a misguided sense of what was right. A "son" of their community was failing to meet his community responsibilities and they were "obliged" to express their displeasure. Jesus forgave them despite how much their rejection hurt, and He moved on.
2. John the Baptist was beheaded by Herod Antipas under outrageous conditions. It would have been so easy to hate Herod for such wanton cruelty to His cousin, but Jesus forgave the misguided Herod and moved on with His ministry.
3. Their rejection in the synagogue at Capernaum hurt them deeply. They would never really be part of that community again. But, to those in the synagogue that day, Jesus was "speaking crazy." They misunderstood; they were misguided by their own revulsion at the part they heard. Jesus forgave them and moved on; the Apostles had not.
4. Passing through the narrow canyon at Megiddo, the awareness of the many Jewish lives lost there at the hands of Egyptians, Babylonians and other invaders was overwhelming, likely stirring up great resentment in their hearts. Forgiving was probably the furthest thing from their minds, but Jesus forgave and moved on.
5. Standing there seeing the ruins of the ancient Jewish town of Dan, brutally destroyed by the Assyrians as they carried

off the "ten lost tribes of Israel" was likely too much for some of them to bear. Tears of hurt and that desire for vengeance again, but Jesus forgave and moved on.
6. The confrontation with the Pharisees and Sadducees in Magdala cut deeply; demanding a sign, regarding Jesus as some magic performer, after all He had done. It would have been so easy to just strike them down, but Jesus forgave and moved on.
7. No sooner had they arrived home when they were confronted by the Temple Tax collectors. Jesus seemed to make the case to them that they should be exempt from the tax. But, He had them pay it anyway. In their zeal, the Temple Tax collectors were misguided. Jesus forgave them and moved on.

The lesson in the parable then was that forgiving others from our hearts, whether they have harmed us in small or in big ways, is an essential part of being in the Kingdom of Heaven. There is no place for vengeance or ill will. Jesus knew that what lay ahead would challenge their ability to forgive from their hearts to their very limits, for unspeakable hurts, to Him and to them.

Jesus gave a startling conclusion to the parable: "Then in anger his master handed him over to the torturers until he should pay back the whole debt." The master "took back" his forgiveness. Forgiveness is on loan, if not used properly God may "take it back." Our Heavenly Father's forgiveness, already given, will be withdrawn at the final judgment from those who have not imitated His forgiveness by their own. Only if we share the forgiveness we receive do we take rightful possession of it. Recall that we heard this same proviso about taking rightful possession in the earlier parable of the Joy of Finding, which was also in Matthew's Gospel.

It's early summer in 32 AD; Jesus' seventh missionary journey has come to an end. And, what a remarkable journey it was, for His companions and us. Along the way, we have seen and experienced Jesus in a way we never had before. Also, a pattern seems to be emerging as we hear more from Jesus about the Kingdom of Heaven (Kingdom of God). It is already "at hand," but to experience it involves an "in-breaking" into our lives, not some cataclysmic event. We take rightful possession of it through some profound "reversal" in our lives. We must see things differently. And, it requires an "action" on our part, we must value things differently, our relationships differently.

There is so much more to come, we can't wait.

9. Jesus' Eighth Journey

In mid-September, 32 AD, Jesus' "brothers" (male family members of Jesus' generation) were in Capernaum [Jn 7:3]. Both Matthew and Mark identified Jesus' "brothers" as James, Joseph, Simon and Judas [Mt 13:55; Mk 6:3]. None of Jesus' "brothers" were Apostles. But, the attitude of Jesus' "brothers" changed drastically following His Resurrection and they joined Mary and the Apostles in the Upper Room to await the Holy Spirit [Acts 1:14]. In addition, St Paul stated that the risen Jesus appeared to James His "brother" [1 Cor 15:7] and from then on James was a leader in the Christian community [Acts 15:13-21] until he was martyred by stoning in 62 AD. [54] St Jerome concluded that this James was also the author of the Letter of James. [55]

But, at this point in their relationship with Jesus, the "brothers" tried to pressure Jesus into going to Jerusalem for the Feast of Tabernacles, which was celebrated October 9 through 15 that year. John says that "*his brothers did not believe in him*" [Jn 7:5] and were trying to coerce Him to go knowing that "*the Jews* [56] *were trying to kill him*" there [Jn 7:1]. Jesus delayed until His detractors had departed for Jerusalem and then Jesus and His disciples left for Jerusalem "*in secret*" [Jn 7:10].

9.1 Leaving Galilee for the Last Time

Jesus was leaving Capernaum for the last earthly time. Both Matthew and Mark say that Jesus left Galilee and "*went to the district of Judea across the Jordan*" [Mt 19:1; Mk 10:1]. However, Luke wrote that Jesus "*resolutely determined to journey to Jerusalem and he sent messengers ahead of him. On the way they entered a Samaritan village to prepare for his reception there*" [Lk 9:51-52].

The district of "Judea across the Jordan" was the common Jewish name for the province of Perea (originally known as Gilead). The name, Perea, which means "beyond," referring to "beyond the Jordan," does not appear explicitly in the Bible, only the name: Judea across the Jordan.

Detail: (route taken to Jerusalem). Luke recounted that they went through Samaria to Jerusalem for the Feast of Tabernacles (or Booths). Luke placed Jesus' journey through Perea after the Feast of Tabernacles. But, Matthew and Mark say they went through Perea, as they headed to Jerusalem. John's Gospel does not indicate which route they took.

Again, Middle Eastern writers used details to fit the message they were trying to convey. Journeying, and being aware of where Jesus and His followers were located, appears to have been important to Matthew, Mark and Luke. Locations and routes taken were meaningful to them and to their first listeners. For a long time, biblical scholars were divided over which route they took on Jesus' final departure from Capernaum. Did they go through Samaria as Luke recounted or did they go through Perea as Matthew and Mark recounted? And, what was the point in these differing details?

One of the pioneers in Middle Eastern Biblical Anthropology was Alfred Edersheim, a Jewish convert to Christianity and Biblical scholar whose most important work, *The Life and Times of Jesus the Messiah,* was published in 1883. Today, many scholars hold to Edersheim's position that the timing was such that their going through Perea was most unlikely.[57]

Edersheim pointed out that Jesus had already delayed until after His "brothers" had left. And, He needed to get to Jerusalem well ahead of the Feast because every able-bodied man was required to make the pilgrimage to Jerusalem for the Feast, and "with his family," to build a small hut, or *sukkoth,* commemorating the huts the Israelites lived in during the Exodus. They were to live in that *sukkoth* in Jerusalem during the festival week. The only practical route through Perea in those days would have taken two full weeks of walking at a steady uninterrupted pace. Yet, the Gospel accounts of Jesus' time in Perea involved large crowds and the sharing of many parables and teachings. For these reasons, Edersheim concluded that the route they took was through Samaria; and, that the journey through Perea occurred sometime after the Feast of Tabernacles, just as Luke recounted it.

Since, there were three events on the Samaria route that only appear in Luke's Gospel, it's clear why Luke would recount that they went through Samaria. But, we're left with the question: why did Matthew and Mark have them going through Perea as they headed to the Feast of Tabernacles? Was it intended to be symbolic of Jesus and His closest followers taking the long Exodus journey before arriving in Jerusalem? This might have been very meaningful to Jewish listeners, but not so to Gentiles. We just don't know. This is another one of those details, used by one or more of the evangelists, whose "message purpose" is beyond our current knowledge.

Luke tells us that, on the way, Jesus *"appointed seventy-[two] others and sent them two by two ahead of him to every town and place where he was about to go"* [Lk 10:1] proclaiming *"the Kingdom of God is at hand"* [Lk 10:9].

Detail: *seventy-[two] were sent*. Some ancient manuscripts read "seventy" and others read "seventy-two." Current translations put the word "two" in brackets. Either interpretation is appropriate. Genesis 8:19 states that all the nations of the world are descended from the three sons of Noah. Chapter 10 of Genesis then names the descendants. Depending on which names are included and which ones are not, Hebrews counted seventy, while Greek translations counted seventy-two. The symbolism is that those sent represented all the nations of the world – a message Luke would want his Gentile listeners to "hear."

A number of early Church Fathers offered lists of who the seventy people were. One of the earliest lists was by Hippolytus, who in his: *On the Seventy Apostles of Christ,* written around 200 AD included the evangelist, Luke, as one of those sent that day. If Hippolytus was correct, that would place Luke in the presence of Jesus at least as early as the fall of 32 AD, some 20 years before he joined Paul in Troas. This suggests that Luke had been a freeman for some time when he met Paul. And, perhaps Luke had been in Israel during the ministry of Jesus. This might account for how one born a Gentile, whose profession was the exclusive service of an extended family, would be so familiar with the land and people of Israel. Luke's writings account for nearly a third of the entire New Testament.

Luke also noted that a Samaritan village would not welcome Jesus *"because the destination of his journey was Jerusalem"* [Lk 9:53]. This would have been an enormous affront. Jesus had been rejected by His original hometown, Nazareth; He had been rejected by His "adopted" hometown, Capernaum; and now in Samaria He was denied even the most basic common courtesy of their times – hospitality to a traveler.

9.2 Hospitality in Ancient Israel

Travel in ancient Israel was very arduous and most often on foot. If food, water and shelter were not freely given by people along the way, most travelers could not have survived. So, hospitality and its associated protocol were central to their culture. It was an obligation of each head of household to respond to the needs of any one "coming to his door," stranger or friend. The Hebrews understood themselves to be 'sojourners' in the world, in need of hospitality [Deu 26:5-11].

When a stranger was encountered, it was expected that they would be greeted. This was to be followed by an invitation to "come and rest awhile." The first invitation was always refused; it was then to be followed by a second invitation that was always accepted. Declining a second invitation was a major social insult. Then, the strangers' feet were washed signifying that they were now guests of the household and they now enjoyed the protection of that head of household. Strangers, now guests, were never questioned; the "host" always let his guests open the conversation first and share what they wished. As strangers departed, they always received a blessing from the host.

This cultural commitment to hospitality to strangers was celebrated each year at the end of the grape harvest on the holiday known as Sukkot, or the Feast of Booths or Tabernacles. During the holiday, each family would build a small hut, or sukkoth, commemorating the huts the Israelites lived in during their 40 years in the desert after leaving Egypt [Deu 16:13-17].

There was also a certain protocol associated with giving a dinner at one's home. Several days before the event, the host would send his servants out to invite the guests, letting them know of the occasion for the event and the date and time.

Accepting this invitation was regarded as essential to sustaining proper hospitality in the village or town. And, this early "heads up" was required in order for people to plan for their attendance and avoid any schedule conflicts.

On the day of the event, if the event was a "banquet," the servants went out to escort the guests to the event to ensure they all made it safely. In the Middle East, shoes were only worn by guests to a banquet; otherwise sandals were the standard footwear. Shoes, in those days, were very uncomfortable and served only to protect the feet from mud and filth while in route to the banquet. This made the foot washing on their arrival, largely ceremonial. It was inexcusable for one to decline to come to a dinner or banquet when "all is ready." Nothing short of a death in the family was acceptable as a reason for not coming.

As each guest arrived, their feet were washed, and any dignitary or special guest was anointed with oil as a symbol of outpouring of blessings upon them. It was the duty of the eldest son to bring each guest to greet his father (the head of household) before the meal began. No one approached the father except through the son [cf. Jn 14:6]. Upon conclusion of a banquet, the guests were always escorted back to their homes by the host's servants.

Fifteen miles south of Mount Tabor was the town of En-gannim ("spring of gardens"). The town was right on the Kishon River, the border between Samaria and Galilee. It was here that, in 842 BC, Ahaziah, king of Judah, was ambushed by other Jews and left for dead. He later escaped but died of his wounds after having crawled away for 20 miles [2 Kings 9:22-28; 2 Chronicles 22:1-9]. Considering that the Samaritans lived only a short walking distance to the south, some biblical scholars have concluded that this is where Jesus spoke the Parable of the Good Samaritan.

9.3 The Parable of the Good Samaritan [Luke 10:25-37]

The text of this parable can be found in section 1.3.4

This parable involves two subjects which we should know a little more about in order to better understand the parable: the role of lawyers in ancient Israel and the Hebrew system of ritual purity.

9.4 The Role of Lawyers in Ancient Israel

In ancient Israel, the *soferim* ("lawyers," also known as "scribes" and "scholars of the law") were Jewish officials whose role was to serve as the interpreters and copyists of God's law. In 539 BC, Cyrus, king of Persia, freed the Israelites from captivity in Babylon but many delayed returning to Israel. By the year 458 BC, progress in reestablishing a functioning people and nation in Israel was progressing so slowly that the later Persian king, Artaxerxes I, sent Ezra the Scribe to Jerusalem to organize efforts there. Ezra took it as his mandate to renew and enforce observance of the Torah. At that time, Ezra declared the Torah the "Law of Moses" and he organized the *soferim* into a formal group whose role was to identify and interpret "God's commandments in the Law."

All the *soferim* belonged to the priestly class: male individuals at least 30 years old who were patrilineal descendants from Aaron, the elder brother of Moses. In Jesus' day, there were 24 families who traced their linage to Aaron (who was of the tribe of Levi). Twice a year for two weeks, selected males from these 24 families served as Temple priests (or *kohanim*). During the balance of the year, they served as *soferim*.

One of their main duties while serving as Temple *kohanim* was to collect the Temple tax from their neighbors. The Temple tax was fixed at 1/10th of their "produce for the year" from their farms or vineyards, businesses, etc. However, it was up to the Temple priest to decide what was each family's "produce for the year." They were often very lenient to one neighbor and grossly unjust to another.

Another principal duty of the *soferim* was to meticulously copy scrolls, hence the title: Scribes. The copying process was so laborious that as they worked they pondered over what the Scripture was saying, day in and day out, year after year after year. They wrestled with the question: "What does this scripture mean?" During the time of Jesus, the Jewish people were very dependent upon the *soferim*. The language of the Jews was passing into the Aramaic dialect, and most of the people, including judges, were unable to understand their own Torah, and gladly accepted the interpretation which was given by the *soferim*.

For many centuries, it was forbidden to compile a definitive list of "God's commandments in the Law" or to write down any sofer's interpretation of the law, thus leaving the matter entirely open to individual interpretations by *soferim*. This was the case in Jesus' day. In many legal disputes, heard before the Sanhedrin or before local elders, *Soferim* were regularly consulted for their interpretations. While they did not decide cases, their interpretations were very influential in the decision.

The first recorded compilation of "God's commandments in the Torah" was in about the year 930 AD by Saadia ben Yosef Gaon, who was the head of a rabbinic academy in Sura (which is in modern day Iraq). Most present-day Jews generally follow the compilation done by Moses Maimonides in 1180 AD of 613 *Mitzvot* or "commandments" in the text *Mishnah Torah*.

9.5 The Hebrew System of Ritual Purity

In the ancient world of the Hebrews, every good thing that happened "was of God," and every bad thing that happened "was of God." With this worldview, the people naturally sought ways to be in harmony with God's wishes, even when they had no idea what God wished. Sometime after the exiles returned from Babylon and rebuilding the Temple was completed (~516 BC), an extensive set of rules associated with ritual purity emerged. The state of "ritual purity" was a prerequisite for those who came to the Temple to offer sacrifices, for those (priests) who regularly officiated at sacrifices, and for any animals which were to be offered as sacrifices.

At one end of the spectrum of order in the world, was God, the "*living God*" [Jer 10:10] at the other end of the spectrum was death.

So, through maintaining ritual purity they sought to keep as far away as possible from things related to death, thereby being as close as possible to God. Ritual purity was seen as a wedge between the forces of death, which were "unclean," and the forces of life which, like God, were "holy."

A person, animal or thing that was not in a condition of ritual purity, "unclean," was said to be "defiled." Depending on an elaborate system of assigning severity to the uncleanness, defilement could be remedied from just staying apart from others for a prescribed period of time all the way to having to perform an extensive sacrifice ceremony, known as the *He'tot*. In the *He'tot*, the blood of a "clean" animal was offered to offset what was lost through defilement. So, every occasion of defilement was seen as having lost some of one's life-giving substance, either literally or figuratively.

Defilement not only affected the "unclean" person, but their state of defilement was seen as degrading the whole land of Israel in the eyes of God. If the state of defilement in the land became too great, God might leave their Temple in disgust.

Yet, being "unclean" had nothing to do with morality or hygiene – it was strictly a matter of ritual. Anyone who was defiled was seen as a threat to those around them. Any contact with a corpse (known as the "father of defilement") was an obvious source of defilement, even when it involved preparing a person for burial.

Also, to be in the same house or enclosure as a corpse defiled; even having the shadow of a corpse pass over someone defiled them. Any form of bleeding, including menstruation and childbirth, defiled; any loss of bodily fluids even in intercourse defiled; eating an animal (such as swine, crustacean, squid, eel) that fed on dead things defiled.

Most biblical historians agree that much of what we know today as the Hebrew ritual purity system was formalized and edited into Leviticus, Numbers and Deuteronomy about the time when Ezra the Scribe declared the Torah as the official Law of Moses in 458 BC. One of the lessons they interpreted from the creation story in the Book of Genesis (~560 BC) was that because God created the world, the world was intended to be orderly and life was to be purposeful.

So, an important part of being purposeful in God's eyes was to act in orderly ways. Thus, in time, the strictures concerning defilement advanced into areas more related to "disorderly things" than related to death.

What was "disorderly" was regarded as breaching the *"hedge of protection around God's people"* [Job 1:10]. In that context, even touching someone who was defiled caused one to be defiled. This was opening oneself to "unclean" spirits. Such actions as a Jew eating with a Gentile, not adhering to the *"tradition of the elders"* [Mt 15:2] in preparing meals or oneself for meals, even touching an object that had been touched by an "unclean" person was regarded as so contrary to proper order that they became defiled.

What had begun in the fifth century BC, on at least primitive theological grounds, morphed over the centuries to become grossly over-burdensome impacting almost every aspect of Jewish life. Jesus vehemently denounced this, saying, *"in vain do they worship me, teaching as doctrines mere human precepts"* [Mt 15:9].

Sadly, one of the most tragic consequences of the Hebrew ritual purity system was that those with mental illness were seen as being possessed by "unclean" spirits and any form of physical deformity was seen as the mark of one who was permanently defiled. These people were banished from the community indefinitely. Any ailment that gave one the appearance of dying, such as skin disorders and leprosy, made one "unclean" [see Leviticus chs.11-15 and Numbers ch.19]. Those banished from the community were literally "cut off" from the people and access to God; they were reduced to being non-persons.

9.6 The Spiritual Lesson in the Parable

The spiritual lesson in this parable can be found in section 1.3.4

A three-day walk south through Samaria would have brought them to the village of Ephraim (known today as Taybeh). This was quite likely the village that rejected Jesus because He was headed to Jerusalem [Lk 9:52]. The town, located on a 2900-foot-high hill, was once the capital of the Land of Ephraim. The Tribe of Ephraim had been at odds with others ever since Moses' blessing of the tribes at the end of the Exodus [Deu 33:17].

As they approached the border with Judea, they would have come to Mount Hazor, a plateau 3400 feet above sea level, where Abraham had built an altar and, for the first time, "*invoked the Lord by name*" [Gen 12:8]. Not far from Mount Hazor, the Shechem Road ascends into the Judean Hills, an area of heavily weathered limestone and red clay. Jesus and His disciples encountered ten lepers on the road. No record has been found of a designated place in Samaria for lepers, so they could have come from any of the myriad of small caves in the Judean Hills. Jesus healed the ten lepers [Lk 17:11]. But, only one of them, a Samaritan, returned to give thanks. About six miles north of Jerusalem, they would have come to a side road to the east that led to what was once the proud city of Gibeah. Gibeah was the home of their first king, King Saul. The name Gibeah means "hill country" and Gibeah served as the royal residence of Saul for 38 years [1 Sam 8:31]. The city was largely destroyed by the Babylonians in 586 BC. All that remained in Jesus' day was a small poor village.

Figure 20: Samarian foothills (colorized 1895 photo)

Although Saul fell from God's favor, he never fell from the favor of his countrymen. Out of respect alone, they likely spent some quiet time at Gibeah. All three Synoptic Gospels recount that as Jesus was going up to Jerusalem, he took the Twelve aside to speak to them away from the others. We don't know for sure that this was the location, but Gibeah would have been an ideal spot for them to pause on the journey for Him to speak to them in private. But, they had not anticipated what Jesus would say:

> "*We are going up to Jerusalem, and the Son of Man will be betrayed to the chief priests and the teachers of the law. They will condemn him to death and will turn him over to the Gentiles to be mocked and flogged and crucified. On the third day he will be raised to life!*" [Mt 20:17-19; Mk 10:33-34; Lk 18:31-33].

This was the third time Jesus told them of His coming passion and death, and the first time He mentioned crucifixion [cf. Mt 20:19]. Luke says that "*they understood nothing of this; the word remained hidden from them and they failed to comprehend what he said*" [Lk 18:34].

Although Jerusalem was at an elevation of 2600 feet above sea level, in the first century, the Judean Hills just north of Jerusalem were covered with oak and carob trees. So, the city would have been hidden from sight until travelers were quite close to the city. Then, suddenly the view would have been before them of the city which Herod the Great had so extravagantly adorned that he nearly bankrupted Judea. But for Jews, all their aspirations were wrapped up in Jerusalem, (which means "provider of peace"). It was their Holy City, God's dwelling place among them. It was the practice of pilgrims, upon the city first coming into their view, to recite with great pride the passage from Isaiah 2:3, "*Many peoples shall come and say: 'Come, let us go up to the Lord's mountain, to the house of the God of Jacob, that he may instruct us in his ways, and we may walk in his paths' for from Zion shall go forth instruction and the word of the Lord from Jerusalem.*'" [58]

The Shechem Road ends at the Gennath Gate in the northwest corner of the Jerusalem city wall. Just before reaching the Gate, they would have passed the rock mound known as Gol'gotha ("place of the skull") on their left. The Romans had a way of holding their executions in very visible locations. Jesus had told His disciples that He was to die on a cross. But, from every indication given by the evangelists His disciples just "didn't get it." Sometimes, when we're presented with something so horrendous, so far from how we want things to be, that denial seems the only response. Was that the case with Jesus' disciples; was the crucifixion of their Messiah just too much for them to get their minds around? We don't really know. We can sympathize with them, we can see how that might have been the case, but we really don't know. However, Jesus had no such mental avoidance. Death on a cross was His accepted destiny; and He likely passed by Gol'gotha that day in a much different frame of mind than that of His companions.

In early-October, 32 AD, they would have arrived in Jerusalem to celebrate Sukkot, the Feast of the Tabernacles. Jerusalem would now be Jesus' new "home base." John says that when the festival week was half over, Jesus openly taught in the Temple, and the Temple authorities *"tried to arrest him, but no one laid a hand upon him, because his hour had not yet come"* [Jn 7:30]. So, Jesus and His disciples withdrew *'to the Mount of Olives"* [Lk 21:37; Jn 8:1]. Since Mount Olivet was regarded as "within Jerusalem," the Mount is likely where they had constructed their booths or sukkot, to stay for the festival week.

John's Gospel [59] says that, upon arriving in the Temple area the next morning, some scribes and Pharisees sought to entrap Jesus. They brought to Him a woman who had been caught in adultery. In responding, Jesus *"bent down and began to write on the ground with his finger"* [Jn 8:6]. The scribes, scholars of their Scriptures, would have immediately recognized what Jesus was doing, recalling to their minds the passage from Jerimiah: *"Those who turn away from thee shall be written in the earth, for they have forsaken the Lord"* [Jer 17:13, RCV]. By this action, Jesus moved their focus from the woman's wrongdoing to their own wrongdoings. Yet, He did so in a non-shaming way; it's unlikely that the crowd would have picked up such a subtle reference. All the accusers backed off leaving none to condemn her. Jesus did not shame her either, saying *"Neither do I condemn you. Go, and from now on do not sin any more"* [Jn 8:11].

Upon leaving the Temple area, Jesus and His disciples came upon a man born blind from birth. In the course of the discourse involved in that encounter, Jesus said to them: *"While I am in the world, I am the light of the world"* [Jn 9:5]. Recall from section 1.3.5 that what is conveyed in dialog is more telling than what is conveyed in narrative. Jesus' use of the phrase "light of the world" would have had special significance to His listeners.

9.7 The Light of the World

In Judaism, the "light of the world" was the huge golden lampstand in the Temple area known as the Holy Place. The lampstand, known today as a *menorah*, was set beside the Table of Showbread (sometimes spelled Shewbread). Showbread ("bread of the presence") was twelve loaves of bread placed every Sabbath in the Temple's Holy Place and consumed by the priests at the end of the week. Ever since God provided manna in the desert during the Exodus, Jews believed that, since God dwelled in the Temple, it was believed that the *Shekhinah* (God's presence) was in the bread.

Recalling Genesis 1:3, *"Then God said: Let there be light, and there was light,"* light was the first thing God created. Light was the first perceptible sign that God existed. Prior to that there was total darkness. Of course, God always existed, but there was no perceptible sign of God before there was light. That's the point of Genesis verse 1:3. (Note: the creation story in Genesis is not a science lesson on how the world was created; it's a faith lesson about the orderly nature of God and His creation and the origin of mankind).

The light from the golden lampstand in the Temple, perpetually shining upon the Showbread, was, to the Jews, the perceptible sign, "entrusted" to the Jews, that God was in the world [cf. Isa 42:6]. But, on that day outside the Temple, Jesus stated, *"While I am in the world, I am the light of the world"* [Jn 9:5]. In His earthly mission, Jesus was the perceptible sign of God in the world, no longer the role of the golden lampstand in the Temple.

At another time (see section 7.12), Jesus said to His disciples, *"You are the light of the world"* [Mt 5:14] – when my earthly mission ends, you will be the perceptible sign of God in the world. If the world cannot see God through you, the world will not know God exists.

Jesus went on to say that he *"came into the world so that the blind may see"* [Jn 9:39]. *"Whoever follows me will never walk in darkness but will have the light of life"* [Jn 8:12], Jesus then healed the man born blind [Jn 9:1-41], but it was on the Sabbath. This led to an ominous confrontation with the Pharisees.

In Galilee, Jesus had faced some very heated confrontations with the Pharisees. But in Jerusalem, the Pharisees went so far as to plot to kill Him [Jn 11:45-57]. Aware that it was no longer safe for them to even spend their nights on Mount Olivet following the Feast, Jesus and the Twelve promptly withdrew to the village of Bethany to the house of Lazarus and his sisters, Martha and Mary [Lk 10:38]. Bethany was on the south-eastern side of Mount Olivet on the Jericho Road.

Detail: In the Gospels, each time Jesus visited Lazarus, Martha and Mary, the evangelists included the name of the community, Bethany. The name Bethany means "house of the afflicted." The village, which was not visible from the Temple mount, was a center for caring for the sick and the destitute that came as pilgrims to Jerusalem, principally from Galilee. [60] Simon the Leper's house was also there [Mk 14:3-10].

Bethany was an ideal place for Jesus and His disciples to avoid confrontation with the Temple authorities. Based on the Gospel accounts, on this occasion, they remained in Bethany until it was time to return to Jerusalem for Hanukkah, the Feast of Dedication, in early December.

By this detail, the evangelists were telling their listeners important information about Lazarus, Martha and Mary. If they accommodated, at their "house," Jesus and His disciples for a period of several weeks, their "house" must have been much larger than typical first-century houses. They likely had several buildings in which they operated in Bethany, the "house of the afflicted," what we would call today, a nursing care facility. This might account for why Jesus had such a deep affection for Lazarus and his sisters.

At some point in their stay in Lazarus' house, Jesus shared with them the Parable of the Friend in Need. But, He did so after first teaching them what has come to be known as the prayer, the Our Father.

9.8 Parable of the Friend in Need [Luke 11:1-13]

Jesus was praying in a certain place, and when he had finished, one of his disciples said to him,
"Lord, teach us to pray just as John taught his disciples."

He said to them, "When you pray, say:
   Father, hallowed be your name,
   your kingdom come.
   Give us each day our daily bread⁻
   and forgive us our sins
   for we ourselves forgive everyone in debt to us,
   and do not subject us to the final test."

And he said to them,
   "Suppose one of you has a friend to whom he goes at midnight and says,
   'Friend, lend me three loaves of bread, for a friend of mine has arrived at my house from a journey and I have nothing to offer him,'

   and he says in reply from within, 'Do not bother me;
   the door has already been locked and my children and I are already in bed. I cannot get up to give you anything.'

   I tell you, if he does not get up to give him the loaves because of their friendship, he will get up to give him whatever he needs because of his persistence.

And I tell you, ask and you will receive; seek and you will find;

knock and the door will be opened to you.

For everyone who asks, receives; and the one who seeks, finds; and to the one who knocks, the door will be opened.

What father among you would hand his son a snake when he asks for a fish? Or hand him a scorpion when he asks for an egg?
If you then, who are wicked, know how to give good gifts to your children, how much more will the Father in heaven give the holy Spirit to those who ask him?"

9.9 The Spiritual Lesson in the Parable

Detail: (context) they had observed before that Jesus prayed in solitude although praying in solitude was most uncommon for Jews. Yet, in the face of mounting hostility to Him, Jesus seemed to draw even more resolute and at peace. Was that coming from His prayer life? It appears that one of the Twelve felt compelled to ask Him to teach them.

The prayer, the "Our Father," speaks to One who delights in supplying his children's needs. In this prayer, there's no pleading, no bargaining which was common in prayer forms of that time, particularly in prayers they had heard among pagans. Instead, this prayer began with praising God in His glory and then follows a simple expression of a present need, and it closed with a request for forgiveness.

Detail: Jesus followed this with a parable. Why a parable? We should expect that the message in the parable will not be obvious at first. There's a much large principle than just how to pray.

Detail: a friend came at midnight. Since Jews did not travel at night, midnight is a most unreasonable time for a guest to arrive. Yet, the neighbor has a cultural duty to provide for the one who has been journeying. But, midnight is also an unreasonable time to be asking for a favor. However, the neighbor expresses a serious, present need not a favor request. In the Middle East no one knocked on a closed door unless there was great urgency. During the day, doors were normally left open.

Detail: He asked for *"three loaves."* The neighbor has an obligation to provide a traveler/guest with abundance.

Detail: *"Do not bother me ... we are in bed."* The neighbor has a duty arising out of cultural expectations. The duty for the man of the house arises out of friendship. Due to the practice of pietas, he has an obligation to his extended family, but to no one else. Whatever response he may offer to his neighbor's serious, present need must arise from their friendship. It doesn't appear that they have much of a friendship.

So, the parable is not primarily calling for persistence in prayer. Rather it expresses, in story form, a divine promise which Jesus summarized in His statement:" If *an unwilling householder can in the end be coerced by a neighbor's shameless persistence into giving him what he needs, you can be sure that God, who is your loving Father, will supply all your needs. Indeed, ask and you will receive; seek and you will find; knock and the door will be opened to you."*

If we don't seem to receive what we asked for in prayer, it's not because God grudgingly refuses to respond; it's because in His love and wisdom He offers something even better. Jesus assured His friends that, with their Heavenly Father, there is no such thing as an unanswered prayer.

Sometime later, they returned to Jerusalem for Hanukkah, the Feast of Dedication [Jn 10:22], which was celebrated on December 16/17 that year.

It's December of 32 AD. Jesus' eighth journey has come to an end; and, what a moving, even troubling journey it was. We saw Jesus leave Galilee for the last time, after being pressured by His "brothers" to go to Jerusalem where it was known that *"the Jews were trying to kill him"* [Jn 7:1]. They secretly took the route through Samaria where He gracefully accepted rejection there as well.

Along the way, He tried again to share with the Twelve His passion and death that lay ahead but *"they failed to comprehend what he said"* [Lk 18:35]. In Jerusalem there was more confrontation, ominous confrontation. Clearly, Jesus was now in direct danger; so, they sought to avoid further confrontation by going to Lazarus' home in Bethany. Along the way, we heard two remarkable parables giving us insights into the loving nature of God which we might not have fully realized before. There are many more parables to go.

We are being drawn deeper and deeper into the life, times and words of Jesus, knowing the glorious outcome. His disciples did not. They were observing danger closing in on Jesus, and possibly on them as well. Yet, they saw glimpses of Jesus' divine power as well; enough to keep them in His company. Perhaps they recalled the words of Jerimiah for assurance:
> *"For thus says the Lord: ... 'I know well the plans I have in mind for you, plans for your welfare and not your woe, so as to give you a future of hope. When you call me, and come and pray to me, I will listen to you''"* [Jer 29:10-12].

Thank you, Jesus, for the divine promise that our prayers never go unheard or unanswered.

10. Jesus' Ninth Journey

In early 33 AD, probably in January or early February, Jesus and His disciples left Bethany and headed into the Province of Perea, a region known to Jews as "Judea across the Jordan." Matthew, Mark and John stated that they first headed to the town of Bethabara [Mt 19:1; Mk 10:1; Jn 10:40], just across the Jordan from Jericho. It was near Bethabara that Jesus had been baptized by John the Baptist; and, it was there that He called His first disciples.

The evangelists did not provide the names of any of the communities they passed through on this journey through Perea. So, we can't be sure of their itinerary. However, the choice of travel routes through Perea in those days was very limited. Since they headed east to Bethabara, there was only one normally traveled route they could have taken through the region. (To follow their journey, see Appendix 1 for a map of Israel in the Time of Jesus)

That route began at Bethabara, then along the eastern leg of David's Highway to where it met the King's Highway in Rabbah (also known as Philadelphia in Perea). Then, it continued a short distance north to the headwaters of the Jabbok ("blue") River; then it followed the river north a few miles where it swung westward back to the Jordan River; and finally, south along the Jordan back to the Jericho crossing. This amounted to more than a 175-mile walk. A number of biblical scholars have concluded that this was their most likely route, and the storylines of a number of the parables Jesus shared along the way fit quite well with the communities they would have passed through.[61]

Considering that the evangelists tell us that Jesus and His disciples encountered a number of crowds along the way, and that this was the period when Jesus shared most of His parables, their journey through Perea must have taken them several weeks to complete.

10.1 Perea, Judea across the Jordan

The earliest information we have on inhabitants in the region of what was known in the Roman Empire as Perea is from some 15th century BC Egyptian records of a nomadic people living there, known as the Shasu. The name, Shasu, is Egyptian for "wanderers." There is some evidence that, like the Israelites, the Shasu worshiped only one god, but no clear connection between those two peoples has been found. [62]

Following the Exodus from Egypt, around 1220 BC, the tribes of Reuben and Gad came to Moses to ask if they could settle in this area, then known as Transjordan [Numbers, chapter 32]. The Israelites later crossed into the Promised Land from Transjordan, most likely at Damia (also known as A'dam), for the Battle of Jericho.

In 39 AD, Emperor Caligula transferred both Perea and Galilee from the disgraced Herod Antipas to Herod Agrippa I (Herod the Great's grandson). In 44 AD, Agrippa's territory was combined with Judea into one province, which was named Judea. So, the name, Perea, was no longer in use by the time the Gospels were written.

Today, what was Perea is the western third of the modern-day Arab kingdom of Jordan. In Jesus' time, Perea was almost entirely Jewish. The region of Perea was largely a desert plateau, ranging from several hundred feet below sea level at the River Jordan on the west and rising to 3900 feet above sea level on the east. The plateau is cut be a number of wadis (seasonal rivers) and two main rivers. The Yarmouk River forms the border with the Decapolis to the north and the Jabbok River cuts through central Perea. All of the wadis and rivers in Perea eventually flow into the Jordan River. Over millions of years, these waterways cut deep ravines through the soft limestone plateau. Except for the banks of the rivers and wadis, the soils in Perea were much better suited to grazing than agriculture.

The major trade route through the region was the King's Highway. The Highway ran along the eastern edge of Perea on a north-south ridge known as the Sharra Highlands. Archeological evidence shows that The King's Highway was in use as far back as 3300 BC. The Israelites used the King's Highway, which they called, D*erekh Ha'Melech* [Numbers 20:17; 21:22].in advancing through Transjordan.

Unlike the Via Maris, the King's Highway traversed much more arid land; therefore, obtaining sufficient water was a constant concern for those on the Highway. Caravans coming from the east would restock their water supplies at the two rivers, the Abana and the Pharpar, at Damascus before heading south through Perea. Except for a few wadis that may have been flowing in the rainy season, it was over 110 miles south to the headwaters of the Jabbok River near the city of Rabbah, where they could again restock their water supplies. And, it was another 90 miles further south after that to reach the town of Karak, where they could restock again. So, except for the northernmost portion of the King's Highway where there might be flowing wadis in the rainy season, it was necessary for travelers on the Highway in Perea to join up with one of these caravans.

For many centuries, poplar and tamarix trees grew along the banks of the rivers and the larger wadis, with forests of oak and olives growing on the nearby hillsides.[63] By the first century, extensive orchards of figs, dates, almonds and peaches were along the banks providing for both domestic and export. Dried figs were the leading export crop of Perea.

Unfortunately, extensive deforestation of these waterway areas over the last hundred years has caused most of the arable soil to be washed downstream as silt into the Jordan River valley. Today, agriculture now amounts to only 3% of the kingdom of Jordan's GDP and the kingdom must import 98% of its food.[64]

Leaving Bethany, Jesus and His disciples' walk to Jericho would have involved descending from about 2500 feet above sea level at Bethany, to some 825 feet below sea level at Jericho, over a distance of about 16 miles. Such a dramatic change in elevation brought with it a startlingly rapid change in environmental conditions that proved exhausting for most anyone making the walk. Jericho was (and remains today) an oasis situated in the midst of a desert.

At a point about 5 miles from Jericho, travelers would encounter a narrow pass, known as the Adummim Pass ("red things" pass) [Joshua 15.7]. St Jerome, who translated the Bible into Latin in the late 4th century, contended that the name of the pass was given because of the blood that bandits repeatedly shed at this place. St. Jerome also argued that there was an inn not far away and that the Adummim Pass was the place Jesus was referring to in the Parable of the Good Samaritan.

After another two-mile walk, near where Herod the Great had built his winter castle, they would have come to the Wadi Qelt. Since it was the rainy season, the Wadi Qelt would have been freely flowing and they would find fresh water. It's unlikely they stayed very long in Jericho; probably only for the night. After wading across the river, the next morning, Jesus and His disciples would have air dried on the east bank and then continued on east to Bethabara.

The Roman historian, Flavius Josephus, related that there was a large community of followers of John the Baptist near where John was baptizing at Bethabara. [65] There are also several places in Scripture that make it clear that there were a number of disciples of John the Baptist still actively ministering long after John's beheading. In Acts of the Apostles, Luke recounted that one of John's disciples, a Jew named Apollos, was teaching in Ephesus at the time Paul arrived. Later, in Acts 19:2-7 Luke tells of a group of John's disciples whom Paul encountered there. That would have been around 54 AD. Further, in the beginning of his Gospel, John the evangelist made the point directly that John the Baptist was not the Messiah [Jn 1:6-8]. John went on to stress that point several times [Jn 1:15, 27, 29, 34]. So, clearly there were disciples of John the Baptist active in Ephesus as late as around 85 AD, and perhaps even later.

Several biblical scholars have concluded that, on this journey, Jesus and His disciples would likely have encountered a number of John the Baptist's disciples in Bethabara. Some of them may have been friends or even family members of some of Jesus' disciples. So, Jesus and His disciples may have stayed some time in Bethabara before moving on with their journey.

Heading east from Bethabara, along David's Highway, the road would rise steadily from about 800 feet below sea level to nearly 3300 feet above sea level near Rabbah (also known as Philadelphia in Perea). The road ran along a narrow, wadi-fed valley, known as *Biq'ah Yitro* (Valley of Jethro). The narrow valley had very fertile soil which supported many small farms and orchards, with vineyards in the higher elevations. Thus, they would have had access to food and water on their journey.

Figure 21: *Biq'ah Yitro* (Valley of Jethro) in Perea

After a full three-day walk, they would have arrived at the city of Gadara ("walled city"). The city was on an 1100-foot-high summit overlooking the fertile valley below. The capital of the region of the Decapolis, just north of Perea, was also named Gadara. Gadara in Perea appears to have been initially settled by the Medians around 750 BC and was then known as Saltus (after a type of raisin made from the pale green sultana grape). Around 330 BC, the Macedonians under Alexander the Great built a large fortress on the summit and renamed the city, Gadara.

As Jesus and His disciples arrived in Gadara, *"great crowds gathered"* [Mt 19:2] and *"children were brought to him that he might lay his hands on them and pray"* [Mt 19:13; Mk 10:13; Lk 18:15]. What a welcome relief this must have been after the very hostile receptions Jesus had received in Judea.

Since children were to be in the company of their mothers until they were considered adults, the presence of children in the crowd meant there were many women there as well. Women had a very mixed status in ancient Judaism. The Torah related that both Israelite men and women were present at Mt. Sinai; however, the covenant was worded in such a way that it bound men to act upon its requirements and to ensure that the members of their household (wives, children, and slaves) met these requirements. So, while women were part of the covenant, it was indirectly. However, women had the responsibility of teaching the children prayer, Scriptures and proper social behavior.

Women also had a role in ritual life. Women (as well as men) were required to make the pilgrimage to the Temple in Jerusalem once a year (men each of the three main festivals) and offer the Passover sacrifice. Women would also do so on special occasions in their lives, such as giving a *todah* ("thanksgiving") offering after childbirth. But, men and women prayed separately and were rarely in the company of one another in public. So, Jesus' disciples, initially, tried to chase the children (and their mothers) away [Mt 19:13; Mk 10:13; Lk 18:15]. But, Jesus said, *"Let the children come to me, and do not prevent them; for the Kingdom of God (Heaven) belongs to such as these"* [Mt 19:14; Mk 10:14; Lk 18:16]. The three evangelists, Matthew, Mark and Luke, not only acknowledged that women were in the company of Jesus, but that women and their children were warmly welcomed by Jesus, in spite of the cultural norms of His time.

Later in Gadara, Jesus spoke the Parable of the Rich Fool in response to a man who called out from the crowd, but also spoke to the self-indulgent mindset of many others in the crowd. Archeologists have established that, in Jesus' time, there was a sizable Epicurean community in Gadara. Around 300 BC, a young Greek philosopher named Epicurus began teaching that the whole purpose of life was to attain freedom from fear through self-indulgence. A very large number of people, including many Jews, were attracted to that line of thinking. And, self-indulgence quickly attained the rank of a religion. Many people who lived self-indulgence as a lifestyle would likely have been among His listeners.[66]

10.2 The Parable of the Rich Fool [Luke 12:13-22]

Someone in the crowd said to Jesus,
"Teacher, tell my brother to share the inheritance with me."

He replied to him, "Friend, who appointed me as your judge and arbitrator?"

Then he said to the crowd, "Take care to guard against all greed, for though one may be rich, one's life does not consist of possessions."

Then he told them a parable.
> "There was a rich man whose land produced a bountiful harvest.
> He asked himself, 'What shall I do, for I do not have space to store my harvest?'
> And he said, 'This is what I shall do:
> I shall tear down my barns and build larger ones.
> There I shall store all my grain and other goods and
> I shall say to myself, "Now as for you, you have so many good things stored up for many years, rest, eat, drink, be merry!"'
>
> But God said to him, 'You fool, this night your life will be demanded of you; and the things you have prepared, to whom will they belong?'
>
> Thus will it be for the one who stores up treasure for himself but is not rich in what matters to God.'"*

10.3 The Spiritual Lesson in the Parable

<u>Detail</u>: *Teacher ("Rabbi"), tell my brother ....* It was common for rabbis to be asked to serve as arbiters of disputes within a family,

but they could not adjudicate inheritance issues. Mosaic Law on the handling of inheritance was quite clear.

Detail: *tell my brother to share the inheritance with me*. What may have happened to the man who cried out is that his brother had decided to follow Jesus, thus abandoning his portion of the inheritance. By Mosaic Law, unless the one who has walked off the land gives it to his brother, it went to the servants who cared for that land during the father's tenure.[67] So, the man's cry "*Teacher, tell my brother to share the inheritance with me*" was not a cry for help, but rather a demand that Jesus instruct His follower to give him the land to prevent it from going to the servants. He was demanding for himself what really should go to others.

Detail: *a rich man whose land produced a bountiful harvest*. The man in the parable, who is already rich, fails to recognize that the bountiful harvest was a 'gift of nature,' not something he caused on his own.

Detail: *What shall I do, for I do not have space to store my harvest?* Their rabbis had long taught that God's purpose in bountiful harvests was that they were to be shared with others. [68]

Detail: *I shall tear down my barns and build larger ones*. His thinking is centered entirely on himself – the mark of an Epicurean.

Detail: *God said to him, 'You fool, this night your life will be demanded of you*. Self-indulgence blinds one to the fact that life itself is a gift of God, which can be lost at any moment. All that we are, all that we have are on loan from God; and it will all return to Him.

Many of us, today, are not familiar with Epicureanism. But, we certainly recognize that self-indulgence as a life style is very much a part of our culture. The general social context in which we live puts strong emphasis on individual achievement. We value independence; and, in our later years we feel that we have "earned" what we have, either through hard work, or frugal behavior, or prudent investments, etc. Epicurean thinking is stitched into the very fabric of how we live. But, we mask much of it from our own consciousness. This parable is as relevant for us as it was for those people in Gadara more than 2000 years ago.

The road heading eastward from Gadara would rise more steeply as they approached the city of Rabbah (the "great city"), also known in Jesus' day as Philadelphia. This is not the Philadelphia referred to in the Book of Revelation. That Philadelphia was in the west central region of what is modern-day Turkey. It would have been a three- to four-day walk to Rabbah, which is now the modern-day city of Ammon, capital of Jordan. David's Highway met the King's Highway trade route at Rabbah.

10.4 Rabbah, the Jewel of the Levant

The Levant is the geographical name for the region occupied today by Israel, Jordan, Lebanon, Palestine, and Syria. During pre-historic times, waves of humans moved out of Africa and into the Levant. They would flourish for a while, decline, and then be replaced by another wave. Remains of anatomically modern Homo sapiens have been found in the area of Mount Carmel, dating from nearly 90,000 BC. One such group of migrating peoples, the Natufians, founded Jericho, around 9500 BC; it is the oldest still-occupied city in the world.

The city of Rabbah was located in about the center of the Levant; and, there was perhaps no city whose strategic situation did more to shape the history of the Middle East. Archeologists contend that Rabbah was initially settled around 2000 BC by a people known as the Ammonites. Soon, trade between Persia to the east and Egypt to the west, along with great wealth was passing through Rabbah along the King's Highway. The first mention of the Ammonites in the Bible is in Genesis 19:37-38. It is stated there that they descended from Ammon, a son of Lot. Throughout the Bible, the Ammonites and the Israelites are portrayed as mutual antagonists.

During the reign of King David, the Ammonites humiliated some of David's messengers and the great siege of Rabbah resulted. This is the siege that is interwoven with the episode of David and Bathsheba [2 Sam 11:1-12:31]. Because the city was on the easternmost edge of the territory of the Tribe of Gad, and the city was so strategic to the trade route, Rabbah managed to avoid serious destruction by the Assyrians and the Babylonians.

Following the death of Alexander, the Great, Ptolemy Philadelphus, who had named himself king of Egypt, captured Rabbah to control the trade route and he greatly expanded the city, from 270 BC to 250 BC. He renamed it Philadelphia and gave the city a distinctly Greek character that was still prevalent in Jesus' time.

Rabbah owed its location to the nearby *Ain Ghazal* ("Gazelle spring"), which is fed by snowmelt from Mount Hermon, via an underground stream over a distance of more than 150 miles. The spring and two small wadis form the headwaters of the Jabbok River. Archeological evidence shows that there was a community near this spring as far back as 10,300 BC. The climate there was more tropical than in the first century and remains of animals found today only in Africa, such as elephants, lions, giraffes and gazelles were found there.

A prolonged drop in the average temperatures and rainfall in that area, and throughout much of the world, occurred around 6200 BC. It eliminated all the "African" animals and vegetation in the Levant and brought about the arid conditions that have prevailed there ever since. [69]

The existence of the Ain Ghazal spring, in that location, is a remarkable example of God's providence. Without that spring, there would have been no King's Highway trade route through that area. Without the King's Highway, the history of the Middle East might have been much different. In addition, there would have been no route for the Israelites to enter the Promised Land from the east. They would have had to pass through the land of the Philistines. But, *"God did not lead them on the road through the Philistine country, though that was shorter. For God said, 'If they face war, they might change their minds and return to Egypt'"* [Ex 13:17]. They were all former slaves with no military training or weapons.

Following the period of Greek conquest, beginning in 334 BC, only Greek was allowed to be spoken, written or read throughout their empire. Later, Greek was the required language of commerce in the Roman Empire at the time of Jesus. Most biblical historians today believe that Jesus, and most of His disciples, were probably fairly proficient in Greek. However, passing along the trade route through Rabbah would have been people speaking Aramaic as well as people from Persia whose native language was Pārsa; people from Mesopotamia speaking Syriac; people from Egypt speaking Coptic; as well as those from Arabia to the south, who spoke a mix of Semitic dialects.

Rabbah would seem to have been an ideal place for Jesus to preach to large crowds. It was more a "crossroads" than even Capernaum was. However, Jesus would have encountered such a wide range of languages there that it would not have been possible to address crowds there in a meaningful way. The Gospels give us no indication of Jesus speaking to any crowds, there; and no mention of any synagogue. They had to pass through Rabbah in order to reach the headwaters of the Jabbok River to continue the rest of their journey. They may not have entered the city of Rabbah at all.

As Jesus and His disciples approached Rabbah, the Castle of the Servant would have come into full view, just west of the city. This grand palace was built around 200 BC by the governor at the time, who was a member of the powerful Tobiad clan in that region.[70]

We don't know the governor's name, only that he referred to himself as the "servant of the king." This was a most disingenuous claim; the Tobaids were not only disloyal to the Greek kings but were a major force in driving them out of power in ancient Israel starting in 140 BC. The Jews hated their Greek oppressors, but they would not have missed the irony that one who falsely proclaimed himself a "servant of the king" would, at the same time, have plotted with others to overthrow the king. This palace, known today by the Arabic name, *Qasr al-Abd*, would have still been in excellent condition at the time Jesus and His disciples were in that area. It appears that this was the place where Jesus shared the Parable of the Vigilant Servants and then in response to Peter the Parable of the Prudent and Wicked Servants as well.

Figure 22: Ruins of Castle of the Servant

10.5 Parable of the Vigilant Servants

This parable is recounted by both Luke and Mark; but Mark used different details to convey a different message than that of Luke.[71]

10.5.1 The Version in Luke's Gospel [Luke 12:35-41]

Jesus said to them,
> "Gird your loins and light your lamps
> and be like servants who await their master's return from a wedding, ready to open immediately when he comes and knocks.
>
> Blessed are those servants whom the master finds vigilant on his arrival.
> Amen, I say to you, he will gird himself, have them recline at table, and proceed to wait on them.
>
> And should he come in the second or third watch and find them prepared in this way, blessed are those servants.
> Be sure of this: if the master of the house had known the hour when the thief was coming, he would not have let his house be broken into.

You also must be prepared, for at an hour you do not expect, the Son of Man will come."

10.5.2 The Version in Mark's Gospel [Mark 13:33-37]

Jesus said to them,
> Be watchful! Be alert! You do not know when the time will come. It is like a man traveling abroad.
>
> He leaves home and places his servants in charge, each with his work, and orders the gatekeeper to be on the watch.
>
> Watch, therefore; you do not know when the lord of the house is coming, whether in the evening, or at midnight, or at cockcrow, or in the morning.
> May he not come suddenly and find you sleeping.
>
> What I say to you, I say to all: 'Watch!'"

10.6 The Spiritual Lesson in the Parable

Detail: (setting). Just ahead of the recounting of this parable, Luke states that "*He said to his disciples*" [Lk 12:22], indicating that Jesus was speaking in private to His companions at this point in their journey. However, Mark has Jesus sharing this parable as part of the Olivet Discourse on Mount Olivet (which we will address in the next chapter). So, Mark intended the parable to support a quite different message than Luke.

At this point, they had been walking and talking together for nearly four days. The evangelists have given us no direct indication of what prompted this parable. There was no crowd, no publicly-posed question; so, there's likely to be some profound insight Jesus wanted His companions to ponder, and so He presented it in parable form.

Detail: "*gird your loins*" – gather up the bottom of your tunic and tie the material around your waist to be ready for something demanding. "*Light your lamps*" – be ready for a time of darkness. Mark's version simply says: "*Be watchful! Be alert!*"

Detail: "*be like servants*" [Lk 12:36]; "*he places his servants in charge*" [Mk 13:34b]. It's the servants, not the steward, who're left in charge. Servants were indentured slaves, not employees who just had a "job to do," rather the servants were totally dependent on their master. Is it just a coincidence that as they would have been near, or at least in sight of, the "castle of the servant" the storyline of Jesus' parables would be about servant loyalty?

Detail: "*who await their master's return from a wedding*" In Luke's version, the master is returning from a wedding. So, the servants would know when to expect him. Wedding feasts lasted a week. However, in Mark's version, the master is returning from "*traveling abroad*." In that case, the master would be away for a very long time and his return would be at an unexpected hour.

Detail: "*Blessed are those servants whom the master finds vigilant.*" The servants who were vigilant (faithful to their master) would be divinely favored upon the master's return.

Detail: "*he will gird himself, have them recline at table, and proceed to wait on them.*" This is a startling statement, reminiscent of the Jewish expectation of the Great Eschatological Feast which was to be hosted by the Messiah. The concept that the "master" would wait on them would have been breathtaking, turning the "natural order" of things upside down in their favor.

Notice that, in Luke's version, there is a grand outcome to the waiting that is part of the storyline. But in Mark's version, there is no description of the outcome to the waiting. Only: "*What I say to you, I say to all: 'Watch!'*"

Detail: "*Be sure of this: if the master of the house had known the hour when the thief was coming, he would not have let his house be broken into.* To be forewarned is to be forearmed – an ancient proverb meant to convey the idea that when one is informed ahead of time, one knows what they are to do.

Luke's version concluded with: *You also must be prepared, for at an hour you do not expect, the Son of Man will come.*"

It's fairly clear from the details and setting Mark used in his account of the parable that, for him and his listeners, it's about being prepared for Jesus' second coming. It's also clear that it's not the message intended in Luke's version. If, as Luke recounted it, this parable was shared by Jesus during His ministry in Perea, then, it's likely, that Jesus was not referring to His second coming either. There was something else intended.

Reviewing the parable: the servants, those totally dependent on their master, were to prepare for something demanding during a period of darkness. Their master would be away for a short while; they would know when he was to return. And, when he returned, the expectations of their lives would be fulfilled. So, since they have been informed beforehand, they know what they are to do.

Jesus had tried three times before, by speaking very directly, to tell them of His impending passion and death. And, that after three days He would rise from the dead. They didn't get it, even after three tries. This parable appears to address the subject from a different direction. In essence, Jesus was saying: "Be prepared for a time of darkness that will demand much of you; for I will be gone from you for a while. But, you know when I will return. And when I do, the expectations of your lives will be fulfilled. I have told you this beforehand that when it happens you know what you are to do." Do *you* think they got it this time?

What is the message in this parable for us, some 2000 years after the events of Passion Week? We might be inclined to think that it's telling us that we need to be prepared for Jesus' coming upon our own death, particularly keying on the concluding statement *"You also must be prepared, for at an hour you do not expect, the Son of Man will come."* That is certainly good advice, but since we don't know the time of our death (the master's return), such an interpretation does not fit the details used in the parable.

The message for us in this parable is not obvious; it was not intended to be obvious. Recall that Jesus' parables are the word of God articulated in an especially challenging manner intended to draw the listeners into a deeper understanding of themselves, of God and of their relationship with one another. This parable calls us to think very deeply about: "what are we, who are totally depended on God, to be prepared for; which will demand much of us; that we know about when it will occur; and, since we have been told beforehand, when it happens, we will know what we as faithful servants are to do?

As noted earlier, just outside of Rabbah are the headwaters of the Jabbok River (known today as the Zarqa River). At the river's origin is the Ain Ghazal spring. From its headwaters, the river flows to the north before heading west. Rising on the western side of the Sharra Highlands ridge, it runs a course of about 75 miles in a deep ravine-like valley before flowing into the Jordan River, at a point 3,576 feet below its origin. At its higher elevations, the river banks are quite steep and canyon-like.

Shortly after sharing the previous parable, Jesus responded to a question from Peter.by sharing the Parable of the Vigilant Servants.

10.7 The Parable of the Prudent and Wicked Servants

This parable is recounted by both Luke and Matthew. Matthew's wording is almost identical to Luke's but then Matthew omits a concluding section that is in Luke's version.

10.7.1 The Version in Luke's Gospel [Luke 12:42-48]

Then Peter said, "Lord, is this parable meant for us or for everyone?"
And the Lord replied,
> "Who, then, is the faithful and prudent steward
> whom the master will put in charge of his servants
> to distribute the food allowance at the proper time?
>
> Blessed is that servant whom his master on arrival finds doing so. Truly, I say to you, he will put him in charge of all his property.
>
> But if that servant says to himself, 'My master is delayed in coming,' and begins to beat the menservants and the maidservants, to eat and drink and get drunk,
> then that servant's master will come on an unexpected day

and at an unknown hour and will punish him severely
and assign him a place with the unfaithful.

That servant who knew his master's will but did not make preparations nor act in accord with his will
shall be beaten severely; and the servant who was ignorant of his master's will but acted in a way deserving of a severe beating shall be beaten only lightly.
Much will be required of the person entrusted with much,
and still more will be demanded of the person entrusted with more.

10.7.2 The Version in Matthew's Gospel [Matthew 24:45-51]

Jesus then said to his disciples,
"Who, then, is the faithful and prudent servant,
whom the master has put in charge of his household
to distribute to them their food at the proper time?"

Blessed is that servant whom his master on his arrival finds doing so. Amen, I say to you, he will put him in charge of all his property.

But if that wicked servant says to himself, 'My master is long delayed,' and begins to beat his fellow servants, and eat and drink with drunkards, the servant's master will come on an unexpected day and at an unknown hour and will punish him severely and assign him a place with the hypocrites, where there will be wailing and grinding of teeth.

10.8 The Spiritual Lesson in the Parable

<u>Detail:</u> (setting). In Luke's account, this parable comes in response to a question from Peter, "*Lord, is this parable meant for us or for everyone?*" Again, Jesus was speaking in private to His companions. There's no honor challenge here, so this is not a pushback intended to pose an even more challenging question. But, it is a parable offered in response to a question, so we should expect that Jesus was addressing more than just Peter's question.

However, Matthew has Jesus sharing this parable as part of the Olivet Discourse, just as Mark had with the previous parable So, Matthew intended the parable to support a quite different message than Luke, even though much of their wording was almost verbatim.

Detail: "*Who, then, is the faithful and prudent steward*" [Lk 12:42] (*servant*" [Mt 24:45]) who is put in charge. The steward is generally in charge in the master's absence; but, the parable offers the prospect that it might be one of the servants who is put in charge. And, he is to "*distribute to them their food at the proper time.*" The phrase "*distribute to them their food at the proper time*" had a particular meaning in the ancient Middle East.

In their culture, meals were not just opportunities for nourishment during which social dialogue might take place. Rather, it was quite the other way around. They were opportunities for bonding through social dialogue and commonly shared etiquette during which nourishment also took place. To them, the power of God was manifested in food: and to feed was to bless. For them to share food in a structured way was God's intended "right order of things." Meals were the forum for much of the communications in their culture. At the meal, there was a specific order to who led the conversations; who led the benedictions; as well as the sequence of serving the food and drink. Even the most "informal" meal had a structure and social purpose. For one to eat alone was the height of rudeness and disorderly behavior.

Consequently, to "*distribute to them their food at the proper time*" was to follow the intended "right order of things" and to maintain the essential social bonds of the group. [72] In short, faithful ones (stewards or servants) were to go on with life in the master's absence, in the same orderly and mutually supportive way as they would if he were present.

Both evangelists likely included this phrase with intent. One of the major problems faced in early Christian communities was that the sharing of meals among Christians of Jewish and Greek heritage was problematic. Greeks (and Romans) eat three meals a day, morning, noon and evening. Whereas, Jews eat two meals a day, sunrise and sunset. And, the different cultures had different etiquette, diet and sequence to their meals. Christians needed to evolve a new "proper" time and order for their common meals.

Detail: *"Blessed is that servant whom his master on arrival finds doing so, he will put him in charge of all his property."* A master entrusting his property to his indentured slaves is a reoccurring theme we will hear in other parables later, as well. In this case, that trust has been granted because the master found those servants faithful in his absence. Notice that they are "Blessed;" the trust granted is a divine favor.

Detail: *"But if that servant says to himself, 'My master is delayed in coming' .... and begins to beat the menservants and the maidservants ..."* Mistreatment of slaves was forbidden under Mosaic Law [Lev 25:43]. Rabbinic interpretation of that passage went so far as to insisted that Jewish slaves should be granted similar food, drink, lodging, and bedding, to that which their master would grant to himself; they should be treated almost like a member of the owner's family.[73]

Detail: *"that servant's master will come on an unexpected day ... and will punish him severely and assign him a place with the unfaithful."* Since the master is always responsible for his servant's conduct, the master would be held accountable by his community. He was culturally required to deal harshly with the wrongdoer. In Luke's version, the wrongdoer was placed with the unfaithful.

The term, "the unfaithful," referred to those who, in Moses' absence on Mount Sinai, fashioned a calf of molded gold to substitute for the invisible God [cf. Ex 32:2-10]. While appearing to be engaging in religious devotion, they were actually trying to reduce God to something they could shape and call upon at their convenience. To be placed with "the unfaithful" was to be left to wander, but never beyond the care and providence of God.

But Matthew changed this detail somewhat. In Matthew's account, the wrongdoer is assigned *"a place with the hypocrites, where there will be wailing and grinding of teeth."* "Hypocrites" was a Greek word for stage actors who played many parts. The actors carried masks so when they played one particular character, they held in front of their face one mask; and when they played another part they held in front of their face the mask of that character. So, hypocrites were people who, by using masks, convinced others that "they are what they are not." The phrase, *"wailing and grinding of teeth"* was also a Greek expression for experiencing anguish, remorse, pain, and misery. Some biblical scholars theorize that there may have been some false teachers in Matthew's community, which he and perhaps others referred to as *hypocrites* who were expelled from the community and were then experiencing *wailing and grinding of teeth.* Matthew has Jesus using this expression on four other occasions as well: Mt 8:12; 13:41-42; 22:11-13; and 25:14-30, so Matthew's community must have been familiar with it.

While persecution was a serious challenge to Christian believers in the first century, it tended to strengthen faith and bring believers together. The biggest threat to Christianity, during time the Gospels were written, was the spreading of false teachings, heresies, which divided communities and pitted believers against one another.

Detail: *"That servant who knew his master's will but ...."* Throughout the Roman Empire, the *Roman Ordo* was the list of crimes and punishments that were to be applied. A judge decided guilt or innocence, but the punishment was proscribed by law and stated in the *Ordo*. Punishment fit the deed. In Judaism, punishment for offenses against Mosaic Law was to be based on the deed and the extent of injury to others [cf. Number 5:5-8]. This was known as the "eye for an eye" rule. In the Jewish view, a wrongful deed "broke faith with God;" the offender's knowledge or intent had no bearing on it. In this portion of the parable, Jesus said quite the opposite. Punishment was to be conditioned by the offender's knowledge and intent. This would have been shocking to first century listeners, most especially Jews.

Notice that this portion of the parable is not in Matthew's version. This is an example of the principle addressed in section 1.3.1. In Middle Eastern storytelling, details are omitted that are not related to, or may distract from, the intended message. Matthew has Jesus sharing this parable as part of the Olivet Discourse during Passion Week. A lesson on punishments for abusing slaves would have distracted from the subject of the end times, so Matthew left it out.

So, indirectly Jesus was telling His Apostles that, unlike in the previous parable, He would also be going away from them for an indeterminate time. He would be placing them in charge. They as faithful ones were to go on with life in His absence, in the same orderly and mutually supportive way as they would if He were physically present with them. He will return "*on an unexpected day and at an unknown hour*" and those who have been unfaithful will be punished. And, that punishment will be conditioned by the offender's knowledge and intent. Clearly this is a different departure and return than He spoke of in the first parable. This is the second indication we have in the Gospels that there will be a Second Coming of Jesus. It's easy to see why Matthew set his recounting of the parable as part of the Olivet Discourse.

Let's pause a few minutes and reflect on what seems to be happening here. We just heard two very profound parables, set in two fairly simple sounding stories, which seem at first to have "appeared out of the blue." Yet, that's not very likely. Looking back on the event on Mount Tabor, a few months earlier, in his account of the Transfiguration, Luke wrote that Moses and Elijah were conversing with Jesus "*and spoke of his exodus that he was going to accomplish in Jerusalem*" [Lk 9:31].

This "exodus" was a clear reference to Jesus' journey, under the watchful eye of the Father, through His passion, death, resurrection, and ascension that would be taking place in Jerusalem, the city of His destiny [cf. Lk 9:51]. Recall that the Transfiguration culminated their long trip through the backcountry of Lebanon and the Decapolis. So, this appears to have been a time for Jesus to build solidarity with His followers and with one another.

We can't literally know the mind of Jesus, but we can pay close attention to what we see and hear with eyes and ears of faith. And, we have the benefit of knowing the outcome as well as having more than 2000 years of the Church's prayerful discernment of Christ's message to humanity. It would certainly seem that, upon coming down from Mount Tabor, Jesus knew the depth of what lay ahead for Him, and what He must expect of His followers, both then and in the years to come.

Jesus and His followers had been on the road in Perea for at least a week, perhaps more. They have been talking with Him and among themselves, as they went. The evangelists have given us no direct insight into what they had been discussing, but it's quite likely that these parables did not "appear out of the blue;" but rather they concluded a discussion that may have been going on for days. While coming upon the "castle of the servant" near Rabbah might have influenced, in some way, the storyline of the parables, their message vastly transcends that setting alone.

What appears to be happening is that we are witnessing Jesus using this journey through Perea as a time for Him to draw His Apostles more deeply into what was expected of Him, and of them, in the weeks and years ahead - as well as what would be expected of the many followers of Jesus yet to come. This was something the Apostles would have had no way of foreseeing at this point.

There was no need for them to stock up on water at Rabbah; there would be plenty of cold clear water in the Jabbok. Unlike a wadi, the Jabbok River was, and still is, perennial (flows year around). It's a very low flow during the dry season and a much heavier flow during the rainy season. The region was well into the rainy season when Jesus and His followers left the headwaters at Rabbah and headed north along the narrow valley that had been cut by the river over millions of years.

There would have been a sweet fragrance in the air from the wildflowers, particularly tulips and cistus, which would have covered many hillsides along the course of the river. Resin from the cistus plant was used to make the ancient medicinal ointment known as "balm of Gilead." [74]

Figure 23: The upper Jabbok River Valley

As they traveled, they were again walking the pages of their history. They were following the same path that Absalom took in fleeing the army of his father, David, after Absalom had led an unsuccessful revolt against David. There certainly was no soft spot in the hearts of Jews for Absalom, but there was for his father, David, and the heart-wrenching tale of David's lamenting the death of his wayward son. [2 Sam 19:1-9].

Along the Jabbok River they would have found small farms and orchards where they could obtain food. Occasionally they would have passed a farmer heading to the trade route in Rabbah with his mule carrying dried fig cakes from their winter fig harvest. Dried fig cakes, called *debelah*, were a delicacy in the ancient world [1 Sam 30:12]. In December-January, the *paggim*, or "green figs" would be picked, dried in the sun, pressure cooked and formed into small round cakes. These were strung like beads in foot-long strings and packed in boxes for export.

Talking along the way, they likely contemplated just what Jesus was telling them in those last two parables. And, did Jesus actually answer Peter's question? After a full two-day walk, they would have arrived at the point where the valley widened as the Chysorrhoas River flowed into the Jabbok from the north.

The Chysorrhoas ("golden flowing") River valley had wheat crops, orchards of figs, plums, and olives and small forests of pine and oak trees. It was in the thick branches of one of those large oaks that Absalom's hair got caught. He was left hanging in midair, while the mule he was riding kept on going. There, he was killed by his pursuers from David's army in the year 979 BC [2 Sam 18:9].

Just north of the junction of the Chysorrhoas and Jabbok, was the city of Gerasa (known today as Jerash). The earliest settlement at Gerasa (Greek for "gift of god") dates from about 6000 BC. The city was largely insignificant in the period of the Assyrians and Babylonians, but it was greatly expanded by the Greeks after the death of Alexander the Great, and further expanded under the Romans. By Jesus' time, the city enjoyed great wealth and importance largely due to the area's fertile lands and year-round fresh water supply. The city had some of the finest Greco-Roman architecture in the world. The Chysorrhoas River flowed right through the center of the city with a grand colonnaded street, known as the *Cardo* along both sides of the river. The city was largely destroyed in a massive earthquake in 749 AD. It lay in ruins until the mid-1500s when it began to be repopulated.

In Gerasa, Jesus was told by someone in a crowd about the death of Galileans at the hands of Pontius Pilate [Lk 13:1]. Apparently, Pilate had reason to suspect some Galilean pilgrims worshiping at the Temple of stirring up unrest among the people. While those Jews were offering up their religious sacrifices, Pilate's men struck them down in the very act of worship. The blood of the slain pilgrims thus was mixed in with the blood of their animal sacrifices.

No historical record of this event has been found, but judging from the description it probably occurred during the Day of Atonement services in late September of the previous year, 32 AD. The Day of Atonement just precedes the Feast of Tabernacles. Recall from section 9.1 that Jesus and His disciples were in Jerusalem for the Feast of Tabernacles that year. Jesus, and just about every Jew in the region, would have known of this outrageous crime. So, this calling out by someone in the crowd was an honor challenge to Jesus along the lines of "Explain why God would allow this?"

Jesus pushed back with a question, *"Do you think that because these Galileans suffered in this way they were greater sinners than all other Galileans? By no means! But I tell you, if you do not repent, you will all perish as they did!"* [Lk 13:2-3]. These were people who believed that every calamity a person experienced was a punishment for his sins. Jesus then followed with the Parable of the Barren Fig Tree.

10.9 The Parable of the Barren Fig Tree [Luke 13:6-9]

And he told them this parable:
"There once was a person who had a fig tree planted in his orchard, and when he came in search of fruit on it but found none, he said to the gardener,

'For three years now, I have come in search of fruit on this fig tree but have found none. So, cut it down. Why should it exhaust the soil?'

He said to him in reply,
'Sir, leave it for this year also, and I shall cultivate the ground around it and fertilize it; it may bear fruit in the future. If not, you can cut it down.'

The parable was offered in response to an honor challenge, so we expect that there's something that calls upon the challenger, and those around him, to think deeply about, thus rendering the challenger silent.

There's a particular reason why Jesus chose the tending of a fig tree for the parable's storyline. So, before we delve into what that message might be, we need to know a little more about the importance of fig trees in their culture.

10.10 The Cultural Position of Fig Trees

In ancient Israel, the fig tree was the most valued tree in the land; it was the symbol of Israel's privilege before God. It was planted in the most favorable locations and received many opportunities to "bear fruit." When things were well in Israel and the people were prosperous, the Bible says, *"every man sits under his own fig tree"* [1 Kgs 4:25]. But, the prophets on the other hand, when predicting judgment on Israel, spoke of the fig trees being destroyed [cf. Jer 5:17].

Normally growing to nearly 20 feet in height and with large leaves, the fig tree provides very pleasant shade. The leaves are as large as a human hand and are hairy on the back side. Minute wasps pollinate these trees, and the fig buds are produced before the leaves emerge. Naturally, therefore, one should expect fruit on a tree in full leaf. This accounts for why Jesus later cursed a fig-tree that had on it nothing but leaves [cf. Mt. 21:18-20].

The flower of the fig tree is never seen, as its many tiny flowers are housed within the fruit bud. It takes three years from its planting for a fig tree to produce fruit. Three crops were produced each year. The first crop, *bikkurah*, ripened in June and was eaten fresh, while the summer crop, *te'enim*, produced the largest harvest in August-September. The winter crop, *paggim*, harvested in December-January was usually dried for export. Also, because the fig tree is the last tree to produce leaves and it does so right before summer, Jesus later used it as an example of nature's way of providing signs of life at work [Mt 24:32; Mk 13:28].

10.11 The Spiritual Lesson in the Parable

Detail: *"a person had a fig tree planted in his orchard."* Notice that it's not a fig tree orchard, but a fig tree that's planted in his orchard. So, this is a highly favored tree consistent with the cultural position of fig trees.

Detail: *"For three years now I have come in search of fruit but have found none."* Since it takes three years from its planting for a fig tree to produce fruit, this tree is six years old. Because God created all things in six days, the number six symbolized fullness of preparation. Everything was ready, and the man waited long enough, but there was no fruit.

Detail: *"cut it down. Why should it exhaust the soil?"* To "exhaust the soil" was to render the soil unfit for other plants because some essential nutrient has been used up. This favored tree had not only produced nothing but was a detriment to the growth of other plants.

Detail: *"the gardener said to him in reply"*. The gardener steps forward to intervene on the tree's behalf.

Detail: *"Sir, leave it for this year also, and I shall cultivate the ground around it and fertilize it." Let me give it even more care than the favored treatment it has already received."* - a most unusual offer. Recall from agricultural practices of those times they did not fertilize, they did not cultivate, they just planted and then let nature take care of itself.

Detail: *"it may bear fruit in the future. If not, you can cut it down."* If the tree does not respond to the gardener's help, then it is ended.

This parable was in response to an honor challenge. We should not expect it to answer the question asked; but rather to pose a concept or idea that required considerable thought. Since the dialog that precedes the parable is about repentance, we might conclude that the parable is about repentance. That conclusion may not be right.

In this parable, we are hearing from Jesus, Himself, the first insights into the Christian understanding of grace. No initiative was required on the part of the tree; it's the intervenor who was going to assist the tree in bearing fruit. The intervener would provide special help, the tree needed only to respond, for its own survival. This special help, from an intervener who comes to our aid and whose aid we must respond to for our own survival, we know today as "grace."

The Gospels don't indicate, at any point, that Jesus used the word, grace. And, Luke is the only evangelist, in both his Gospel and Acts of the Apostles, to use the word grace (actually the Greek word, *charis*). An example is in the angel's words to Mary: "Hail, full of grace, the Lord is with you." Luke's use of *charis* is more accurately translated, favored, rather that grace, as we understand grace today. And, the more recent *New American Bible* translation of the angel's words: are "*"Hail, favored one, the Lord is with you"* [Lk 1:28].

Jesus' listeners that day were mostly, if not all, Jews. Jews called themselves: *am ha'sefer* ("people of the book"). And the "fertilizer" or nourishment that God provided for them was their Scripture. Every time they prayed, they read Scripture; they didn't recite rehearsed prayers. For a Jew, reading Scripture was the cultivation that he/she gets from God that they might bear fruit. The Jewish concept of grace was what they received because they were good and kept God's commandments. One earned grace by performing *mitsvot* (those acts required by Mosaic Law). Jesus was bringing together, for the first time, two seemingly unrelated ideas to Jews, divine help and grace – certainly something for His listeners to ponder deeply. It would be many centuries after Jesus that Christians would articulate an understanding of grace as divine help.

10.12 Grace and How It Works in Our Lives

The *Catechism of the Catholic Church* teaches that God's grace may be broadly divided into Habitual, or "sanctifying" grace, which brings about or sustains holiness in us; and Actual, or "actualizing" grace, which aids us in particular actions in our life [cf. *Catechism of the Catholic Church* #1996-2005].

Prior to the Reformation, "grace" was understood only in very general terms. Owing to the teachings of St Paul, grace was understood to be a gift of God that was essential to our living a Christian life, that is, essential to our bearing fruit as Jesus called us to do. But, it wasn't until the late 1600s that a definitive picture evolved of how grace works in us for that purpose and the distinction between grace that "actualizes" and grace that "sanctifies."

A remarkable advance in our understanding of grace came from a most unlikely circumstance. In February 1431, Joan of Arc was on trial in Rouen, France. The Inquisitor, or Prosecutor, Jean Beaupere, was convinced that Joan was being led and supported by local sympathizers. So, he tried to force Joan to identify them.

But, she kept insisting that it was the grace of God that led her. In his effort to "break her," he had an amazing insight into the workings of grace that pre-dated the great theological debates of the Reformation by more than 200 years.

Throughout most of the Old Testament, "grace" was seen as God's favor earned through proper living. But St. Paul came to see that "grace" is not something we earn or gain as a reward for doing good. Rather, "grace is the means by which God empowers us to share in His work in the world" [cf. *Catechism of the Catholic Church* #1997]. St. Paul wrote extensively on "sin" being the misuse or rejection of God's grace. However, he wrote relatively little defining grace itself. So, this led to a long period in the Church when the theology focused more on the destructive nature of sin than on the empowering nature of grace. Beaupere, however, saw grace as being almost a 'force' from God which acted on a person, countering the forces of desires and ambitions that arise from within one's Self and the pressures and expectations that arise from one's Environment. This is illustrated in the diagram below.

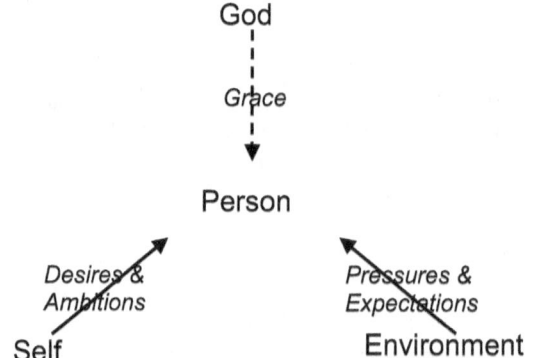

In his early investigations and prison interviews with Joan of Arc, it was clear to him that she was not being driven by desire or ambitions. She insisted that it was God's grace that was propelling her forward. He, however, was convinced that she was being driven by secret supporters in the English-held territory. These he wanted identified by putting her on trial in Rouen. But, Joan consistently talked about it being God's grace that gave her the inspiration and insights that were regularly leading her to defeat the English in battle. In his prosecution of Joan, Beaupere couldn't appear to be "attacking" an agent of God; so, he staged the trial before the local bishop, Pierre Cauchon. In the end, Beaupere never 'broke her story' and he settled for having her condemned as a witch and she was burned at the stake on May 30, 1431. Tragic!

Yet, we are able to learn a great deal from this tragic episode in history. The simple diagram depicting Beaupere's view of grace helps us visualize how grace fits in the struggle that goes on within us involving God, our Environment and our Selves. But, we should quickly notice a serious flaw in Beaupere's view. In Beaupere's view, the Person was just a passive object being acted on by three opposing forces. Free will was absent from Beaupere's theory.

In 1635, about 200 years after Joan's trial, a Belgian bishop by the name of Cornelius Jansen questioned, "How can an all-persuasive force like grace, which can impose such potent influences on the human person and elicit from them such good works, co-exist with free will?" He concluded that free will was much less important than had been previously taught. Out of this grew the heresy that would be known as Jansenism, which claimed that our free will was really quite minimal.

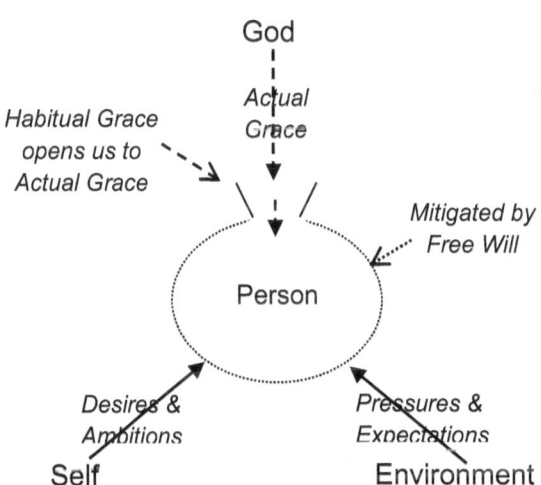

Out of the Church's struggles against Jansenism, the understanding was reinforced that grace is not an all-pervasive "force" but an ever-present gift. It is freely offered by God and it must be freely accepted by a person in order for it to have any effect on that person. This was explained more fully through the concepts of Actual Grace and Habitual Grace.

When we accept Habitual, or "sanctifying" grace, it brings about or sustains holiness in us, opening us to Actual grace, which calls and empowers us to act in accordance with the will of God.
"Actual" grace gets its name, from the Latin ad *actum*, meaning "to action."

Given this essential refinement, it's remarkable how close Beaupere came to the ultimate understanding of grace, without any theological training at all.

Just as a father prompts and empowers his children, God prompts and empowers us via Actualizing grace. Actualizing grace covers the whole range of human needs and endeavors. So, discernment is essential to our taking the right actions in response to God's prompting.

Discernment is the interior search for answers in our relationship with God; not only to the broader question of one's vocation in life, but also to the ever-present more specific question of "what's God calling me to do in response to this prompting I'm feeling?" It's that same Inquisitor's Question that was asked of Joan of Arc: "How do you know that God is prompting you to do something?" It is that 'stirring within' that signals His call. God rarely speaks overtly; no voice from a cloud, no burning bush, no Special Delivery letter. It's via 'stirrings within' that Actualizing grace most often manifests itself.

Basically, the lesson taught by St. Paul was that discernment involves making right judgments about our impulses – what is emanating from God, what is emanating from ourselves, or what is emanating from those around us. Picture again Beaupere's Insight, but with that essential ingredient: free will.

Habitual, or Sanctifying grace is needed for us to make right judgments; for the task cannot be accomplished entirely on our own. In addition to our trying to interpret 'stirrings within,' it's further complicated by the fact that not all our ambitions are wrong, and not all expectations of us by others are wrong.

With this deeper understanding of grace, gained over many centuries, we are much better able today to understand the message in Jesus' Parable of the Barron Fig Tree. Jesus had intervened for us, and provided divine help, just as the gardener in the parable intervened for and helped the favored fig tree that was not bearing fruit. That divine help we call grace. And, we must be open to, accept and act on that grace if we are to "survive" this life and enter eternal life with God.

We can only imagine what Jesus' first listeners might have thought. Many of them may have just dismissed the parable with "I didn't get it" and moved on with their lives. But, there must have been some who passed this parable on for years for it to later reach Luke; who himself was likely discerning "what is the divine help Jesus spoke of and how does it work in our lives?"

Sometime later, near Gerasa, Jesus shared the Parable of the Mustard Seed. This parable is recounted in all three Synoptic Gospels, but neither Matthew, nor Mark nor Luke gave any clear indication of who Jesus was speaking to - a crowd or to His disciples privately. He shared His first parable about the Kingdom of God with a crowd in Tiberias. The second, He shared with a crowd in Magdala. But since then, Jesus shared three more such parables, but only with His disciples in private. Jesus may have concluded that such parables were lost on crowds. So, this parable, also about the Kingdom of God, as well as the one after it, were most likely shared with His disciples in private.

10.13 The Parable of the Mustard Seed

10.13.1 The Version in Matthew's Gospel [Matthew 13:31-32]

Jesus proposed another parable to them.
> "The kingdom of heaven is like a mustard seed
> that a person took and sowed in a field.
> It is the smallest of all the seeds, yet when full-grown it is the largest of plants. It becomes a large bush, and the 'birds of the sky come and dwell in its branches.'"

10.13.2 The Version in Mark's Gospel [Mark 4:30-32]

Jesus said,
> "To what shall we compare the kingdom of God,
> or what parable can we use for it? It is like a mustard seed that, when it is sown in the ground, is the smallest of all the seeds on the earth.
> But once it is sown, it springs up and becomes the largest of plants and puts forth large branches, so that the birds of the sky can dwell in its shade."

10.13.3 The Version in Luke's Gospel [Luke 13:18-19]

Then Jesus said,
> "What is the kingdom of God like? To what can I compare it? It is like a mustard seed that a person took and planted in the garden.
> When it was fully grown, it became a large bush and 'the birds of the sky dwelt in its branches.'"

10.14 The Spiritual Lesson in the Parable

Detail: *"The kingdom of heaven is like a mustard seed that a person took and sowed in a field."* In Mark, it was sown *in the ground*; in Luke it was sown *in a garden*. In ancient Israel, mustard (*"chardal"*) grew so abundantly in the wild that it was not normal to deliberately plant it, whether in a field, in a garden or just in the ground. So, the Kingdom of God (Kingdom of Heaven) results from someone doing something quite unexpected.

In ancient times, chardal was a medicinal substance, not a spice – when ground into a paste and wrapped in a cloth it was applied to areas of the body hurting from an injury or arthritis. [75]

Detail: *It is the smallest of all the seeds, yet when full-grown it is the largest of plants."* The mustard seed was small but not the smallest; and it produced a very large bush, but not the largest. We are hearing emphasis through exaggeration: from very humble beginning something spectacular resulted in the Kingdom of Heaven.

Detail: *"and the 'birds of the sky come and dwell in its branches."* The oil from the leaves of the mustard bush is so chemically active that birds do not nest in it. So, unexpected behavior will be observed in the Kingdom of Heaven.

To bring about the Kingdom of Heaven, God did something most unexpected, He came into the world as man. From humble beginnings (an infant born in a stable in an insignificant place in the world) it will result in something spectacular (people living out the will of God in great numbers). And in the Kingdom, there will be unexpected behavior (all will be welcomed at the table).

Notice how far from the original Jewish Messianic expectation of the Kingdom of God, Jesus' description has come. And also notice that the pattern we observed in Jesus' parables about the Kingdom of God is evident in this one as well. It begins with a humble "in-breaking" into the world, not a cataclysmic event. There is a profound "reversal" in the lives of many as the Kingdom becomes a reality throughout the earth. And, it requires an "action:" people valuing relationships differently.

Jesus then continued by sharing the Parable of the Yeast. This parable is recounted in the Gospels of Matthew and Luke.

10.15 The Parable of the Yeast

10.15.1 The Version in Matthew's Gospel [Matthew 13:33]

He spoke to them another parable.
> "The kingdom of heaven is like yeast that a woman took
> and mixed with three measures of wheat flour
> until the whole batch was leavened."

10.15.2 The Version in Luke's Gospel [Luke 13:20-21]

Again, Jesus said,
> "To what shall I compare the kingdom of God?
> It is like yeast that a woman took
> and mixed in with three measures of wheat flour
> until the whole batch of dough was leavened."

10.16 The Spiritual Lesson in the Parable

Detail: *yeast*. Actually, the Greek word, *zume*, which is translated here as "yeast," is better translated as, "leaven." Yeast did not exist as a substance in the ancient world.

Leaven was a small portion of dough from the previous round of bread-making which was mixed with a small amount of freshly pressed grape juice and set aside for several days. The dough would gather microbes from the air which would feed on the sugar provided by the fruit juice to multiply many times over in the dough wad. This dough wad, or leaven, then served as the starter for the next round of dough preparation.

Ancient peoples had no idea of the microbiology at work in the dough wad, only that this process of making leaven (Hebrew: *se'or*), originally learned from the Egyptians, was necessary for yielding bread that would rise during baking. It was not until the late 1860's that the active element in leaven was found to be a living organism which could be isolated and cultured to produce what is known today as baker's yeast.

The symbolism of the leaven in this parable is that the Kingdom of Heaven (the reign of God in the hearts of man on earth) did not arise out of nothing. It required the essential "starter" provided by the Jewish people from whom the world received the Messiah.

Detail: *"three measures of wheat"* An *ephah* would yield, when properly leavened, about 150 loaves of leavened bread, enough for a sizable fellowship meal. Jews would have immediately recognized an *ephah* as the amount used by Sarah to bake bread when she and Abram were visited by the three angels [cf. Gen 18:6]. Cultural hospitality required that Abraham and Sarah could not have a dinner for just three guests alone; they were expected to invite their whole extended family.

So, in the Kingdom of God, "bread" is prepared, leavened by the faithful people of old, that feeds the whole family of God in the world. Jesus' disciples have heard, yet again, that the Kingdom of God welcomes everyone and will feed them all. Of course, on this day in late February, 32 AD, outside of Gerasa, they had no concept of the Eucharist, but that will come all too soon for them.

This is a profound parable, something Jesus' first listeners might have pondered for years. For the Jews who were listening, Jesus offered a great re-orienting of their thinking. For us Christians today, He gave us a great reminder of the debt we owe to the Jewish people. They are truly the leaven on which the beginnings of the Kingdom of God relied. For, they kept the faith in the one true God, for generations after generations, under almost impossible conditions. And, from them the world received the Messiah and Savior.

As St. Paul put it, some 25 years after Jesus' resurrection, in speaking to the Romans about the Jewish people:
> *"theirs is the adoption, the glory, the covenants, the giving of the law, the worship, and the promises; theirs the patriarchs, and from them, according to the flesh, is the Messiah"* [Rom 9:4-5].

Later, while still in Gerasa, Jesus was invited on the Sabbath to dine at the home of a Pharisee. There, he shared the Parable of the Invitations.

10.17 The Parable of the Invitations [Luke 14:7-14]

Jesus told a parable to those who had been invited,
noticing how they were choosing the places of honor at the table.

> "When you are invited by someone to a wedding banquet,
> do not recline at table in the place of honor.
> A more distinguished guest than you may have been invited
> by him, and the host who invited both of you may approach
> you and say,
> 'Give your place to this man,'
> and then you would proceed with embarrassment to take the
> lowest place.
>
> Rather, when you are invited,

> go and take the lowest place so that when the host comes to you he may say,
> 'My friend, move up to a higher position.'
> Then you will enjoy the esteem of your companions at the table.
>
> For everyone who exalts himself will be humbled, but the one who humbles himself will be exalted."

Then he said to the host who invited him,
> "When you hold a lunch or a dinner, do not invite your friends or your brothers or your relatives or your wealthy neighbors, in case they may invite you back and you have repayment.
>
> Rather, when you hold a banquet, invite the poor, the crippled, the lame, the blind; blessed indeed will you be because of their inability to repay you.
> For you will be repaid at the resurrection of the righteous."

10.18 The Spiritual Lesson in the Parable

<u>Detail:</u> (setting) dining at the home of a Pharisee on the Sabbath. On the Sabbath, no one could work, so all the food had to be prepared the day before and kept hot. Then, everything had to be served just before the second star was seen in the sky, which commenced the Sabbath. Consequently, putting on a dinner on a Sabbath was quite a feat and it put servants to a great effort. So, this Pharisee was deliberately showing off.

Also, Jesus observed the guests jockeying for positions of honor. As we've seen before, such dinners were held in the courtyard at the host's house. The guests would recline in a large U-shaped arrangement with the fireplace in the center. The host sat at the head of the U-shape, the most honored position was to his right and the second most honored position at his left. The third, fourth, fifth, etc. positions ran to the host's right all the way to the end of the U-shape. The sequence then continued up the other end of the U-shape such that the "lowest" position was to the left of the second highest position (two positions to the host's left). So, to be asked to relocate from a higher position to one of the lowest positions would involve moving many people at the "table," a huge annoyance and embarrassment.

Detail: "*When you are invited to a wedding banquet.*" Notice it's a wedding banquet, not a fellowship dinner. Therefore, each guest is escorted to his/her place at the "table" by the groom.

Detail: "*do not recline at table in the place of honor. ... you might have to proceed with embarrassment to take the lowest place.*" To select your place at the "table" or change your place once the groom has positioned you was more than poor etiquette it was an outrageous affront to the host, an undermining of the very purpose of a wedding banquet: unity between the families of the bride and groom.

Detail: "*Rather ... go and take the lowest place so that when the host comes to you he may say, 'My friend, move up to a higher position.'*" Why? Because, "*everyone who exalts himself will be humbled, but the one who humbles himself will be exalted.*" Jesus will use this same message in the later Parable of the Pharisee and the Tax Collector [Lk 18:14]; as well as when He cautions His disciples not to follow the example of the Pharisees [Mt 23:12].

This part of the parable, using emphasis through exaggeration of poor table etiquette; cautions those who were willing to listen against an exaggerated sense of self-importance. Spiritual riches only come to those who admit their spiritual poverty. There's a second part to the parable, which Jesus addressed to the host.

Detail: "*When you hold a lunch or a dinner, do not invite (those who can reciprocate).*" By Jesus' time, the long-held practices of Middle Eastern hospitality had undergone a serious twist. For the elite of ancient Israel, hospitality had morphed into: "I'll do that for you if you will do this for me." There was a Latin saying among Romans, *do ut des* ("I give so that you will give back"). The saying began as a Roman prayer as they made offerings to their gods. But, the mentality embodied in that prayer was not limited to the Romans; it had spread throughout the whole Mediterranean area. That's common of traditions that start out as very good and wholesome practices but, over generations, they morph into something quite different.

<u>Detail</u>: *"Rather ... invite (those who cannot reciprocate)."* Why? Because *"you will be repaid at the resurrection of the righteous."*

This part of the parable cautions the host, and those who were willing to listen, against false graciousness. God gave the ultimate because He *"so loved the world"* [Jn 3:15a]. By the first century, the Jewish view was that "the resurrection" would involve a restoration of the nation of Israel, not each individual person. However, there would be some who would benefit from the fact that the resurrection took place. There was not common agreement on how they would benefit. Would they actually come back to life? Or, was some other benefit in store for them?

The first group who would benefit was the *Sheluchim*, those who not only spoke on God's behalf but also acted on His behalf (Moses, Elijah, etc.). The second group would be the *tsedeq* ("righteous"), those who held justice and charity in right balance. So, the ultimate reward for a Jew was to be part of the "righteous" at the resurrection. The message of the second part of the parable was that one must be genuinely gracious in order to hold justice and charity in right balance and thereby receive the ultimate reward, in their level of understanding. They had no concept, yet, of eternal life.

A typical first century courtyard could accommodate approximately two dozen guests reclined at "table." Considering the host was trying to impress his extended family and neighbors, it's unlikely that any of the Apostles were invited guests. They would have stood around the periphery of the courtyard as "spectators' along with the other locals who were not invited guests.

On first hearing, this sounds like a two-part parable, instructions on table etiquette followed by instructions on hospitality. And, that may have been how most of Jesus' listeners that evening took it. But, the Apostles were accustomed at this point to the subtleties Jesus packed His parables with. The message may have been directed more to them than those absorbed in their own way of life. We, having the benefit of knowing the outcome, see a connection to the Eucharistic banquet. God hosts a Eucharistic banquet every day; and, all are invited. All His guests are indeed the poor, the infirmed, and the needy – perhaps not physically but certainly spiritually. And, we have no way of reciprocating. God does the very things Jesus asks us to do.

We don't know how long Jesus and His disciples stayed in or near Gerasa, but at some point, they went back south along the Chysorrhoas River to where it joins the Jabbok. They then headed west toward the Jordan River. And, they were again walking the pages of their history.

Around the year 1775 BC, growing tensions between Jacob's household and that of his uncle, Laban, prompted Jacob to pack up his entire household, all his herds and abruptly leave Padan-aram, headed into the '*hill country of Gilead* (Perea) [Gen 31:21]. Eventually, they made their way down the Chysorrhoas River to where it joins the Jabbok River. They then headed west along the north bank of the Jabbok toward the Jordan River. Jesus and His disciples were walking that same path. To ancient Israelites, their past was their present. In their minds' eye, it was "only yesterday" that Jacob passed by here. Great challenges lay ahead for Jacob on that route, and great challenges lay ahead for Jesus, as well.

The Jabbok River valley widens to the west and Jesus and His disciples would have encountered many more farms and orchards. Also, since it was likely mid-March, they would have also encountered pilgrims heading to Jerusalem for Passover. As Luke put it, "*Great crowds were traveling with Jesus*" [Lk 14:25a]. The owners of farms and orchards west of the junction of the Chysorrhoas and the Jabbok would have been accustomed to having pilgrims passing through, year after year. So, they were quite adept at providing food, and where possible, lodging for them; especially for families traveling with small children.

The crowds around Jesus and His disciples would likely have slowed their progress to the extent that it would have taken about four full days walking for them to reach the site of Mahanaim. Mahanaim is where a host of angels came to comfort Jacob on his journey, and Jacob said of the place, "*This is God's campsite*" [Gen 32:2]. It was from here that Jacob sent messengers ahead of him to request peace from his brother Esau, who still lived at their father's house near Hebron. While Jacob awaited a response, he became concerned that Esau might still be seeking revenge against him, so he divided his household up into two camps in the hope that one camp might survive an attack by Esau. The name, Mahanaim means "two camps." After a while, Jacob and his household moved on further west to a place named Penuel.

Following the Exodus, around 1220 BC, Mahanaim was settled by the tribe of Manasseh and it was renamed Jabesh-Giliead. Over time, it grew to be a prominent city in the area. And, it was the men of this town who, in 1004 BC, recovered the body of King Saul from the walls of Beisan and burned his body so his bones could be quickly buried beneath a tree in Jabesh-Giliead [1 Sam 31:13]. King David later exhumed Saul and reburied him at Zelah, north of Jerusalem [2 Sam 21:14]. By Jesus' time, military conflicts, earthquakes and river erosion had taken their toll on the city. Other than a few farms and orchards nearby, there was little left at Mahanaim but ruins. Today, there is so little remaining that some question the precise location of Mahanaim. Most accept that it was 9 miles east of where the Jabbok enters the Jordan River valley. [76]

At some point along the way, Jesus shared with the crowd accompanying Him the Parable of the Costs of Discipleship.

10.19 The Parable of the Costs of Discipleship [Luke 14:25-33]

Great crowds were traveling with Jesus, and he turned and addressed them,
> "If any one comes to me without hating his father and mother, wife and children, brothers and sisters, and even his own life, he cannot be my disciple.
>
> Whoever does not carry his own cross and come after me cannot be my disciple.
>
> Which of you wishing to construct a tower does not first sit down and calculate the cost to see if there is enough for its completion?
> Otherwise, after laying the foundation and finding himself

unable to finish the work the onlookers should laugh at him and say, 'This one began to build but did not have the resources to finish.'

Or what king marching into battle would not first sit down and decide whether with ten thousand troops he can successfully oppose another king advancing upon him with twenty thousand troops? But if not, while he is still far away, he will send a delegation to ask for peace terms.

In the same way, every one of you who does not renounce all his possessions cannot be my disciple."

10.20 The Spiritual Lesson in the Parable

Detail: "*If any one comes to me without hating his (extended family) and even his own life, he cannot be my disciple.*" To Middle Easterners, pietas required of them a profound responsibility for the guidance and care of each member of their extended family, even before themselves.

Detail: "*Whoever does not carry his own cross and come after me cannot be my disciple.*" Crucifixion was the most horrible, painful, torturous, and humiliating form of execution possible. It was reserved for those regarded as a threat to Roman power and was intended to be so humiliating that it was regarded as the most effective deterrent to others who threatened Roman power. Only those for whom a grand public spectacle was planned were required to "carry their cross." The typical Roman cross weighed about 300 lbs., so those condemned could only carry the cross beam or literally drag their cross to their execution.

With this in mind, the crowd must have been stunned into silence. They certainly hated the Romans, but they didn't see themselves as a threat to Roman power. So, why would they have their own cross to carry? And, why come after him? They didn't get it.

Detail: "*wishing to construct a tower ... unable to finish the work the onlookers should laugh at him.*" One constructed a tower for the protection of a vineyard, orchard or community. It served as the lookout point for potential intruders, animal or man, as well as early warning of a fire. To not complete the tower would be far more than an embarrassment, it would have been catastrophic. So, we are hearing an exaggeration.

Detail: *"what king marching into battle ... with ten thousand troops ... opposing another with twenty thousand troops,"* a two-to-one disadvantage. Considering the location where they were standing, this was an understatement. Esau had approached Jacob with 400 armed men; Jacob had none at all [Gen 33:1].

Detail: *"every one of you who does not renounce all his possessions cannot be my disciple."* To renounce one's possessions was to abandon one's inheritance. This left one totally vulnerable in the world – a really extreme position for someone in the ancient world to deliberately put themselves in.

Every master teacher in antiquity had disciples, i.e., "intentional learners." Typically, these disciples sought to learn the ways and wisdom of their master. Not much more was asked of them. But, on this day, Jesus said that to be His disciple, one must: *hate his (extended family) and even his own life; carry his own cross and come after him;* and *renounce all his possessions.*

And, in the middle of this, Jesus used a typical "Hebraism" whereby the comparison of two things is expressed by the exaggeration of the first (the greater) and the understatement of the second (the lesser). Accurately assessing what one is getting into is made the greater while preparing oneself for opposition is made the lesser. [77]

The crowd was likely mystified, "what is he talking about?" But, as the Apostles stood there, near the ruins of Mahanaim, memories might have returned of that day in late October of the previous year when they were resting near the ruins of Gibeah and Jesus had said to them that in Jerusalem He would be *mocked and flogged and crucified.* At the time, *"they failed to comprehend what he said"* [Lk 18:34]. Here they were again crossing the tragic path of their King Saul. Again, they were standing in the ruins of what was once a proud city of their past. And, again Jesus was speaking of His crucifixion.

Did His message finally break through to them? "What lies ahead will challenge you far beyond your limits. Unless you commit yourself to Me above all else, you will turn away." Jesus' eyes had not lost their caring look, but His face seemed to have a determination they hadn't seen before. And, more and more, His words cut to the quick.

While continuing west toward the Jordan River, at some point Jesus' disciples approached Him and asked, "Who is the greatest in the kingdom of heaven?" Jesus replied with the Parable about Being Like a Child.

10.21 The Parable about Being Like a Child

This parable is recounted in both Matthew's Gospel and Mark's Gospel; however, Mark used a little different wording and a considerably different setting. So, we should expect that the message Mark sought to convey, using the parable, was quite different than Matthew's.

10.21.1 The Version in Matthew's Gospel [Matthew 18:1-5]

At that time the disciples approached Jesus and said,
"Who is the greatest in the kingdom of heaven?"
He called a child over, placed it in their midst, and said,
> "Amen, I say to you, unless you turn and become like children,
> you will not enter the kingdom of heaven.
> Whoever humbles himself like this child is the greatest in the kingdom of heaven.
> And whoever receives one child such as this in my name receives me."

10.21.2 The Version in Mark's Gospel [Mark 9:33-37]

They came to Capernaum and, once inside the house, he began to ask them, "What were you arguing about on the way?" But they remained silent. They had been discussing among themselves on the way who was the greatest.

Then he sat down, called the Twelve, and said to them,

"If anyone wishes to be first, he shall be the last of all and the servant of all."

Taking a child, he placed it in their midst,
and putting his arms around it he said to them,
"Whoever receives one child such as this in my name, receives me; and whoever receives me, receives not me but the One who sent me."

10.22 The Spiritual Lesson in the Parable

Detail: (Matthew's setting) *The disciples asked: "Who is the greatest in the kingdom of heaven?"* On the basis of the Gospel accounts, this was the eighth time Jesus spoke to His disciples about the Kingdom of Heaven, but it was the first time they brought up the subject. So far, they've heard how different the Kingdom is from their long-held expectations. So, they looked to what they thought would surely be in agreement. Upon the commencement of the Kingdom the first to rise was to be the *Sheluchim,* the holy ones. And, the greatest of the holy ones was Moses, *"there was no other prophet who arose in Israel like Moses, whom the Lord knew face to face"* [Deu 34:10]. *"Moses was able to converse with God whenever he so wished"* [Num 9:8]. Certainly, Moses must be the *greatest in the kingdom of heaven.* Or, so they would have thought.

(Mark's setting) *"Jesus asked them, 'What were you arguing about on the way?' ... They had been discussing among themselves who was the greatest."* Mark places them in Capernaum, right after Jesus had told them, for the second time, about His passion and death. Mark says that they not only did not understand what Jesus was saying but that they were quibbling over who was the greatest among them. So, in this setting, Jesus' response: *"If anyone wishes to be first, he shall be the last of all and the servant of all."* was not intended to give insight into the Kingdom of God, but insight into their own ministry; which may have been an issue in Mark's community at the time.

Detail: *"He called a child over."* Jesus did not just speak about a child; He called one over to Him. Since children were always in the company of their mothers until they were considered adults;

the child's mother had to be nearby. Mark was again reminding his listeners that women not only accompanied Jesus during His travels and ministry but were drawn to Him in His teaching. So, while Jesus was speaking privately to His disciples, other pilgrims in route for the Passover were not far away.

Detail: *"unless you turn and become like children, you will not enter the kingdom of heaven."* The basis resources of every family were their land and their children. And, children were just that, a resource for the ongoing survival of the family. They were not persons. They were innocent, trusting, and essentially powerless. So, one could not even enter the Kingdom of Heaven unless they became innocent, trusting, and essentially powerless.

Detail: *"Whoever humbles himself like this child is the greatest in the kingdom of heaven."* So, Moses is not the greatest in the Kingdom of Heaven, as they expected. Rather, it is anyone who humbles himself like a child, who intentionally wills them self to become insignificant.

Detail: *"whoever receives one child such as this in my name receives me."* The phrase, "receive a child" had a particular meaning in the ancient world. As soon as a baby was born, it was washed by the midwife and wrapped in coarsely woven linen strips, referred to as "swaddling clothes." She would then present the baby to the father. If he "received the child" i.e., embraced the child and claimed the child as his own, the child became part of the family. If the father did not "receive the child," the midwife placed the child in a clay pot and deserted it outside the front door or on the roadway. A woolen strip was tied around the pot if the child was a female; an olive branch was tied around the pot if it was a male.

While this practice seems barbaric in our times, in ancient times a child was not a resource but a burden to the family until he/she was old enough to productively work for the family. There were many situations where a family simply could not support another burden. Most often these infants were 'adopted" by a neighbor or passerby simply by their claiming the child. Sadly, if the child had a deformity; then nothing was tied around the pot and these infants usually died of exposure. The abandonment of infants to exposure was outlawed in the Roman Empire in 374 AD.[78]

So, to "receive a child" involved far more than hospitality; one was accepting the responsibility to care for and nurture someone who was most in need and could not repay the kindness. To receive one in Jesus' name was to act for one who is most in need, for Jesus' sake. Jesus identified Himself with those who are most insignificant to such an extent that He would be mysteriously present in the one being received.[79]

Mark's account has the additional phrase: *"and whoever receives me, receives not me but the One who sent me."* In this, Jesus was telling His disciples that their acceptance of the most insignificant among them, their acceptance of Him, was the measure of their acceptance of God Himself.

Within less than a day's walk from Mahanaim Jesus and His disciples would have come to the place known as Penuel (sometimes spelled: Peniel). Jesus was very familiar with Penuel. Each year since He was a child, He passed through Penuel to and from Jerusalem for the Jewish holidays.

Penuel was a place steeped in Jewish history. When Jacob arrived at the "ford of the Jabbok" [Gen 32:23], the location where the Jabbok River flows into the Jordan, he pitched camp on the northern bank of the Jabbok. That night, Jacob arose, took his two wives, with the two maidservants and his eleven children, and crossed over to the southern bank of the river. He left them there and went off by himself. During the night, the "Angel of the Lord" wrestled with Jacob [Gen. 32:24-32] and because Jacob prevailed, the Lord changed his name to Israel (which means "wrestles with God"). In the morning, Israel (Jacob) named the place Penuel (which means "face of God") *"because I have seen God face to face," he said, "yet my life has been spared"* [Gen 32:31]. Well, Israel (Jacob) need not have worried, Esau came for reconciliation with his brother. Jews regularly remind themselves that if God had not guided Esau's heart to reconciliation, there would have been no Israelite people.

Following the Exodus, around 1200 BC, Penuel was settled by the tribe of Manasseh. Over time, it grew to be a prominent city. Around the year 1135 BC, the Jewish military leader, Gideon, with 300 men was in pursuit of the army of two Midian kings. At Penuel, Gideon asked the people for provisions for his warriors, but they refused and taunted him. After capturing the two kings, Gideon punished the people of Penuel by destroying their tower and killing all the men there [Judges 8:17]. Slowly the city recovered and in 931 BC, Jeroboam I, the first king of the northern Israelite kingdom, greatly expanded and fortified Penuel and made it his "capital beyond the Jordan" [1 Kings 12:25]. But, in 924 BC, the Egyptian king, Shishak, completely destroyed the city of Penuel.[80] After that, Penuel was never rebuilt and it remained just a pilgrimage site and meeting place for people heading along the Jordan to and from the holy days in Jerusalem.

Figure 24: Bedouin Tents at Site of Ancient Penuel

So, to the many pilgrims passing through Penuel, they were on holy ground. For it was there that their namesake had wrestled with God and lived to tell about it. And, ever since, his descendants have wrestled with God and their scriptures tell about it. To those people, their past really was their present. The image of Israel (Jacob) and his next of kin standing on the southern bank of the Jabbok, seeing his brother's entourage approaching in the distance, would have been as vivid to them in the first century as it was on the day it happened.

Penuel was a convenient location for people to rest in their trek to and from Jerusalem. People were coming from Galilee and the diaspora to the north and east, as well as from northern Perea. It's likely that there were several inns at Penuel along with other accommodations offered by the permanent residents who were there. So, Jesus and His disciples would have encountered crowds. And, as Luke put it, *"tax collectors and sinners were all drawing near to listen to him, but the Pharisees and scribes began to complain, saying, 'This man welcomes sinners and eats with them.'"* So, Jesus responded with the Parable of the Lost Sheep.

10.23 The Parable of the Lost Sheep

This parable is recounted in both Luke's Gospel and Matthew's Gospel. However, as we will see Matthew had a different purpose in recounting the parable than did Luke.

10.23 1 The Version in Luke's Gospel [Luke 15:1-7]

The tax collectors and sinners were all drawing near to listen to him,
but the Pharisees and scribes began to complain, saying,
"This man welcomes sinners and eats with them."
So, to them he addressed this parable.
> "What man among you having a hundred sheep
> and losing one of them would not leave the ninety-nine in the
> desert and go after the lost one until he finds it?
> And when he does find it, he sets it on his shoulders with great
> joy and, upon his arrival home, he calls together his friends
> and neighbors and says to them, 'Rejoice with me because I
> have found my lost sheep.'

I tell you, in just the same way there will be more joy in heaven over one sinner who repents than over ninety-nine righteous people who have no need of repentance.

10.23.2 The Version in Matthew's Gospel [Matthew 18:12-14]

Then he said to them: "What is your opinion?

> If a man has a hundred sheep and one of them goes astray, will he not leave the ninety-nine in the hills and go in search of the stray? And if he finds it, amen, I say to you, he rejoices more over it than over the ninety-nine that did not stray.
>
> In just the same way, it is not the will of your heavenly Father that one of these little ones be lost."

10.24 The Spiritual Lesson in the Parable

Detail: (Luke's setting) There's a large crowd around and some Pharisees and scribes complain: "*This man welcomes sinners and eats with them.*" This is clearly an honor challenge, so we should expect the parable offered in response to be very subtle. In their culture, the more subtle the response to an honor challenge, the more effective the pushback was regarded. Recall that Jesus' first parable recounted in the Gospels (see section 4.2) was in response to this very same charge from Pharisees.

The Greek word, *dechomai,* which was translated here as "welcomes," is more accurately translated as "receives." As we've seen earlier, in the Middle East, to "receive" a child involved far more than hospitality or welcoming. Likewise, to "receive" an adult also involved far more than hospitality or welcoming. To "receive" an adult was to offer brotherhood, trust and peace. [81] To "receive" sinners was unthinkable to Pharisees, but to eat with them was utterly repugnant. Table fellowship in the Middle East was serious business. The host would begin the meal by showering his guests with a long series of compliments on the honor brought to his home by their presence. This was followed by each guest invoking the honor of God upon the host and affirming their great honor in having the host with them. The host would then respond with even more elaborate praises; followed by each guest responding in kind. And, this went on for quite a while before food was served. For a Pharisee to speak of the honor of being in the presence of sinners was just 'too much' for them. There even was a rabbinic prohibition against it: "Let not a man associate with sinners even to bring them near to the Torah."[82] So, for Jesus to eat with sinners is regarded by many theologians as one of the most meaningful expressions of the redeeming love of God.[83]

(Matthew's setting) Matthew sets this parable as Jesus' response to a question from His disciples in Peter's house in Capernaum. So, there's no honor challenge involved. Matthew's use of the parable calls his community to seek out and bring back those who have strayed. Indeed, in Matthew's account, the shepherd didn't lose the sheep, the sheep went astray. No fault is suggested on the part of the shepherd. But, in Luke's account, the shepherd bears responsibility for losing the sheep.

Detail: *"What man among **you** having a hundred sheep."* Jesus addresses the Pharisees directly as though they were shepherds, shocking their sensitivities. Moses, the greatest of the great, was a shepherd for most of his adult life. And, a *midrash* (rabbinic interpretation) of Exodus Chapter 3 described Moses searching for a lost kid goat when he encountered God in the burning bush.[84] So, the figure of a shepherd was a noble symbol from antiquity. But, by the first century, shepherds were regarded as *am ha'aretz* ("people of the land") rather than *am ha'sefer* ("people of the book"). To Pharisees, this placed shepherds outside the community, unwanted remnants of their past.

Detail: *"and **losing** one of them."* The shepherd bears responsibility for losing the sheep, implying that he was negligent.

Detail: *"would not leave the **ninety-nine** in the desert and go after the **lost** one until he finds it?"* Typically, one shepherd could manage about a dozen sheep. In a herd of 100, there would have been at least seven other shepherds there. To own 100 sheep was to be quite wealthy, so this herd was most likely owned by an extended family. The shepherd was not abandoning the 99, but rather leaving them in the care of the other shepherds and departing immediately while they were still *in the desert* to search for the one he had lost.

Detail: (the shepherd's response on finding the sheep). The natural thing for the shepherd to have said was "I have found it!" Instead the parable presents a lengthy and unnatural construct of words with more details than are needed for the storyline. As we learned in section 1.3.4, this is a good hint that we are hearing a chiasm. Recall that a chiasm is a repetition of similar ideas, first presented in a forward sequence then repeated in the reverse

Walking the Parables of Jesus

sequence. The objective of the chiasmic construct is to point to a central idea, which is in the center between the two sequences.

Sure enough, just as the Parable of the Good Samaritan was presented in chiasmic form, so too this parable was presented in chiasmic form. Therefore, the central idea in the parable is contained in the phrase *"upon his arrival home, he calls together his friends and neighbors."* The structure of this parable is a little more complex than that of the Good Samaritan. This chiasm is set between two parallel stanzas that repeat the same three words, *you, one* and *ninety-nine*. In addition, it uses poetic rhyme with the Aramaic words, *hadh* and *hadhwa*. This same three-stanza parallelism construct appears in Jesus' teaching on prayer right after He taught His disciples the Our Father, as recounted by Luke [Lk 11:9-13].

Table 5: Chiasmic Structure of the Parable of the Lost Sheep [85]

A	What man among <u>you</u> having a hundred sheep (15:4a)
B	and losing <u>one</u>[(a)] of them (15:4b)
C	would not leave the <u>ninety-nine</u> in the desert (15:4c)
1	and go after the <u>lost</u> one (15:4d)
2	until he <u>finds</u> it, and when he does <u>find</u> it (15:5a)
3	he sets it on his shoulders with great <u>joy</u>[(b)] (15:5b)
4	**upon his arrival home, he calls together his friends and neighbors** (15:6a)
3'	and says to them, 'Rejoice[(b)] with me (15:6b)
2'	because I have <u>found</u> my sheep (15:6c)
1'	which was <u>lost</u>. (15:6d)
A'	I tell <u>you</u>, in just the same way there will be more <u>joy</u>[(b)] in heaven (15:7a)
B'	over <u>one</u>[(a)] sinner who repents (15:7b)
C'	than over <u>ninety-nine</u> righteous people who have no need of repentance. (15:7c)

(a) Aramaic word, *hadh*
(b) Aramaic word, *hadhwa*

It's not obvious what the central idea is that's contained in: *"upon his arrival home, he calls together his friends and neighbors."*

That's to be expected; chiasms were intended to draw the listeners into deep reflection on just what the speaker/writer was saying.

From the setting, Jesus was responding to a charge from the Pharisees that He was not fit to be a religious leader because He *receives sinners and eats with them*. And, they leveled that charge in a very insulting way. But, as Peter would later say about Jesus: "*When he was insulted, he returned no insult*" [1 Peter 2:23a]. So, while this parable is a pushback, it is not a counter charge or an insult, but rather it calls Jesus' challengers to reflect on just what being fit to be religious leaders really entails. And, indirectly He was addressing all who claim to live their faith.

In the parable, when the shepherd finds the lost sheep, *he set it on his shoulders with great joy*. Why great joy? A lost sheep would just lie down helplessly and would have to be carried back to safety. An adult sheep weighed about 130 lbs.; that's quite a load to put on one's shoulders. (It's also just about the weight of the cross beam of a Roman cross). But, this shepherd rejoiced as he began the arduous task of restoring the lost one to its "proper place." The word, redeem, means to bring back to its proper place. So, the shepherd was "redeeming" the sheep who was lost. In this parable, Jesus was telling His listeners that the task of redeeming, restoring the lost to their "proper place," while a very difficult, demanding task, is a joy-filled effort.

The role of religious leaders, indeed all who live out their faith, is to seek out the lost and labor to bring them back to their "proper place." This was the role the Pharisees, the religious leaders of their times, were called to. Indeed, it's the role they once filled in the days of the Babylonian Captivity. But, that was in their past. And, the undertaking of redemption is joy-filled. But, the Pharisees were now living a joyless existence.

Jesus' listeners could not have known; but He was speaking to them that day within less than a month of His own carrying of the Cross, and yet He was approaching it with a spirit of joy. Why? The parable answers that question. Because Jesus knew that when it was over, the lost would be redeemed, and there would be even greater joy. And the same will be true for every lost one who is sought out and brought back to his/her "proper place" in the community. All their friends and neighbors, everyone, is to be called to share in that great joy.

It's likely that among those Pharisees that day were at least a few rabbis ("teachers"). Rabbis were quite adept at parables as well as recognizing and discerning chiasms. So, some of them may well have understood what Jesus was saying, because Jesus immediately followed the Parable of the Lost Sheep with the Parable of the Lost Coin.

10.25 The Parable of the Lost Coin [Luke 15:8-10]

> "Or what woman having ten coins and losing one would not light a lamp and sweep the house, searching carefully until she finds it?
>
> And when she does find it, she calls together her friends and neighbors and says to them,
>
> 'Rejoice with me because I have found the coin that I lost.'
>
> In just the same way, I tell you, there will be rejoicing among the angels of God over one sinner who repents."

10.26 The Spiritual Lesson in the Parable

Detail: *"Or what woman."* Jesus again rejected Pharisaic attitudes toward groups of people in their society, first it was shepherds, now women.

Detail: *"having ten coins and losing one."* At her betrothal, a wife received the *mohar* as her "social security" in the event of her husband's death or their divorce. The *mohar* was normally converted into silver coins which she kept with her at all times. Bedouin women wore their *mohar* in the form of coins hanging from her veil while village women wore them as a necklace.[86] Ten silver coins would have been worth about $600 dollars then, so for a woman to lose even one coin was a very sizable loss.

Detail: *'light a lamp and sweep the house, searching carefully until she finds it."* Since the movement of peasant women in a village was very limited, she was reasonably assured that it was in the house somewhere. But, it would likely take considerable effort to find it in the darkened interior of a house.

Detail: (the woman's response on finding the coin). Again, we hear an extended response which includes *calling together her friends and neighbors* for rejoicing (including the same Aramaic word, *hadhwa*), just as in the first parable. The first parable was in chiasmic form. Sure enough, Jesus repeated the use of the chiasmic form in this parable, as well.

Table 6: Chiasmic Structure of the Parable of the Lost Coin [87]

Or what woman having **ten** coins, (15:8a)

A   and losing one, (15:8b)
B   would not light a lamp and sweep the house, searching carefully until she finds it? (15:8c)
C   **And when she does find it, she calls together her friends and neighbors and says to them, 'Rejoice[a] with me** (15:9a)
B'   because I have found the coin (15:9b)
A'   that I lost.' (15:9c)

In just the same way, I tell you, there will be rejoicing[a] among the angels of God
over **one** sinner who repents." (15:10)

(a) Aramaic word, *hadhwa*

This second parable increased the relative value of what was lost: it was one in ten; whereas it was one in a hundred in the first parable, Also, the area of the search was confined to a house not the entire wilderness, increasing the assurance that what was lost can be found if one was willing to put in sufficient effort. Also, the burden of the effort was not as extreme as carrying an adult sheep (or a cross beam). And again, redemptive effort leads to communal rejoicing. This second parable reinforces the message in the first parable.

Jesus followed the second parable with yet another, what is known today as the Parable of the Prodigal Son. In speaking to a mostly Jewish crowd, Jesus began the parable with the phrase: "*there was a man who had two sons*" [Lk 15:11]. Most of His listeners in Penuel that day would have recognized that phrase.

10.27 "The Man Who Had Two Sons"

In their ancient Jewish experience, the "man who had two sons" was their patriarch, Isaac, whose two sons were Esau and Jacob. Theirs was a family torn apart over the handling of inheritance - the main plot line of the parable Jesus was about to share.

Among the people of the Middle East, when a man died, the oldest son received twice as much inheritance as the other sons [cf. Deu 21:17]. This was called the oldest son's "birthright" and it included the "father's blessing" for a long life and prosperity. This blessing also created in the one who received it, a special relationship with God, regardless of whether mankind might judge him as being "worthy." In that culture, the oldest son had the obligation to carry on the family and continue the support of the family farm, or flocks, or business providing for others, including their servants and slaves. So, the oldest would receive a larger portion of resources to accomplish that. In the case of Esau and Jacob, Esau would have received 2/3rd and Jacob 1/3rd of Isaac's estate.

But, Jacob convinced Esau to sell him his inheritance share for a meal when Esau was exceedingly hungry. Then later, Jacob tricked his father, Isaac, into giving him the "father's blessing" instead of to Esau [cf. Gen 27:1-40]. This so infuriated Esau and deeply saddened Isaac that Jacob fled to Haran, a city north of the Euphrates River in modern-day Turkey [Gen 29:29] where he remained for 20 years [Gen 31:38-41]. This area was known then as Padan-aram.

As we heard earlier, around the year 1755 BC, Jacob sought to reconcile with his brother and he sent messengers to him with gifts [Gen 32:1-5]. And then Jacob headed south to meet his brother Esau who was headed north. At the "ford of the Jabbok" (Penuel) Jacob and his family spent the night [Gen. 32:9-12]. There Jacob wrestled with God. Because Jacob strove mightily with God and prevailed, the Lord changed his name to *Israel*, the namesake of the Israelites. The next morning, Esau arrived, and the two brothers reconciled. And, Israel (Jacob) promised Esau he would follow him back to their family homestead in Seir (also known as Mamre), near the town of Hebron, to see their father, Isaac [Gen 33:1-15].

But, after Esau went on ahead, Israel (Jacob) reneged on his promise and instead headed west to settle in Shechem [Gen 33:16-20]. It was some thirteen years later that Israel (Jacob) returned to his father's home to join his brother, Esau, burying their father, Isaac, in the Cave of Machpelah (where Abraham, his wife Sarah, and Isaac's wife Rebecca were already buried).

It is not clear from Genesis 35:27-29 whether Israel (Jacob) made it in time to see his father alive, but most rabbis have interpreted that he did not, thus failing to ask his father's forgiveness.[88] In Jesus' day, it had long been a sore spot in the hearts of Israelites that they were named after a man who, though he was deeply loved and protected by God, who even successfully wrestled with God, was unable to bring himself to go home, in spite of his promise to his brother, to seek his father's forgiveness. Jesus took this troubling story and recast it into one of hope and repentance in the Parable of the Prodigal Son. Even the most flawed character; the most egregious offender can find forgiveness if they will only seek it.

10.28 The Parable of the Prodigal Son [Luke 15:11-32]

Then he said,

> "A man had two sons, and the younger son said to his father, 'Father, give me the share of your estate that should come to me.' So, the father divided the property between them.
>
> After a few days, the younger son collected all his belongings and set off to a distant country where he squandered his inheritance on a life of dissipation. When he had freely spent everything, a severe famine struck that country, and he found himself in dire need.
>
> So, he hired himself out to one of the local citizens who sent him to his farm to tend the swine. And he longed to eat his fill of the pods on which the swine fed, but nobody gave him any.
>
> Coming to his senses he thought, 'How many of my father's hired workers have more than enough food to eat, but here am I, dying from hunger. I shall get up and go to my father and I shall say to him, "Father, I have sinned against heaven and against you. I no longer deserve to be called your son; treat me as you would treat one of your hired workers."'
>
> So, he got up and went back to his father. While he was still a long way off, his father caught sight of him, and was filled with compassion. He ran to his son, embraced him and kissed him. His son said to him, 'Father, I have sinned against heaven and against you; I no longer deserve to be called your son.'
>
> But his father ordered his servants, 'Quickly bring the finest robe and put it on him; put a ring on his finger and sandals on his feet. Take the fattened calf and slaughter it. Then let us celebrate with a feast, because this son of mine was dead, and has come to life again; he was lost and has been found.' Then the celebration began.

Now the older son had been out in the field and,
on his way back, as he neared the house,
he heard the sound of music and dancing.
He called one of the servants and asked what this might mean.

The servant said to him,
'Your brother has returned, and your father has slaughtered the fattened calf because he has him back safe and sound.'

He became angry, and when he refused to enter the house, his father came out and pleaded with him.
He said to his father in reply, 'Look, all these years I served you and not once did I disobey your orders; yet you never gave me even a young goat to feast on with my friends.
But when your son returns who swallowed up your property with prostitutes, for him you slaughter the fattened calf.'

He said to him, 'My son, you are here with me always; everything I have is yours. But now we must celebrate and rejoice, because your brother was dead and has come to life again; he was lost and has been found.'"

10.29 The Spiritual Lesson in the Parable

Detail: (setting) Recall that Jesus was speaking in response to a charge that He was not fit to be a religious leader because He *"receives sinners and eats with them."* Jesus responded by pointing out what was really required of religious leaders, indeed all who claim to live their faith: seeking out the lost and bringing them back to their "proper place." This might well be a very arduous experience, but it should also be a very joy-filled experience.

Detail: *"and the younger said to his father, 'Father, give me the share of your estate that should come to me.'"* This son was expressing his wish that his father was dead. One did not receive inheritance until his father died.

Detail: *"So, the father divided the property between them."* This set an extremely bad example in the village. In that culture, it was the eldest son's duty to be the reconciler in the family. He should have stepped in between them to stop this. But, he was silent.

Detail: *"After a few days, the younger son collected all his belongings."* The youngest son's inheritance was land, crops in the field, flocks in pasture. He could not sell them because inheriting sons must live on the father's estate for one year after his death before anything may be sold. It was the father who had to sell a third of his estate! And, sell to whom, in only a few days? his neighbors. They were the only ones nearby with use for his land, his crops and his herds – along with all the hired men and slaves who cared for that land, crops and herds. This was an act of grave humiliation for this father for the sake of his son's demand.

Detail: *"and he set off to a distant country."* That phrase meant that he had left Judaism to live among Gentiles. He's left his father, his brother and now his religion. His selfishness was blinding him to all his mother had taught him. From a boy's infancy to the age of twelve it was his mother who taught him in the faith and the ways of proper relationships. Such an act, in the face of one's mother, was unconscionable to Jews. This detail was most likely a way of telling the listeners that the mother was no longer alive.

Detail: *"And, there he squandered his inheritance in extravagant living."* The worst offense a Jew could commit against his community was to sell or lose his inheritance to Gentiles. This act lets pass back into the hands of Gentiles that which Jews have collectively fought and died for over many centuries.

Learning of such an offense, the community would conduct a ceremony called a *qesasah* ("cutting off"). In the ceremony, the villagers would gather beans into a large clay pot in the village center. Then they would smash the pot spilling the beans on the ground. They would vehemently stomp the beans into the ground and declare the young man "dead" – cut off from the community.

Should the person attempt to return to the village he would most certainly be met with great hostility, or even mortal attack. If the son's villagers learned that *"he squandered his inheritance"* they would have certainly conducted a *qesasah* ceremony, much to the humiliation of his father. [89]

Detail: *"After he had spent everything, there was a severe famine in that whole country, and he found himself in dire need."* A famine doesn't happen all of a sudden! It takes a few years to build. So, it's been some years since he left his home. Why hasn't his brother found him yet? A spendthrift Jew in a Gentile land could easily be found via the "gossip line," everybody knows everybody else's business in the Middle East. In their culture, it was the eldest son's duty to keep his siblings safe from danger or want. The older brother should have located his brother and brought him home but there's no indication in the parable that he made any such attempt.

Detail: *"So the young man went and hired himself out to a citizen of that country, who sent him to his farm to feed the pigs."* No self-respecting Jew would ever touch pigs let alone feed them. Pigs were regarded as the abode of devils. So, he has no self-respect left; he's lost; he's descending into his own hell.

Detail: *"And, he longed to fill his stomach with the pods that the pigs were eating, but no one gave him anything."* Typically, pigs were fed scrub berries. A person couldn't eat enough of scrub berries to stay alive; there was too little nourishment. And, he even failed at begging.

Detail: *"Coming to his senses, the young man said, 'How many of my father's hired men have food to spare, and here I am starving to death!'"* "Coming to his senses;" his behavior had been so bizarre that he was viewed as being "out of his mind" – all the more reason, the obligations under pietas, for his older brother to seek him out and bring him home. But, he did not.

Detail: *"And, he said, 'I will set out and go back to my father and say to him: 'Father, I have sinned against heaven and against you.'"* He had the moral obligation to care for his father in his old age and he didn't do that.

Detail: *"I am no longer worthy to be called your son; make me one of your hired men."* **Make** me one of your hired-men!! He was going to order his father to take him on as a hireling. As a hireling he would receive one denarius a day; it was out of his father's generosity that the hirelings were fed each day.

Detail: *"So he got up and went back to his father. Now, while he was still far off, his father caught sight of him and was filled with compassion."* It's been several years since he left, yet his father still looked for him.

Detail: *"and he ran to his son, embraced him and kissed him."* This was a matter of great cultural significance. No dignified man in that culture ran. Ben Sirach wrote that *"A man is known by his gait"* [Sir 19:30]. Each man in the village was recognized from a distance by his manner of walking. So, for the father to run was to humiliate himself. And, for the father to embrace and kiss him was to "receive" him as a guest, an extraordinary gesture under the circumstances.

Detail: *"Father, Father, I have sinned against heaven and against you. I am no longer worthy to be called your son."* There was no audible word of welcome; the father's arms "said it all." So, repentance is not about deep sorrow, but about deep surrender. The son had repented in the arms of his father, not in the pig sty.

Detail: *"Then, the father called to his servants, 'Quickly! Bring the best robe and put it on him.'"* The servants have chased after the father, sure that something was very wrong; and the villagers weren't far behind. For, from the son's appearance alone, he had lost it all, to Gentiles! They would want to kill him. Righteous anger breeds violence. Putting the father's robe on him signaled that the son was now under his father's protection. *"cloth him in the robe of salvation"* [Is 61:10], for my son is alive, he has been saved.

Detail: *Put a ring on his finger and sandals on his feet.'* Only a slave went barefoot. By putting the father's ring with the family seal on it all will know that his son has full authority. The father has placed his son above himself in the community. The father was taking extreme measures to ensure his son's safety and acceptance back into the village.

Detail: *"Take the fattened calf and slaughter it. Let us celebrate with a feast. This son of mine was dead but has come to life again; he was lost and has been found."* A fattened calf would feed the whole village, so all were invited to the celebration. No one would dare turn down this invitation, regardless of how they felt about the prodigal son.

Detail: *"Then the celebration began. Meanwhile, the older son had been out in the field and, as he neared the house, he heard the sound of music and dancing."* The fact that the celebration was underway without the oldest son being there tells us that the oldest son has also "gone away" from his father, not literally but figuratively. In their culture, it was the duty of the oldest son to serve as the majordomo ("principal of the house") for such events. The oldest son's role was to bring each guest to his father that he/she might be properly welcomed to the father's home. The only time a younger son would perform such a duty was if it was the younger one's wedding banquet. There's been a huge breech in the relationship between the oldest son and his father that's exposed by this detail in the parable.

Further, their culture highly valued each person doing what was expected of them, no more and no less. The oldest son did not belong "in the field" when everyone else had already come in. It was the duty of the field foreman to be the last to leave the field each day. To usurp that duty was to dishonor the foreman. So, the oldest son was not only at odds with his father, but also with others, as well.

Detail: *"So, he called one of the young boys and asked what this might mean. They said to him, 'Your brother has returned, and your father has killed the fattened calf because he has him back safe and sound.'"* The celebration would have been taking place in the courtyard of the father's house; only the Romans ate indoors. Children did not attend such events; they would congregate outside the entrance to the courtyard, enjoying the music and festive atmosphere. They would have been the first villagers the oldest son would have encountered as he approached his father's house. The maturity and insightfulness of the young boys' response would not have gone unnoticed by Jesus' listeners.

Detail: *"He became angry, and when he refused to enter the house, his father came out and pleaded with him."* The oldest son has chosen to further humiliate his father by quarrelling with him in full view of the guests. While this would be considered a grave insult in most cultures, it was far worse than that among Jews. To disrespect one's father was a capital crime, which could be punished by stoning should the father choose to bring charges against him before the village elders.[90]

Jesus' listeners expected the father to at least banish the older son from the village. Such conduct could not be tolerated and set a terrible example for other sons in the village. Instead, Jesus said that the father *pleaded with him* to do the little that was expected of him as the eldest son. The lengths this father will go to in trying to "bring them back" to him were astounding to Jesus' listeners.

Detail: *"The older son answered his father, 'Look! All these years I've been slaving for you.'"* The son doesn't even address him properly as "Father." And, he claims to have been *slaving for* him. An outrageous insult followed by an outrageous claim. This was the same attitude that the Pharisees were exhibiting. They saw themselves as "slaving" for God and getting no appreciation for it. They were not lost in a far-off land like the younger son; they were lost in their own hearts like the older son.

Detail: *"And, he said, 'I've never disobeyed your orders. Yet you never gave me even a young goat to feast on with my friends. But when this son of yours, who swallowed up your property with prostitutes returns, for him you slaughter the fattened calf.'"* The son is so bitter he charged his father with a crime. If a son dishonors his family with prostitutes, Mosaic Law required that the father kill the son [Deu 21:18-21]. But, Jesus had said that the younger one *squandered his inheritance in extravagant living;* nothing was said about prostitutes.

Detail: *"The father said, "My son, you are here with me always; everything I have is yours. But now we must celebrate and rejoice, because your brother was dead and has come to life again; he was lost and has been found.'"* The father still calls him "son" This father will not give up; he offers this one the same love in humiliation that he offered the younger one. In full view of all the guests, the father was crying from his heart, "please be my son, do the little I ask of you."

Detail: there was no concluding stanza – the ending of the story is missing; the listeners were left "hanging." The pushback question Jesus silently posed to His listeners was: "Did the older son repent and do what was asked of him? What would you do?"

Let's briefly review, Jesus was responding to a charge from the Pharisees that He was not fit to be a religious leader because He *receives sinners and eats with them*. So, Jesus responded with a parable that called His challengers to reflect on just what being fit to be religious leaders really entails. They are to seek out the lost and labor to bring them back to their "proper place" – that is, they are to redeem the lost. And, the undertaking of redemption is joy-filled. All their friends and neighbors, everyone, is to be called to share in that great joy. Jesus followed up with a second parable which reinforced the message of the first parable. It had the effect of increasing the assurance that what was lost can be found if one was willing to put in sufficient effort. And again, redemptive effort leads to communal rejoicing. Both of these parables were presented in chiasmic form increasing the need for listeners to reflect more deeply on what Jesus was saying.

Then, Jesus related to them what many biblical scholars refer to as a "dual parable," a parable that has two different messages for two different groups of listeners at the same time.[91] In addition to the Pharisees and scribes who had challenged Jesus, there was a large crowd, many of whom were pilgrims headed to Jerusalem.

In the first two parables, nothing was required of the one (sheep or coin) that was lost. The focus was on the search and find mission. But, the first half of the Parable of the Prodigal Son focused on what is required of a person who is lost: repentance. The story Jesus used illustrated that repentance begins with "going back home to the father" – turning back to God.

The lesson of the Adam and Eve story is that sin arises out of the disposition of the heart. The lesson of the first half of the Parable of the Prodigal Son is that repentance must also arise out of the disposition of the heart. Forgiveness awaits those whose hearts "go back home to the father." Recall that the first words of the parable awakened in their minds that their namesake, Israel (Jacob), failed to go back home to his father and he never received the forgiveness he so much needed in his life.

At the beginning a living father was wished dead; at the end a "dead" son was found alive through his response to the father's unexpected love. In our times, we think of the younger son as "prodigal" – one who acts in an unrestrained and extravagant way. But, in the culture of Jesus' first listeners, it was the father who was "prodigal." He was expected to be harsh and judgmental, just as they envisioned God; but the father acted in a most unexpected way.

The Pharisees and scribes listening to the telling of the parable were compelled to see themselves in the character of the oldest son and conclude, "I am just like him." The second half of the parable tells of the unprecedented offer of love the father makes to that oldest son, in spite of his failings. God's unprecedented love and forgiveness awaits them if they will just "go back home to the father," re-discover their ancient roots as the true religious leaders the people needed so much.

These three parables show us again that Jesus was a master at engaging His listeners' imaginations. Often referred to as the "Gospel within the Gospel,"[92] these three parables are meant to be heard together as one unit, as we just did. We will need to reflect a very long while on just what this "Gospel within the Gospel" means in our lives, for the third parable in the set is just as unfinished for us as it was for Jesus' first listeners.

Because of the large number of people who would have been heading to Jerusalem for the Passover, there would have been hundreds walking along with Jesus and His disciples as they continued south from Penuel along the east rim of the Rift Valley trench. It most likely took them a full day to reach the site known as Damia, about 9 miles north of Jericho. In the 13th century, an Arab sultan built a stone bridge across the Jordan River at Damia; and, bridges have been destroyed and re-built, again and again, at that site ever since. While it was regarded as the place where the Israelites first crossed into the Promised Land for the Battle of Jericho, in Jesus' day, there was little more than a small settlement at Damia. So, there would have been a lot of people "sleeping under the stars" that night. The inhabitants of Damia would have extended the same hospitality to travelers that was part of their cultural tradition, preparing for the many pilgrims they would see passing through year after year.

Several miles beyond Damia, Jesus and His fellow travelers would have come to a place where the Rift Valley trench rim slopes down to a site on the river enabling crossing. We don't know the precise location of that site. As we learned earlier, the crossing point at Jericho was moved several times. The Jordan carries a lot of silt downstream and deposits of it made wading through it very difficult. Also, the riverbed shifts in that area.

When Jesus and His disciples crossed the Jordan a few weeks earlier, heading west into Perea, the crossing site was largely deserted. But, with Passover approaching, there were now thousands crossing east bound every day. The more the riverbed was stirred up by river crossers, the more muddy and slippery the footing became. This was another reason why they were forced to regularly relocate the crossing point. On this day, there would have been a number of heavy ropes strung across the river from one bank to the other, forming crossing lanes. The less surefooted would hold on to a rope as they made their way across the river.

Most years, in mid-March, the river level would have been at least waist high on an adult, so the men would be carrying their women and children across one-by-one on their shoulders. Perhaps Jesus may have fondly recalled the years when He would watch Joseph gently carry Mary across the river headed to Jerusalem for Passover. The pack animals would be crossed further downstream to avoid collisions with people who were crossing. The scene would have been quite festive as anticipation of the last day or so of their journey drew near.

After wading across the river, Jesus and His fellow travelers would have air dried and then continued south on the west bank to the entrance to the city of Jericho. The city had served as the private estate of Alexander the Great between 336 BC and 323 BC after his conquest of the region. Alexander heavily fortified the city with high stone walls. Later, Herod the Great had his winter palace in Jericho and he added an extensive date plantation just north of the city. Jesus and His fellow travelers would have passed that plantation as they made their way along the west bank to enter through the main gate to the city.

Jericho was a very cosmopolitan city with many places for lodging, from palatial to very modest. It would have been a very long and exhausting day, so it's likely Jesus and His disciples stayed over in Jericho before heading out the next day. As they were leaving, with a large crowd with them, they encountered a blind beggar [Lk 18:45]. Mark tells us that the man's name was Bartimaeus (which means "son of the unclean") [Mk 10:46], reflecting the bias in those days against those with disabilities that were considered inherited from their parents due to a parental fault or sin.

Matthew recounted that there were two blind beggars [Mt 20:29-30]. There's no general agreement on what Matthew intended in reporting two men instead of one. In any case, Jesus healed the blind beggar(s) and the crowd likely became even more exuberant than before. It was then that Jesus encountered a tax collector named Zacchaeus [Lk 19:1].

10.30 The Encounter with Zacchaeus

One of the principles in Middle Eastern storytelling is that we have to follow the details very closely. While Jericho was the 'Palm Springs' of the Middle East, and they clearly were "out of place" there, they had to pass through Jericho in order to get to the road to Jerusalem. As Luke tells us, *"there was a man there named Zacchaeus who was the chief tax collector and also a wealthy man. He was seeking to see who Jesus was, but he could not see him because of the crowd, for he was short in stature"* [Lk 19:2-3].

Detail: Recall that in Middle Eastern storytelling, the person's name provides hints in how to interpret what the person says or does. We don't know what this tax collector's real name was. It could've been Zacchaeus which is Greek for *"pure of heart."* So,

Luke is telling us that while this man was a tax collector, indeed he was the chief tax collector, he was a man who was 'pure of heart.' Jesus had said about those who were *"pure of heart"* that they *"shall see God"* [Mt 5:8]. So, Zacchaeus was going to see God.

But as a tax collector, he was the most hated man in town *"so he ran ahead and climbed a sycamore tree in order to see Jesus, who was about to pass that way"* [Lk 19:4].

Detail: Every detail in a Middle Eastern story is there for a reason. In ancient Israel, a "sycamore tree" was a sycamore fig tree. It was not an edible fig. For many centuries, it was the practice that only trees with edible fruit were planted inside the city walls. In case the city was under siege, the edible fruit would provide food for the people who were inside the city. So, Luke was telling his listeners that the tree is outside the walls of the city.

Part of the "contract" for being a tax collector for Rome, particularly a chief tax collector, was that Zacchaeus would receive the protection of the Roman guard stationed in the city. But, this applied only when he was within the city. If he went outside the city limits, he was "on his own."

Through this detail, Luke was telling his listeners that Zacchaeus was risking his life in climbing that tree. In fact, if he was recognized, and that was quite likely due to the large crowd there, Zacchaeus might be killed by a mob. He has gone that far to see Jesus, because he was "pure of heart." This man wanted to see Jesus so much, that he took such extraordinary action.

Detail: *"When he reached the place, Jesus looked up and said to him 'Zacchaeus, come down quickly for today I must stay at your home.'"* In the Middle East, no one ever invited themselves to somebody else's home. Hospitality was to operate the other way around; one was invited by the host (homeowner), one did not invite them self. By this action, Jesus was rescuing Zacchaeus in calling the man down out of the tree and into His company. As long as he was in Jesus' company, no one in the crowd, who just witnessed a miracle, would dare touch him.

Detail: "*He came down quickly and received him with joy. When they all saw this, they began to grumble: 'he's going to stay at the house of this sinner.'*" Notice that they were grumbling against Jesus, now not against the tax collector.

But, Zacchaeus "*stood there and said to the Lord* (not to them, he speaks to Jesus) *'Behold half of my possessions, Lord, I shall give to the poor and if I have extorted anything from anyone I shall repay it four times over.'*" His entire wealth came from extorting others, that's what tax collecting was all about. Tax collectors weren't paid by the Romans; they were "paid" by how much they were able to overcharge others. And, there was no appeals court!!

If Zacchaeus was literally going to do as he claimed, he was about to give everything away. Recall that Jesus had said to others "*give what you have to the poor and follow me*" [Mt 19:21; Mk 10:21; Lk 18:22]. And, that's exactly what Zacchaeus was going to do. This is remarkable, but Luke "explained" why this man was doing that, by telling us at the very beginning that he was "pure of heart." It was necessary for Luke, in relating the story, to tell us the man's name and the type of tree he climbed, or the man's actions would've made little sense.

Detail: "*Then Jesus said to him, 'today salvation has come to this house because this man too is a descendent of Abraham.' For the Son of Man has come to seek and save what was lost.*" Underlying Luke's depiction of Zacchaeus as a "descendant of Abraham," the father of the Jews, is his recognition as a Gentile of the central place occupied by Israelites in the plan of salvation.

So, Jesus and His disciples stayed another night in Jericho. At some point, Jesus had an opportunity to speak to His disciples in private where He shared the Parable of the Shrewd Steward.

10.31 Parable of the Shrewd Steward [Luke 16:1-8]

We encountered the text of this parable in section 1.3.2 under the subject of the paramount importance of honor in Middle Eastern culture. The story involves debtors who had debts essentially impossible to pay off.

By the first century, virtually all small farmers were tenant farmers on a large landowner's property. It generally started by the farmer initially receiving a relatively small loan. If he had a poor crop that year, he needed to be able to plant the following year. So, he would obtain a loan of some olive oil which he could then sell. With the proceeds he could then plant the following year. This debt was separate from the rent he paid the landowner (master) for use of the land.

Tenancy deals were usually for a certain percentage of one's harvest which was to be paid to the landowner. Sadly, over the course of time, given that there were good years and bad years, in some years one was unable to pay off both debt and rent. In time, it built up to an enormous, almost impossible debt to pay off.

The Eastern Mediterranean waters normally rotate counterclockwise due to the currents in the Atlantic. This brings moist air off the southern Mediterranean over Palestine in the evenings. But, about every seven or eight years the Atlantic currents move further west causing the waters of the Mediterranean to rotate in the other direction (clockwise) bringing colder water near Palestine so that the air did not absorb anywhere near as much water. And so, there was drought in the Middle East roughly every seven or eight years.

The currents in the Atlantic shift side-to-side, just like they do in the Pacific where we get El Niños, because the earth wobbles on its axis as it rotates. This is called precessing. If the drought lasted two years or more, tenants in the Middle East could run up serious debts. Egypt however had the magnificent Nile River, fed from annual snows in the mountains of east central Africa. Egypt rarely had a problem with drought. That's how Egypt became the "Breadbasket of the Middle East." They were not particularly vulnerable to famines - except the one that came in the time of Joseph. That was a most unusual occurrence.

10.32 The Spiritual Lesson in the Parable

Recalling from section 1.3.2, Jesus was not praising the steward for being dishonest. What mattered most, in that man's life circumstances, was to restore the honor of his master. The steward was praised for applying himself to what mattered most. When all seemed lost, the steward turned to what matters most.

Every one of us owes the fullest of full of safety and sustenance to God. There's no way we can pay that back, so God generously forgives us. We must apply our efforts to the things that matter most in life. If we were really honest with ourselves, the things we apply our most attention to are our own safety and sustenance, the health of our family or our business or our social security/pension. What should matter most in our life?

When we consider the circumstances under which Jesus shared this parable, we realize that in only a few short weeks ahead, the Apostles would have to recognize and apply themselves to what matters most in their life circumstances. Very soon, all was going to seem lost.

Sometime later, when Jesus and His disciples were again confronted by Pharisees in public, He spoke the parable known as the Parable of the Rich Man and Lazarus. In that parable, Lazarus goes to "the bosom of Abraham." What does that phrase mean?

10.33 The "Bosom of Abraham"

To first century Jews, God alone dwells in heaven. There was no concept that they would ever dwell with God. God was going to come and dwell with them. In their minds, one didn't go to heaven when he/she died; one went to a place which the Jews called *Sheol* (in Greek: "Hades").

For many years, the term, Sheol (Hades), was translated as Hell. But in the modern translation, it's the "netherworld." Netherworld is an invention in the English language to mean neither heaven nor hell. It's that other place: the "place of the dead." So, to Jews, all who died went to this place; if one was righteous one was invited to a great banquet being hosted by Abraham. If one was not judged to be righteous, he/she was left out of the banquet. In the parable, Abraham was able to talk to the rich man and the rich man was able to talk to Abraham. They're in the same place, *Sheol*, but the rich man was not in the banquet with Abraham.

Recall the seating pattern at a formal dinner or banquet. The host sat in the center position, at his right hand was position number one. At his left was position number two. Number three was at Number one's right. The very last, the least favored position was to number two's left. The phrase being at "the bosom of Abraham" meant that you were in position number one. When one was eating, one reclined on their left and ate with their right hand. This meant that one who was in position number one was literally right at the front of the host as they were reclined. To speak with the host number-one merely leaned back against the host's bosom.

In the Western world, such close contact at table would be considered "invading one's private space." But, that's not the case in the Middle East at all. For one to pull back from someone in the Middle East is an enormous affront. Nobody tried to yell across the table to somebody else. Most conversations were limited to the person at one's left and the person at one's right. That's why it was so important to be seated at the "bosom of Abraham." To be at the "bosom of Abraham" would be to sit in the most favored position at the banquet being held by Abraham in *Sheol* (Hades).

10.34 Parable of the Rich Man and Lazarus [Luke 16:19-31]

Jesus said to them,
"There was a rich man who dressed in purple garments
and fine linen and dined sumptuously each day.

And lying at his door was a poor man named Lazarus,
covered with sores, who would gladly have eaten his fill of the
scraps that fell from the rich man's table.
Dogs even used to come and lick his sores.

When the poor man died, he was carried away by angels to the
bosom of Abraham.

The rich man also died and was buried, and from the
netherworld, where he was in torment, he raised his eyes and
saw Abraham far off and Lazarus at his side. And he cried out,
'Father Abraham, have pity on me.
Send Lazarus to dip the tip of his finger in water and cool my
tongue, for I am suffering torment in these flames.'

Abraham replied, 'My child, remember that you received what was good during your lifetime while Lazarus likewise received what was bad; but now he is comforted here, whereas you are tormented.

Moreover, between us and you a great chasm is established to prevent anyone from crossing who might wish to go from our side to yours or from your side to ours.'

He said, 'Then I beg you, father, send him to my father's house, for I have five brothers, so that he may warn them, lest they too come to this place of torment.' But Abraham replied, 'They have Moses and the prophets. Let them listen to them.'

He said, 'Oh no, father Abraham, but if someone from the dead goes to them, they will repent.' Then Abraham said, 'If they will not listen to Moses and the prophets, neither will they be persuaded if someone should rise from the dead.'"

10.35 The Spiritual Lesson in the Parable

Detail: "*Jesus said to them.*" He is speaking to a crowd where there are a number of judgmental Pharisees looking on.

Detail: "*There was a rich man who dressed in purple garments and fine linens and dined sumptuously each day.*" Only the super wealthy could afford to wear purple vestments. Actually, they were a blue-purple, called *tekhelet*, a dye that came from Eastern Mediterranean murex snails. Fishermen took these little snails and squeezed them to get a few drops of dye out of them. They would have to squeeze thousands and thousands of snails to get enough to dye one garment.

Detail: "*And lying at his door was a poor man named Lazarus.*" We are told that the man's name was Lazarus, Greek for Eliezer. The name means "God is my help." This is the only parable in which Jesus gives a character a name. The poor man was literally lying at the rich man's door. This detail tells Jesus' listeners that there was no excuse for the rich man not knowing about Lazarus. He had to step over him to get in and out of his house.

Second, this detail also tells Jesus' listeners that the rich man was eating alone because if people were coming to eat with him, they would have to climb over Lazarus, which guests certainly would not do. For a Jew, the ultimate in loneliness was to eat alone.

Detail: *"He was covered with sores and would have gladly eaten his fill of the scraps that fell from the rich man's table. The dogs even use to come and licked his sores."* Dogs were regarded as the lowest form of animal life in the Middle East. To us, it was like saying that rats came and used to lick his sores.

Detail: *"When the poor man died he was a carried away by angels to the bosom of Abraham. The rich man also died and was buried, and from the netherworld, where he was in torment, he raised his eyes and saw Abraham far off and Lazarus at his side."* Here we encounter what is the one of the biggest controversies about this parable over the past few centuries. Many argue that this is a story about heaven and hell; that the poor man went to heaven and the rich man went to hell. However, going to heaven with God was a concept they didn't have, certainly not the Pharisees.

Detail: *"The rich man was buried and from the netherworld where he was in torment, ..."* In the Pharisees' teachings about Sheol (Hades), there was no fire. The man was in torment because he then realized that he will never share in the banquet with Abraham, and he's terrified. His mouth was dry from fear. That could also be the torment of hell - the realization that "I will never be with God."

Jesus was clearly incorporating into the story the Pharisees' answer to "what happens in the afterlife?" He was playing back to them their own explanation and using it as a lesson to show them that they, the Pharisees, did not follow their own teachings. The Pharisees' explanation about *Sheol* (Hades) and the grand banquet hosted by Abraham did not come from their Scriptures; rather it was from the *Mishnah*, the rabbinic explanations of scripture used in synagogues from the period 536 BC to around 220 AD.

To the Sadducees, there was no afterlife because there is no mention of it in the Torah. But to the Pharisees, there 'had to be one,' based on the Book of Wisdom:

> *The souls of the just are in the hands of God and no torment shall touch them, they seem in the view of the foolish to be dead but they're passing away was thought of as an affliction and their going forth from us utter destruction. But, they are in peace* [Wis 3:1-3].

Notice that this passage indicates that God is in control, but there's no mention about the souls going to God. The Pharisees concluded that there must be some place or situation intended for the souls of the righteous. Over the course of centuries, rabbis attempting to answer the question, "what happens in the afterlife," came up with the banquet of Abraham explanation. Among Jews, there was and still is no teaching authority akin to the magisterium in Catholicism, so Jews might encounter variations on the afterlife story depending upon which synagogue they attended.

Detail: "*He raised his eyes and saw Abraham far off and Lazarus at his side and he cried out 'Father Abraham, have pity on me. Send Lazarus to dip the tip of his finger in water and cool my tongue I am suffering torment in these flames.' Abraham replied 'my child, remember that you received what was good during your lifetime while Lazarus likewise received what was bad. But now he is comforted here whereas you are in torment.'*" The concept, in those days, was that a person was rich because he/she had God's favor; and was a righteous person. But, Jesus was teaching that the situation is quite the other way around; one has abundance so that he/she may share that abundance. The more one has the greater one's responsibility to share. And, that's precisely where this rich man failed. Notice that even, in his distress, the rich man is still giving orders, "*send Lazarus to ...*"

Detail: "*Abraham continued: 'Moreover between us and you a great chasm is established to prevent anyone from crossing who might wish to go from our side to yours or from your side to ours.'*" Final realization was the chasm, knowing that he had failed and now there was no way to correct it.

Detail: *"He said: 'then I beg you Father send him to my father's house, for I have five brothers, so that he may warn them.'"* Why five brothers? In the ancient world, the number five signified trouble. Recall that the Woman at the Well had five husbands; The Samaritans had five gods. He has five brothers!! Also, his brothers were living in his father's house; therefore, his father was still alive. By Mosaic Law, sons were to remain in their father's house until one year after his death. This man should be in his father's house, as well. This detail tells us that he is alienated from his extended family. He is not living up to his obligations of a son, just as the Pharisees were not living up to their obligations as "sons of Abraham."

Detail: *"'Lest they too come to this place of torment.' But, Abraham replied 'they have Moses and the prophets, let them listen to them.'"* The Pharisees claimed that Moses and the prophets were their source. Thus, Jesus was addressing the Pharisees directly. "Listen to Moses and the prophets not your teachings because you're not even following your own teaching."

Detail: *He said: Oh no father Abraham, but if someone from the dead goes to them they will repent. But Abraham said "If they will not listen to Moses and the prophets, neither will they be persuaded by someone who should rise from the dead.* What a starling thing to say: "if someone from the dead goes to them they will repent." Jesus was later going to raise a man named Lazarus from the dead; was Jesus referring to Lazarus or was He referring to Himself? We don't know.

This parable was a story about a great deal of pain: the pain of misery on the poor man's part, the pain of loneliness and isolation on the rich man's part; culminating in the rich man's eternal pain realizing that he would never experience what was the goal of righteous Jews. The rich man didn't mean Lazarus any harm; he was oblivious to Lazarus' existence. He was so absorbed in and bitter over his own misery that he was unable to see the misery that was literally at his own doorstep.

The parable also speaks of the Pharisees' pain. Although they positioned themselves as opponents of Jesus, He had compassion for them. They too lived a joyless, isolated life. The fastidiousness which they taught and went about their daily lives only added to the already miserable conditions their fellow Jews were living under. That hadn't always been the case.

About 70% of the Jewish people in Jesus' day followed the teachings of the Pharisees. The Pharisees were portrayed in the Gospels as being "the bad guys." But historically, the Pharisees were the people who saved Judaism. When the Temple was destroyed in 587 BC, thousands were hauled off into captivity in Babylon. They no longer had a place of worship. It seemed to Jews that their relationship with God had ended.

In Babylon, the Pharisees began as a lay movement which basically said, "We are People of the Book, so let's gather every day to read from the Book and hold onto what we were raised with." Thus, the Pharisees began the synagogue experience in Babylon. The daily reading of the Book in the synagogues literally saved Judaism. But, over the course of generations, with the restored Temple in Jerusalem under the control of the Sadducees, the Pharisee leaders became so involved in holding onto their own authority and the strictures associated with ritual purity, that they had become "the bad guys" by Jesus' day. While their authority was generally recognized, they were socially despised by the people and lived in their "own world," much like the rich man in the parable. If even a few of them "saw themselves" in the story and reflected on what it meant in their lives, the parable achieved its purpose.

This parable was meant for us, as well. Have we become so isolated and turned inward as we deal with our own life circumstances that we don't see the misery at "our doorsteps?" We don't mean them harm any more that the rich man in the parable did. But, the effect of not noticing is still the same.

Sometime later, messengers from Mary and Martha, the sisters of Lazarus of Bethany, came to Jesus and said: *"Master, the one you love is ill"* [Jn 11:3]. But, much to the puzzlement of the Apostles, *"he remained for two days in the place where he was"* [Jn 11:6] before they headed up the Jericho Road to Bethany. It was likely years later that they realized the lesson: sometimes God seems to delay when we ask His help, for He has a greater purpose in mind.

As they neared the outskirts of Bethany, Jesus *"found that Lazarus had already been in the tomb for four days"* [Jn 11:17]. Recall that in the Jewish understanding of death, one was not dead-dead until the third day.

Just outside of Bethany, Jesus was met by Martha. In the course of their conversation, Martha said to him, *'I know he will rise, in the resurrection on the last day"* [Jn 11:24]. Jesus told her, *"I am the resurrection and the life; whoever believes in me, even if he dies, will live, and everyone who lives and believes in me will never die"* [Jn 11:25-26].

10.36 "Whoever believes in me will never die"

The exchange between Martha and Jesus, in verses 24 thru 26 of John's Gospel, is often used as "Jesus' words supporting justification by faith alone." In properly interpreting those verses we need to keep two things in mind:

1. One of the central principles in Biblical interpretation, as stated in the *Catechism of the Catholic Church*, article 112, is that there is a unity to the whole of Scripture. Every verse in Scripture cannot contain the entirety of God's revelation. Consequently, Jesus' words must be interpreted in the context of His whole teachings.

In that light, there are numerous passages in the Gospels that clearly show that the phrase: *believes in me* means much more than "having faith in Jesus." For example:
> *"If you love me, you will keep my commandments"* [Jn 14:15]
> *"Amen, amen, I say to you, whoever keeps my word will never see death"* [Jn 8:51]
> *"The hour is coming in which all who are in the tombs will hear the Son of Man's voice and will come out, those who have done good deeds to the resurrection of life, but those who have done wicked deeds to the resurrection of condemnation"* [Jn 5:28-29]

> *"If you wish to enter into life, keep the commandments"* [Mt 19:17]
> *"Not everyone who says to me, 'Lord, Lord,' will enter the kingdom of heaven, but only the one who does the will of my Father in heaven"* [Mt 7:21]
> *"For the Son of Man will come with his angels in his Father's glory, and then he will repay everyone according to his conduct"* [Mt 16:27]

2. Catholics and many Protestants are in substantial agreement on the theological meaning of "justification" [see *Joint Declaration on the Doctrine of Justification,* 1999]. But they tend to see the means of gaining justification differently. As the *Catechism of the Catholic Church,* article 2017, puts it, "The grace of the Holy Spirit confers upon us the righteousness of God. Uniting us by faith and Baptism to the Passion and Resurrection of Christ, the Spirit makes us sharers in his life." Catholics see that as a lifelong process of growing in righteousness through cooperating with God's grace. Whereas, some Protestants see that as occurring at the beginning of the Christian life when God forgives one's sins and declares one righteous. Here's where the *keep my commandments;* and *those who have done good deeds,* and *only the one who does the will of my Father,* and *he will repay everyone according to his conduct* come in. We do not need to do good works in order to come to God and be forgiven, but we need to do more than simply say: "I believe in Jesus as my Lord and Savior." We need to live in the ways of Christ during our lifetime if we wish to share in eternal life with Him.

Jesus raised Lazarus from the dead, much to the delight of his family and friends, but much to the trepidation of many onlookers. John said of them: *"some of them went to the Pharisees and told them what Jesus had done. So, the chief priests and the Pharisees convened the Sanhedrin and said, "What are we going to do? This man is performing many signs. If we leave him alone all will believe in him and the Romans will come and take away both our land and our nation"* [Jn 11:46-48]. *"So, from that day on they planned to kill him"* [Jn 11:53]. Jerusalem was now more dangerous than when they left.

Dcn. Bob Evans

It was March of 33 AD; Passover was only weeks away. Jesus' ninth journey has come to an end; and, what a challenging journey it was. The walk was more than 175 miles and it lasted several weeks. Jesus and His disciples encountered great crowds along the way, at Gadara, Gerasa, Mahanaim, Penuel and Jericho. And as they followed the Jabbok River, they were joined by hundreds of pilgrims headed to Jerusalem for Passover. The number of pilgrims grew to thousands as they crossed the Jordan at Jericho.

On this journey, we had the opportunity to hear Jesus share fourteen parables, the most we've heard on a journey, so far. Some were to large crowds, some were to confrontational Pharisees and scribes, and some were to His disciples in private. Jesus used the time in Perea to draw His Apostles more deeply into what was ahead for Him, and for them. But, He did so through the use of parables. To them, His parables spoke of being prepared for a time of darkness, but they would know when He would return; and, when He returned the expectations of their lives would be fulfilled. To them, He shared the first insights into the Christian understanding of grace and how it works in our lives. His parables were increasingly more moving and more challenging. They likely remained in the listeners' minds and hearts for a very long time, including our own.

But, what must have been a wonderful experience for His disciples came to an ominous end in Bethany when some onlookers were alarmed when they saw Jesus raising Lazarus from the dead. The Sanhedrin was now plotting to kill Jesus; the Apostles had to have been very worried for His safety, and their own.

11. Jesus' Final Mission Journey

It's likely that the euphoria Martha and Mary experienced over Jesus' restoring their brother Lazarus to life quickly became joy of service to others as more and more pilgrims arrived for Passover, since Bethany was the "house of the afflicted." Families with members who were physically challenged often left for Jerusalem more than a month before Passover. [93] Roads were quite poor in the Roman Empire, especially during the rainy season, and progress could be very slow at times.

As we learned earlier, all those celebrating Passover were required to spend Passover night in Jerusalem. Over the centuries, the crowds at Passover grew to the point that Temple authorities had to expand the boundaries of "in Jerusalem" to include Mount Olivet and the towns of Bethphage and Bethany. Therefore, many of those who were physically challenged stayed in Bethany for Passover, quite likely at a facility operated by Lazarus, his sisters and some volunteers, including Jesus and His disciples. At some point, Jesus shared the Parable about the Attitude of a Servant with His Apostles.

11.1 Parable about the Attitude of a Servant [Luke 17:7-10]

He said to the Apostles
"Who among you would say to your servant
who has just come in from plowing or tending sheep in the
field, 'Come here immediately and take your place at table'?

Would he not rather say to him, 'Prepare something for me to eat. Put on your apron and wait on me while I eat and drink. You may eat and drink when I am finished'?

Is he grateful to that servant because he did what was commanded?

So, should it be with you. When you have done all you have been commanded, say, 'We are unprofitable servants; we have done what we were obliged to do.'"

11.2 The Spiritual Lesson in the Parable

Detail: (setting). Jesus was speaking in private to His Apostles, no crowd was present. Since He chose to use a parable to convey His message, we should expect that this was more than a "teaching moment" but something we must think deeply about.

Detail: The parable did not begin with: "There was a man who had a servant;" rather it began: *"Who among you would say to your servant."* At first, it might seem odd that Jesus would say this to His Apostles. We tend to think that only the wealthy had servants. But, in ancient Israel, servants were indentured debt-slaves. It is estimated that, in the time of Jesus, every 1 in 5 persons in the Roman Empire was an indentured debt-slave. People in indentured servitude were a regular part of everyday life in the Middle East. So, it's quite likely that at least some of the Apostles had servants, or their extended families had servants.

Detail: *"plowing or tending sheep in the field."* Plowing and shepherding were normally performed by members of the family, not the servants. The long-term sustainability of the family enterprise relied on these tasks being performed well. For servants to be given such trust and responsibility would have been quite unusual.

Detail: *"Come here immediately and take your place at table."* The proper posture for slaves was to stand when they ate. To "take one's place at table" was much more than sitting down to have a meal, it made one an honored guest of the host.

Detail: *"Would he not rather say to him, 'Prepare something for me to eat. ... You may eat and drink when I am finished.'"* This was not denigrating the servant; it was the culturally-appropriate "proper order" of things.

Detail: *"Is he grateful to that servant because he did what was commanded?"* While the servant was engaged in tasks unusual for a servant, the servant would not have taken them on of his own volition. He would have responded to an authoritative order or command. To be "grateful" was more than to show appreciation;

but, it was to receive with thankfulness. The unspoken question to be pondered: "Why did the master act in the way he did?"

Detail: *"So should it be with you. When you have done all you have been commanded, say, 'We are unprofitable servants; we have done what we were obliged to do.'"* The Jewish expectation was that the more righteous deeds you performed, the more favored you would be with God.

Since Peter would later say to Jesus: *"We have given up everything and followed you. What will there be for us?"* [Mt 19:27; Mk 10:28; Lk 18:28], we take from this that the Apostles did not understand the parable; probably because they had not answered the unspoken question. Jesus replied that *"many who are first will be last, and the last will be first"* [Mt 19:30; Mk 10:31]. But, they needed the lessons of later events to fully comprehend this.

In our case, we are able to look back on the death and resurrection of Jesus and see that, just as God "received us" out of pure love, the "master" in the parable acted out of love for his servant which neither we nor the servant had earned. All the faithful followers of Christ are offered the same gift of love - eternal life. We are called to act without expecting recognition in this life. Recognition may be nice to receive, but the faithful followers of Jesus should not expect it. And, there's no preferential treatment in eternal life with God; which by human standards just "doesn't seem right." But, eternal life with God is so magnificently beyond what each one of us could ever imagine, that preferential treatment has no meaning.

The joy in Lazarus' household was short lived, however. Word came to them from Jerusalem that the Sanhedrin had ordered the arrest of Jesus. As John put it in his Gospel: *"So Jesus no longer walked about in public among the Jews, but he left for the region near the desert, to a town called Ephraim, and there he remained with his disciples"* [Jn 11:54]

The town of Ephraim was in Samaria near the border with Judea. It was a very unlikely place for the Temple guards to look for

Jesus. The Tribe of Ephraim had been at odds with others ever since Moses' blessing of the tribes at the end of the Exodus [Deu 33:17]. But, it was also quite likely the town that had rejected Jesus just a few months earlier as they passed through Samaria. So, in going there they had to avoid the notice of the local townspeople or pilgrims who were passing through.

As a practical matter, where they went to stay near Ephraim had to be able to accommodate what was quite likely about twenty people for a period of a week or more. First century homes were not large enough for that; so biblical scholars have concluded they had to have stayed somewhere outside the town of Ephraim. There was a location that would fit that situation very well; just south of Ephraim was Mount Hazor. Rising some 3400 feet above sea level, Mount Hazor is more a tilted plateau than a mountain; it has excellent grazing land. As far back as the time of King David, it was common for a wealthy landowner to operate an *eder-machaneh* ("sheep-camp") on the plateau, which was known then as Baal-hazor ("husband of grass"). A sheep-camp consisted of pastures, pens, shearing-houses and dwellings all on one property. [94] Since Jesus and His disciples had to leave Bethany in haste, it's most likely that Lazarus, or a very close friend of his, owned such a sheep-camp on Mount Hazor. Consequently, it's quite likely that Martha and Mary, Lazarus' sisters, were with them although John tells us that Lazarus remained in Bethany [Jn 12:1].

Since shearing season was not until May-June, [95] Jesus and His disciples likely had a good bit of leisure time to walk the pastures of Mount Hazor. And, as they walked they would have again crossed the tragic path of David and his son Absalom. Absalom was born of Maacha, King David's third wife. Maacha also bore David's only daughter, Tamar (not to be confused with Jacob's daughter-in-law who was also named Tamar and is mentioned in the genealogy of Jesus [Mt 1:3]).

Tragically, David's eldest son, Amnon, raped Tamar, his half-sister [2 Sam 13:14]. But, King David did nothing to punish Amnon [2 Sam 13:21]. This infuriated Absalom. *"Two years went by. It was sheep-shearing time for Absalom in Baal-hazor near Ephraim, and Absalom invited all the king's sons"* [2 Sam 13:23], including Amnon. At the feast celebrating the conclusion of shearing, Absalom had his brother Amnon killed, and all the guests fled in horror [2 Sam 13:28-29]. This was the beginning of Absalom's revolt against his father, which led to a brutal civil war that almost destroyed the kingdom.

Throughout their history since the time of Cain and Abel, brother has killed brother. It happened twice in David's family alone, Absalom killed his brother Amnon, and later, Solomon killed his brother Adonijah. Thoughts of these tragedies would have weighed heavily on them as Jesus and His disciples walked the pastures stained by the blood of their ancestors.

We might wonder how events that happened as much as a thousand years earlier could still be on their minds and in their conversations as they walked along. But, today we don't have anywhere near the rootedness in history those people had. Their past was very much their present. They read their scriptures every day; they heard the stories again and again; they talked about them as though they happened yesterday. They were not rehashing old tragedies but re-learning old lessons. There had evolved "proper ways" to handle conflicts within families; but when those ways were ignored, violence, anguish and heartache was the result.[96]

It was late March and Passover was drawing closer. It seems from Jesus' recent words that He was very much aware that this was the Passover when it would all happen. He had accepted His Father's will that He *"must suffer greatly and be rejected by the elders, the chief priests, and the scribes, and be killed and on the third day be raised"* [Lk 9:22]. The salvation of mankind was Jesus' destiny, and no one could take that from Him. But, whether His legacy of bringing about the Kingdom of God on earth would continue was not that certain. As the leading rabbi of those times, Gamaliel, would point out to the Sanhedrin: many popular movements, led by ones thought to be the Messiah, came to an early end as soon as their leader was executed [cf. Acts 5:36-39]. The same could happen to Jesus' followers, as well.

There was one thing that Jesus had no control over, by His choice: man's free will. Free will is God's way of ensuring that those who will spend eternity in His presence will be there by their own choice. But, free will is very much a two-edged sword. It had been the undoing of Satan and his band, and they have been wreaking havoc on God's creation ever since [cf. Rev 12:7-12]. Jesus knew that His followers would be challenged to their very limits. He would use every opportunity to bring them to a deeper understanding of His Heavenly Father and what was being asked of them. And, He would give them His very self in the Eucharist to see them through their darkest hours. But, ultimately, each disciple's free will would work in the decision, made again and again, to continue or to abandon Jesus' mission in the world. This all must have weighed heavily on Jesus as the time grew near for Him to head back to Jerusalem, for the last time.

And, He must have known at this point that there was something not right with Judas Iscariot. Jesus had chosen Judas to be an Apostle and had shared with him everything that He had shared with all the others. But, Jesus also could read the hearts of man like no one else ever could. We have no way of knowing how often and in what ways Jesus reached out to Judas. These are details known only to God. We've seen Jesus' compassion, not just for those who were hurting, those on the very margins of life, but even for the Pharisees who mostly showed Him contempt. Jesus' heart must have ached for Judas long before that fatal kiss in the Garden [cf. Mt 26:47-50; Mk 14:43-45; Lk 22:48-49].

We know from the Gospels that Mary, the mother of Jesus, was with Him during His passion, death and resurrection in Jerusalem. But, the evangelists gave us no direct information on when Mary met up with Jesus for that final Passover. From what little information we have, there appears to have been only two locations where their being re-united might have occurred: at Lazarus' home in Bethany or at this place outside of Ephraim. Since Jesus' "brothers" were also in Jerusalem that Passover [Acts 1:14], it's possible that Mary traveled with them from Galilee. And, since there would have been a number of adult males in the group, they could have taken the Shechem Road through Samaria to Ephraim and reunited there; we just don't know. But, we do know that during the most difficult days in Jesus' life his mother, Mary, was there with Him.

Jesus likely spent much time in prayer while near Ephraim. Indeed, He may have spoken about it with His disciples, either together or in one-on-one conversations, because at some point He shared two parables on understanding prayer in a much different way that they had been accustomed to. Jesus began with the Parable of the Persistent Widow.

11.3 The Parable of the Persistent Widow [Luke 18:1-7]

Then Jesus told them a parable about the necessity for them to pray always without becoming weary. He said,

> "There was a judge in a certain town who neither feared God nor respected any human being. And a widow in that town used to come to him and say, 'Render a just decision for me against my adversary.'
>
> For a long time, the judge was unwilling, but eventually he thought, 'While it is true that I neither fear God nor respect any human being, because this widow keeps bothering me I shall deliver a just decision for her lest she finally come and strike me.'"

The Lord said, "Pay attention to what the dishonest judge says. Will not God then secure the rights of his chosen ones who call out to him day and night? Will he be slow to answer them?"

11.4 The Spiritual Lesson in the Parable

Detail: (setting) Jesus was speaking to His disciples; a group who would certainly have been considered devout Jews. As we learned earlier, prayer among devout Jews had long been something that was done primarily in public. Prayer, fasting and almsgiving were the ways in which a Jew showed his/her faith. Jesus began, through His own example, to teach His disciples about praying in solitude. Using this parable, Jesus addressed yet another dimension of prayer that they were not familiar with.

Luke began his recounting the parable with the statement: *"Jesus told them a parable about the necessity for them to pray always without becoming weary"* [Lk 18:1]. It was most unusual for a Middle

Eastern storyteller, in this case Luke, to state the purpose in telling the parable. This may have simply been Luke's way of making clear to his listeners his purpose in recounting the parable, because the parable relies a good deal on insights into Jewish scriptures and prayer practices.

Detail: *"There was a judge in a certain town who neither feared God nor respected any human being."* The usual forum for Jews to resolve "legal" disputes was to bring the issue before the local elders. The community elders were charged with upholding the rights of those in their community. This was a sacred duty and the place where they convened their hearings was regarded as a frontier where the divine plane and the human plane met. In rural settings, they convened on the floor of the main threshing barn; in urban settings, it was at the gates to the community. One initiated their case by simply going before the elders and shouting "justice, justice!" [97]

But in this parable, the woman is not before the community elders; instead, she is before a "judge." In the Roman Empire, a *praetor* (Latin for "judge") was an official appointed to hear legal disputes between Roman citizens and foreigners. So, this woman's adversary was a Roman citizen over whom the community elders had no jurisdiction.

In outlying areas of the Empire, such as ancient Israel, most judge appointees were unpaid, and many enriched themselves through bribes. They decided cases based on who paid the larger bribe. The phrase, *neither feared God nor respected any human being,* suggests that this judge's judgment was influenced by bribes. The corruptness of judges in Israel was such a part of their everyday lives that it was spoken of frequently in their rabbinic commentaries.[98] So, this woman was in an essentially impossible situation, having to present her case against a Roman citizen before a Rome-appointed judge.

Detail: *"a widow in that town used to come to him and say, 'Render a just decision for me against my adversary.' For a long time, the judge was unwilling."* The judge was delaying to see how large a bribe she would offer. This showed how uninformed the judge was about the woman's circumstances. In ancient Israel, the only thing a widow could own was her *mohar*, which she received at the time of her marriage as her "social security" in the event of her husband's death. Evidently, her adversary had extorted or cheated her out of some or all of her *mohar*. She couldn't have paid a large bribe even if she were inclined to. And, she was not - rather, she kept reiterating her case and calling for justice.

There was a backdrop story from their scriptures that Jesus was paralleling with this parable. It comes from the Book of Sirach, long known as Ecclesiasticus Liber ("church book"), which was often read in their synagogues.[99]

> *For God always repays and will give back to you*
> *sevenfold. But offer no bribes; these he does not accept!*
>
> *Do not trust in sacrifice of the fruits of extortion,*
> *For he is a God of justice, who shows no partiality.*
>
> *He shows no partiality to the weak*
> *but hears the grievance of the oppressed.*
> *He does not forsake the cry of the orphan,*
> *nor the widow when she pours out her complaint.*
>
> *Do not the tears that stream down her cheek*
> *cry out against the one that causes them to fall?*
>
> *Those who serve God to please him are accepted;*
> *their petition reaches the clouds.*
>
> *The prayer of the lowly pierces the clouds;*
> *it does not rest till it reaches its goal;*
> *Nor will it withdraw till the Most High responds,*
> *judges justly and affirms the right.*
>
> *God indeed will not delay,*
> *and like a warrior, will not be still*
> *Till he breaks the backs of the merciless.*
>
> [Sir 35:13-22].

<u>Detail:</u> "eventually he thought, 'While it is true that I neither fear God nor respect any human being ...'" The basic elements of a

widow crying out for justice, the issue of extortion, the subject of bribes, and a deliberative judge are in both the prototype story in Sirach and in Jesus' parable. But in the parable, the deliberative judge is corrupt.

Jesus repeated the phrase: *neither fear God nor respect any human being* to emphasize through repetition, that the judge was corrupt and felt no shame for it. In the Middle Eastern culture, one who felt no shame had no sense of honor to which anyone could appeal. This underscores the hopelessness of the widow's situation in the parable as compared to the widow's situation in the prototype story. This detail is intended to prepare the listeners for something most unexpected.

Detail: "*because this widow keeps bothering me I shall deliver a just decision for her lest she finally come and strike me.*" In the prototype story in Sirach, the deliberative judge was God and the way to influence God in your favor was to do things that pleased God [Sir 35:20]. That is, one had to earn God's favor in prayer. That was the prayer-lesson Jesus' listeners had heard in their synagogues for generations.

In the parable, the widow's conviction and unwavering trust that she would receive justice, even in the face of what seemed to be a hopeless situation, so intimidated the dishonest judge that he ruled in her favor. Jesus' listeners would have been astonished; they knew that the judge's concern was entirely unrealistic. The Roman policy of *vastatio* ("retaliate a hundred-fold") was well-known. For a Jew ("foreigner" under Roman Law) to attack a Roman official would be disastrous, for the attacker and the whole community around him/her.

Jesus concluded with the statement: "*Pay attention to what the dishonest judge says. Will not God then secure the rights of his chosen ones who call out to him day and night? Will he be slow to answer them?*" There is no need to earn God's favor in prayer. If a dishonest judge could be persuaded in your favor by conviction and unwavering trust in justice, will not our loving God be even more ready to answer our prayers?

In only a matter of days, Jesus' disciples would need to remember this parable. They will need to see prayer differently from what they had been accustomed to. For, things will seem hopeless; it will seem that God is not listening. But, there would be no need to earn God's favor; conviction and unwavering trust that God's will is at work was what they needed.

After bidding farewell to those who had so graciously provided for them near Ephraim, "*six days before the Passover,*" which was Nisan 9 (March 28/29), 33 AD, "*Jesus came to Bethany where Lazarus was*" [Jn 12:1]. No sooner had they arrived, and Jesus was invited to dine as the guest of Simon the Leper [Mt 26:6-13; Mk 14:3-10]. John tells us that Lazarus and his sisters were there. At the dinner, Mary anointed Jesus' feet and dried them with her hair. The disciples, at the instigation of Judas, were indignant at this seeming waste of ointment [Jn 12:4-8]. It seems that, at this point, Mary was the only one in the group who had understood what Jesus had been saying about His impending suffering and death.

When many others learned that Jesus was in Bethany, a great crowd assembled there, not to see Jesus only but also Lazarus; hence the Chief Priests thought of killing Lazarus too [Jn 12:9-10]. Confronting them, Jesus spoke the Parable of the Pharisee and the Tax Collector.

11.5 Parable of the Pharisee and Tax Collector [Luke 18:9-14]

Jesus then addressed this parable to those who were convinced of their own righteousness and despised everyone else.

1. "Two people went up to the temple area to pray;
   one was a Pharisee and the other was a tax collector.
2.   The Pharisee took up his position and spoke this prayer to himself, 'O God, I thank you that I am not like the rest of humanity—
3.   greedy, dishonest, adulterous—or even like this tax collector.
4.   I fast twice a week, and I pay tithes on my whole income.'

5.   But, the tax collector stood off at a distance and would not even raise his eyes to heaven,
6.   but beat his breast and prayed,
      'O God, be merciful to me a sinner.'
7. I tell you, the latter went home justified, not the former.

For everyone who exalts himself will be humbled, and the one who humbles himself will be exalted."

11.6 The Spiritual Lesson in the Parable

Detail: (Setting) Luke said that Jesus was addressing *"those who were convinced of their own righteousness and despised everyone else"* – a clear reference to the Pharisees in the crowd. Again, Luke states the purpose in telling the parable; but there's more to the parable than a lesson on self-righteousness.

Detail: (literary construct) In listening to the parable, we may note that there appears to be more details than the storyline needs and suspect that we are hearing a chiasm. But, on further examination, we find that, although there is parallelism the subjects presented in the forward sequence are not repeated in the reverse sequence. The construct is a seven-stanza ballad rather than a chiasm. We will later encounter a seven-stanza balled in the Parable of the Feast as recounted in Luke's Gospel.

The object of this construct is to increase the contrast between competing concepts or characters. In the 1st stanza, two went up to pray; in the 7th stanza, two went down, but the Pharisee was mentioned first in the 1st stanza while the tax collector was mentioned first in the 7th stanza. The 2nd stanza describes the Pharisee's prayer posture; while the 6th stanza describes the tax collector's prayer posture. The 3rd stanza states the Pharisee's impression of the tax collector, while the 5th stanza states the reality of the tax collector. Lastly, the 4th or middle stanza is the Pharisee's justification for why he thinks he's a righteous man. [100]

Detail: *"Two people went up to the temple area to pray; one was a Pharisee and the other was a tax collector."* The two were specifically going to pray in the Temple. There was one service in the Temple in the early morning and a second service in the late afternoon. The Temple was "a house of prayer" [Lk 19:46]. Community worship and prayer were one and the same thing; prayer in the Temple was out loud, very public and not in unison. There were often hundreds, if not thousands, of others also praying in the same area; many overhearing each other's prayers. The two were at opposite ends of the social spectrum but going to pray in the same area.

Detail: *"The Pharisee took up his position and spoke this prayer to himself."* In principle, everyone was equal in the Temple. But, in practice this one's "position" was likely front-and-center for dramatic effect. The phrase: "spoke this prayer to himself" meant that he was praying to himself, not to God. It does not mean that he was engaged in silent prayer.[101]

Detail: *"O God, I thank you that I am not like the rest of humanity —greedy, dishonest, adulterous—or even like this tax collector."* Jewish prayer always began with thanks and praise of God, not praise of one's self. Such religious superiority by the Pharisees was precisely what Jesus cautioned His followers against. "Greedy" and "dishonest" were directed at the tax collector; then the Pharisee threw in "adulterous" just for good measure. To Jews, the Pharisee was not praying; there is no Psalm or Scripture passage that remotely resembles what the Pharisee was saying. He was making a public accusation against a fellow worshiper in their holy Temple, under the pretext of praying.

Detail: *"I fast twice a week, and I pay tithes on my whole income."* The Pharisee was clearly preaching to the lowly *am ha'aretz* ("people of the land") standing within ear-shot of him. A day's fast was required only on the Day of Atonement [Lev 25:29; Num 39:7]. To fast <u>twice a week</u> was extreme, even for the most fastidious Pharisee. Initially, tithes were only required on grain, wine and oil [Lev 27:30; Num 18:27]. Later, the Mishnah extended it to anything used as food.[102] By claiming to tithe on <u>everything,</u> the Pharisee was claiming a place among the *Sheluchim,* the holy ones (Moses, Isaiah, etc.). Jesus was using a very extreme example here to make His point.

Detail: *"But the tax collector stood off at a distance and would not even raise his eyes to heaven but beat his breast and prayed."* In sharp contrast to the Pharisee was this repentant man standing, not front-and-center but, off on the periphery. His posture was completely the opposite that of the Pharisee. The posture for prayer in the Temple was to stand with hands crossed over the chest and eyes cast down. To beat one's breast was an expression of great anguish; and, it is never mentioned in the Old Testament.[103] It only appears in this parable and as an expression by the witnesses upon the death of Christ on the cross [Lk 23:48]. This was the contrasting extreme example with regard to the tax collector.

Detail: *"O God, be merciful to me a sinner."* Jews would recognize the tax collector as praying; he was expressing the essence of Psalm 51:3. They did not attempt to recite their Scriptures verbatim; rather they sought the essence of each passage. For a Jew to ask God's mercy was more than a request for forgiveness or compassion. Their word for mercy was *hesed*, which literally meant to 'hold close to the heart.' The tax collector was begging God to hold him close to His heart for he had no merit of his own to commend him as being righteous.

Detail: *"I tell you, the latter went home justified, not the former."* The Temple service was concluded, a lamb had been sacrificed for the sins of those present, the people prayed, and the officiating priest had given them the benediction blessing. Since both the Pharisee and the tax collector *went home*, they were likely at the late afternoon service. The tax collector *went home justified*; the Pharisee did not. The Hebrew word, *tsadaq* ("justified"), literally meant to be in right balance. For the tax collector to go home from the Temple justified meant that he was in right balance with God, he was forgiven his transgressions and was now worthy to be in God's presence again.

Jesus concluded with the statement: *"everyone who exalts himself will be humbled, and the one who humbles himself will be exalted."* There are two other occasions recounted in the Gospel where He used those same words: in Mt 23:12 and in Lk 14:11. The Pharisees couldn't have missed that this parable was directed to them and their frequent displays of self-righteousness.

But, there's a much more profound message in this parable that many of those who were listening may never have thought of before. From the parable, the Temple service itself did not make the participants justified; it was the disposition of their hearts that made them justified. This is the same lesson Jesus shared with the Pharisees in Penuel only a few weeks earlier. Recall that the lesson of the first half of the Parable of the Prodigal Son was that repentance must arise out of the disposition of the heart.

The communal rites were an integral part of their communion with God. But for those rites to be fully effective the participants had to be properly disposed. This principle applies in the Church to this day. The sacraments are said to be efficacious, that is: they are successful in producing their intended result.

> *From the moment that a sacrament is celebrated in accordance with the intention of the Church, the power of Christ and his Spirit acts in and through it, independently of the personal holiness of the minister. Nevertheless, <u>the fruits of the sacraments also depend on the disposition of the one who receives them.</u>*
> [see article 1128 in the *Catechism of the Catholic Church*]

On the following day, Nisan 10, Jesus and His disciples set out for Jerusalem. "*As they approached Jerusalem and came to Bethphage on the Mount of Olives, Jesus sent two disciples, saying to them, 'Go to the village ahead of you, and at once you will find a donkey tied there, with her colt by her. Untie them and bring them to me*" [Mt 21:1; Mk 11:1; Lk 19:29-30]. This was in fulfillment of the words of Zechariah: "*See, your king comes to you, righteous and victorious, lowly and riding on a donkey, on a colt, the foal of a donkey*" [Zech 9:9]. A donkey was the symbol of peace. The village most likely was En-shemesh ("spring of the sun"). It was about a mile east of Bethany and the only spring on the road to Jericho. Archaeologists have concluded that it got its name due to the spring being in the direct sun light the whole day long.

A great crowd quickly surrounded them waving palm branches and shouting *"Hosanna"* (which meant "Lord, grant salvation" from Psalm 118:25). The waving of palm branches was prescribed for expressing rejoicing [Lev 23:40]. However, shouting *Hosanna* would have been regarded as treasonous by Romans, since the only living person who could be publicly acknowledged as a deity was Caesar. But, Romans would have been well out-of-sight in Jerusalem during Passover for fear of inciting public unrest.

As they rounded Mount Olivet on the Jericho Road and the city of Jerusalem first came into view, the crowd would have begun reciting with great pride the passage from Isaiah 2:3, as was their custom. But, Luke tells us that, Jesus *"saw the city and wept over it, saying, 'If this day you only knew what makes for peace—but now it is hidden from your eyes'"* [Lk 19:41-42]. How grand and sweeping was His power, yet how particularly personal was His love. He poured Himself out to every person He touched. Yet for many, that was not enough. His beloved Holy City not only rejected Him but would kill Him in the most hateful and grotesque manner imaginable. He wept not for Himself but for them and all they could have experienced had they *"recognized the time of their visitation"* [Lk 19:44].

It's difficult for many of us who did not grow up in the Jewish tradition to fully appreciate the deep visceral connection Jews of all times, Jesus and His disciples included, had for Jerusalem. From the ardent longing when they were away, to the aspirations breathed into almost every synagogue service, to the awe they would experience each time their Holy City came into view, no place on earth had such a hold on the psyche of a people than did Jerusalem in the time of Jesus.[104] But, on this occasion, Jesus wept. God Himself, in the flesh, had walked in their streets and they did not recognize Him.

11.7 Jerusalem and the Temple in the Time of Jesus

The area known today as Jerusalem was originally a cluster of three moderate sized mountains with fairly deep valleys between them. There was Mount Olivet (2641 feet above sea level), Mount Zion (2534 ft.) and Mount Moriah (2438 ft.). The first settlement in the area dates from about 4500 BC near the Gihon ("gushing")

Spring. The spring was located in a cave in the Kidron Valley which separates Mount Olivet from Mount Moriah. The spring flowed only intermittently. So, a large reservoir, later called the Pool of Siloam, was dug to store water during periods of draught. Later, large aqueducts brought water from the Pools of Solomon, located southwest of Bethlehem.

The Tyropoeon Valley separated Mount Zion from Mount Moriah. The Hinnom Valley ("Gehenna" in Greek) was west and south of Mount Zion and merged with the Kidron Valley south of the city. In approximately 1850 BC, Abraham came to Mount Moriah [Gen 22:2] to sacrifice his son, Isaac, as God had commanded. At the last moment, Abraham was prevented from carrying out the sacrifice and he named the place *Yahweh-yireh* ("the Lord will provide") [Gen 22:14]. This was later shortened to *Yireh*. It was in a nearby area called Salem ("peace"), where the priest-king, Melchisedek, went out to meet Abraham and bless him. The name Yireh-Salem later became Jerusalem ("provider of peace").

In 1010 BC, King David captured the city from the Jebusites and declared it his capital. David built his palace on Mount Zion. It was later replaced by King Herod's palace. In 6 AD, Herod's son, Archelaus, was replaced by a Roman governor and the palace was renamed, the Praetorium ("commander's tent"). In 26 AD, Pontius Pilate became prefect (governor) of Judea and the Praetorium became Pilate's house when he was in Jerusalem. On the east side of the Praetorium was the Bema ("judgment seat"), which John referred to in his Gospel by its Hebrew name, *Gabbatha* [Jn 19:13]. It was from the bench on this elevated stone platform that Pilate condemned Jesus to death by crucifixion [Mt 27:23-24; Mk 15:14-15; Lk 23:23-24; Jn 19:16]. The remains of that platform were unearthed by archeologists in the 1970's.[105]

Northeast of the Praetorium was the Gennath Gate which opened onto the Shechem Road. It was through that Gate that Jesus carried His cross on the way to Gol'gotha ("place of the skull") [Mt 27:33; Mk 15:22; Lk 23:33; Jn 19:17]. The Church of the Holy Sepulcher has covered that site and the nearby Tomb of Jesus since 326 AD. In 1883, while visiting Jerusalem, a well-known military leader named Charles George Gordon strongly supported a popular argument at the time that Gol'gotha was actually Skull Hill. Skull

Hill came to be known as Gordon's Calvary. He also claimed that a nearby Garden Tomb was the actual burial place of Christ. This did not gain much support from the archeological community; however, these sites remain popular places of pilgrimage among Protestants. In about 962 BC, David's son, Solomon, had built the First Temple on Mount Moriah. Each king after David added his own palace, so by Jesus' day, Jerusalem had become a "city of marble palaces." Not even imperial Rome exceeded Jerusalem in architectural splendor in the first century. As enlarged by Herod the Great, the Temple, with its snowy white limestone, ornamented with gold plating and gilded pinnacles, with a gabled cedar roof with gold spikes on it, occupied an approximate square of roughly 1,000 feet on a side. This was more than one-half greater that the length of St Peter's Basilica in Rome. [103]

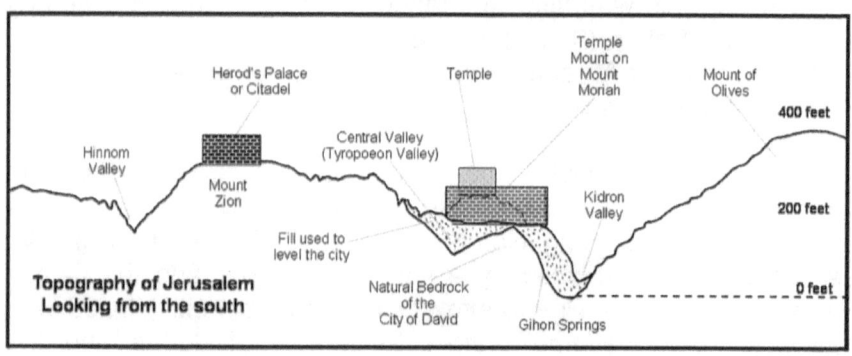

Figure 25: Topography of Jerusalem in the First Century

With the initial construction of Solomon's Temple; completed around in 962 BC; its subsequent destruction by the Babylonians in 587/586 BC; its rebuilding around 516 BC, and the subsequent expansion of the Temple by King Herod begun in 17 BC, considerable rock, rubble and dirt were used in filling portions of the Kidron and Tyropoeon valleys to level the land somewhat.

Mount Olivet ("mount of olives") was always fresh and green even during the dry season and the foliage of olive trees provided a leafy canopy overhead for the many that leisurely walked its pathways. There were no cultivated gardens, as we use the term "garden;" they let nature adorn the area as it saw fit. What is known as the Garden of Gethsemane ("oil press") was a small area near the base of Mount Olivet where all the olive trees had been originally planted from the same parent plant. [106]

In addition to olive trees, there were also wild berry bushes, a number of fig and fruit trees and a few cypress trees scattered about. There was also a cluster of palm trees on the Jericho Road ascending the east side of Mt Olivet

During most of the year, approximately 500,000 residents occupied some 6 1/3 square miles of the city. But, during Passover, nearly 2.5 million people were in Jerusalem in the first century. The city walls had nearly a hundred lookout towers surrounding the city, built by King Herod when he lavishly embellished the city as his legacy. The main streets of the city were very narrow, cobble stone paved, with an elevated footway along one side for those who had purified themselves in a *mikvah* as they headed to the Temple. Everyone else walked in the lower street way.

The city streets were named after the city gate that opened onto that street. The houses and shops were packed together with no apparent plan, typical of ancient cities. Every few houses there were narrow passageways giving access to shared courtyards behind. Ladders behind the houses led to canopy-covered roofs where the family would sleep during hot weather and pilgrims would sleep when they were in the city. There was a great rock ledge on the western slope of the Hinnom Valley that provided a stunning panoramic view of the Temple and the whole city below.

The Antonia Fortress, at the northwest corner of the Temple, had a subterranean passageway into the Temple. The Roman soldiers used this as an avenue into the Temple's Court of Gentiles to quickly take control of the Temple to quell any public disturbance there. On the southern slope of Mount Moriah was the area known as Ophel, where the Temple priests resided when they were in the city on Temple duty.

Dcn. Bob Evans

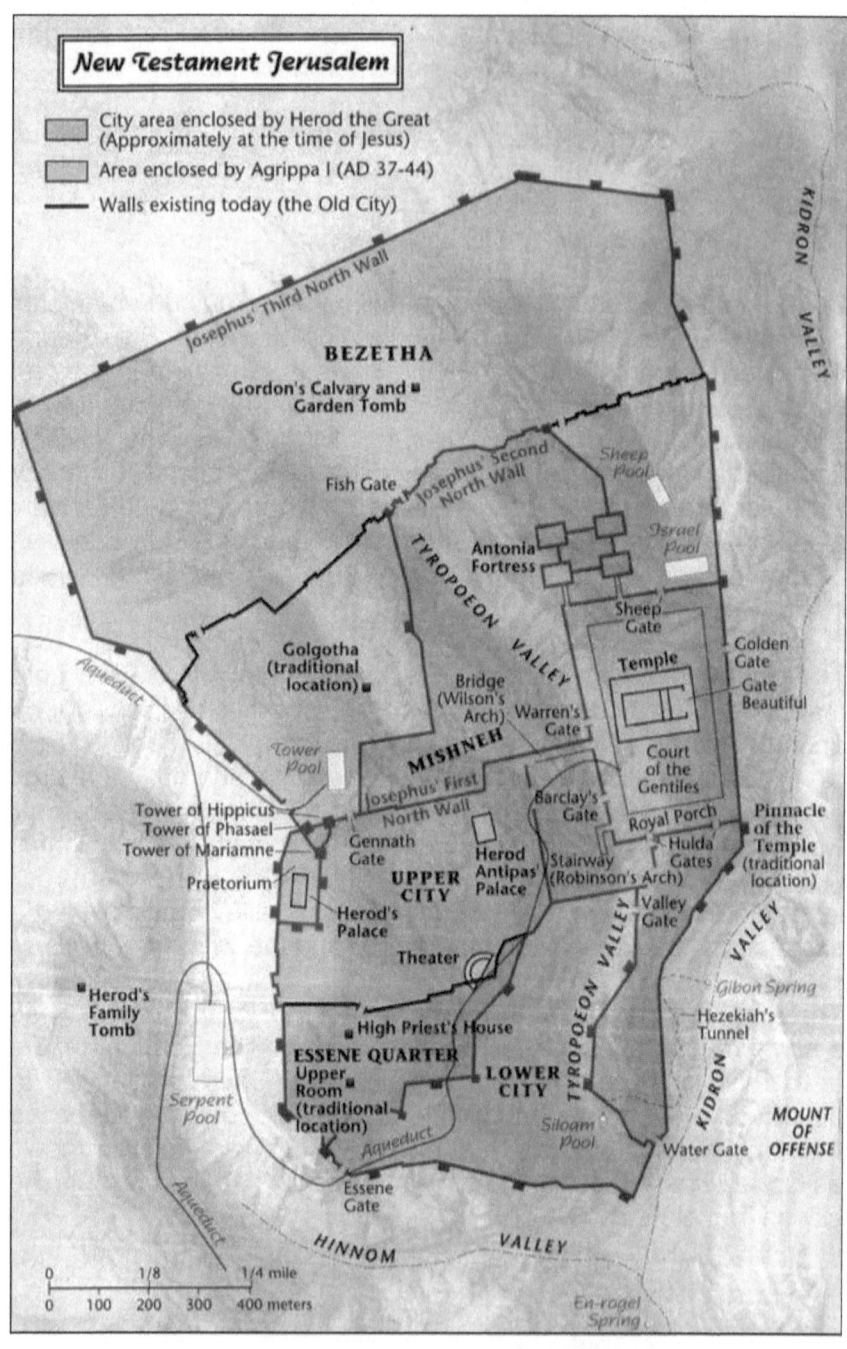

Figure 26: New Testament Jerusalem map

Southwest of the Temple, on the side of Mount Zion, was the Palace of the High Priest, with a large courtyard below, which was overlooked by a grand porch. It was in this courtyard that Peter denied Jesus three times. East of the Palace of the High Priest was the immense public square, known as The Xystus, surrounded by a covered colonnade. It was here that Peter addressed the crowd on Pentecost. Immediately south of The Xystus was The Maktesh, where all the bazaars connected with the Temple were located. Directly south of the Temple was the Water Gate which opened to the Kidron Valley and Mount Olivet.

The Temple was located on a plateau that had been formed at immense cost and labor on Mount Moriah. Beneath the Temple was a very large rectangular substructure that had been excavated for several hundred feet down and then built out in stone to ensure that there were no ancient human remains buried there that would have defiled the Temple. The Temple itself rose terrace-by-terrace upon this substructure.

One of the architectural wonders of its day was the Royal Bridge that crossed the Tyropoeon Valley from Mount Zion to the porch area of the Temple. The Royal Bridge still stood from the days when the queen of Sheba marveled at it [1 Kgs 10:5]. It was 50 feet wide and consisted of a series of 40-foot arches, carefully constructed of stone blocks, each weighing nearly 100 tons. The amount of engineering and physical effort required to transport and place those stones rivaled the building of the pyramids in Egypt. It was across this bridge that they led Jesus, in sight of all of Jerusalem, from the Palace of the High Priest to the meeting chamber of the Sanhedrin in the Temple. Over the centuries since, so much rubble and dirt has been used to fill in the Tyropoeon Valley that the remains of the Royal Bridge are now more than a hundred feet below ground level.

The porch area of the Temple ran all around the inside of the Temple wall, bounding the Court of the Gentiles. The porch was lined with marble pillars each cut from a single block of marble 37 feet high. The porch area was the community meeting place where people sat on benches often "debating" for hours on end.

The most popular area was known as Solomon's Porch (or the Portico of Solomon) which ran along the eastern wall of the Temple. It was most likely in one of these areas on the porch that Mary and Joseph found the young Jesus "*sitting in the midst of the teachers, listening to them and asking them questions*" [Lk 2:46]. This was also the place where, on the Feast of Dedication in December of 32 AD, Jesus was confronted by the Temple authorities demanding to know if He was the Messiah [cf. Jn 10:23]. Later, during Passover of 33 AD, He was again confronted by the Temple authorities there [Mt 21:23; Mk 11:27; Lk 20:1].

There were four main entrances to the Temple from the west and two long archways from the south, known as the Hulda Gates. People entered a Temple gate on the right and exited on the left. The outer court, The Court of the Gentiles, was paved with the finest variegated marble. It was the furthest a Gentile could go in the Temple, under pain of death. There were a series of small apartments in this area where Levites resided when they were on Temple duty. It was in this area that animals for sacrifice were sold and the money-changers conducted business, where Jesus vehemently drove them out [Jn 2:14; Mt 21:12-13; Mk 11:15-17; Lk 19:45-46].

From the Court of the Gentiles, nine staircases of fourteen steps led up to a barrier terrace, called the *Chel*, which surrounded the upper courts. The first upper court was the Court of Women, which as the name implies was the furthest women could proceed in the Temple. They entered the Court of Women through what was called the Beautiful Gate. It was in front of this gate that Peter cured the crippled beggar [Acts 3:1-10].

Along the north and south walls of the Court of Women was the Temple Treasury. It consisted of thirteen large wooden boxes with trumpet-shaped bronze funnels. The funnels guided the coins into the box and the sound these coins made against the metal would indicate how much people offered to the Temple. Recall that almsgiving was a very public act. It was here that Jesus observed the poor widow putting her last two coins in the Temple Treasury [Mk 12:41-44].

Walking the Parables of Jesus

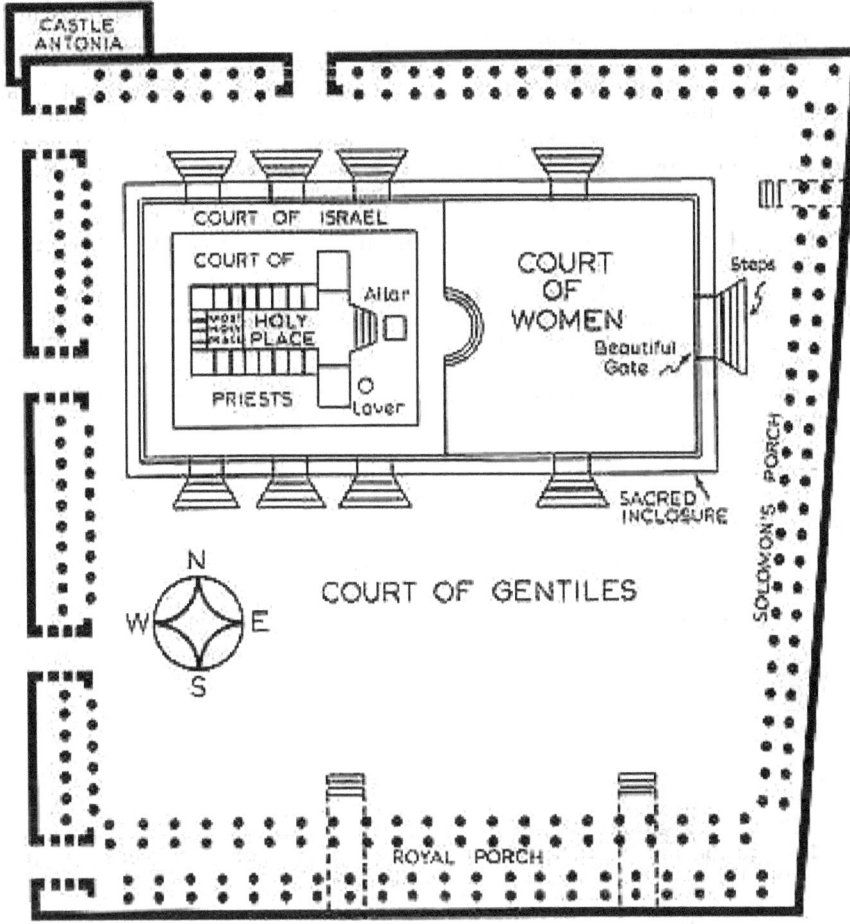

Figure 27: Map of the Temple in the First Century

A curved stairway of fifteen steps, led from the Court of Women to the Nicanor Gate, through a pair of huge bronze doors, into the Court of Israel, which was for all males who were not clergy. The doors were so large that it required the united strength of 20 men to open and close them. It was on this curved stairway that mothers presented their first-born sons to God, and the presentation of Jesus by Mary took place [Lk 2:22-40].

The Court of Israel surrounded the Court of Priests where was located the Altar of Burnt Offerings and the Laver of Cleansing (also known as the Brazen Sea) which rested upon twelve bulls cast in bronze. Just beyond the Altar of Burnt Offerings was a curtain, embroidered with a map of the then known world; which concealed from view the Holy Place where only priests on Temple duty could enter. The Holy Place contained a golden altar at which incense was offered and next to it was the golden lampstand, the Light of the World, and a table with the twelve loaves of Showbread (which were replaced by fresh ones every Sabbath).

Within the Court of Priests, behind the massive, priceless Temple Curtain, lay the Holy of Holies, where none except the High Priest was allowed to enter, and he only on the Day of Atonement. The Holy of Holies contained a stone designating the place where once the Ark of the Covenant had stood.

Proceeding on the Jericho Road, around the southwestern slope of Mount Olivet, in full view of the magnificent Temple, Jesus and the crowd would have crossed the Kidron Valley and, most likely, entered the city through the Water Gate, which was where the Jericho Road ended, and it was the main gate to the Temple area. It was in the square in front of this same gate, in the year 458 BC, that the all the people gathered to hear Ezra the Scribe read to them the entire Torah and declared it the official Law of Moses [cf. Neh 8:1-12]. This was a much-needed new beginning for the people in Ezra's day.

On this festive day, as the jubilant crowd entered the Water Gate with Jesus, a new beginning was at hand for them, as well. But, they would turn on Him in a matter of a few days and their new beginning slipped through their fingers. Once through the gate, they would have proceeded by the Xystus Square where even more people would have joined them. They most likely entered the Temple through one of the very popular Hulda Gates on the south side of the Temple.

Sometime after entering the Temple area, a group of Greeks *"who had come up to worship at the feast"* [Jn 12:20], approached Philip asking to see Jesus. They wanted to know if Jesus was the Messiah. Jesus gave a reply that startled them all: *"The hour has come for the Son of Man to be glorified. Amen, amen, I say to you, unless a grain of wheat falls to the ground and dies, it remains just a grain of wheat; but if it dies, it produces much fruit"* [Jn 12:23-24]. The insight that only Peter had professed on the road from Caesarea Philippi, that the Messiah was also the Son of Man who must sacrifice himself for the redemption of all [cf. Mt 16:13-16; Mk 8:27-29; Lk 9:18-20] was now professed to Jews and Gentiles alike. Mark tells us that soon after entering the Temple area, Jesus *"looked around at everything and, since it was already late, went out to Bethany with the Twelve"* [Mk 11:11].

The next day, Nisan 11, perhaps a little after their sunrise meal, in preparation for His leaving, Jesus and Mary would have recited together the *Tefilat HaDerekh*, or "Traveler's Prayer." Facing each other, each with their head and shoulders covered by a *tallit*, or "prayer shawl," Mother and Son softly praying. God's plan was moving quickly now; it was not clear when she would see Him again. We don't know what they said to each other that day about what lay ahead, for either of them. It was for them to cherish and only God to know. On receiving Mary's blessing, Jesus departed from her and, with His disciples, left Bethany for the last time.

Along the way, they came upon a barren fig tree. In early April, the first fig crop of the year, the *bikkurah*, would not have been fully ripened [Mk 11:13b], but one would expect some fruit on a tree that was in full leaf. However, there was none at all. In frustration, Jesus "cursed" the fig tree [Mt 21:18-20; Mk 11:12-14]. "Cursing" the fig tree was a parable in action representing Jesus' judgment on the long-favored Jerusalem and its Temple which now "bore no fruit."

Later, upon entering the Court of Gentiles, Jesus drove the buyers and sellers from the Temple area for the second time [Mt 21:12-13, Mk 11:15-17; Lk 19:45-46]. This infuriated the Temple authorities who profited handsomely from these transactions.

That evening, they went to stay on Mount Olivet where they had stayed before. They would have no evening meal; they would have to make do with what fruit and berries they could pick while there was still light. There would be no way to cook anything.

Campfires were never lit in or near Jerusalem. The people were ultra-careful with open fires. In its entire history, Jerusalem never experienced a devastating fire that had not been set by an invading army. It was there, that evening on Mount Olivet, that Jesus shared the Parable of the Workers with His disciples.

11.8 The Parable of the Workers [Matthew 20:1-16]

Jesus said to His disciples,
> "The kingdom of heaven is like a landowner
> who went out at dawn to hire laborers for his vineyard.
> After agreeing with them for the usual daily wage,
> he sent them into his vineyard.
>
> Going out about nine o'clock, he saw others standing idle in the marketplace, and he said to them, 'You too go into my vineyard, and I will give you what is just.' So, they went off.
>
> And he went out again around noon, and around three o'clock, and did likewise.
>
> Going out about five o'clock, he found others standing around, and said to them, 'Why do you stand here idle all day?' They answered, 'Because no one has hired us.' He said to them, 'You too go into my vineyard.'
>
> When it was evening the owner of the vineyard said to his foreman, 'Summon the laborers and give them their pay, beginning with the last and ending with the first.'
>
> When those who had started about five o'clock came, each received the usual daily wage. So, when the first came, they thought that they would receive more, but each of them also got the usual wage.
>
> And on receiving it they grumbled against the landowner, saying, 'These last ones worked only one hour, and you have made them equal to us, who bore the day's burden and the heat.'

> He said to one of them in reply, 'My friend, I am not cheating you. Did you not agree with me for the usual daily wage? Take what is yours and go. What if I wish to give this last one the same as you? Am I not free to do as I wish with my own money? Are you envious because I am generous?'

Thus, the last will be first, and the first will be last."

11.9 The Spiritual Lesson in the Parable

Detail: *"The kingdom of heaven is like."* Jesus was again speaking of the Kingdom of Heaven to His disciples in private. So, this was not about Heaven, eternal life or anything to do with the afterlife. *"The Kingdom of Heaven (God) is at hand"* [Mk 1:15; Mt 3:2, 4:17], in this life.

Detail: *"a landowner who went out at dawn to hire laborers for his vineyard."* Ordinarily, the field foreman hired the daily workers. For the landowner to go out and hire his workers indicated very unconventional behavior.

Detail: *"agreeing with them for the usual daily wage"* - one denarius. This indicated conventional thinking; there was nothing to bargain about, one denarius was the standard wage. As we've learned earlier, a denarius a day was a subsistence level pay, one could just about feed a small family on that.

Detail: *"Going out about nine o'clock ... and he went out again around noon and around three o'clock ... going out about five o'clock."* The landowner went out <u>five</u> times during the day to hire workers, something most unconventional. Recall that the number five was symbolic of trouble.[134]

Detail: *"he saw others standing idle in the marketplace ... 'Why do you stand here idle all day? ... You too go into my vineyard.'"* This indicated the conventional way of thinking by landowners about hirelings - they are lazy and avoid work and need to be told what to do.

Detail: The landowner said to the later hirelings: *"I will give you what is just."* Jesus' listeners' concept of righteousness involved holding mercy and justice in balance, as God does. Their leaning was very much in the direction of justice. Their scriptures were full of passages extolling God as a God of justice. For example: *"The Rock! His work is perfect, for all his ways are just"* [Deu 32:4a]; *"I, the Lord, love justice"* [Isa 61:8a]; *"The Almighty will not pervert justice"* [Job 34:12b]; *"The strength of the King loves justice"* [Ps 99:12]; *"The Lord has established His throne for judgment"* [Ps 9:7]. They lived in a world of extreme injustice, so it was comforting for God to be a God of justice.

There were also passages extolling God's mercy, but much of the rabbinic commentary the people heard for generations leaned in the direction of justice. So, the expectation of Jesus' listeners was that the landowner would do the "just" thing: pay each worker in accordance with his effort – the conventional way of thinking.

Detail: *"The owner of the vineyard said to his foreman, 'Summon the laborers and give them their pay, beginning with the last and ending with the first.'"* The foreman would do the paying of each worker, which was the conventional way of thinking. But, the accepted order in paying workers was the first hired were paid first, the last hired were paid last.[107] This was from rabbinic interpretation of Deuteronomy 24:14-15:

> *You shall not exploit a poor and needy hired laborer, whether one of your own kindred or one of the resident aliens who live in your land, within your gates.* On each day you shall pay the laborer's wages before the sun goes down, since the laborer is poor and is counting on them. Otherwise the laborer will cry to the Lord against you, and you will be held guilty.

Detail: *"And on receiving it they grumbled against the landowner, saying, 'These last ones worked only one hour, and you have made them equal to us, who bore the day's burden and the heat.'"* This was outrageous behavior. A day laborer would never dare address a landowner in this way if he ever wished to work again in that region. Again, we hear of unconventional behavior.

Detail: *"He said to one of them in reply, 'My friend, I am not cheating you. Did you not agree with me for the usual daily wage? Take what is yours and go. ... Are you envious because I am generous?'"* Shocking, the landowner addressed the day laborer as "Friend" and acted out of generosity, not justice. Yet, the thinking displayed is conventional: "you agreed to a usual wage and that's what you were paid, Go."

There is a pattern to what the details have conveyed. We are hearing another common literary construct often used in biblical times, called a *semukha* ("juxtaposition").[108] Juxtaposition took two distinct forms: (1) Duality – placing two things in contrast to each other so that their characteristics become more evident, such as: good-evil, light-dark, divine-human, etc. And, (2) Antithesis [109] – placing in contrast two loosely related or contradictory ideas to draw attention to an underlying principle, such as: Jesus placed *"You shall not commit adultery"* [Mt 5:27b] in juxtaposition to *"whoever looks with lust on another has already committed adultery in his heart"* [Mt 5:28] to point out the underlying principle that we are to keep sacred relationships sacred. [110] The sexual relationship between man and woman is sacred; it is God's empowerment of mankind to share in His life-giving work.

In this parable, Jesus has placed conventional thinking in juxtaposition to unconventional behavior to point to an underlying principle. The underlying principle was hinted at but was not explicitly stated; it's up to the listener to discern the principle being taught. Recall that, in Middle Eastern storytelling, dialogue is more telling than narrative.

The hint is in the landowner's words: *"I will give you what is just ... Are you envious because I am generous?"* The listeners expected him to act in a way that heavily leaned to justice (pay the laborers based on their effort), but, he acted in a way that heavily leaned to mercy (pay each what he needed that day to support his family). Jesus was teaching His listeners, those there that evening, and all of us today, that in the Kingdom of Heaven mercy takes precedence over justice. If His followers are truly to be righteous people, that is, hold mercy and justice in balance, as God does, then, we must place mercy well above justice in our dealing with one another.

History has shown that the lesson in this parable is of enormous importance. In the lifetime of Jesus' first listeners, there was the threat of a great split in the Church over whether those who had not been circumcised should be "allowed" to be Christians. After much debate, mercy took precedence over justice and circumcision was not made a requirement to be Christian. In the following generation, an even bigger conflict arose. During the period of the Reign of Terror, 90-96 AD, there were many thousands of apostates (those who renounced the faith in the face of persecution). When Emperor Domitian was assassinated by the Roman Senate, the Reign of Terror ended. And, many apostates wanted to come back into the Church. The Church struggled for decades over: "Are we to accept apostates back; and if so, how do we do that?" In the end mercy prevailed. In our own times, there are many whose "behavior and lifestyles" cause them to be rejected as being "outside the Church." The very sustainability of the Church in the twenty-first century may depend on whether the lesson of this parable again prevails.

Jesus concluded the parable with the phrase: *"the last will be first, and the first will be last"* [Mt 20:16]. That statement appears to have been used to connect two seemingly unrelated events to teach a common lesson. The previous use of the phrase, stated in reverse order, was in response to Peter's attempt to understand the Parable about the Attitude of a Servant (see section 11.2). God's values and ways are not the same as earthly values and ways. To live our earthly life as God intended, we much adopt God's values and ways.

The following morning, Nisan 12, Jesus and His disciples would have sought out hospitality in the city for their morning meal and they headed for the Temple. There, Jesus was confronted by the Temple authorities who demanded: *'By what authority are you doing these things; who gave you this authority?'"* [Mt 21:23; Mk 11:27; Lk 20:1].

This was clearly an honor challenge; basically, they were saying "who gave you the authority to do this? We're in charge here; how dare you come in and chase these people out." Recall that the culturally appropriate manner to deal with an honor challenge is to pushback with an even bigger question. So, Jesus said: "*I shall ask you one question, and if you answer it for me, then I shall tell you by what authority I do these things. Where was John's baptism from? Was it of heavenly or of human origin?*" [Mt 21:24-25]. Because they feared the crowd who believed that John was a prophet, they replied: "**We do not know**" [Mt 21:27a; Mk 11:33a; Lk 20:7].

That was the most humiliating response for someone of that culture to answer. Normally, in the Middle East someone will offer an answer even if they don't know. Their culture says that they are to respond with what the listener expects. That's their natural inclination. "*So, he said to them: 'neither shall I tell you by what authority I do these things'*" [Mt 21:27b; Mk 11:33b; Lk 20:8]. The Temple authorities showed themselves to be incapable of speaking with authority; hence Jesus refused to discuss with them the grounds of His authority.

The "Temple authorities" were selected and directed by the 72-member Jewish Supreme Court, the *Sanhedrin*. The court was composed of three groups: the Chief Priests, the Elders and the Scribes. Each group held 24 seats on the court. The Chief Priests were all from the tribe of Levi, and in addition were to be direct descendants of Zadok, the High Priest during Solomon's reign. However, by the first century there were a number of High Priests who were not Zadokites. The Chief Priests were the religious elite of Israel.

In contrast, the Scribes were the religious scholars whose role it was to serve as the interpreters and copyists of God's law. They came from the "priestly" class: male individuals at least 30 years old who were patrilineal descendants of Aaron, the elder brother of Moses. Then there were the Elders, senior leaders of the most powerful clans in Israel. They were not clerics. They held power by virtue of their tribal influence and extensive land holdings. They were the aristocrats of Israel.

Dcn. Bob Evans

Both Mark and Luke report that it was the "*chief priests, the scribes, and the elders*" [Mk 11:27; Lk 20:1] who confronted Jesus that day in the Temple. However, Matthew reported that it was the "*chief priests and the elders*" [Mt 21:23]. It's not clear why Matthew did not include the Scribes; the religious scholars, as being among Jesus' challengers that day. This is one of those details whose purpose is now lost to history.

Although Jesus would not discuss with the Temple authorities the grounds for His authority, He went on to share with them two parables. We may wonder why. Jesus had successfully silenced His challengers. Why not just leave it at that and walk away? But, He did not. As we hear the two parables, we will see one of Jesus' most remarkable acts of compassion. Reflecting back on the purpose of Jesus' parables, they were to lead listeners to a fuller understanding of themselves, of God, and of their relationship with one another. Jesus' parables invited His listeners to introspection: to seeing themselves differently, free from the consuming effects of their everyday lives.

The two parables Jesus shared with the Temple authorities, His most vehement adversaries, were particularly intended to invite their introspection. These two parables were reminiscent of the Parable of the Poor Man's Ewe Lamb, told by the prophet Nathan to King David. It was Nathan's attempt to get David to see the error of his ways in impregnating Bathsheba, the wife of Uriah the Hittite and, David "got the message" and repented [2 Sam 12:1-15].

Jesus' attempting something similar with the Temple authorities would not change the course of God's plan of salvation. In the end, they would be responsible for Jesus' crucifixion. But, there was the possibility of changing the course of at least some of their lives. And, Jesus was willing to take that chance. We know of at least one Chief Priest, Nicodemus, whose life was changed by Jesus' teachings [Jn 3:1-21; 7:50-51; 19:39-42]. There may have been others. Nicodemus went on to become a saint whose feast day is celebrated on August 3rd.

Matthew tells us that Jesus began by sharing the Parable of the Two Sons.

11.10 Parable of the Two Sons [Matthew 21:28-32]

Jesus said to them "what is your opinion,
>A man had two sons.
>He came to the first son "Go out and work in the vineyard today." But he said in reply "I will not."
>But afterward, he changed his mind and he went.
>
>The man came to the other son and gave the same order. And he said in reply "Yes." But he did not go.

"Which of the two did his father's will?"
They answered, "The first."

Jesus said to them, "Amen, I say to you, tax collectors and prostitutes are entering the kingdom of God before you.

When John came to you in the way of righteousness, you did not believe him; but tax collectors and prostitutes did. Yet even when you saw that, you did not later change your minds and believe him.

11.11 The Spiritual Lesson in the Parable

Detail: (setting) Many of the Temple authorities lived lavish lifestyles while the average Jewish peasant struggled to survive. By the first century, the temple taxes combined with taxes imposed by Herod and by Rome were threatening the existence of the Jewish people. The people were carrying a burden they could scarcely bear or tolerate. Israel had become a powder keg waiting to ignite. So, the Temple authorities never moved about except in a group. This was the second confrontation Jesus had with them. The first was during the Feast of Dedication in December of 32 AD, when Jesus was confronted by them demanding to know if He was the Messiah [cf. Jn 10:23]. That previous confrontation, and this one as well, most likely took place in the area known as Solomon's Porch (or the Portico of Solomon). This means that there was a very large number of people who would have witnessed this confrontation.

Detail: *"Jesus said to them 'what is your opinion.'"* There was no mistaking; the parable was addressed to the Temple authorities. They were the challengers, and this parable is a continuation of His pushback. So, we should expect the parable to pose a profound question to the challengers. Recalling the Parable of the Good Samaritan, the question posed by the parable was not the question asked by Jesus at the conclusion of that parable. We should expect the same pattern here.

Detail: *"A man had two sons. He came to the first son "Go out and work in the vineyard today."* In this story, there is an exchange between a father and his son, not a landowner and his servant. This is crucial to understanding the parable. The father is not just sending his son out to work; he is sending him into the family vineyard. Every vineyard needed competent vine-keepers to properly prune the vines, to select the right canes as the fruiting canes for the current year and those that will be the fruiting canes for next year. The vine-keepers also removed any leaves that shaded the fruit buds from the sun. The role of vine-keepers was so essential to the quality of the resulting wine that the task was only performed by members of the family and most often only by the vineyard owner's sons. So, the father was calling on his son to perform a very essential and responsible duty that the whole family depended on.

Detail: *"But he said in reply 'I will not.'"* The commandment: "Honor your father and your mother" was not just care for or be obedient to – but honor. The highest virtue in the Middle East was honor. This son has dishonored his father. In their culture, to dishonor one's father was a capital crime. If the father chose to, he could bring his son up on charges in front of the village elders. If they found him guilty, he would be stoned to death.[111] That is how serious dishonoring one's father was.

The underlying principle behind "honor your father and your mother" is not just a matter of courtesy or politeness; we are to honor legitimate authority. For most of human history, the only authority that existed was one's parents. There was no police force; there was no government; it was parents who maintained order and civilization. They instructed the children on what was right behavior, what was not right behavior, and each one was required to always follow their parents' directions. These people know that they had to enforce proper honor and respect for parents or civilization would come apart. That's why "honor your father and your mother" was so important. For most of human history, it was essential to the very survival of civilization.

Detail: *"But afterward, he changed his mind and he went."* Repentance is about the recognition that one has gone too far; one has to 'turn-around and go back.' Guilt probably arose in the son, but he did more than feel guilty - he repented (turned around) and did what his father directed. Guilt is an emotion that has a way of undoing things, of being more of an impediment than a benefit. God does not ask of us a sense of guilt. In fact, quite the contrary, God would much rather we repented and accept His forgiveness and move on in life.

Detail: *"The man came to the other son and gave the same order. And he said in reply 'Yes.' But he did not go."* This son also dishonored his father by deceiving him. Recall from the Parable of the Shrewd Stewart that, in this culture, the one being deceived is the one dishonored, not the one doing the deceiving (see section 1.3.2). Further, he did not go; so, he disobeyed his father intensifying the dishonor. So, in this parable, both sons dishonored their father, in a matter of grave importance to the entire household.

Jesus then asked the Temple authorities: "which of the two did his father's will." They answered, "the first." That's true. The first did ultimately do his father's will. But, the unstated question posed by the parable was "Why did the first son change his mind, while the second one did not?" Just as in the Parable of the Good Samaritan, Jesus did not give enough information to come to a conclusion about the character in this story. The listeners can only come to a conclusion about themselves in the position of the one in the story – precisely the introspection the parable was intended to prompt.

And, Jesus didn't just leave the question hanging; He pushed them to some conclusion by pointing out:
"Amen I say to you; tax collectors and prostitutes are entering the Kingdom of God before you. When

> *John came to you in the way of righteousness you did not believe him, but the tax collectors and prostitutes did. And yet even when you saw that you did not change your mind and believe him."*

Both sons sinned grievously, but one changed his mind (i.e. repented) when he realized what he had done. "Why did you Temple authorities not change your minds? Do you not realize what you are doing?" What an incredibly kind way for Jesus to speak to them. This was part of His pushback, but it was not done in a hurtful way. Jesus had given them, those entrusted with a sacred duty to lead God's people, an opportunity to gracefully respond that "we didn't know." But, they remained silent. So, Jesus followed with another parable, the Parable of the Wicked Tenants. This parable was recounted by Matthew, Mark and Luke.

11.12 Parable of the Wicked Tenants

11.12.1 The Version in Matthew's Gospel [Matthew 21:33-46)]

Jesus then said to them, "Hear another parable.
> There was a landowner who planted a vineyard, put a hedge around it, dug a wine press in it, and built a tower.
> Then he leased it to tenants and went on a journey.
>
> When vintage time drew near, he sent his servants to the tenants to obtain his produce.
> But the tenants seized the servants and one they beat, another they killed, and a third they stoned.
> Again, he sent other servants, more numerous than the first ones, but they treated them in the same way.
>
> Finally, he sent his son to them, thinking,
> 'They will respect my son.' But when the tenants saw the son, they said to one another, 'This is the heir.
> Come, let us kill him and acquire his inheritance.'
>
> They seized him, threw him out of the vineyard, and killed him.

"What will the owner of the vineyard do to those tenants when he comes?"

They answered him, "He will put those wretched men to a wretched death and lease his vineyard to other tenants who will give him the produce at the proper times."

Jesus said to them, "Did you never read in the scriptures: 'The stone that the builders rejected has become the cornerstone; by the Lord has this been done, and it is wonderful in our eyes'?

Therefore, I say to you, the kingdom of God will be taken away from you and given to a people that will produce its fruit. [The one who falls on this stone will be dashed to pieces; and it will crush anyone on whom it falls.]"

When the chief priests and the Pharisees heard his parables, they knew that he was speaking about them.
And although they were attempting to arrest him, they feared the crowds, for they regarded him as a prophet.

11.12.2 The Version in Mark's Gospel [Mark 12:1-12]

Jesus began to speak to them in parables.
> "A man planted a vineyard, put a hedge around it, dug a wine press, and built a tower. Then he leased it to tenant farmers and left on a journey.
>
> At the proper time he sent a servant to the tenants to obtain from them some of the produce of the vineyard. But they seized him, beat him, and sent him away empty-handed. Again, he sent them another servant. And that one they beat over the head and treated shamefully. He sent yet another whom they killed. So, too, many others; some they beat, others they killed.
>
> He had one other to send, a beloved son.
> He sent him to them last of all, thinking, 'They will respect my son.' But those tenants said to one another, 'This is the heir. Come, let us kill him, and the inheritance will be ours.'

So, they seized him and killed him, and threw him out of the vineyard."

"What then will the owner of the vineyard do? He will come, put the tenants to death, and give the vineyard to others.

Have you not read this scripture passage:
'The stone that the builders rejected has become the cornerstone; by the Lord has this been done and it is wonderful in our eyes'?"

They were seeking to arrest him, but they feared the crowd, for they realized that he had addressed the parable to them. So, they left him and went away.

11.12.3 The Version in Luke's Gospel [Luke 20:9-19]

Then Jesus proceeded to tell the people this parable.
"A man planted a vineyard, leased it to tenant farmers, and then went on a journey for a long time.

At harvest time he sent a servant to the tenant farmers to receive some of the produce of the vineyard. But they beat the servant and sent him away empty-handed. So, he proceeded to send another servant, but him also they beat and insulted and sent away empty-handed. Then he proceeded to send a third, but this one too they wounded and threw out.

The owner of the vineyard said, 'What shall I do? I shall send my beloved son; maybe they will respect him.' But when the tenant farmers saw him they said to one another, 'This is the heir. Let us kill him that the inheritance may become ours.' So, they threw him out of the vineyard and killed him."

What will the owner of the vineyard do to them? He will come and put those tenant farmers to death and turn over the vineyard to others."

When the people heard this, they exclaimed, "Let it not be so!"

> But he looked at them and asked, "What then does this scripture passage mean: 'The stone which the builders rejected
> has become the cornerstone'?
> Everyone who falls on that stone will be dashed to pieces;
> and it will crush anyone on whom it falls."

The scribes and chief priests sought to lay their hands on him at that very hour, but they feared the people, for they knew that he had addressed this parable to them.

11.13 The Spiritual Lesson in the Parable

Detail: *"There was a landowner who planted a vineyard, put a hedge around it, dug a wine press in it, and built a tower. Then he leased it to tenants and went on a journey."* Why so much detail? Recall at Penuel when Jesus began the Parable of the Prodigal Son: "There was a man who had two sons." His listeners immediately thought of Isaac and his two sons, drawing on their knowledge of a prior event in their history. Well, here Jesus relied on the Temple authorities' knowledge of the passage in Isaiah chapter 5 known as the "Song of the Vineyard."

> *"Now let me sing of my friend, my beloved's song about his vineyard.*
> *My friend had a vineyard on a fertile hillside; He spaded it, cleared it of stones, and planted the choicest vines. Within it he built a watchtower, and hewed out a wine press. Then he waited for the crop of grapes."* [Isa 5:1-2]

The term, "vineyard," was frequently used as a metaphor for God's people [Isa 27:2; Ps 80:9,14,15; Jer 2:21; Jer 12:10; Ezk 17:7; Hosea 10:1; Nahum 2:2]. And, many of those present in the crowd would also have recognized the Song of the Vineyard.

In Isaiah's text, the man went and looked for a crop of grapes, but it yielded only wild grapes. The main problem with growing grapes is that one must prune a great deal to concentrate the energy of the plant into a few fruiting branches, or canes. If the vine is allowed to just grow at will, all the fruit will be bitter. So, one must select the branches, usually those closest to the main stalk, that have the best buds on them and then remove all the rest. This eliminates that which would detract from feeding what will bear the best fruit.

Isaiah's prophecy of the destruction of Jerusalem by the Babylonians follows the vineyard song. Jews regarded Isaiah's vineyard song as a lead in to the downfall and destruction of Jerusalem; and, Jesus was relying on that as he began this parable.

Mark's version begins with essentially the same words. However, Luke's version begins with: *"A man planted a vineyard, leased it to tenant farmers, and then went on a journey for a long time."* Luke's listeners had no knowledge of the "Song of the Vineyard," so there was no point in his repeating the details from the vineyard song.

<u>Detail</u>: *"When vintage time drew near, he sent his servants to the tenants to obtain his produce."* The tenancy agreement, then, involved paying a portion of their produce as rent, which was a very common arrangement. Mark's version and Luke's version both say that the landowner sent <u>one</u> servant not a group of servants (as in Matthew's version). This starts to make the parable parallel Jesus' own story.

<u>Detail</u>: *"But the tenants seized the servants and one they beat, another they killed, and a third they stoned."* This was how they treated the prophets. In Mark's version and Luke's version the violence against the servant builds over time but he was not killed (as in Matthew's version). Later, it was the son who was killed, further pointing to Jesus' own story. Luke's listeners were unfamiliar with the fate of the prophets. The Gentiles had no history of prophets.

<u>Detail</u>: *"Finally, he sent his son to them, thinking, 'They will respect my son.'"* Mark made the point that there was only <u>one</u> son, a beloved son, to send, paralleling Jesus' story. Using a little different wording, Luke also makes the point that it was the man's one "beloved son."

Detail: *"they said to one another, 'This is the heir. Come, let us kill him and acquire his inheritance.'"* For a man who had only one son, if his son dies, those who tend the land for the father receive the inheritance. [112] So, they're right. If they killed the son, they would take over the inheritance. With slightly different words, Mark's and Luke's versions are essentially the same.

Detail: *"They seized him, threw him out of the vineyard, and killed him."* In Matthew's account, the son was thrown out of the vineyard first and then killed. Jews killed outside their city walls, which was why Golgotha was outside of the Jerusalem wall. Luke reports the same sequence. But, in Mark's version, the sequence was the other way around. In Mark, they killed the son and then they threw him out of the city. Mark was writing to Jews in the area in and around Rome. Most of the Jews there were several generations removed from Palestine. So, they've adopted more to Roman-like thinking. This was the Romans' approach: they killed in the most public way possible and then just discarded the body outside the city. So, Mark gave a Roman twist to the story.

Jesus concluded with the question: *"What will the owner of the vineyard do to those tenants when he comes?"* They answered Jesus, *"He will put those wretched men to a wretched death and lease his vineyard to other tenants who will give him the produce at the proper times."*

Jesus then replied, *"Did you never read in the scriptures:*
'The stone that the builders rejected has
become the cornerstone; by the Lord has this
been done, and it is wonderful in our eyes?'"
[Psalm 118:22-23].

The Temple authorities, Jesus was speaking to, recite the Psalms every single day. They knew exactly what He was referring to.

Detail: Jesus continued: *"Therefore, I say to you, the kingdom of God will be taken away from you and given to a people that will produce its fruit."* What a shocking thing to say to the Temple authorities. They considered themselves as the most entitled to be in the Kingdom of God. That is, their expectation of the Kingdom of God; the Temple authorities and the crowd around them (except for Jesus' closest disciples) were unfamiliar with Jesus' teachings on the Kingdom of God. This subject will come up again shortly.

Jesus had drawn the parallel clearly for them. The Temple authorities were like tenant caretakers on the Father's land who had been entrusted with responsible duties they were refusing to perform. When the prophets came to their predecessors, they mistreated and killed them. They have dishonored the Father by disregarding His will and they have proclaimed their own judgment. The Son is going to die: the builders are going to 'reject the cornerstone.'"

There is an additional statement that appears in Jesus' response: [*The one who falls on this stone will be dashed to pieces; and it will crush anyone on whom it falls.*]" [Mt 21:44]. It appears in brackets because it is absent from most early texts of Matthew's Gospel. It's not clear whether that sentence was in Matthew's original work or it was not. It appears to have been a later addition, but it has been retained in current translations because it also appears in Luke's version.

That phrase was referring to the cornerstone: Jesus Christ. To "fall upon the stone" referred to how the Temple authorities "fell upon him" to kill Him. "They will be crushed, and they will be dashed to pieces." Upon Jesus' death upon the cross, the earth quaked, tombs opened, and buildings fell upon many in Jerusalem.

Jesus had made the introspective connection for them. The parable spoke of the very circumstances they were presently in. Would they see that and change their minds? Some may have, but as Matthew put it: "*When the chief priests and the Pharisees heard his parables, they knew that he was speaking about them. And although they were attempting to arrest him, they feared the crowds, for they regarded him as a prophet*" [Mt 21:45-46].

Jesus had given them an opportunity to see themselves, and what they were thinking, differently. Luke added the statement: "*When the people heard this, they exclaimed, 'Let it not be so!'*" [Lk 20:16b]. Luke's message was that the people in the crowd made the connection that the Temple authorities did not.

The Temple authorities, at a point earlier in their history, were a very trusted group. They cared for the house of the Lord and for widows and orphans. But, this trusted group had lost their way. And, because they lost their way they would lose out on the Kingdom of God.

At the very end of this parable, there is another change of details by the evangelists that's worth noting. Matthew wrote: *"When the chief priests and the Pharisees heard his parables, they knew that he was speaking about them"* [Mt 21:45]. Initially, Matthew had omitted the Scribes from among those who confronted Jesus that day. At the conclusion, the Elders have been replaced by the Pharisees. At the time Matthew's Gospel was written, the Pharisees were the only "authorities" left in Judaism and they were expelling Christians from the synagogues. So, Matthew was indicating to his listeners that the "authorities" of his day also did not get that Jesus was the son in the parable who was killed.

At the conclusion, Mark referred to the Temple authorities simply as *"they"* [Mk 12:2a]. Whereas, Luke omits the Elders and referred to the Temple authorities as: *"the scribes and chief priests"* [Lk 20:19a]. In Luke's Gentile world, there was no group comparable to the Elders. There were leaders of powerful families who had political influence, but they had no role in religious matters.

Some of the Temple authorities, that day, may have been sufficiently moved by what Jesus said to reconsider their thinking; but, the evangelists tell us that most of them went away to plot how they would kill Jesus. The large crowd that had witnessed the exchange must have been stunned into near silence. No one had ever addressed the Temple authorities like that before. It was in a firm but not hostile way. Many of them might have wanted it to be more hostile, but that was not Jesus' way. Turning to the large crowd, Jesus shared with them the Parable of the Feast.

11.14 Parable of the Feast

This parable was recounted by Matthew and Luke; however, Luke presented it in an entirely different setting. Luke intended a much different message than Matthew, and we will consider the spiritual lesson in each version separately. There are enough differences in the two versions that some biblical scholars have suggested that they might be two different parables. Some have referred to the version in Luke's Gospel as the Parable of the Seven Speeches.[113]

11.14.1 The Version in Matthew's Gospel [Matthew 22:1-14)]

Jesus again in reply spoke to them in parables, saying,

> "The kingdom of heaven may be likened to a king
> who gave a wedding feast for his son.
> He dispatched his servants to summon the invited guests to the feast, but they refused to come.
>
> A second time he sent other servants, saying,
> 'Tell those invited: "Behold, I have prepared my banquet,
> my calves and fattened cattle are killed, and everything is ready; come to the feast."'
>
> Some ignored the invitation and went away, one to his farm, another to his business. The rest laid hold of his servants, mistreated them, and killed them.
>
> The king was enraged and sent his troops, destroyed those murderers, and burned their city. Then he said to his servants, 'The feast is ready, but those who were invited were not worthy to come. Go out, therefore, into the main roads and invite to the feast whomever you find.'
>
> The servants went out into the streets and gathered all they found, bad and good alike, and the hall was filled with guests.
>
> But when the king came in to meet the guests
> he saw a man there not dressed in a wedding garment.
> He said to him, 'My friend, how is it that you came in here without a wedding garment?'
>
> But he was reduced to silence. Then the king said to his attendants, 'Bind his hands and feet, and cast him into the darkness outside, where there will be wailing and grinding of teeth.' Many are invited, but few are chosen."

11.14.2 The Spiritual Lesson in the Parable

Detail: *"The kingdom of heaven may be likened to ..."* Jesus had introduced to His listeners, that day, the subject of the Kingdom of God (Kingdom of Heaven) in the previous parable. The last seven parables about the Kingdom had been shared only with Jesus' disciples in private. Here, Jesus tried again to make known the Kingdom to those present who might be willing to listen with an open mind.

Detail: may be likened to a *"king who gave a wedding feast for his son."* Their scriptures told of four great feasts that were hosted by their king: David [2 Sm 6:19], Solomon [1 Kgs 8:65], Hezekiah [2 Chr 30:24-26], and Josiah [2 Chr 35:7-18]. None of them were wedding feasts; so, Jesus was putting an unexpected twist on a familiar story. Understanding this parable will rely on knowing ancient Jewish wedding customs (see section 2.5).

Also, recall that the motif of a great feast hosted by their king had great significance to Jesus' listeners in another regard. It was the expected event when their Messiah would gather all the righteous together and they would enjoy a great feast in complete joy while all non-believers (Gentiles) were driven away. It's ironic that the porch area in the Temple, where this crowd was gathered, led into what was known as the Court of the Gentiles. There was a place for Gentiles in the Temple (God's house), but they expected to have no place for them at the Great Banquet.

Detail: *"He dispatched his servants to summon the invited guests to the feast, but they refused to come."* At a wedding feast, the family of the bride is united with the family of the groom, in this case, the royal family. So, no one in their right mind would refuse such an "invitation." Jesus was using great exaggeration for emphasis. Also, in ancient Middle Eastern hospitality, the guests knew well in advance when a feast was going to be - often as much as a week to 10 days prior.

Detail: *"A second time he sent other servants, saying, 'Tell those invited: "Behold, I have prepared my banquet, my calves and fattened cattle are killed, and everything is ready; come to the feast."'* Some ignored the invitation and went away, one to his *farm, another to his business. The rest laid hold of his servants, mistreated them, and killed them."* Notice the mistreatment and killing of the servants. There is a striking similarity between this parable and the previous one shared with the Temple authorities. Only, in this one they're guests invited to a wedding feast.

Detail: *"The king was enraged and sent his troops, destroyed those murderers, and burned their city."* Burned their city! The Babylonians burned their city, Jerusalem, in 587 BC. Was Jesus foretelling that Jerusalem would be burned again? It was burned by the Romans in 70 AD.

Detail: *"Then he said to his servants, 'The feast is ready, but those who were invited were not worthy to come. Go out, therefore, into the main roads and invite to the feast whomever you find.' The servants went out into the streets and gathered all they found, bad and good alike, and the hall was filled with guests."* It was the extended families who were to be part of a wedding feast. The families could not be fully united if many of them were not there.

Those who rejected the king's invitation were replaced by the least likely guests, gathered off the streets – a most unexpected uniting of families. Recall from the Parable of the Weeds and the Wheat and the Parable of the Fishing Net that during the time of the Kingdom, both the *"bad and good alike"* would co-exist.

Detail: *"But when the king came in to meet the guests he saw a man there not dressed in a wedding garment."* The wedding garment, in Jewish weddings, was provided by the groom when each guest arrived. The wearing of the wedding garment was symbolizing that "we're all members of the same family." It seems that after joining the feast, this man cast the garment aside, willing to enjoy the feasting but unwilling to be part of the family.

Detail: *"He said to him, 'My friend, how is it that you came in here without a wedding garment?' But he was reduced to silence."* Notice that the king's initial approach was to call this man, "My friend," leaving open the possibility that he might have misplaced the wedding garment. But, in the Middle East, silence was the response of shame.

Detail: *"Then the king said to his attendants, 'Bind his hands and feet, and cast him into the darkness outside, where there will be wailing and grinding of teeth.'"* Recall that this is a parable about the Kingdom of Heaven, not about Heaven or the afterlife. The Kingdom is *"at hand"* [Mk 1:15; Mt 3:2, 4:17]; it is a present reality here on earth. So, for those who refuse to be united with those in the Kingdom, they will not only be excluded from the brightness, glory and joy of the Kingdom, but they will also be rendered unable to act under their own power (i.e., deprived of sanctifying grace). Those who have willfully refused to wear the "wedding garment," that is, refused to act in a manner that corresponds to God's invitation and grace, will not experience the reign of God in their hearts (instead "there will be wailing and grinding of teeth").

Detail: *"Many are invited, but few are chosen."* Many are called or invited into the Kingdom, but none are able to come on their own. God must draw the hearts of those who come; otherwise they will not come [cf. Jn 6:44]. A puzzling parable for Jesus' listeners: they were under the impression that they were the "chosen" and the only ones called or "invited."

There would have been thousands of people in the Temple that day, and certainly hundreds within earshot of Jesus' speaking. The Temple authorities had gone away, most of them angry, leaving these people to ponder what they had seen and heard. It's hard for us to imagine what they might have concluded from this parable. It was so much unlike what they expected to hear concerning a banquet hosted by a king. Did they not sing of their being part of the "family' of their king: God, in Psalms 2, 15, 24, 74, 95, 145? If they wanted to be part of the Kingdom, as Jesus described it, they could not refuse to wear the "wedding garment." They would have to ponder a very long while to come to some conclusion about what that meant.

For us, the modern-day "wedding garment" is the white garment that we are baptized in. That's the symbol that we are members of the same family; at Baptism, we become members of the family of Jesus Christ. Of course, we don't walk around each day in our baptismal gowns. Therefore, we have to make our membership in the family of Jesus Christ more "observable" through our actions.

11.14.3 The Version in Luke's Gospel [Luke 14:15-24]

One of his fellow guests said to Jesus, "Blessed is the one who will dine in the kingdom of God." He replied to him,

"A man gave a great dinner to which he invited many.

1. When the time for the dinner came, he dispatched his servant to say to those invited, 'Come, everything is now ready.' But one by one, they all began to excuse themselves.
2. The first said to him, 'I have purchased a field and must go to examine it; I ask you, consider me excused.'
3. And another said, 'I have purchased five yoke of oxen and am on my way to evaluate them; I ask you, consider me excused.'
4. And another said, 'I have just married a woman, and therefore, I cannot come.'
5. The servant went and reported this to his master. Then the master of the house in a rage commanded his servant, 'Go out quickly into the streets and alleys of the town and bring in here the poor and the crippled, the blind and the lame.
6. The servant reported, 'Sir, your orders have been carried out and still there is room.'
7. The master then ordered the servant, 'Go out to the highways and hedgerows and make people come in that my home may be filled.

For, I tell you, none of those men who were invited will taste my dinner.'"

11.14.4 The Spiritual Lesson in the Parable

Luke presented this parable in an entirely different setting. In Luke's Gospel, they were not standing in the Temple; rather Jesus was at the home of a leading Pharisee and one of his fellow guests said to Him: "Blessed is the one who will dine in the Kingdom of God." It was the fellow-guest who brought up the subject of the Kingdom of God, not Jesus. There is a vailed question here that is being posed in public: "Why is your description of the Kingdom of God not consistent with the Great Banquet we've heard of for years?" This is an honor challenge. Jesus pushed back by replying with a parable which presented an even more profound question.

In Luke's version of the parable, there's no wedding feast; it's a dinner, because Luke's community, principally Gentiles, was not very familiar with Jewish wedding customs. In their culture, a dinner was a fellowship event rather than a celebration.

In Matthew's version, the invited ignore the invitation even mistreated and killed the host's servants. In Luke's version, when the host's servant came to escort them to the dinner, they asked to be excused; but they offered ridiculous reasons. The preparation of such a dinner relied on knowing how many guests would be attending. So, the host of this dinner has already received commitments days earlier from the invitees. When "all was ready," the host's servants then went to escort each guest to the dinner. Consequently, there was always a double invitation to a fellowship dinner. So, to fail to come to such a dinner was a huge breach of social protocol.

Detail: (literary construct) In Luke's version, the telling of the parable is presented as a seven-stanza ballad. We encountered this literary form earlier in the Parable of the Pharisee and the Tax Collector. The parable is divided into seven speeches. Recall that the object of this literary construct is to increase the contrast between competing concepts or characters.

Detail: (1st stanza) *"When the time for the dinner came, he dispatched his servant to say to those invited, 'Come, everything is now ready.' But one by one, they all began to excuse themselves."* The host sent his servant to escort his original guests, but he met with excuses. Notice that the host is not a king, but "a man" (one who is like us), and he sent out only one servant to escort the invited guests. The 1st stanza established the pattern for each speech: *Action, Because, Excuse*.

Detail: (2nd stanza) *"The first said to him, 'I have purchased a field and must go to examine it; I ask you, consider me excused.'"* This was a nonsense excuse. In that culture and area, there were so few plots of agricultural land available that one did not purchase a field until after they had already examined it, tested the soil, and walked every hill and furrow. [114] The excuse also implies that the land was more important to the invitee than the host's friendship – a huge insult.

Detail: (3rd stanza) *"And another said, 'I have purchased five yoke of oxen and am on my way to evaluate them; I ask you, consider me excused.'"* An equally nonsense excuse! One did not buy a team of oxen, let alone five pairs, until they made sure the teams worked together.[115] Also, recall that the symbolic meaning of the number five was trouble.[134] So, in that culture, one would never buy five of something. Again, the oxen were more important to this invitee than the host's friendship. And, the insult was even more biting: the first man said that he "must go," but this one said he was already "on my way."

Detail: (4th stanza) *"And another said, 'I have just married a woman, and therefore I cannot come.'"* This statement was shocking. Indeed, it would have been regarded as vulgar. In their culture, a man never mentioned the women in his family when he was away from his home.[116] Furthermore, if he was recently married he should not have accepted the original invitation. His duty was to be with his wife; procreation was the principal purpose of marriage in their culture. And, the insult became extreme; this man didn't even ask to be excused.

Detail: (5th stanza) *"The servant went and reported this to his master. Then the master of the house in a rage commanded his servant, 'Go out quickly into the streets and alleys of the town and bring in here the poor and the crippled, the blind and the lame.'"* The master responds not with a call for vengeance but with remarkable grace. He directs the servant to bring in the marginalized of the community to replace those who have gravely rejected him. Notice that this is not an invitation, which would normally precede the event by a number of days. The servant is to "*bring in*" any who are willing to come. This is most unexpected behavior. It's the same amazing expression of compassion in the face of great humiliation that characterized the father in the Parable of the Prodigal Son. In Matthew, they brought in the "*good and the bad."* But in Luke, it was the *"poor, the crippled, the blind, the lame"* who were brought in. To Luke, Jesus most favored the marginalized, the very socio-economic class Luke was writing to.

Detail: (6th stanza) *"The servant reported, 'Sir, your orders have been carried out and still there is room.'"* The pattern of: *Action, Because, Excuse* continues. The servant did what he was commanded. He was not successful, however, because the community had too few willing to come - there is still room for more in the master's house.

Detail: (7th stanza) *"The master then ordered the servant, 'Go out to the highways and hedgerows and make people come in that my home may be filled.'"* This statement is astounding. Robbers and beggars are on the highways and hedgerows, the reprobates of society, as well as Gentiles. Furthermore, the servant is to "make" them come to the master's house. The pattern that was established in the first six stanzas was broken in the seventh. The *Action* was to find and make them come in; the *Excuse* was that the master's home was still not full. But, the *Because* part of the master's final speech is missing; he gave no reason why reprobates and Gentiles should be brought into a fellowship dinner.[117] This pointed to the question posed by the parable to Jesus' challenger. The challenger had asserted that: *"Blessed is the one who will dine in the Kingdom of God."* How could the master regard not only the marginalized, but the reprobates, even the Gentiles as "blessed?"

One last point, after the host still had room, he ordered his servant to "make" others come. Since one servant couldn't very well force people to come, this likely meant that he wanted the servant to be compelling in his manner and earnestness. But, it could also have been a reference to something more akin to actually "compelling" them. In the early centuries, if a head of household accepted Christianity and was baptized, everyone in his household was also baptized. So, in that sense, many were "compelled" to join. This could have been happening, to some extent, in the communities around Antioch, which might be why Luke used a phrase like this.

All three Synoptic evangelists tell us that, shortly after His confrontation with the Temple authorities, Jesus was confronted by a group of Pharisees and Herodians. They had likely heard about how He had silenced the Temple authorities and were going to show their superiority by stumping Jesus with what they thought to be a very clever question [Mt 22:15-22; Mk 12:13-17; Lk 20:19-26]. Some biblical scholars argue that this alliance between the Herodians and Pharisees did not take place until after 44 AD when Herod Agrippa II came to power. After 70 AD, the Pharisees were the only authorities left in Judaism. The Herodians were included by the three evangelists as co-conspirators with the Pharisees against Jesus because, in the time when the Gospels were written, an alliance between Herod Agrippa II and the Pharisees to eliminate Christianity was a formidable danger that their listeners would have immediately recognized.[118]

The conspirators asked Jesus: "Is it lawful to pay the census tax to Caesar or not?" Clearly this was an honor challenge. Jesus used a question: *"Show me the coin that pays the census tax ... whose image is this and whose inscription?"* to surface a more penetrating question. The coin they produced had the image of Tiberius Caesar who had declared himself to be a god. The pushback question was: "Why do you have on your possession, in the Temple (God's house), this object that bears the image of a false god? This was a shocking revelation; they were silent.

Jesus concluded with: *"Repay to Caesar what belongs to Caesar and to God what belongs to God."* We cannot truly give ourselves to God until we accept how God sees us. [119] It is that anxious struggle with which we hang onto and "protect" the image we want others to see, that gets in the way of our accepting ourselves. It's the very struggle these men were experiencing. They wanted so much to be seen as superior even to the Temple authorities that they failed to recognize their long-awaited Messiah standing right in front of them.

No sooner had these conspirators walked away in shame but a group of Sadducees came forward to confront Jesus [Mt 22:23-33; Mk 12:18-27; Lk 20:27-40]. This was a most unusual exchange, quite unlike the exchanges Jesus had with any other group.

The Sadducees were the wealthy power brokers in Judaism and they controlled the Jewish court, the *Great Sanhedrin*. They drew their name from Zadok, the first High Priest of ancient Israel in the time of Solomon. The Sadducees accepted only the Torah (Law of Moses) and rejected the other Hebrew Scriptures as being "mere traditions" promoted by the Pharisees. They denied that there would be any bodily resurrection, because there was no mention of it in the Torah. They denied the existence of angels as well as the sovereignty of God over human affairs. They taught that man was the master of his own destiny.[120]

The Sadducees saw themselves as masters of debate. So, they didn't take the approach of posing a classic Middle Eastern honor challenge to Jesus. Rather, they resorted to a debating style more common among the Greeks; probably figuring that they would have the upper-hand against an itinerate preacher from Galilee. They set up what they thought would be grounds for a sure-win by first quoting from the Torah, saying: *"Moses said, 'If a man dies without children, his brother shall marry his wife and raise up descendants for his brother'"* [Mt 22:24; Mk 12:19; Lk 20:28]. Then, they posed a hypothetical situation in which a woman was widowed in turn by seven brothers. They then asked: *"at the resurrection whose wife will that woman be?"* [Mt 22:29; Mk12:23; Lk 20:33].

This was a classic debating tactic called a *non-sequitur*. Non-sequitur is Latin for "it does not follow." In this tactic, the debater posed a question that they're confident has no right answer. Then, they quickly jump to the charge: "if you can't answer *this* correctly, well then, you're not correct in *anything else* either." Of course, whose wife the woman would be following the resurrection of the dead had no bearing at all on whether there will be any resurrection of the dead. That's the *non-sequitur* aspect of their hypothetical case.

The fallacy in the Sadducees' case was their limiting scriptures (the Word of God) to just the Torah. The scriptural basis they were ignoring was from the Book of Daniel:
> *Many of those who sleep in the dust of the earth shall awake; some to everlasting life, others to reproach and everlasting disgrace.* [Daniel 12:2]

Notice here that the Jewish expectation was not for all to rise at the resurrection, only that "many" would rise, when Israel would be restored upon the coming of the Messiah. [121] Jesus immediately pointed out the fallacy in their case, saying: *"You are misled because you do not know the scriptures or the power of God"* [Mt 22:29; Mk 12:24]. This part of Jesus' response does not appear in Luke's account, most likely because Luke's Gentile listeners would not have been familiar with the Book of Daniel and therefore would not see the point in this part of Jesus' response.

We marveled when, a few months earlier in Jericho, Jesus was confronted by some Pharisees, how compassionately He instructed them following the Parable of the Rich Man and Lazarus. Now, we hear that great compassion again. He had soundly defeated these would-be 'masters of debate,' these men who will plot His death, and yet He instructed them on *the power of God* explaining that the risen bodies at the resurrection will be the creative work of God and there will be no need for procreation by man and woman. Recall that, in ancient Israel, procreation was the principal purpose of marriage, so their question: "whose wife would she be" really had no relevance.

Notice that the Sadducees were defeated by truth, not the skill of the debater, Jesus. Luke noted that: *"Some of the scribes said in reply, "Teacher, you have answered well." And they no longer dared to ask him anything"* [Lk 20:39-40]. The scribes among them would have been very familiar with the critical passage in the Book of Daniel that the debaters were ignoring.

Then, one of the scribes stepped forward to speak with Jesus and we hear another remarkable exchange. The scribe said: *"Teacher, which commandment in the law is the greatest?"* [Mt 22:34; Mk 12:28]. This exchange was not recounted by Luke, possibly because it relies on knowledge of the Torah that most Gentiles would not have had.

At first, the scribe's question might sound like another classic public honor challenge. But, there must have been something in the scribe's tone or manner that signaled that he was not challenging Jesus but rather giving Him an opportunity to continue compassionately instructing. Because Jesus answered the question asked, as though it had been asked in private.

Jesus' reply, as recounted by Mark, was:
> "*You shall love the Lord your God with all your heart, with all your soul, with all your mind, and with all your strength. The second is this: You shall love your neighbor as yourself*" [Mk 12:30-31a].

And, as it was recounted by Matthew was:
> "*You shall love the Lord, your God, with all your heart, with all your soul, and with all your mind*" ... *The second is like it: You shall love your neighbor as yourself*'" [Mt 22:37-39]

This illustrates a point we encountered earlier with the Parable of the Pharisee and the Tax Collector. The Jews did not attempt to recite their Scriptures verbatim; rather they sought to express the essence of each passage. The quoted passages in the Torah read:
> "*You shall love the Lord, your God, with your whole heart, and with your whole being, and with your whole strength*" [Deu 6:5]. "*You shall love your neighbor as yourself*" [Lev 19:18b].

Basically, Jesus took the opportunity this scribe had offered by instructing all who would listen that the love of God must engage the whole person and extend to everyone around us. The scribe replied to Jesus: "*Well said, teacher. You are right in saying, 'He is One and there is no other than he.' And 'to love him with all your heart, with all your understanding, with all your strength, and to love your neighbor as yourself' is worth more than all burnt offerings and sacrifices*" [Mk 12:32-33].

In their culture, the style and marking on your clothing indicated your occupation and religious affiliation. As we learned earlier, during weekday morning prayers, all males wore, on their forehead and left arm, a *tefillin* or phylactery, which was a black leather box containing scrolls of parchment inscribed with verses from the Torah. They also wore tassels, called *tzizit*, attached to the corners of their garments to serve as reminders to keep the

Lord's commandments. But, as Jesus pointed out to His disciples, Pharisees *"widen their phylacteries and lengthen their tassels"* [Mt 23:5] to show off their piety.

Seeing a group dressed in that manner, knowing them to be Pharisees, Jesus put this question to them: *"'What is your opinion about the Messiah? Whose son is he?' They replied, 'David's.' He said to them, 'How, then, does David, inspired by the Spirit, call him 'lord'"* [Mt 22:42-43; Mk 12:35; Lk 20:41-44]. Jesus was not denying His Davidic sonship. Rather He was pointing out to them what they should have recognized in their piety, if it were genuine, that although He was the Son of David, He was someone much greater, the Son of Man and Son of God. And, He was recognized as being greater even by David who calls him "my lord." This group too was left standing there in silence.

Jesus and His disciples had come to the Temple to pray as part of their celebrating Passover. According to the rabbis, three things were required of those celebrating the Passover: (1) their presence in Jerusalem on Passover night to share in the Paschal Banquet; (2) joyousness, no matter how bad life seemed to be, Passover was a time of joy; and, (3) the *Chagigah* ("festival offering"). The *Chagigah* was a two-fold peace offering to be made on festival occasions as a burnt-offering in the Temple. During the Passover festival, the first offering was to take place during the week of preparation and the second was to take place on Passover Day, Nisan 15.

A "burnt-offering" involved, first, selecting and purchasing a lamb in the Court of Gentiles. Then, having it inspected for blemishes by a Temple priest; taking it to the Altar of Burnt Offerings in the Court of Priests; having the lamb slaughtered there and one-third consumed by fire on the Altar as an offering to God, one-third given to the Temple priests, and taking the remaining one-third to be consumed that evening with family and friends. So, sacrificial lambs were very large animals specifically raised for that purpose.[122]

The first *Chagigah* was voluntary and was typically offered on Nisan 12; the second offering, on Nisan 15, was required. It was this second *Chagigah* that the Jews were later afraid they might be unable to eat if they contracted defilement by entering Pontius Pilate's house [Jn 18:28]. The peace-offering lambs were in addition to those sacrificed on Nisan 13 and shared at the Paschal Banquet at sundown that began Nisan 14. It is estimated that about 250,000 lambs were sacrificed each year, in the time of Jesus, at the Passover festival alone. [123]

Since Jesus and His disciples were devout Jews, they most likely made the voluntary *Chagigah*. So, proceeding along with many others from the Solomon's Porch area they would have gone into the Court of Gentiles and there purchased a lamb, had it inspected by a Temple priest, and continued up the stairs and through the Beautiful Gate into the Court of Women. They would then be in a place of prayer and those women in their group, of which there may well have been several, would have remained in the Court of Women. The men would have continued up the curved stairway to the Nicanor Gate, through the huge bronze doors into the Court of Israel, where they would wait with hundreds of other men.

From the Court of Israel, they would have been admitted in groups of 30 men into the Court of Priests and the massive doors closed behind them. A three-fold blast on silver trumpets would begin the sacrifice ceremony. A huge plume of incense would rise, and a Levite would lead the group in singing the *Hallel* ("praise"). The *Hallel* was Psalms 113 thru 118 with Psalm 136 sung antiphonally by the Levite. During the singing, the lambs were slaughtered, flayed, salted and one-third was place in the fire of the Altar of Burnt-offerings. The salt intensified the flames. The portion given to the Temple priests was then taken away and the remaining lamb meat wrapped in the sheepskin was placed on the shoulders of a pair of men to be taken and consumed by family and friends. The sheepskin was a valuable item; typically, out-of-towners gave it to the family that hosted them during their stay in Jerusalem. As the massive doors were opened, the group of 30 men was quickly replaced by the next group of 30.

This burnt-offerings process went on in the Temple, all day, from the end of the community sin-offering sacrifice at sunrise until the evening community sin-offering sacrifice, just before sunset. The community sin-offerings were presided over by the High Priest, who imparted his blessing on all at the conclusion of the services.

Both Mark and Luke tell us that when Jesus and His disciples were leaving, Jesus *"sat down opposite the treasury and observed how the crowd put money into the treasury"* [Mk 12:41]. Jesus observed "some wealthy people putting their offerings into the treasury" [Lk 21:1]. As we learned earlier, the Temple treasury was along the north and south walls of the Court of Women. It consisted of thirteen [124] large wooden boxes with trumpet-shaped bronze funnels. The funnels guided the coins into the box and the sound these coins made against the metal would indicate how much people offered to the Temple. This amount of sound was not seen as a measure of one's generosity but as an indication of one's favor with God. The noise was intended to shame those who could give only very little.

Jesus also *"noticed a poor widow putting in two small coins'* [Mk 12:42; Lk 21:2]. This made Him furious because the Temple authorities had convinced poor widows that it was their obligation to support the Temple; whereas, in fact it was the Temple's obligation to support them. So, with that, Jesus stormed out of the Temple disgusted.

They would spend the night on Mount Olivet, but, they would have had to fully consume, shortly after sundown, the lamb that had been sacrificed in the Temple. Since there could be no open fires on Mount Olivet, they most likely went to the home of a disciple who lived in the city of Jerusalem to cook and share the meal.

At sundown, Nissan 13 began. Upon their returning to Mount Olivet, they would have come to a level area on the western slope that overlooked the city of Jerusalem. From that spot, they could easily see the Temple in all its glory. Still furious over the Temple officials literally lining their pockets by convincing widows that they had to support the Temple, Jesus told His disciples *"not a stone will be left upon a stone that will not be thrown down"* [Mt 24:2; Mk 13:2], referring to the destruction of the Temple. As they headed further on the Mount of Olivet, advancing by torch light, it was too dark to really make out who was there and who was not. This was most likely the time when Judas slipped off into the darkness and returned to the city to plot the betrayal of Jesus.

After Jesus and His disciples had settled in where they would stay the night, Jesus began what is known today as the "Olivet Discourse." The Olivet Discourse is a lengthy answer to their question about the destruction of the Temple, "when's this going to happen?" The Discourse was a combination of a prophecy of the end times and the destruction of Jerusalem. The two subjects seemed to be so intermixed in the Discourse that it's difficult to tell which of Jesus' remarks apply to the end times and which apply to the destruction of Jerusalem.

Many find this very disconcerting. We want to treat those things which Jesus said that related to the destruction of Jerusalem as "no longer of concern," because that event is behind us. We want to know what to expect as the end times approach, because that lies ahead of us. What we don't realize is that our sense of time is incompatible with the Middle Eastern sense of time and comprehending the Olivet Discourse (as well as those parables Jesus shared as part of the Discourse).

Time is a construct of the physical world that provides a framework for understanding cause-effect, the sensation of waiting, and more recently the physics concepts of entropy and general relativity. For much of the history of mankind, there was no understanding of cause-effect and the earliest connection between time and physics was made by the scientist, Ludwig Boltzmann, in the 1870s.

Our concept of time as a linear-progression originated with the Greek philosophers in Athens in the early 3rd century BC. Their line of thinking, known as Stoicism, was predominantly a philosophy of personal ethics: for one to live a good life, one had to understand the rules of the natural order. And, one of those rules was that the past is behind us, we can't change the past, one's destiny was in the future. In their line of thinking, then, time must be a linear progression from the past, through the present and into the future.

For most of human history, there were no fixed units of time. For example, in Jesus' day, an "hour" was one-twelfth of the daylight or one-twelfth of the darkness. So, during the summer, an "hour" during the day was much longer than an "hour" during the night. During the winter, the reverse was true. To Middle Easterners, who did not hold to Stoic thinking, time was "compressed" such that, for them, the past, the present and the future were all one and the same. What happened in the past is happening now and will happen in the future. Yet, there was the sensation of waiting that needed some explanation. So, waiting was regarded as a pause rather than as a passage of time. [125]

The Middle Eastern concept of time was expressed very well by the author of the Second Letter of Peter:

"do not ignore this one fact, beloved, that with the Lord one day is like a thousand years and a thousand years like one day. The Lord does not delay his promise, as some regard 'delay,' but he is patient with you, not wishing that any should perish but that all should come to repentance."*

[2 Pet 3:8-9]

In short, he was saying that to comprehend the ways of the Lord, one must adopt the Lord's way of thinking about time – which happened to be the way Middle Easterners think about time. It is the Middle Eastern sense of time that we need to bring to our listening to the parables Jesus shared as part of the Olivet Discourse. But, we also recognize that we may not be able to fully relate what Jesus had to say that evening to our comprehension of time. When mystery is dispelled there is nothing left but words.

Early in the Discourse, Jesus spoke of His "*coming upon the clouds of heaven with power and great glory*" [Mt 24:30b; Mk 13:26; Lk 21:27 and then He shared with them the Parable of the Fig Tree.

11.15 Parable of the Fig Tree

This parable was recounted almost verbatim by all three Synoptic evangelists, Matthew, Mark and Luke.

11.15.1 The Version in Matthew's Gospel [Matthew 24:32-34]

Jesus said to them,
> "Learn a lesson from the fig tree.
> When its branch becomes tender and sprouts leaves,
> you know that summer is near.
>
> In the same way, when you see all these things,
> know that he is near, at the gates.
>
> Amen, I say to you, this generation will not pass away
> until all these things have taken place."

11.15.2 The Version in Mark's Gospel [Mark 13:28-30]

Jesus said to them,
> "Learn a lesson from the fig tree.
> When its branch becomes tender and sprouts leaves,
> you know that summer is near.
>
> In the same way, when you see these things happening,
> know that he is near, at the gates.
>
> Amen, I say to you, this generation will not pass away
> until all these things have taken place."

11.15.3 The Version in Luke's Gospel [Luke 21:29-32]

Jesus taught them a lesson.
> "Consider the fig tree and all the other trees.
> When their buds burst open, you see for yourselves and know
> that summer is now near;
>
> in the same way, when you see these things happening,
> know that the kingdom of God is near.
>
> Amen, I say to you, this generation will not pass away
> until all these things have taken place."

11.16 The Spiritual Lesson in the Parable

Detail: *"Learn a lesson from the fig tree."* We have encountered the subject of fig trees before (see section 10.10). Recall that fig buds are produced before the leaves emerge and fig leaves are very large. And, the flower of the fig tree is never seen, as its many tiny flowers are housed within the fruit bud. So, when looking at a fig tree all one sees are the leaves. The fruiting process goes on unseen until very near ripening. In a sense, a fig tree is a natural example of the compression of time: the fruiting process appears to happen all at once.

Detail: *"When its branch becomes tender and sprouts leaves, you know that summer is near."* The fig tree is the last tree to produce leaves and it does so right before summer.

Detail: *"In the same way, when you see all these things, know that he is near, at the gates."* When an enemy was prepared to attack, such as the Romans in 70 AD, they were said to be "at the gates." So, the "he" in this statement might have meant the Roman General (later Emperor) Titus or it might have meant the Son of Man, or it might have meant both. The statement could be eschatological: the destruction of the Temple by the Romans in 70 AD interpreted as the beginning of the end times.

But, we also must bear in mind that we are to *"learn a lesson from the fig tree."* The signs ancient Middle Easterners looked for in fig trees were not alerts to what was to come, but assurances of what was already happening, but was unseen. God was advancing the growth of fruit even though it could not be seen.

Luke rephrased this detail as: *"in the same way, when you see these things happening, know that the kingdom of God is near"* to give more emphasis to his listeners of the "fig tree lesson" and less emphasis on the eschatological aspects. In the Kingdom of God, through the Eucharist, we consume Jesus' flesh and blood and become His flesh and blood in the world. The Word became flesh to make us *"partakers of the divine nature"* [2 Pet 1:4]. Therefore, the Incarnation lives on in us. Jesus came, Jesus comes, Jesus will come, is one and the same.

Detail: *"Amen, I say to you, this generation will not pass away until all these things have taken place."* "All these things have taken place" might have meant the destruction of the Temple or it might have meant the end times. But, it might have meant the love-sharing works of the Body of Christ in the Kingdom of God that went on essentially unseen by the larger world. Many of Jesus' first listeners that evening, "*this generation*," saw the destruction of the Temple. Many were also instrumental in the early fostering of the Kingdom of God on earth. And, many of them experienced "Jesus with us" in the Eucharist. For them, Jesus' *"coming upon the clouds of heaven with power and great glory"* was seen not as the event of His return but as the culmination of making the Kingdom of God on earth fully realized.

When heard with a Middle Eastern sense of time, we realize that Jesus has answered their question: "when's this going to happen?" in a way that renders that question irrelevant. Their concerns about discerning the signs of the end times were poorly placed; their future, and ours, rested in doing their best to bring about the Kingdom of God (Kingdom of Heaven) in their time and place. That is why Jesus' focus on the Kingdom, again and again, was so important to Him.

Jesus then shared with them another parable about the Kingdom of Heaven, the Parable of the Ten Virgins. To understand the point of this parable we need to be familiar with the role of virgins in ancient Israel.

11.17 The Role of Virgins in Ancient Israel

The term, virgin, had a much different meaning in ancient Israel then it does in our times. A virgin (or *"betulah"* in Hebrew) was the most politically significant role in ancient Israel. She was the visible symbol of the honor of her family, and in particular of her father. A *betulah* (virgin) was a woman who was both eligible for marriage and virginal (had never experienced intercourse).

In those times, virginity was a badge of honor, not one of moral character. Recall that honor (i.e. the esteem in which one was held by others) was the virtue in highest regard in the Middle East. To maintain his honor, the father (as head of household) had the supreme duty to provide for, guard and protect those virgins in his household. The number of married women in his household symbolized his prosperity; but the number of virgins symbolized his honor in the community.

Any time a family was called upon to serve as a witness to some legal transaction, it was one of the virgins in the family who served that duty. When there were no female virgins in the household, a male who was eligible to marry and virginal was declared "Virgin" for the purpose of serving as a witness.

For a virgin to lose her virginity put her whole household at risk. In the cultural setting of ancient Israel, when a virgin was raped, the attack was regarded as being against the father, not the woman (even though she was clearly a victim). The father was greatly shamed and was regarded as unfit for the community to rely on to maintain proper conduct and order.

The virginity of the virgins within his household was the legal guarantee of the father's continued possession of the family's property. In King David's time, the property of a dishonored household was taken over by the assailant's household. This led to enormous injustices and, in time, there evolved a means of restoring the honor of the shamed household. The shamed father was required to kill the daughter and one of the males in her family had to kill the assailant. For the most part, the rapes and retaliations recounted in the Bible are to be seen as power challenges by one family against another, not primarily as sexual attacks. The rape of a married woman was seen as an attack against the honor of her husband, not an attack against her person.

Regarding virginity, as we learned earlier, a *betulim* ("proof cloth") was placed under the bride during the consummation of her marriage. It was the physical evidence that the father of the bride had lived up to his obligations to the community and the family of the groom [cf. Deu 22:17]. The bride's father retained the "proof cloth" against any possible later claims that he had not provided a true virgin in marriage. Consequently, it was essential to have formal witnesses, independent of the bride's family, examine the "proof cloth" immediately after consummation and swear to the evidence. Serving as such an official witness was a primary duty of a virgin.

11.18 The Parable of the Ten Virgins [Matthew 25:1-13]

Jesus said,
> "Then the kingdom of heaven will be like ten virgins
> who took their lamps and went out to meet the bridegroom.
> Five of them were foolish and five were wise.
> The foolish ones, when taking their lamps, brought no oil with them, but the wise brought flasks of oil with their lamps.
>
> Since the bridegroom was long delayed,
> they all became drowsy and fell asleep. At midnight, there was a cry, 'Behold, the bridegroom! Come out to meet him!'
>
> Then all those virgins got up and trimmed their lamps.
> The foolish ones said to the wise, 'Give us some of your oil, for our lamps are going out.' But the wise ones replied, 'No, for there may not be enough for us and you. Go instead to the merchants and buy some for yourselves.'
>
> While they went off to buy it, the bridegroom came
> and those who were ready went into the wedding feast with him. Then the door was locked.
>
> Afterwards the other virgins came and said,
> 'Lord, Lord, open the door for us!' But he said in reply,
> 'Amen, I say to you, I do not know you.'
> Therefore, stay awake, for you know neither the day nor the hour.

11.19 The Spiritual Lesson in the Parable

Detail: *"like ten virgins who took their lamps and went out to meet the bridegroom."* The ten virgins were to be the witnesses to truth: that the bride was a virgin. They were waiting to receive from the groom the "proof cloth." When the couple had consummated the wedding; the groom would come out of the *chuppah* (tent-like marriage chamber) and hand the "proof cloth" to the witnesses. Each of them, individually, had to examine it carefully and swear "yes, I saw it myself." And, ten of them were the official witnesses at this wedding. The number ten had the symbolic meaning: complete or sufficient,[134] so this was a very significant wedding in this community because all the witnesses they would ever need were enlisted. Ten families had put their reputations on the line by sending one of their virgins to "witness" the consummation of this wedding. Each had her own lamp so that, in the dark, she had sufficient light to examine the "proof cloth." If they had no lamps, they would fail at their duty to witness.

Detail: *"Five of them were foolish and five were wise. The foolish ones when taking their lamps brought no oil with them. But, the wise brought flasks of oil with their lamps."* Five of them – the number five symbolized "trouble," half of the official witnesses were about to dishonor their families on a monumental scale.

Detail: *"Since the bridegroom was long-delayed, they all became drowsy and they fell asleep."* The error of their ways is compounded. They were totally unprepared for their paramount duty at that point in their life.

Detail: *"Behold, the bridegroom! ... The foolish ones said to the wise "give us some of your oil for our lamps are going out but the wise ones replied: 'No, for there may not be enough for us and you go instead to the merchants and buy some for yourselves."* Each had a solemn duty to perform, and if they shared their oil there would be a danger that all ten of them would fail to fulfill their duty.

Detail: *"While they went off to buy it, the bridegroom came. Those who were ready went into the wedding feast with him. Then the door was locked."* Locking of the door symbolized that the families were all inside and potential intruders are excluded. So, the foolish virgins, who failed in witnessing to the truth, are not just barred from the festivities, they have been excluded from the families.

Detail: *"Afterward, the other virgins came and said, 'Lord, Lord open the door for us.'"* Recall that, for Jews, the Lord would have the door of the Great Feast guarded against "outsiders" (Gentiles). After all Gentiles were eliminated, the Lord would throw the door open and the Kingdom of Heaven would live on forever. That was the Jewish expectation of the commencement of the Kingdom of Heaven.

Detail: *"But, he said in reply: 'Amen I say to you I do not know you."* They have failed in their paramount duty in life, so they are not "part of the family."

Detail: *"Therefore, stay awake for you know neither the day nor the hour."* Be alert, for you do not know when you will be called upon to serve as a witness to the truth.

In the Kingdom of Heaven, which Jesus was inaugurating, His Apostles would be the official witnesses to the truth, that "*God so loved the world that he gave* his only Son, so that everyone who believes in him might not perish but might have eternal life" [Jn 3:16]. Jesus was telling His Apostles directly, and us indirectly, that "You are to be the "virgins" of Christianity. Your primary duty will be to stand for the Father's honor by witnessing to the truth; don't let others deter you from it."

Jesus knew the end was near; He would be crucified in less than two days. So, the lesson in this parable was profoundly demanding and His Apostles would need something very powerful. So, He shared with them another parable, the Parable of the Talents.

11.20 Parable of the Talents

11.20.1 The Version in Matthew's Gospel [Matthew 25:14-30]

Jesus told his disciples this parable.
> "A man going on a journey
> called in his servants and entrusted his possessions to them.
> To one he gave five talents; to another, two; to a third, one—
> to each according to his ability. Then he went away.
> Immediately the one who received five talents went and traded with them and made another five.
> Likewise, the one who received two made another two.
> But the man who received one went off and dug a hole in the ground and buried his master's money.

After a long time, the master of those servants came back and settled accounts with them. The one who had received five talents came forward bringing the additional five. He said, 'Master, you gave me five talents. See, I have made five more.' His master said to him, 'Well done, my good and faithful servant. Since you were faithful in small matters, I will give you great responsibilities. Come, share your master's joy.'

Then the one who had received two talents also came forward and said, 'Master, you gave me two talents. See, I have made two more.' His master said to him, 'Well done, my good and faithful servant. Since you were faithful in small matters, I will give you great responsibilities. Come, share your master's joy.'

Then the one who had received the one talent came forward and said, 'Master, I knew you were a demanding person, harvesting where you did not plant and gathering where you did not scatter; so out of fear I went off and buried your talent in the ground. Here it is back.

His master said to him in reply, 'You wicked, lazy servant! So, you knew that I harvest where I did not plant and gather where I did not scatter? Should you not then have put my money in the bank so that I could have got it back with interest on my return?

Now then! Take the talent from him and give it to the one with ten. For to everyone who has, more will be given, and he will grow rich; but from the one who has not, even what he has will be taken away. And throw this useless servant into the darkness outside, where there will be wailing and grinding of teeth.'"

11.20.2 The Spiritual Lesson in the Parable

<u>Detail:</u> *"A man going on a journey called in his servants and entrusted his possessions to them."* Since the man was going on a journey, the time of his return was uncertain. Yet, he entrusted all of his possessions to his indentured slaves (servants) before he left.

Detail: *"To one he gave five talents; to another, two; to a third, one to each according to his ability. Then he went away."* The Greek word, *talanton*, from which we get the English word, "talent," was a specific weight in gold. One talent was 130 pounds of gold, worth about two and a half million dollars - an astounding amount in Jesus' day. Private individuals didn't have that kind of money, only national treasuries. So, Jesus was using extreme exaggeration here to emphasize that each servant in the story was entrusted with something whose value was far beyond all imagination, what each was given was priceless! So, their ability was not the gift, ability was the measure by which the master judged how much to give each servant. No servant was given a greater responsibility than the master felt the servant could handle.

Notice that this man with enormous wealth had only three servants. The symbolic meaning of the number three was: full circle or spiritual perfection.[134] At the outset, this man had all he needed, but one of them would fail him in a most dishonoring way. Was this a reference to the sin of Adam; was it a hint of the impending betrayal by Judas; or, was it a reference to all those who would dishonor God through grievous sin? We don't know.

Detail: *"Immediately, the one who received five talents went out and traded with them and made another five. Likewise, the one who received two made another two. But the man who received one went off and dug a hole in the ground and buried his master's money."* The storyline was that the first two servants profitably applied what they were entrusted with. But, to say that through trading they doubled what they had been given was clearly more extreme exaggeration. Only treasuries had talents for storing national wealth, not for trade; and certainly not with slaves. So, this detail is saying that the first two servants acted far outside normative behavior for their culture and apparent circumstances. In contrast, the third servant dug a hole and buried what he had been given. This was normative behavior. The best place for him to protect his something of great value was to bury it on his master's land. Culturally, he took the "right" action. The behavior of the other two would have been seen as reckless, even dangerous.

We are hearing an antithesis, the placing in contrast of two very contradictory things to draw attention to an underlying principle. We encountered this literary construct earlier in the Parable of the Workers where Jesus had placed conventional thinking in juxtaposition to unconventional behavior. In this parable, He has placed boldly acting outside the prevailing norms to cautiously acting strictly within the prevailing norms in order to point to an underlying principle. And, typically, that underlying principle is not directly stated, the listener has to figure it out.

We also saw how antithesis was used by the author of Genesis in the Fall of Man story (see footnote 109). This parable may be drawing on that story, which Jesus' listeners knew well. In that story, we found the hints to the underlying principle in the dialog; we should look for hints in the dialog in this parable as well.

Detail: *"the master of those servants came back and settled accounts with them. The one who had received five talents came forward bringing the additional five. He said, 'Master, you gave me five talents. See, I have made five more.'"* Basically, he was saying: Master, you entrusted to me something of enormous value, and I have returned to you even more.

Detail: *"His master said to him, 'Well done, my good and faithful servant. Since you were faithful in small matters, I will give you great responsibilities. Come, share your master's joy.'"* Wow, this incredible feat was seen by the master as a "small matter." Yet, because he had done well in a "small matter," the servant would be given "great responsibilities" and share in his "master's joy." It appears that responsibility handled well leads not to reward but to joy and more responsibilities.

Detail: *"Then the one who had received two talents also came forward ..."* The dialog between the second servant and the master is virtually identical to the previous dialog. The same point: responsibility handled well leads not to reward but to joy and more responsibilities, was repeated for emphasis.

Detail: *"Then the one who had received the one talent came forward and said, 'Master, I knew you were a demanding person, harvesting where you did not plant and gathering where you did not scatter; so out of fear I went off and buried your talent in the ground. Here it is back.'"* There was no indication given in the parable that would've suggested the master with a demanding person. On the contrary, he had entrusted his entire wealth to his slaves. So, this statement would have brought to the minds of Jesus' listeners Eve's answer to the question from the serpent who said: "*Did God really say, 'You must not eat from any tree in the garden'?*" [Gen 3:1]. Eve replied: "*it is only about the fruit of the tree in the middle of the garden that God said, 'You shall not eat it or even touch it, or else you will die'*" [Gen 3:3]. This was a gross distortion of God's instructions; this servant has also grossly distorted his master's instructions. This discloses the disposition of this servant's heart. Recall that sin arises out of the disposition of the heart. So, burying the talent was an act of sin, not an act of fear. Although the servant claimed it was fear, he dishonored the master by refusing to do the master's will.

Detail: "*His master said to him in reply, 'You wicked, lazy servant! So, you knew that I harvest where I did not plant and gather where I did not scatter? Should you not then have put my money in the bank so that I could have got it back with interest on my return?'*" The master regarded this servant, who initially he entrusted with great wealth, as being "wicked and lazy." The master even repeated back to the servant the distortion of his instructions the servant had verbalized – again, emphasis through repetition. The disposition of the servant's heart was at the center of the lesson being taught here.

Since all temples throughout the Roman Empire maintained guarded treasuries, temples also served as banks. The Temple in Jerusalem operated a bank; the Chief Priests were also bankers, called in Latin, *mensarii*. The *mensarii* kept track of deposits and they loaned money for interest, but they did not pay interest on deposits. In those days, banks were not insured, so when a loan was made, with a depositor's approval, the bank and the depositor shared in the interest paid.[126] Consequently, for the third servant to have gained interest on his master's money, the servant had to be willing to place the money at risk, which he would not do. That servant wanted the safest possible arrangement; most in his culture would have done the same.

Detail: *"Now then! Take the talent from him and give it to the one with ten. For to everyone who has, more will be given, and he will grow rich; but from the one who has not, even what he has will be taken away."* The servant who had ten didn't "grow rich" in the usual understanding of "rich." He gave the entire amount back to the master and remained an indentured slave. So, there's some other form of "rich" referred to here in which having much gains more but having a little leads to loss.

Detail: *"And throw this useless servant into the darkness outside, where there will be wailing and grinding of teeth."'* Those who have acted in the manner this servant did (refused to do the master's will) will be barred from the Kingdom of Heaven.

If we can identify what the priceless gift (talents) were, in the spiritual realm, we may be able to discern the underlying principle Jesus presented in this parable. Many attempts have been made concerning the talents in biblical commentaries ever since they first appeared in English. In the early 1700's, the master giving out the talents was seen as a metaphor for God commanding that each person should have engaging work.[127]

In the late 1800s, the term "talents" was literally interpreted as personal talents or abilities which were to be used for the benefit of all.[128] By the mid-1970s, being given the "talents" was seen as a metaphor for each person being given life-long responsibilities by God.[129] In 1988, the Catholic authors of the Gospel of Matthew commentary in the Navarre Bible series saw the talents, the precious gift, as God's grace.[130]

The term "grace" hadn't appeared in any previous commentaries at all, even up through the great evangelizer, William Berkeley in 1975; the word "grace" wasn't mentioned in connection with this parable. We encountered the first insights into the Christian understanding of grace in Jesus' parable of the Barren Fig Tree (see section 10.12). As we learned then, God's grace consists of "sanctifying" grace, which brings about or sustains holiness, and "actualizing" grace, which aids us in particular actions in our life [cf. *Catechism of the Catholic Church*, #1996-2005].

Through our understanding of grace, the underlying principle presented by Jesus in this parable appears to be that grace was the priceless gift. Grace empowers one to boldly act outside the prevailing norms of the world around them; to unconditionally love, even their enemies. One who accepts grace and acts on it receives more grace and takes on even more "responsibilities;" whereas, one who does not act on the grace they have will lose even that. One grows "rich" in the Kingdom of Heaven through grace, yet we all remain indentured servants of God. God has entrusted to us His entire wealth, His creation. So, we receive an unbelievable amount of grace to care for His creation. The parable goes on to teach that to reject God's grace is to sin in a manner that greatly dishonors God.

This is a wonderful example of how the Holy Spirit continues to work enabling us to hear the Word of God more clearly with each new generation. Jesus gave the first insights into grace nearly two thousand years ago. Over the centuries since, with the guidance of the Holy Spirit, we have come to a fairly well-articulated understanding of grace. We are fortunate in that we benefit from the exegetic efforts of many others, over those years, to gain such insights. And, as the Holy Spirit continues to work in our midst, our children and grandchildren will have even deeper insights than we've been blessed with.

The prevailing understanding of grace among Jews of Jesus' time was that they received because they were righteous and kept God's commandments. One earned grace by performing *mitsvot* (those acts required by Mosaic Law). The Parable of the Talents was also recounted by Luke, but most Gentiles had no concept of grace, so Luke used the parable in teaching a different lesson.

11.20.3 The Version in Luke's Gospel [Luke 19:11-28]

While they were listening to Jesus speak,
he proceeded to tell a parable because he was near
Jerusalem and they thought that the Kingdom of God
would appear there immediately.

So, he said,

Dcn. Bob Evans

"A nobleman went off to a distant country to obtain the kingship for himself and then to return. He called ten of his servants and gave them ten gold coins and told them, 'Engage in trade with these until I return.

His fellow citizens, however, despised him and sent a delegation after him to announce, 'We do not want this man to be our king. 'But when he returned after obtaining the kingship, he had the servants called, to whom he had given the money, to learn what they had gained by trading.

The first came forward and said, 'Sir, your gold coin has earned ten additional ones.' He replied, 'Well done, good servant! You have been faithful in this very small matter; take charge of ten cities.'

Then the second came and reported, 'Your gold coin, sir, has earned five more.' And to this servant too he said, 'You, take charge of five cities.'

Then the other servant came and said, 'Sir, here is your gold coin; I kept it stored away in a handkerchief, for I was afraid of you, because you are a demanding man; you take up what you did not lay down and you harvest what you did not plant.' He said to him,

'With your own words I shall condemn you, you wicked servant. You knew I was a demanding man, taking up what I did not lay down and harvesting what I did not plant; why did you not put my money in a bank? Then on my return I would have collected it with interest.'

And to those standing by he said, 'Take the gold coin from him and give it to the servant who has ten.' But they said to him, 'Sir, he has ten gold coins.' He replied, 'I tell you, to everyone who has, more will be given, but from the one who has not, even what he has will be taken away.

Now as for those enemies of mine who did not want me as their king, bring them here and slay them before me.'"

11.20.4 The Spiritual Lesson in the Parable

Detail: *"While they were listening to Jesus speak, he proceeded to tell a parable because he was near Jerusalem and they thought that the Kingdom of God would appear there immediately."* Luke relates the same parable (although some scholars contend that this is a different parable); however, Luke's purpose appears to have been on setting-straight expectations regarding the Kingdom of God.

Detail: *"A nobleman, went off to a distant country to obtain the kingship for himself and then to return."* What we are hearing is of a real-life event from the time of Jesus' listeners that Luke is using in his recounting the parable. When Herod the Great died in 4 BC, his son, Archelaus, was to take over Samaria and Judea. But, he had to go to Rome and claim his kingship from the hand of Caesar. However, a group of men in Jerusalem decided they didn't want Archelaus, so they hurried to Rome before Archelaus and said to Caesar "We don't want him, he's not fit to rule." But, Caesar replied, "He's my choice." Soon after, Archelaus returned to Jerusalem. He had all those men brought in and executed before him. We will need to hear more details in order to discern why Luke was using this real-life event in his recounting the parable.

Detail: *"He called ten of his servants and gave them ten gold coins and he told them engage in trade with these until I return."* In Luke's version, the servants receive the same amount. And, they received gold coins, not talents. A gold coin, or *aureus*, was equivalent to 25 denarii or 25 day's wages - not a trivial amount, but it was not an unbelievable amount of money either.

Notice that the number "ten" was used in this detail. The number ten had the symbolic meaning: complete or sufficient.[134] Yet, the parable will only tell us about three servants, as in Matthew's version. So, *ten* was being used symbolically to indicate that the full complement of this nobleman's servants was given a sufficient amount to profitably *engage in trade*. Therefore, Luke presents the story as being about managing trust, not priceless gifts.

It was certainly unusual for slaves to be trading on behalf of their master, but not too far outside the norms of their times, as we saw in Matthew's version of the parable. Indeed, some of this nobleman's servants may have been merchants prior to their indentured servitude.

Detail: *'His fellow citizens, however, despised him and sent a delegation after him to announce, 'We do not want this man to be our king.'"* This confirms that it's the Archelaus event that's being referred to. As we learned earlier, Middle Eastern storytellers often gave characters names to help the listeners interpret the characters' words and actions. Here, Luke is using the listeners' knowledge of Archelaus to signal the character of the nobleman in the parable.

Detail: *"He had the servants called, to whom he had given the money, to learn what they had gained by trading. The first came forward and said, 'Sir, your gold coin has earned ten additional ones.' He replied, 'Well done, good servant! You have been faithful in this very small matter; take charge of ten cities.'"* This servant's efforts increased the value of what he was entrusted with by ten-fold. He was put in charge of ten cites. Stewards were put in charge of things, not slaves. So, this indicates that this servant was given more responsibilities in proportion to his having fulfilled the master's directions.

Detail: *"Then the second came and reported, 'Your gold coin, sir, has earned five more.' And to this servant too he said, 'You, take charge of five cities.'"* This servant's efforts increased the value of what he was entrusted with by five-fold. And, he was further tasked accordingly.

Detail: *"Then the other servant came and said, 'Sir, here is your gold coin; I kept it stored away in a handkerchief. For I was afraid of you because you are a demanding man, you take up what you did not lay down and you harvest what you did not plant.'"* In Matthew's version, there was no indication given that the nobleman was demanding. In Luke's version, the tie to the Archelaus event tells the listeners that the nobleman in the parable is indeed a demanding man, even a tyrant. This servant was rightly concerned about losing the gold coin in a bad business deal.

The Greek word, *soudarion*, translated into English as "handkerchief" more accurately was a sweat-cloth, or *keffiyeh*. Adults in the Middle East wore a white cloth over their head, particularly in the heat, that hung to their shoulders and was held in place by a sweatband around their forehead. So, this servant kept what he was entrusted with hidden on his person. Again, hiding the coin rather than putting it at risk was the culturally appropriate thing for him to do.

Detail: *"He said to him, 'With your own words I shall condemn you, you wicked servant. You knew I was a demanding man, taking up what I did not lay down and harvesting what I did not plant; why did you not put my money in a bank? Then on my return I would have collected it with interest.'"* This is essentially the same response as in Matthew's version except this servant was not labeled as "lazy."

Detail: *"And to those standing by he said, 'Take the gold coin from him and give it to the servant who has ten.' But they said to him, 'Sir, he has ten gold coins.' He replied, 'I tell you, to everyone who has, more will be given, but from the one who has not, even what he has will be taken away.'"* Those who do not apply themselves to the task their master (God) assigned will be barred from the Kingdom of God. Notice that some of the by-standers objected saying, *"Sir, he has ten gold coins."* The by-standers' protest reinforces in the listeners' minds that this servant had done the culturally appropriate thing and not put the gold coin at risk.

Luke's use of this parable was intended to set-straight expectations. The Kingdom of God is not entered by entitlement or playing-it-safe, but by diligently applying oneself to doing the will of God. Gentiles saw faith and salvation differently from Jews. Prior to being Christian, Gentiles did not have a concept of an afterlife or resurrection. Most of them came from belief in multiple impersonal gods. For them, just learning about God was a precious gift.

Detail: *'Now as for those enemies of mine who did not want me as their king, bring them here and slay them before me.'"* This detail makes doubly sure that the listeners recognize that the nobleman was a dangerous tyrant and the servant who hid the gold coin had good reason to fear. The lesson was that doing the will of God is sometimes very dangerous. But, that danger cannot deter us in the task God sets before us. The threat of persecution may have been a great concern for Luke's community at the time he was writing his Gospel.

Luke may have seen the giving of a gold coin as one's receiving Baptism. The newly baptized then went out and "invested" their faith leading to taking on greater responsibility. Great responsibility, to the people of Antioch, was spreading the word with the zeal they once had decades earlier. Then, Antioch was the center of missionary life. That's where Paul and Barnabas started out. But, a few decades later, Rome had destroyed the Temple and much of Jerusalem. Thousands of Jews had flooded into the Antioch area.

Luke appears to have used his account of this parable as a way of reminding his faith community about this gift that they've received, this new understanding of God. They had never before been given something to "invest." Sadly, some will foolishly hold it to themselves and thereby lose it. In understanding the parables, we need to interpret what Jesus was saying, in the context in which He was speaking. And, we also must interpret how the evangelists related what Jesus said, in the context in which they were writing.

They probably didn't sleep well that night; it had been a day like no other. There were several confrontations in the Temple, and there was the firmness yet amazing compassion with which Jesus spoke to His adversaries. They had made their *Chigigah* offering, shared the meal with others and then retired to Mount Olivet. On this day, they had heard six parables, each one more challenging than the previous. We don't know at what point Judas returned or how much, if any, he heard of the Olivet Discourse and its three parables. Might some of it have changed his mind? We don't know. We don't know Judas' motive in betraying Jesus. There is so much we don't know about Judas; but Jesus knew, and He loved him anyway.

Early in the morning of Nisan 13, the first day of the Feast of Unleavened Bread, Jesus sent Peter and John to make preparations for the group's eating the Paschal Banquet [Mt 26:18; Mk 14:13; Lk 22:9]. The Paschal Banquet was to be eaten just after sundown, which began Nisan 14, in accordance with the Law of Moses [Lev 23:5]. Jesus said to them:

> "Go and make preparations for us to eat the Passover." They asked him, 'Where do you want us to make the preparations?' And he answered them, 'When you go into the city, a man will meet you carrying a jar of water. Follow him into the house that he enters and say to the master of the house, 'The teacher says to you, 'Where is the guest room where I may eat the Passover with my disciples?' He will show you a large upper room that is furnished. Make the preparations there." [Lk 22:8-12].

This made Peter head-of-household for the preparations, since a furnished room was being provided but not hosted by a disciple in Jerusalem. There were many important duties for the head-of-household.

First, the head-of-household (Peter) had to search the house in which the meal was to be eaten for any traces of leaven. This was to be done by candle light in accordance with rabbinic interpretation of Zephaniah 1:12, *"At that time, I will search Jerusalem with lamps, I will punish the people who settle like dregs in wine, who say in their hearts, 'The Lord will not do good, nor will he do harm.'"* And, this was to be done with special prayers and great ceremony.

Then, the head-of-household had to go to the Temple, along with about 200,000 other heads-of-household and select and purchase a spotless lamb; then have it inspected by a Temple priest. After much waiting in line, he would take the lamb into the Court of Priests and there, under the supervision of a Chief Priest, slaughter the lamb and catch the blood in a basin. The priest would toss the blood at the base of the Altar of Burnt Offerings.

Then the head-of-household would skin the lamb and remove the fat and internals, so they could be placed on the Altar and burned. At that point, he would wrap the lamb in the sheepskin, place it on his shoulders and those of another man (in this case, John), so that they could carry it to the place where the meal would be shared. The requirement was that the lamb had to be shared with not less than 10 or more than 20 people. The sacrifice had to be concluded by 3 pm so that the meal could be fully prepared by sundown; and it was early April. The sun would set at about 6:15 pm that day.

The head-of-household had to oversee the roasting of the lamb over an open fire. In addition, preparations also included jars of water, bitter herbs, unleavened bread, a fruit-and-nut paste, and a raw vegetable dipped in a tart dressing. Also, abundant wine had to be purchased. Timing and attention to details were critical in the preparation of the Passover Banquet.[131]

For those not directly involved in preparations, Nisan 13 was a day of prayer and reflection. From their *Mishnah*: "In every generation, a person is obligated to regard himself as if he personally left Egypt. This is the purpose of the *seder* on Pesach Eve: to provide every individual with an opportunity to experience an exodus from his own personal bondage." [132] So, The Paschal Banquet became their once-a-year re-experiencing the Exodus.

Jesus and His disciples (except Peter and John) spent the day on Mount Olivet, often standing in small groups sharing *avodah* ("prayer") together. His disciples didn't know this at the time, but that evening, Jesus' final observance of Passover, He would merge both the elements of their annual Paschal Banquet and their daily community meal into a single experience of "eating and drinking in God's presence, at His invitation." [133] This is why the Catholic Catechism states: the Eucharistic celebration is both a Paschal banquet and a community meal, in which Christ is consumed, and we are filled with grace" [*Catechism of the Catholic Church*, article 1323].

At some point during the day, Jesus shared his last parable with his disciples, the Parable of the Final Judgment.

11.21 The Parable of the Final Judgment [Matthew 25:31-46]

Jesus said to them,
"When the Son of Man comes in his glory,
and all the angels with him, he will sit upon his glorious
throne, and all the nations will be assembled before him.
And he will separate them one from another, as a shepherd
separates the sheep from the goats.

He will place the sheep on his right and the goats on his left.

Then the king will say to those on his right, 'Come, you who
are blessed by my Father. Inherit the kingdom prepared for
you from the foundation of the world. For I was hungry, and
you gave me food, I was thirsty, and you gave me drink, a
stranger and you welcomed me, naked and you clothed me,
ill and you cared for me, in prison and you visited me.'

Then the righteous will answer him and say, 'Lord, when did
we see you hungry and feed you, or thirsty and give you
drink? When did we see you a stranger and welcome you, or
naked and clothe you? When did we see you ill or in prison,
and visit you?'

And the king will say to them in reply, 'Amen, I say to you,
whatever you did for one of these least brothers of mine, you
did for me.'

Then he will say to those on his left, 'Depart from me, you
accursed, into the eternal fire prepared for the devil and his
angels. For I was hungry, and you gave me no food, I was
thirsty, and you gave me no drink, a stranger and you gave
me no welcome, naked and you gave me no clothing, ill and
in prison, and you did not care for me.'

Then they will answer and say, 'Lord, when did we see you
hungry or thirsty or a stranger or naked or ill or in prison, and
not minister to your needs?'

He will answer them, 'Amen, I say to you, what you did not do
for one of these least ones, you did not do for me.' And these

will go off to eternal punishment, but the righteous to eternal life."

11.22 The Spiritual Lesson in the Parable

Detail: *"When the Son of Man comes in his glory, and all the angels with him, he will sit upon his glorious throne, and all the nations will be assembled before him."* The meaning of the term, *all the nations*, has been argued about for centuries. Some contend that it meant all the world, however, others point out that in four other places in his Gospel, Matthew used the term, "the nations," to refer to non-believing Gentiles [Mt 4:15; 6:32; 10:5; 12:18]. This interpretation would imply that only non-believers would face final judgment. We will need to hear more details to discern what was intended.

Here, Jesus was clearly speaking about the end times, when the Kingdom of God on earth has concluded and He returns in glory. The first indication we had in the Gospels that there will be a Second Coming of Jesus was in Jesus' mystifying response to Peter on the road to Caesarea Philippi; the second was in the Parable of the Prudent and Wicked Servants. Now, this is the third time.

Detail: *"And he will separate them one from another, as a shepherd separates the sheep from the goats. He will place the sheep on his right and the goats on his left."* We learned from the Parable of the Weeds among the Wheat that the good and the bad will co-exist in the Kingdom until the "end of the age." And, we learned that the good and the bad will then be separated. Also, from the Parable of the Feast, we learned that, in the Kingdom, we become members of the same family (the family of Christ) at our baptism and it's symbolized by the white garment. Therefore, as St Paul would later write: in God's eyes there is no distinction between Jew and Gentile [see Gal 3:28; Rom 10:12]. Consequently, "all the nations" must refer to the entire world and all people face final judgment.

Here, Jesus used the familiar practice, at the end of each grazing season, of each shepherd claiming his herd in order to pay the grazing fees based on headcount. Each herd had both sheep and goats with roughly one goat for every dozen lambs. In the roundup pens, there was a passageway leading in that had a narrow gate on the side where the shepherd would personally pull the goats in and a wider gate at the end where the sheep passed in. Symbolically, this depicts the separation of the good (on the shepherd's right) from the bad (on the shepherd's left). In their culture, to be on the *right* symbolized an honorable place, whereas, to be on the *left* was to be excluded.

Detail: (separation criteria) *"Inherit the kingdom prepared for you from the foundation of the world. For I was hungry, and you gave me food, I was thirsty, and you gave me drink, a stranger and you welcomed me, naked and you clothed me, ill and you cared for me, in prison and you visited me. ... Amen, I say to you, whatever you did for one of these least brothers of mine, you did for me."* This had to have been a sobering message for Jesus' listeners. Most of their lives they had been expecting that God's favor would be on those who meticulously performed *mitsvot* (met the requirements of Mosaic Law). That would "entitle" them to be included in the Kingdom of God, which would go on forever. But, in the last three years, they have been hearing from Jesus something much different.

Jesus has moved His disciples, all of whom were Jews, from their initial expectation of the Kingdom of God to something much different. Instead of stating on a single occasion "what you previously understood is wrong, the Kingdom will really be like 'this,'" He has used an incremental approach. Here, Jesus concludes that approach by telling them, and us, that the salvation plan from the foundation of the world has been that those who care for the least in God's creation will share eternal life with Him. Those who fail to care for the least in God's creation will not share eternal life with Him.

Late that afternoon, as the sun went down in the western sky, the long shadow of the Temple moved across the Kidron Valley and was advancing up the side of Mount Olivet. Soon, they would be sharing the Paschal Banquet and most likely there was a sense of joyousness as they began to make their way along the path down the slope that led to the valley below and the city gate. To avoid being seen by the Temple guards, who were still looking to arrest Jesus, they likely broke up into small groups and blended in with the many pilgrims heading into the city on the Jericho Road. The road ended at the Water Gate. From there they would make their way by the Pool of Siloam, along the wall around what would later be called the Lower City, through Xystus Square and into the Essene Quarter. There, the Upper Room, known today as the *Cenacle*, was located (at least as best as archeologists can determine). At that location they would be only a few hundred feet from the Palace of the High Priest. A location the Temple guards were not likely to look for them.

We know where this was all headed. When we set out on this journey, we knew where it was headed, to Jesus passion, death and resurrection. We took the journey hoping to draw closer to Him and hear the Word of God more clearly than we have ever heard it before.

Along the way we saw and heard Jesus, fully human and fully divine. There were many times when His humanity was so evident. He labored, He tired, He was prayerful, He was determined, He was joy-filled, He wept. He was firm, yet, He confronted adversaries with kindness and compassion. He was a master of parables and we learned so much. He tried again and again to get His followers prepared for what lay ahead, for Him and for them. There were times when His divinity was so evident. He walked on water, He miraculously cured, He raised the dead, He was transfigured before the eyes of His closest Apostles. And, there were times when we saw both God and Man in profound expressions of mercy and love; love beyond all telling.

> *"For God so loved the world that he gave his only Son, so that everyone who believes in him might not perish but might have eternal life"* [Jn 3:15-16].

Jesus' glory still lay ahead of Him that late afternoon as He and His small band of followers headed off into the shadows of the Kidron Valley ahead of us.

Walking the Parables of Jesus

Don't let your journey end here; there is so much more. Get your Bible; open it to Matthew 26:20 or Mark 14:17 or Luke 22:14 or John 13:1, which ever suits you, and join them in your imagination as they enter into their final Paschal Banquet, which Jesus transformed into the Last Supper. Then follow Jesus through His passion, death and resurrection - the greatest act of love the world has ever known. You know how to do this; Jesus wants you with Him. So, go; hurry now; they will be reaching the Upper Room soon.

12. Closing Thoughts

We have arrived, not at the end but at the beginning. With a desire to better understand Scripture, and particularly the teachings of Jesus in His parables, we set out on a journey into His life, times and words that we might draw closer to Him in our own lives.

Using the inspired writings of the evangelists and some background on the Middle East, we "walked along" with Jesus' disciples hearing Him proclaim His parables. In our imagination, we followed them from one town to another. In each place, we considered the social mix Jesus encountered there and the history of the place and how that might have influenced the 'storyline' of His parable, as well as how they might have understood His message, the same message that was intended for us.

As Jesus said to His disciples near Magdala, "*Blessed are the eyes that see what you see. For I say to you, many prophets and kings desired to see what you see, but did not see it, and to hear what you hear, but did not hear it*" [Lk 10:23-24]. In our imagination, we were able to 'see and hear,' and it has increased so much our understanding of Jesus' parables.

Yet, we are only at the beginning, if we will just continue this journey into the Word of God. Let this book be more than just an 'interesting read.' Let it be a door that opened for you, or re-opened for you, a greater desire to hear the Word of God more clearly in Scriptures. There are opportunities for you to do this, in your parish, your neighborhood bookstore, near-by community college, in on-line classes, and in faith communities and study groups around you. There is a great resurgence in Bible Studies; make it a bigger part of your life.

As I mentioned at the start of our journey, the prophet Jeremiah once wrote: "*When I found your words, Lord, I devoured them; and they became the joy and happiness of my heart*" [Jer 15:16]. May the Word of God become the joy and happiness of your heart.

Notes

1. See Vatican II, *Dei Verbum*, 1965, article 12.

2. See "Parables," in *The Catholic Encyclopedia*, 1911.

3. from Augustine's *Questiones Evangeliorum* cited in C. H. Dodd, *The Parables of the Kingdom*, 1961.

4. W. F. Lynch, *Images of Hope: Imagination as Healer of the Hopeless*, 1965.

5. Robert Alter, *The Art of Biblical Narrative*, 1983.

6. V. Matthews and D. Benjamin, *Social World of Ancient Israel*, 1993.

7. Joachim Jeremias, *Jerusalem in the Time of Jesus*, 1969.

8. Ibid.

9. K. Bailey, *Jesus Through Middle Eastern Eyes: Cultural Studies in the Gospels*, 2008.

10. David A. Dorsey, *Literary Structure of the Old Testament*, 2004 and, John Breck, *The Shape of Biblical Language (New Testament)*, 2008.

11. Nils W. Lund, "The Presence of Chiasmus in the Old Testament," in *American Journal for Semitic Languages* 46, 1929.

12. K. Bailey, *Through Peasant Eyes*, 1980.

13. Robert Alter, *The Art of Biblical Narrative*, 1983.

14. G. M. Burge, *Jesus, the Middle Eastern Storyteller*, 2009.

15. A. J. Blass, et. al. (eds), *Handbook of Early Christianity, Social Science Approaches*, 2002.

16. P. J. Thompson. *The Christian Story: Past, Present, and Future*, 2009.

17. Josephus, *Antiquities* of the Jews, XVII, viii, 1.

18. Josephus, *Antiquities of the Jews*, IV, 4; viii, 4.

19. Ibid.

20. V. Matthews and D. Benjamin, *Social World of Ancient Israel*, 1993.

21. J. F., Strange, "Nazareth" *in Anchor Biblical Dictionary*, 1992.

22. Arye, Ben-David, *Talmudic Economy, the economy of Jewish Palestine at the time of the Mishnah and the Talmud*, 1974.

23. The Torah is the first five books of Hebrew Scripture. In 458 BC, Ezra the Scribe declared the Torah the "Law of Moses;" and, a formal group, called the *soferim,* was formed whose role was to identify and interpret "God's commandments in the Law."

24. J. Herzog and P. Schaff , "Hebrew Dress and Garments," in *The Encyclopedia of Religious Knowledge*, 1914.

25. Jordan River Basis," *United Nations Inventory of Shared Water Resources in Western Asia*, 2014.

26. J. Magness, *The Archaeology of Qumran and the Dead Sea Scrolls*, 2002.

27. Robert Cardinal Sarah, *The Power of Silence*, 2017.

28. K. C. Hanson, "The Galilean Fishing Economy and the Jesus Tradition" in *Biblical Theology Bulletin*, 1997.

29. Josephus, *Antiquities of the Jews*, 18:29-30.

30. J. A, Montgomery, *The Samaritans, the earliest Jewish sect: their history, theology and literature,* 1907

31. CBS News, *60 Minutes Overtime*, April 29, 2017.

32. Augustine, *City of God*, Book XXI, chap. 8, 415 AD.

33. Mohr Siebeck, *Settlement and History in Hellenistic, Roman and Byzantine Galilee*, 2009.

34. Ten Top Discoveries," in *Biblical Archaeology Review*, Jul-Oct 2009.

35. J. Jeremias, *Jerusalem in the Time of Jesus*, 1962.

36. H. W. Hoehner, *Chronological Aspects of the Life of Christ*, 1977.

37. S. B. Sage, *Biblical Numismatics*, 2001.

38. Josephus, *Bellum Judaicum*, 75 AD, 6.422.

39. For example, F. G. Martinez and E. J. C. Tigchelaar, "Rule of the Congregation" (Scroll 1QSa) translated in *The Dead Sea Scrolls Study Edition*, 2000.

40. For example, H. Hoehner, *Chronological Aspects of the Life of Christ*, 1977.

41. There were 150 psalms in the Hebrew Scriptures. At the time the Greek Empire included the Middle East, Greek was the only language allowed in public, so the Hebrew Scriptures were translated into Greek. That translation is known as the Septuagint ("the work of seventy"). Completed in 132 BC, the Septuagint also contained 150 psalms, but they were number slightly different from the original Hebrew because of multiple versions of several of the psalms in use at the time. Today, Jews, Catholics, Lutherans, Anglicans, and Calvinists follow the Hebrew numbering, while other Christian denominations and the Greek Orthodox follow the Greek numbering.

Table 7: Numbering of the Psalms

Hebrew Numbering	Greek Numbering
1-8	1-8
9	9:1-21
10	9:22-39
11-113	10-112
114	113:1-8
115	113:9-26
116:1-9	114
116:10-19	115
117-146	116-145
147:1-11	146
147:12-20	147
148-150	148-150

From 382 AD to 405 AD, St Jerome translated the Septuagint into Latin, known as the Vulgate. He followed the Greek numbering of the psalms. In 1943, Pope Pius XII's encyclical *Divino Afflante Spiritu*, called for translations from original texts rather than the Vulgate. Catholic texts prior to 1943 had followed the Greek numbering.

There is also a second difference in numbering, the enumeration of the verses. Most of the psalms begin with a superscription that identifies the ascribed author, the circumstances of its composition and notes about its musical accompaniment. The Greek word, *psalmoi*, means "words for music." Most Catholic Bibles, such as the popular *Catholic Study Bible*, have assigned a verse number to these superscriptions. Consequently, for those psalms, the verse numbers used in the Catholic Liturgy are at least one number higher than in many other Christian texts [cf. *The Psalms, New Catholic Version*, 2002].

42. Slavery in the Roman World," in *Ancient History Encyclopedia*, 2013.

43. Josephus, *Antiquities of the Jews*, 13:8:1.

44. J. B. Green, *The Gospel of Luke*, 1997.

45. W. Foerster, *Palestinian Judaism in New Testament Times*, 1964.

46. K. E. Bailey, "Women in the New Testament: A Middle Eastern Cultural View," *Theology Matters,* Jan/Feb 2000

47. Haim Watzman, *A Crack in the Earth: A Journey up Israel's Rift Valley*, 2007.

48. See article 114 in the *Catechism of the Catholic Church*.

49. Josephus, *Bellum Judaicum*, 75 AD, 3:10.

50. F. Josephus, *Antiquities of the Jews,* 18:2.

51. K. Larsen, *Recognizing the Stranger, Recognition Scenes and the Gospel of John*, 2008.

52. B. Pixner, *Paths of the Messiah*, 1991.

53. The number seven symbolized completeness. The statement that Mary Magdalene was possessed by seven demons indicates that she was completely under the control of demonic power; she was essentially paralyzed, either by illness or a mental condition like epilepsy. Consequently, she could not have been a prostitute as she has been incorrectly characterized for many centuries.

54. F. Josephus, *Antiquities of the Jews*, 20.9.1.

55. Jerome, *De Viris Illustribus*, 390 AD.

56. This point has been made many times before by others, but it bears repeating. The term, "the Jews," as used in John's Gospel, did not refer to the Jewish people. It referred to the Jewish authorities. In the time of Jesus, the Jewish authorities were the Sadducees who ran the Temple in Jerusalem. In the time of John's first listeners, it was the synagogue officials who denounced those Jews who believed in Christ as *minim* (which

means "heretics") and had them expelled from the synagogues. For a Jew to be expelled from the synagogue cut them off from their cultural and community roots. It set them adrift in the ancient Middle East, which was very much a community-oriented world. The mere mention of "the Jews" in John's Gospel likely brought pain to the hearts of his first listeners, and it was definitely not an anti-Semitic reference.

57. F. Farrar, *The Life of Christ*, 2008.

58. A. Edersheim, *The Temple, Its Ministry and Services as They Were at the Time of Jesus Christ*, 1880.

59. In the *New American Bible, revised edition,* the footnote to this passage, John 8:1-11, states that the story of the woman caught in adultery is a later insertion, absent from all early Greek manuscripts. It is a Western text-type insertion, attested mainly in Old Latin translations. There are many features in the language of this passage that are not characteristic of John. While John most likely did not write this passage, it is certainly characteristic of Jesus. The Catholic Church accepts this passage as canonical scripture. This is a good illustration the principle that being "an inspired author of Scripture" is not an attribute of the person, it is an act of God. There are many books in the Bible which are the work of several authors and many which were not written by the one to whom the book is ascribed.

60. J. H. Charlesworth (ed.), *Jesus and Archaeology*, 2006.

61. H. T. Ong, *The Multilingual Jesus and the Sociolinguistic World of the New Testament*, 2016.

62. R. D. Miller, *Chieftains of the Highland Clans: A History of Israel in the 12th and 11th Centuries B.C.*, 2005].

63. V. J. Philippe, *Reclamation's History of the Jordan River Basin in Jordan*, 2003.

64. International Trade Administration, "Jordan - Agricultural Sectors" in *Jordan Country Commercial Guide*, February 22, 2017.

65. Josephus, *Antiquities of the Jews*, 18.116-119.

66. F. Stern, *A Rabbi Looks at Jesus' Parables,* 2006.

67. Bruce Wells, *Inheritance Laws in Ancient Israel*, 2010.

68. Brad Young, *The Parables, Jewish Tradition and Christian Interpretation*, 1998.

69. T. Kobashi, "Precise timing and characterization of abrupt climate change 8,200 years ago" .in *Quaternary Science Reviews*. 26, 2007.

70. Josephus, *Antiquities of the Jews*, 12:4.

71. The details and the settings depicted in these two versions are enough different that some authors have regarded them as two different parables rather than the same parable used to convey two quite different messages.

72. J. H. Neyrey, "Meals, Food and Table Fellowship," in *The Social Sciences and New Testament Interpretation*, 1996.

73. C. Hezser, *Jewish Slavery in Antiquity.* 2005.

74. L. J. Musselman, *Jordan in Bloom: Wildflowers of the Holy Land*, 2000.

75. G. Vaughan & J.S. Hemingway, *The Utilization of Mustards*, 1959.

76. D. F. Buhl, *Geographie des alten Palestina*, 1896.

77. C. A. Lapide, *The Great Commentary*, 1887.

78. J. E. Boswell, "Exposition and Oblation: The Abandonment of Children and the Ancient and Medieval Family" in *American Historical Review,* 1984.

79. M. Healy, *The Gospel of Mark, Catholic Commentary on Sacred Scripture,* 2008.

80. Y. Aharoni, *The Land of the Bible: A Historical Geography,* 1962.

81. K. E. Bailey, *Poet and Peasant,* 1976.

82. C. G. Montefiore, *Rabbinic Literature and Gospel Teachings,* 1930.

83. J. Jeremias, *New Testament Theology,* 1971.

84. W. O. E. Oesterley, *The Gospel Parables in the Light of their Jewish Background,* 1936.

85. K. E. Bailey, *Poet and Peasant,* 1976.

86. I. Sa'id, *Commentary on the Gospel of Luke,* 1970.

87. K. E. Bailey, *Poet and Peasant,* 1976.

88. *Book of Jubilees,* ~150 BC.

89. K. E. Bailey, *Poet and Peasant,* 1976.

90. J. D. M. Derrett, *Law in the New Testament,* 1970.

91. J. Jeremias, *The Parables of Jesus,* 1963.

92. K. E. Bailey, *Finding the Lost Cultural Keys to Luke 15,* 1992.

93. A. Edersheim, *The Temple, Its Ministry and Services as They Were at the Time of Jesus Christ,* 1880.

94. F. H. Wright, *Manners and Customs of Bible Lands,* 1953.

95. G. M. Mackie, *Bible Manners and Customs,* 1898.

96. R. Littlejohn, "The Hebrew Concept of Time," in *Biblical Illustrator*, Winter 1999-2000.

97. V. Matthews and D. Benjamin, *Social World of Ancient Israel*, 1993.

98. K. E. Bailey, *Through Peasant Eyes*, 1980.

99. The Book of Sirach was widely read in synagogues as part of their *Ketuvim* ("wisdom writings") from around 132 BC on. However, some time before 200 AD, all texts believed to have been written in Greek, including Sirach, were dropped from the Hebrew canon of scripture [D. Senior, et. al. (eds), Sirach (Ecclesiasticus) Reading Guide in The Catholic Study Bible, 1990].

100. K. E. Bailey, *Through Peasant Eyes*, 1980.

101. I. H. Marshall, *The Gospel of Luke*, 1978.

101. S. Safrai and M. S. Judith (eds), *The Jewish People in the First Century*, Section One, Volume One, 1976.

103. A. Edersheim, *The Temple, Its Ministry and Services as They Were at the Time of Jesus Christ*, 1880.

104. Ibid.

105. J. W. Charlesworth (ed), *Jesus and Archaeology*, 2006.

106. ABC News, "*Jerusalem olive trees among oldest in world*," October 20, 2012.

107. W. R. Herzog II, *Prophet and Teacher*, 2005.

108. A. Goldberg, *The Semukha – a Compositional Form of the Rabbinic Homily*, 1985.

109. The *semukha* in the Fall of Man story [Genesis 3:1-13] is an excellent example of the use of antithesis by biblical authors. The temptation by the *nachash* ("shiny one"), interpreted as Satan, is placed in juxtaposition to the sin of Adam and Eve. A

common misinterpretation is that the temptation "<u>caused</u>" their sin. While the concept of cause-effect was quite common as far back as Aristotle, it was not a concept held by ancient Jews. They saw God as the sole and direct cause of everything, so they did not look for cause-effect connections. [R. Gilmour, *Juxtaposition and the Elisha Cycle*, 2014 and G. F. Moore (ed), *Judaism in the First Centuries of the Christian Era*, 1927]. Therefore, the underlying principle in the Fall of Man story could not be that temptation causes sin. Generally, the scripture authors did not give hints to the underlying principle, leaving discernment entirely to the listeners. However, the author of Genesis gave two hints; (1) Adam's silence betrayed the disposition of his heart. (2) How Eve referred to God and exaggerated His command betrayed the disposition of her heart. The underlying principle in the Fall of Man story is that sin arises from the disposition of our heart. Temptation may play on our weaknesses, but it does not cause sin.

110. The Ten Commandments state, in simple "Biblical wording" profound underlying principles of behavior [cf. *Catechism of the Catholic Church*, #2081].

Table 8: The Moral Principles Underlying the Ten Commandments

No. (a)	(b)	(c)	Exodus 20:	Expressed in "Biblical wording"	The underlying moral principle (d)
1	1	Preface	2	I am the Lord your God.	Adore God alone, for He is the only god
	2	1	3	You shall have no other gods before me.	
		2	4-6	You shall not make for yourself an idol.	
2	3	3	7	You shall not take the name of the Lord, your God, in vain	Respect the mystery of God in your speech

3	4	4	8-11	Remember the Sabbath and keep it holy	Imitate God in your use of time
4	5	5	12	Honor your father and mother	Honor legitimate authority in your life
5	6	6	13	You shall not murder	Guard the sanctity of life
6	7	7	14	You shall not commit adultery	Keep sacred relationships sacred
7	8	8	15	You shall not steal	Preserve others' property rights
8	9	9	16	You shall not bear false witness against your neighbor	Preserve others' dignity and good name
9	10	10	17b	You shall not covet your neighbor's wife	Be pure of heart with others
10			17a	You shall not covet your neighbor's goods.	Be poor in spirit, relying only on God

(a) Numbering used by Catholics and Lutherans, based on St Augustine's *Questions on Exodus, Book II*, 419 AD.
(b) Numbering used by Orthodox, Anglicans and other Christians based on Origen of Alexandria's *Homilies of Origen*, 245 AD.
(c) Numbering used by Jews and Muslims, based on *The Talmud*, ~200 AD.
(d) Abstracted from *Catechism of the Catholic Church*, Part Three, Section Two, *The Ten Commandments*.

111. F. Stern, *A Rabbi Looks at Jesus' Parables*, 2006.

112. B. Wells, *Inheritance Laws in Ancient Israel*, 2010.

113. K. E. Bailey, *Through Peasant Eyes*, 1980.

114. W. M. Thomson, *The Land and the Book*, Vol II, 1871.

115. I. Sa'id, *Commentary on the Gospel of Luke*, 1970.

116. W. M. Thomson, *The Land and the Book*, Vol II, 1871.

117. K. E. Bailey, *Through Peasant Eyes*, 1980.

118. B. W. Bacon, "Pharisees and Herodians in Mark," in *Journal of Biblical Literature*, Vol. 39, 1920.

119. H. Nouwen, *Life of the Beloved*, 1992.

120. F. Josephus, *Antiquities of the Jews*, 13.10.6.

121. D. R. Schwartz, *Studies in the Jewish Background of Christianity*, 1992.

122. A. Edersheim, *The Temple, Its Ministry and Services as They Were at the Time of Jesus Christ*, 1880.

123. J. Jeremias, *Jerusalem in the Time of Jesus*, 1962.

124. The ancient symbolic meaning of the number thirteen was both authority and rebellion [J.J. Davis, *Biblical Numerology*, 1968]. So, having thirteen boxes for contributions in the Temple treasury may have been a play on the name, *Israel*, which means: wrestles with God.

125. R. Littlejohn, "The Hebrew Concept of Time," in *Biblical Illustrator*, Winter 1999-2000.

126. J. Andreau, *Banking and Business in the Roman World*, 1999.

127. Matthew Henry, *Henry's Commentary*, 1706.

128. C. Spurgeon, *Spurgeon's Commentary*, 1892.

129. W. Barkley, *Daily Study Bible Series: The Gospel of Matthew*, 1975.

130. J. M. Casciaro, et. al., *Navarre Bible Series, The Gospel of Matthew*, 1988.

131. A. Edersheim, *The Temple, Its Ministry and Services as They Were at the Time of Jesus Christ*, 1880.

132. *Mishnah,* "Pesachim," 10:5.

133. Brant Pitre, *Jesus and the Jewish Roots of the Eucharist,* 2011.

134. J. J., Davis, *Biblical Numerology: A Basic Study of the Use of Numbers in the Bible,* 1968.

Bibliography

ABC News, *"Jerusalem olive trees among oldest in world,"* October 20, 2012.

Aharoni, Yohanan, *The Land of the Bible: A Historical Geography,* 1962.

Alter, Robert, *The Art of Biblical Narrative,* 1983.

Ancient History Encyclopedia, "Slavery in the Roman World," 2013.

Andreau, Jean, *Banking and Business in the Roman World,* 1999.

Augustine, *City of God,* Book XXI, chap. 8, 415 AD.

Augustine, *Questiones Evangeliorum* cited in C. H. Dodd, *The Parables of the Kingdom,* 1961

Bacon, B. W., "Pharisees and Herodians in Mark," in *Journal of Biblical Literature,* Vol. 39, 1920.

Bailey, Kenneth E., *Finding the Lost Cultural Keys to Luke 15,* 1992.

Bailey, Kenneth E., *Jacob & the Prodigal,* 2003.

Bailey, Kenneth E., *Jesus Through Middle Eastern Eyes: Cultural Studies in the Gospels,* 2008.

Bailey, Kenneth E., *Poet and Peasant*, 1976.

Bailey, Kenneth E., *Through Peasant Eyes*, 1980.

Bailey, Kenneth E. "Women in the New Testament: A Middle Eastern Cultural View," *Theology Matters,* Jan/Feb 2000.

Barkley, William, *Daily Study Bible Series: The Gospel of Luke*, 1975.

Barkley, William, *Daily Study Bible Series: The Gospel of Matthew*, 1975.

Barkley, William, *The Parables of Jesus*, 1970.

Barton, George A., *Archaeology and the Bible*, 1946.

Bengel, Johann A., *Gnomin Novi Testamenti*, (Exegetical Annotations on the New Testament), 1742.

Ben-David, Arye, *Talmudic Economy, the economy of Jewish Palestine at the time of the Mishnah and the Talmud*, 1974.

Berkhof, Louis, *New Testament Introduction*, 2016.

Biblical Archaeology Review, "Ten Top Discoveries," Jul-Oct 2009.

Blasi, A, J., et. al. (eds), *Handbook of Early Christianity, Social Science Approaches*, 2002.

Book of Jubilees, ~150 BC.

Boswell, John Eastburn, *"*Exposition and Oblation: The Abandonment of Children and the Ancient and Medieval Family*"* in *American Historical Review,*1984.

Breck, John, *The Shape of Biblical Language (New Testament)*, 2008.

Buhl, D. F., *Geographie des alten Palestina*, 1896.

Burge, Gary M., *Jesus, The Middle Eastern Storyteller*, 2009.

Burge, Gary M., *The Bible and the Land*, 2009.

Casciaro, Jose M., et. al., *Navarre Bible Series, The Gospel of Matthew*, 1988.

Catechism of the Catholic Church, 1997.

Catholic Encyclopedia, "Parables," 1911.

CBS News, *60 Minutes Overtime*, April 29, 2017.

Charlesworth, James W. (ed), *Jesus and Archaeology*, 2006.

Cheung, Vincent, *The Parables of Jesus*, 2014.

Clements, Ronald Ernest (ed), The World of Ancient Israel, 1989.

Davis, John J., *Biblical Numerology: A Basic Study of the Use of Numbers in the Bible*, 1968.

Derrett, J. D. M., *Law in the New Testament*, 1970.

Dorsey, David A., *Literary Structure of the Old Testament*, 2004.

Edersheim, Alfred, *Sketches of Jewish Social Life in the Days of Christ*, 1876.

Edersheim, Alfred, *The Life and Times of Jesus the Messiah*, 1883.

Edersheim, Alfred, *The Temple, Its Ministry and Services as They Were at the Time of Jesus Christ*, 1880.

Ellickson, R.C, and C.D. Thorland, "Ancient Land Law: Mesopotamia, Egypt, Israel," in *Yale Law Faculty Scholarship Series*, 1995.

Farrar, Frederic, *The Life of Christ*, 2008.

Feldman, Louis H. and Meyer Reinhold (eds), *Jewish Life and Thought among Greeks and Romans*, 1996.

Finger, Reta H., *Of Widows and Meals, Communal Meals in the Book of Acts*, 2007.

Foerster, Werner, *Palestinian Judaism in New Testament Times*, 1964.

Gardner, Gregg E., *The Origins of Organized Church in Rabbinic Judaism*, 2005.

Gibson, Simon, *The Final Days of Jesus: The Archeological Evidence*, 2009.

Gilmour, Rachelle, *Juxtaposition and the Elisha Cycle*, 2014.

Gottlieb, Isaac, *Order in the Bible*, 2009.

Goldberg, Arnold, *The Semukha – a Compositional Form of the Rabbinic Homily*, 1985.

Green, Joel B., *The Gospel of Luke*, 1997.

Guardi, Romano, *The Lord*, 1937.

Hanson, K.C., "The Galilean Fishing Economy and the Jesus Tradition" in *Biblical Theology Bulletin*, 1997.

Healy, Mary, *The Gospel of Mark, Catholic Commentary on Sacred Scripture*, 2008.

Harding, Gerald L., *The Antiquities of Jordan*, 1959.

Henry, Matthew, *Henry's Commentary*, 1706.

Herzog, Jakob and Philip Schaff, "Hebrew Dress and Garments," in *The Encyclopedia of Religious Knowledge*, 1914.

Herzog II, William R., *Prophet and Teacher*, 2005.

Hezser, Catherine, *Jewish Slavery in Antiquity*. 2005.

Hirsch, Emil G. and Henry Hyvernat, "Fig and Fig-Tree," in *Jewish Encyclopedia*, 1906.

Hoehner, Harold W, *Chronological Aspects of the Life of Christ*, 1977.

Holden, Joseph and Norman Geisler, *The Popular Handbook of Archaeology and the Bible*, 1960.

International Trade Administration, "Jordan - Agricultural Sectors" in *Jordan Country Commercial Guide*, February 22, 2017.

Jeremias, Joachim, *Jerusalem in the Time of Jesus*, 1962.

Jeremias, Joachim, *Jesus and the Message of the New Testament*, 2002.

Jeremias, Joachim, *New Testament Theology*, 1971.

Jeremias, Joachim, *The Parables of Jesus*, 1963.

Jerome, *De Viris Illustribus*, 390 AD.

Jewish Encyclopedia, "Day of Atonement or Yom Kippur," 1960.

Jewish Virtual Library, "Bethsaida," 1998.

Jordan River Basis," *United Nations Inventory of Shared Water Resources in Western Asia*, 2014.

Josephus, Flavius, *Antiquities of the Jews*, ~94 AD.

Josephus, Flavius, *Bellum Judaicum*, ~75 AD.

Keener, Craig S., *A Commentary on the Gospel of Matthew*, 1999.

Kend, Charles F., *Biblical Geography & History*, 1911.

Kobashi, T. et al., "Precise timing and characterization of abrupt climate change 8,200 years ago".in *Quaternary Science Reviews*. **26**: pp. 1212–1222, 2007.

Lapide, Cornelius A., *The Great Commentary*, 1887.

Larsen, Kasper, *Recognizing the Stranger, Recognition Scenes and the Gospel of John*, 2008.

Lebanese Ministry of the Environment, "Rivers of Lebanon," 2005.

Littlejohn, Ronnie, "The Hebrew Concept of Time," in *Biblical Illustrator*, Winter 1999-2000.

Lund, Nils W, "The Presence of Chiasmus in the Old Testament," in *American Journal for Semitic Languages* 46, 1929.

Lynch, William F., *Images of Hope: Imagination as Healer of the Hopeless*, 1965.

Macarthur, John, *Parables, The Mysteries of God's Kingdom Revealed Through the Stories Jesus Told*, 2015.

Mackie, George M., *Bible Manners and Customs*, 1998.

Magness, Jodi, *The Archaeology of Qumran and the Dead Sea Scrolls*, 2002.

Maline, Bruce, *The New Testament World, Insights from Cultural Anthropology*, 1981.

Marshall, I. Howard, *The Gospel of Luke*, 1978.

Martin, Francis and William Wright IV, *The Gospel of John, Catholic Commentary on Sacred Scripture*, 2015.

Martin, George, *Bringing the Gospel of Luke to Life*, 2011.

Martinez, F. Garcia and E. J. C. Tigchelaar, "Rule of the Congregation" (Scroll 1QSa) translated in *The Dead Sea Scrolls Study Edition*, 2000.

Matthews, Victor and Don Benjamin, *Social World of Ancient Israel,* 1993.

McNutt, Paula M., *Reconstructing the Society of Ancient Israel,* 1999.

Milgrom, Jacob, *Leviticus 1-16,* 1998

Miller, Robert D. *Chieftains of the Highland Clans: A History of Israel in the 12th and 11th Centuries B.C.,* 2005.

Mishnah, "Pesachim," 10:5.

Mitch, Curtis and Edward Sri, *The Gospel of Matthew, Catholic Commentary on Sacred Scripture,* 2010.

Moore, George F. (ed), *Judaism in the First Centuries of the Christian Era,* 1927.

Montefiore, C. G., *Rabbinic Literature and Gospel Teachings,* 1930.

Montgomery, James Alan, *The Samaritans, the earliest Jewish sect: their history, theology and literature,* 1907.

Musselman, Lytton J., *Jordan in Bloom: Wildflowers of the Holy Land,* 2000.

New American Bible, revised edition, 2010.

Neyrey, Jerome H., "Meals, Food and Table Fellowship," in *The Social Sciences and New Testament Interpretation,* 1996.

Nouwen, Henri, *Life of the Beloved,* 1992.

Nun, Mendal, *The Sea of Galilee and its Fishermen in the New Testament,* 1989.

Ong, Hughson T., *The Multilingual Jesus and the Sociolinguistic World of the New Testament,* 2016.

Osborne, Grant R., *The Hermeneutical Spiral*, 2007.

Oesterley, W. O. E., *The Gospel Parables in the Light of their Jewish Background*, 1936.

Philippe, Venot J., *Reclamation's History of the Jordan River Basin in Jordan*, 2003.

Pitre, Brant, *Jesus and the Jewish Roots of the Eucharist*, 2011.

Pitre, Brant, "Jesus, the Messianic Banquet, and the Kingdom of God" in *Letter & Spirit* 5 (2009): pp. 145–166.

Pixner, Bargil, *Paths of the Messiah*, 1991.

Plaut, W. G., et. al., *The Torah, a Modern Commentary*, 1981.

Raphael, Simcha, *Living and Dying in Ancient Times*, 2015.

Ratzinger, Joseph (Pope Benedict XVI), *Teaching and Learning the Love of God*, 2016.

Rose, Tov, *Jesus in the Targums*, 2016.

"Rule of the Congregation" (Scroll 1QSa) translated by F. G. Martinez and E. J. C. Tigchelaar in *The Dead Sea Scrolls Study Edition*, 2000.

Russell, David S., *The Method and Message of Jewish Apocalyptic 200 BC – 100 AD*, 1964.

Safrai, Shmuel and M. Stern Judith (eds), *The Jewish People in the First Century*, Section One, Volume One, 1976].

Sage, Shirley B., *Biblical Numismatics*, 2001.

Saint Augustine, *City of God*, Book XXI, chap. 8, 415 AD.

Sa'id, Ibrahim, *Commentary on the Gospel of Luke*, 1970.

Sarah, Robert Cardinal, *The Power of Silence*, 2017.

Schurer, Emil, *A History of the Jewish People in the Time of Jesus Christ*, 1890.

Schwartz, Daniel R., *Studies in the Jewish Background of Christianity,* 1992.

Scott Jr., J. Julius, *Jewish Backgrounds of the New Testament*, 1995.

Senior, Donald, et. al. (eds), "Sirach (Ecclesiasticus) Reading Guide" in *The Catholic Study Bible*, 1990.

Senior, Donald, et. al. (eds), "The Book of Psalms" in *The Catholic Study Bible*, 1990.

Sheed, Frank J., *To Know Christ Jesus*, 2014.

Sheen, Fulton J., *Life of Christ*, 1958.

Siebeck, Mohr, *Settlement and History in Hellenistic, Roman and Byzantine Galilee*, 2009.

Silva, Moises, *Biblical Words and Their Meaning*, 1983.

Spurgeon, Charles, *Spurgeon's Commentary*, 1892.

Strange, James F, "Nazareth" in *Anchor Biblical Dictionary*, 1992.

Stern, Frank, *A Rabbi Looks at Jesus' Parables,* 2006.

Ten Top Discoveries," in *Biblical Archaeology Review*, Jul-Oct 2009.

The Psalms, New Catholic Version, 2002.

Thompson, Peter J., *The Christian Story: Past, Present, and Future*, 2009.

Thomson, William M., *The Land and the Book*, Volumes I and II, 1871.

Thorsen, Steffen, *Time and Date AS*, 1998, at timeanddate.com.

Tverberg, Lois, *Walking in the Dust of Rabbi Jesus*, 2012.

Vatican II, Dei Verbum ("the Word of God"), Dogmatic Constitution on Divine Revelation, 1965.

Vaughan, J. G. and J.S. Hemingway, *The Utilization of Mustards*, 1959.

Vermes, Geza, *The Complete Dead Sea Scrolls in English*, 1962.

Watzman, Haim, *A Crack in the Earth: A Journey up Israel's Rift Valley*, 2007.

Wells, Bruce, *Inheritance Laws in Ancient Israel*, 2010.

Wright, Fred H., *Manners and Customs of Bible Lands*, 1953.

Young, Brad, *Jesus, The Jewish Theologian*, 1995.

Young, Brad, *The Parables, Jewish Tradition and Christian Interpretation*, 1998.

Zaslow, David, *Jesus, First Century Rabbi*, 2014.

Credits

Figure 1: Remains of paved section of Via Maris in Galilee, photo by Dr. William Pelletier at biblescienceguy.wordpress.com/2012/03/21/9-hike-the-bible-via-maris/.

Figure 2: Looking South into Samaria, permission to use courtesy of Dr, Todd Bolan at bibleplaces.com.

Figure 3: Looking East from Jerusalem, permission to use courtesy of Dr, Todd Bolan at bibleplaces.com.

Section 1.6.1 on "Estimated Dates in Jesus' Life" and Section 1.6.2 on "Estimated Dates of the Events in Holy Week" were principally drawn from H. W. Hoechner, *Chronological Aspects of the Life of Christ*, 1977.

Figure 4: Topographical View of Israel, permission to use courtesy of Dr, Todd Bolan at bibleplaces.com.

Figure 5: The Town Well in Nazareth (1894 photo), in public domain, photo taken prior to January 1923.

Figure 6: The Jordan River south of the Sea of Galilee, permission to use courtesy of Dr, Todd Bolan at bibleplaces.com.

Figure 7: Al-Maghtas: The Traditional Site of Jesus' Baptism, from wikipedia.com; used under the Creative Commons Attribution - Sharealike 3.0 Unported License

Figure 8: David's Falls at Ein-Gedi, from wikipedia.com; used under the Creative Commons Attribution - Sharealike 3.0 Unported License

Section 2.5 on "Ancient Jewish Wedding Customs" was principally drawn from: Victor H. Matthews and Don C. Benjamin, *Social World of Ancient Israel*, 1993.

Figure 9: Jacob's Well (1920 photo), in public domain, photo taken prior to January 1923.

Dcn. Bob Evans

Section 3.3 on "The Roots of Hometown Expectations" was principally drawn from Victor H. Matthews and Don C. Benjamin, *Social World of Ancient Israel*, 1993.

Figure 10: The Caves of Arbela, permission to use courtesy of Israel–Extreme Tours at www.israel-extreme.com.

Section 4.1 on "The Day of Atonement or Yom Kippur," was principally drawn from: *The Jewish Encyclopedia*, 1960.

Section 5.1 on "Fishing on the Sea of Galilee" was principally drawn from: Mendal Nun, *The Sea of Galilee and its Fishermen in the New Testament*, 1989.

Figure 11: A Musht Fish from the Sea of Galilee, image from Sept 1989 article: *Fish and the Sea of Galilee*, by Mendel Nun, at www.jerusalemperspective.com/4311/

Section 5.2 on "Agriculture in Ancient Israel" was principally drawn from Victor H. Matthews and Don C. Benjamin, *Social World of Ancient Israel*, 1993.

Figure 12: View from Mt Eremos, Traditional Site of Sermon on the Mount, photo by Kyle Gilbert in April 2014 article: *My Visit to Israel, Part 2*, at kylesrandom.com/2014/04/my-visit-to-israel-part-2/

Section 6.1 on 'The Jewish Expectation of the Kingdom of God" was principally drawn from D. S. Russell, *The Method and Message of Jewish Apocalyptic 200 BC –100 AD*, 1964 and B. Pitre, "Jesus, the Messianic Banquet, and the Kingdom of God" in *Letter & Spirit* 5 (2009): pp. 145–166.

Section 7.1 on Ancient Jewish Burial Practices, was principally drawn from Simcha Raphael, *Living and Dying in Ancient Times*, 2015.

Figure 13: First Interment Caves near Nain, from panoramio.com, used under the Creative Commons Attribution - Sharealike 3.0 Unported License

Section 7.3 on Debtors, Servants and Slaves in Ancient Israel, was principally drawn from Joachim Jeremias, *Jerusalem in the Time of Jesus*, 1962.

Section 7.15 on Land "Ownership" in Ancient Israel, was principally drawn from V.H. Matthews and D.C. Benjamin, *Social World of Ancient Israel*, 1993 and R.C. Ellickson and C.D. Thorland, "Ancient Land Law: Mesopotamia, Egypt, Israel," in *Yale Law Faculty Scholarship Series*, 1995.

Figure 14: The Remains of Magdala (1900 colorized photo) in public domain, photo taken prior to January 1923.

Figure 15: The Shoreline near Gergesa, photo by Janet Frankovic, at www.jerusalemperspective.com/2771/, permission to use courtesy of David N. Bivin at Jerusalem Perspective.com.

Section 8.2 on 'Bethsaida, Childhood of Jesus' First Disciples," was principally drawn from *Jewish Virtual Library*, "Bethsaida," 1998.

Figure 16: Ruins of Roman Pools at Bethsaida from wikimedia.org; used under the Creative Commons Attribution - Sharealike 3.0 Unported License

Figure 17: Aerial View of Tyre (1934 French Army photo) from wikimedia.org; used under the Creative Commons Attribution - Sharealike 3.0 Unported License

Figure 18: The Leonites River in the Mount Lebanon Foothills from wkimedia.org; used under the Creative Commons Attribution - Sharealike 3.0 Unported License

Figure 19: Mount Tabor (colorized 1890 photo) in public domain, photo taken prior to January 1923.

Section 9.5 on The Hebrew System of Ritual Purity was principally drawn from Jacob Milgrom, *Leviticus 1-16*, 1998.

Figure 20: Samarian foothills approaching Judea (colorized 1895 photo) in public domain, photo taken prior to January 1923.

Figure 21: *Biq'ah Yitro* (Valley of Jethro) in Perea photo from wikimedia.com; used under the Creative Commons Attribution - Sharealike 3.0 Unported License

Section 10.4 on Rabbah, the Jewel of the Levant was principally drawn from Gerald L. Harding, *The Antiquities of Jordan*, 1959.

Figure 22: Ruins of Castle of the Servant photo from wikipedia.com; used under the Creative Commons Attribution - Sharealike 3.0 Unported License.

Figure 23: The upper Jabbok River Valley photo from wikimedia.com; used under the Creative Commons Attribution - Sharealike 3.0 Unported License.

Section 10.10 on The Cultural Position of Fig Trees was principally drawn from Emil G. Hirsch and Henry Hyvernat, "Fig and Fig-Tree," in *Jewish Encyclopedia*, 1906.

Figure 24: Bedouin Tents at Site of Ancient Penuel, photo from wikimedia.com; used under the Creative Commons Attribution - Sharealike 3.0 Unported License.

Section 10.27 on "The Man Who Had Two Sons" was principally drawn from W. G. Plaut, et. al., *The Torah, a Modern Commentary*, 1981.

Section 10.33 on the "Bosom of Abraham" was principally drawn from Frank Stern, *A Rabbi Looks at Jesus' Parables*, 2006.

Section 11.7 on "Jerusalem and the Temple in the Time of Jesus" was principally drawn from Alfred Edersheim, *The Temple, Its Ministry and Services as They Were at the Time of Jesus Christ*, 1880.

Figure 25: Topography of Jerusalem in the First Century, permission to use courtesy of Galyn Wiemers at generationword.com.

Figure 26: New Testament Jerusalem map, image free to use from wiki--travel.com: map of jerusalem new testament #444576.

Figure 27: Map of the Temple in the First Century, permission to use courtesy of Galyn Wiemers at generationword.com.

Section 11.17 on "The Role of Virgins in Ancient Israel" was principally drawn from V. H. Matthews and D. C. Benjamin, *Social World of Ancient Israel*, 1993.

Glossary

abarah	Hebrew, meaning "crossing." A place for crossing a river.
adelphoi	Greek, meaning "brothers." Male members of the same generation in ones extended family.
Adoptionism	A heresy that taught that Jesus was adopted as the Son of God upon His resurrection because of his sinless devotion to the will of God. Some early proponents held that the adoption occurred at Jesus' Baptism.
Adummim Pass	Hebrew, meaning "red things" pass. A narrow pass on the Jericho Road, about five miles from Jericho, where the rock formation has red streaks in it. St Jerome, who translated the Bible into Latin in the late 4th century, contended that the name of the pass was given because of the blood that bandits repeatedly shed at this place. He also argued that there was an inn not far away and that the Adummim Pass was the place Jesus was referring to in the Parable of the Good Samaritan.
Aelia Capltolina	Roman name for Jerusalem following their destruction of the Temple and much of the city in 70 AD.
Ain Ghazal	Hebrew, meaning "Gazelle spring." The spring near Rabbah that, with two small wadis, forms the headwaters of the Jabbok River. Archeological evidence shows that there was a community near this spring as far back as 10,300 BC.
allegory	Greek, meaning "figurative." A literary device in which each person, event and detail in a story stands for something or someone else.

alma	Hebrew, meaning "maiden." Usually translated into Greek as parthenos ("virgin").
Al-Maghtas	Arabic, meaning "baptism." The traditional spot on the Jordan River where Jesus was baptized. It is about 5 miles north of where the Jordan flows into the Dead Sea.
am ha'aretz	Hebrew, meaning "people of the land." A derogatory term used by the Pharisees to refer to the uneducated masses.
am ha'sefer	Hebrew, meaning "people of the book." An endearing term used by the Pharisees to refer to the faithful of God.
anagnorisis	Greek, meaning "to know again." The point in the plot of a Greek tragedy at which the protagonist makes known his or her true identity or discovers the true nature of his or her own life situation.
antithesis	Greek, meaning "to set against." A literary device that places in contrast two apparently contradictory concepts to draw attention to an underlying principle.
Antonia Fortress	A garrison at the northwest corner of the Temple in Jerusalem which had a subterranean passageway into the Temple. The Roman soldiers used this as an avenue into the Temple's Court of Gentiles to quickly take control of the Temple to quell any public disturbance there.
apostate	Greek, meaning "defection." One who denies their faith, often when faced with persecution, the loss of their family, their children or loved ones.

assēs	The earliest Roman coins to replace Greek coins in the lands conquered by Rome. The metal content in assēs changed a number of times over the history of the Roman Empire.
avodah	Hebrew, meaning "prayer."
Beautiful Gate	see Court of Women
Beelzebub	Hebrew, meaning "lord of the flies." A derogatory name for Satan ("accuser" or "adversary"). Satan was regarded as like dung and those around him like filth-ladened flies. To be acting by the power of Beelzebub was to be an enemy of the people in the worst possible way.
Beisan	Hebrew, meaning "house of rest." A town located near the principal crossing point on the Jordan River just south of the Sea of Galilee. It has been in use since at least 1500 BC. It was also known by its Greek name: Scythopolis.
beit-knesset	Hebrew, meaning ""house of assembly" (Greek: *synagogue*). Building, initially houses, for regular gatherings for prayer and reflection on scriptures
berakhah	Hebrew, meaning "blessing."
Bethabara	Hebrew, meaning "across the river." A location on the Jordan River, not far from Jericho, where John the Baptist ministered and the place where Jesus called his first six disciples. Also known as Bethany-across-the-Jordan.
Bethany	Hebrew, meaning "house of the afflicted." A village on the south-eastern side of Mount Olivet on the Jericho Road which served as a center for caring for the sick and the destitute who came as pilgrims to Jerusalem, principally from Galilee.

Dcn. Bob Evans

Bethel	Hebrew, meaning "house of God." A city in Samaria near the border with Judea. It was there that Jacob, fleeing from the wrath of his brother Esau, fell asleep on a stone and dreamed of a ladder stretching between Heaven and Earth. He named the site, Bethel. Later, following the Exodus, the Ark of the Covenant was kept in Bethel. Over the centuries, Bethel figured prominently in the ministries of the prophets: Samuel, Elijah, Elisha, Hosea and Jeremiah.
Bethesda	Hebrew, meaning "house of healing." A pool in Jerusalem probably fed by an underground geyser. It had a portico around it; and people would gather around and wait for the water to stir, thinking that an angel was there stirring up the water. If they hurried and entered the pool while the water was still moving, they believed that they would be healed.
Bethphage	Hebrew, meaning "house of green figs." A walled village on Mount Olivet that served as a meeting place for the Great Sanhedrin for decisions about what was holy and what was not holy. It was to Bethphage that the Messiah was expected to first appear.
Bethsaida	Hebrew, meaning "house of fishing." A city situated on a large mound of Jordan River silt just east of where the river enters the Sea of Galilee. It was once a great city but had declined to little more than a town by the first century. Jesus' first six disciples, John, James, Andrew, Simon Peter, Philip and Nathanael grew up in Bethsaida
betulah	Hebrew, meaning "virgin." (Greek: parthenos).

betulim	Hebrew, meaning "marks of virginity." The "proof cloth," a white linen cloth on which the new bride bled providing proof of her virginity. The proof cloth was retained by the bride's father to counter any later claims that his daughter was not a virgin at the time of her marriage.
bikkurah	Hebrew, meaning "early fig." The first fig crop of the year, harvested in June and eaten fresh.
Biq'ah Yitro	Hebrew, meaning "Valley of Jethro." A narrow, wadi-fed valley running east from the Jordan River and rising steadily from about 800 feet below sea level to nearly 3300 feet above sea level near Rabbah (also known as Philadelphia).
Birah Ebhedh	Hebrew, meaning "Castle of the Servant." A grand palace, built around 200 BC near Rabbah, by the governor at the time, who was a member of the powerful Tobiad clan in that region. The governor referred to himself as the "servant of the king" although he and his clan actively plotted against the Greek king. This palace is known today by the Arabic name, Qasr al-Abd.
Book of Jubilees	A set of 50 volumes of rabbinic expansion on and restatement of the Book of Genesis and early Exodus, written around 150 BC.
burnt-offering	An offering made in the Temple which involved selecting and purchasing a lamb in the Court of Gentiles. Then, having it inspected for blemishes by a Temple priest; taking it to the Altar of Burnt Offerings in the Court of Priests; having the lamb slaughtered there and one-third consumed by fire on the Altar as an offering to God, one-third given to the Temple priests, and taking the remaining one-third to be consumed that evening with family and friends.

Caesarea Philippi	A Roman mountain-retreat city located at the headwaters of the Banias River on the southwestern slope of Mount Hermon, near the Via Maris. It was adjacent to a spring, grotto and related shrines dedicated to the Greek god, Pan. The Greeks called the city Paneas ("city of Pan").
Caesarea	A city on the Mediterranean coast. In 22 BC, Herod the Great began this site as a Roman seaside resort in honor of Caesar Augustus. It was in Caesarea, that Pontius Pilate lived and operated the administrative center of Judea during Jesus' day.
Canaanite	A member of a Semitic people that inhabited parts of ancient Palestine and were conquered by the Israelites and largely absorbed by them. Canaan was the name of the fourth son of Ham, the youngest son of Noah. Like Canaan, the Canaanites were considered a cursed people.
Capernaum (also spelled Capharnaum)	A town situated where the Upper Jordan River enters the Sea of Galilee. It was a strategic import-export site and major crossroads in northern Israel. It was "home base" for Jesus during His Galilee ministry period. The fishing docks and fish brokers in northern Galilee were located in Capernaum.
Cave of Machpelah	Hebrew, meaning cave of the "double tombs." A cave at Mamre near Hebron which was purchased by Abraham as the family place of second internment. Abraham, Isaac, Jacob, Sarah, Rebecca, and Leah are all buried there. The only one who is missing is Rachel, who was buried near Bethlehem where she died in childbirth.

Caves of Arbela	Caves at the foot of Mount Arbel, just west of Magdala, which were the first-century dwelling places in Galilee of those, principally lepers, who were banished as being "permanently unclean."
Cenacle	From the Latin word for "dining room." A house with an upper room located in the David's Tomb Compound in the Essene Quarter of Jerusalem. It is traditionally held to be the site of the Last Supper. It is unclear when the current building on the site was constructed.
Chagigah	Hebrew, meaning "festival offering." A two-fold peace offering to be made on festival occasions as a burnt-offering in the Temple. During the Passover festival, the first offering was to take place during the week of preparation and the second was to take place on Passover Day, Nisan 15. The first Chagigah was voluntary and was typically offered on Nisan 12; the second offering was required.
chardal	Hebrew, meaning "mustard." A bush that grew so abundantly in the wild that it was not normal to deliberately plant it. In ancient times, it was not a spice; rather, when ground into a paste and wrapped in a cloth it was applied to areas of the body hurting from an injury or arthritis. Also known by the Greek name, sinapi.
chatan	Hebrew, meaning "to tie or connect." The name for the groom or son-in-law.
Chel	Hebrew, meaning "fortress." The barrier in the Temple which surrounded the upper courts from the lower, Count of Gentiles. Nine staircases of fourteen steps led up to the Chel from the Court of Gentiles.

chiasm	A Middle Eastern literary construct in which there was a repetition of similar ideas, first presented in a forward sequence then repeated in the reverse sequence. The objective of the chiasmic construct was to point to a central idea, which was in the center between the two sequences.
chuppah	Hebrew, meaning "covering." A tent-like structure in which the couple consummated their marriage before entering the wedding banquet.
Chysorrhoas River	Greek, meaning "golden flowing." A river arising in the foothills of the Mount Hermon range which flows south into the Jabbok River just south of the city of Gerasa in Perea.
cistus	A flowering plant found in dry or rocky soils throughout the Mediterranean region. It is also known as rockrose. Resin from the cistus plant was used to make the ancient medicinal ointment known as "balm of Gilead."
Court of Israel	The second of the upper courts in the Temple that was for all males who were not clergy. They entered the Court of Israel via a curved stairway of fifteen steps, which led to the Nicanor Gate. It was on this curved stairway that mothers presented their first-born sons to God.
Court of Priests	The third of the upper courts in the Temple. It contained the Altar of Burnt Offerings and the Laver of Cleansing (also known as the Brazen Sea) where animal sacrifices took place. Just beyond the Altar of Burnt Offerings was a curtain which concealed the Holy Place from view.

Court of the Gentiles	The outer court of the Temple which was paved with the finest variegated marble. It was the furthest a Gentile could go in the Temple, under pain of death. There were a series of small apartments in this court where Levites resided when they were on Temple duty. It was in this area that animals for sacrifice were sold and the money-changers conducted business
Court of Women	The first of the upper courts in the Temple, which as the name implies was the furthest women could proceed in the Temple. They entered the Court of Women through what was called the Beautiful Gate.
Damia	Latin, meaning "goddess of the forces of nature." Believed to be the site where the Israelites first crossed the divided Jordan River into the Promised Land for the Battle of Jericho. The site was initially known as A'dam.
Dan	Hebrew, meaning "judge." An ancient city situated on the floor of the Rift Valley trench. It is where Abraham traveled to rescue his nephew Lot. It was the birthplace of Samson, the strongman who valiantly fought against the Philistines around 1100 BC. Dan was destroyed by the Assyrian king, Tiglath Pileser III, in 732 BC, and it was never rebuilt. The city was also known as Laish.
darnel	A weed that looks almost identical to wheat, but it is not edible.
debelah	Hebrew, meaning "lump." A dried fig cake made from *paggim* ("green figs"). These were the leading export crop of Perea.

Decapolis	Greek, meaning "ten cities." A group of ten cities on the eastern frontier of the Roman Empire in the southeastern Levant. The cities each functioned as an autonomous city-state. The Decapolis was a center of Greek and Roman culture in a region which was otherwise ancient Semitic-speaking peoples. Which cites were part of the Decapolis changed several times over the course of history.
denarius	Latin, meaning "contains ten." A small silver coin first minted about 211 BC which was originally worth 10 assēs. In the first century, it was worth 16 assēs. From 14 AD to 37 AD, the standard daily wage for day laborers throughout the Roman Empire was one denarius.
Docetism	From the Latin word meaning "to seem." A heresy that taught that that Jesus was fully God, but He was not fully human; therefore, his bodily sufferings were only apparent.
eder-machaneh	Hebrew, meaning "sheep-camp." A sheep-camp consisted of pastures, pens, shearing-houses and dwellings all on one property.
Ein Gedi	Hebrew, meaning "spring of the kid goat." One of only four locations where the aquafer beneath the Judean Wilderness comes to ground level. This is the place where David hid when fleeing from King Saul who was trying to kill him.
Ein Karem	Hebrew, meaning "spring of the vineyard." A village a few miles west of Jerusalem. Today, there are five churches and monasteries located around the village, including the site of the birthplace of St. John the Baptist and site of the Visitation.

Elders	The senior leaders of the most powerful clans in Israel. They were not clerics. They held power by virtue of their tribal influence and extensive land holdings. They were the aristocrats of Israel.
En-gannim	Hebrew, meaning "spring of gardens." A village in Galilee at the border with Samaria. It was here that, in 842 BC, Ahaziah, king of Judah, was ambushed by other Jews and left for dead. He later escaped but died of his wounds after having crawled away for 20 miles.
En-shemesh	Hebrew, meaning "spring of the sun." A small village about a mile east of Bethany and the only spring on the road to Jericho.
ephah	Hebrew, meaning "three measures." An amount of wheat sufficient for about 150 loaves of leavened bread. It was the amount used by Sarah to bake bread when she and Abram were visited by the three angels [cf. Gen 18:6].
Ephraim	A village perched on a prominent hill top with an extensive view of the Samarian countryside. It was also known as Ophrah. (The name of this village was changed from Ephraim to Taybeh around 1187).
erusin	Hebrew, meaning "betrothal." The betrothal began when the woman drank the cup of wine, called the Cup of Acceptance, offered to her by the groom. At that point, they became legally married. During the erusin period, the bride remained in her father's house while the groom prepared a place for her in his father's house. This often took several months to a year.

Essenes	Hebrew, meaning "pious ones." A sect of Judaism that flourished from the 2nd century BC to the 1st century AD. They were celibate, practiced voluntary poverty, and daily immersion. They had stricter purity laws than those of other Jews. So, they tended to live apart from others.
Essene Quarter	An area in southwest Jerusalem that got its name from about 50 Essene *kohanim* (priests) who lived there from about 30 BC and 70 AD.
ezohr	Hebrew, meaning "help." A girdle-style belt wound several times around the waist to bind the clothing tightly to the body.
ezrat nashim	Hebrew, meaning "women's court." The small room at the back of the synagogue where the women were separated from the men based on a long-standing rabbinic interpretation of Zechariah 12:12-14.
Gabbatha	Hebrew, meaning "judgment seat." (Latin: Bema). The bench on an elevated stone platform on the east side of the Praetorium where Pilate rendered judgments.
Gadara in Decapolis	Greek, meaning "walled city". The capital of the region of the Decapolis, just north of Perea. It is now known as Umm Qays.
Gadara in Perea	Greek, meaning "walled city". A city in Perea located on an 1100-foot-high summit overlooking the Valley of Jethro. It was originally known as Saltus after a type of raisin made from the pale green sultana grape.
Galileearea	A small town at the foot of Mount Tabor where Jesus healed a boy with epilepsy, at the pleading of the boy's father.

Gamala	Hebrew, meaning "camel." A town in the Golan Heights situated on a steep hill shaped like the back of a camel, from which the town derived its name. It is the traditional site of the Feeding of the 4000. Following its destruction by the Roman army in 71 AD, the town was lost to history until the site was excavated in 1968.
Garden of Gethsemane	Hebrew, meaning "oil press." A small area near the base of Mount Olivet where all the olive trees had been originally planted from the same parent plant. The foliage of olive trees provided a leafy canopy overhead for the many that leisurely walked its pathways.
Garis	A fairly affluent community in the Jezreel Valley. Because of its fertile soil nearby, Garis was the center of agricultural commerce in Lower Galilee.
garum	Latin, meaning "fish-sauce." A very pungent fish sauce which was cured in the afternoon sun. Garum was packed in clay pots, put into wooden boxes, loaded on mules and taken along the Via Maris to Ptolemais, which was the shipping port of Galilee. Revenue from the exporting of garum was how Herod Antipas gathered enough money each year to pay his taxes to Rome.
Gennath Gate	Hebrew, meaning "of gardens," The gate in the northern wall of the city of Jerusalem opening onto the Shechem Road. It also leads to Gol'gotha.
Gennesaret	Greek form of the Hebrew name Kinneret, meaning "a harp." A town just west of Capernaum on the shore of the Sea of Galilee. The small Plain of Gennesaret, which surrounds the community has been called, from its fertility and beauty, "the Paradise of Galilee."

Gerasa	Greek, meaning "gift of god." A city in Perea on the Chysorrhoas River. In the first century, the city enjoyed great wealth and importance largely due to the area's fertile lands and year-round fresh water supply. The city had some of the finest Greco-Roman architecture in the world.
Gergesa	Hebrew, meaning "place of fighters." A town on the eastern shore of the Sea of Galilee located on a cliff overlooking the sea, in the area known then as the Decapolis.
Gezer Almanac	An inscribed limestone tablet, discovered in 1908, which dates from around 925 BC, or shortly after the time of King Solomon. It provides a good deal of information about early Middle Eastern farming methods and experiences.
Gibeah	Hebrew, meaning "hill country." A city six miles north of Jerusalem. It was the home of King Saul and it served as the royal residence of Saul for 38 years [1 Sam 8:31]. The city was largely destroyed by the Babylonians in 586 BC.
Gihon Spring	Hebrew, meaning "gushing." A spring located in a cave in the Kidron Valley which separates Mount Olivet from Mount Moriah. The spring flowed only intermittently; so, a large reservoir, later called the Pool of Siloam, was dug to store water during periods of draught.
Gol'gotha.	Hebrew, meaning "place of the skull." The rocky mound outside the northern wall of Jerusalem where crucifixions where carried out.

Great Eschatological Feast	The Jewish expectation, loosely based on Isaiah 25:6-9, of a great "feast for the righteous" hosted by their Messiah. Only righteous Jews would be entitled to attend. While the banquet was going on, God would descend on the world, "level the mountains," "fill in the valleys" and eliminate all non-believers so that when the banquet was over, the faithful would walk out into the Kingdom of God devoid of all poverty, oppression and hatred. Then, God would reign; and there would be endless peace in the world. The arrival of that Kingdom of God would be this cataclysmic event in which only the believers remained. It was this misguided expectation about the Kingdom of God that Jesus sought to correct by His teachings on the Kingdom of God (or Kingdom of Heaven as Matthew called it).
Great Sanhedrin	Hebrew, meaning "sitting together." The ruling religious assembly of 72 men in Jerusalem. The assembly was dominated by Sadducees. The court was composed of three groups: the Chief Priests, the Elders and the Scribes. Each group held 24 seats on the court.
Hallel	Hebrew, meaning "praise." A prayer consisting of Psalms 113 thru 118 with Psalm 136 sung antiphonally.
Hinnom Valley	Hebrew, meaning "evil." (Greek: Gehenna). A valley west and south of Mount Zion and merges with the Kidron Valley south of the city of Jerusalem. It had been the place where the idolatrous Jews burned their children alive to the pagan gods Moloch and Baal. A particular part of the valley was called *Tophet*, or the "fire-stove," where the children were burned.

hirelings	Non-trade day laborers. Since the standard daily wage for hirelings throughout the Roman Empire was at a subsistence level, there were no brokers involved in retaining hirelings.
hittah	Hebrew, meaning "wheat" (also means "sustenance").
Holy of Holies	The innermost court in the Temple where only the High Priest was allowed to enter, and he only on the Day of Atonement. The Holy of Holies contained a stone designating the place where once the Ark of the Covenant had stood.
Holy Place	The fourth of the upper courts in the Temple where only priests on Temple duty could enter. The Holy Place contained a golden altar at which incense was offered and next to it was the golden lampstand, the Light of the World, and a table with the twelve loaves of Showbread.
Hosanna	Hebrew, meaning "Lord, grant salvation," from Psalm 118:25.
Hulda Gates	Two long archways for entering the Temple in Jerusalem from the south.
Jabbok River	Hebrew, meaning "blue" river. A river in Perea whose origin is the Ain Ghazal spring. From its headwaters, the river flows to the north before heading west. Rising on the western side of the Sharra Highlands ridge, it runs a course of about 75 miles in a deep ravine-like valley before flowing into the Jordan River, at a point 3,576 feet below its origin. It is known today as the Zarqa River.
Jericho	Hebrew, meaning "fragrant." A city on the west bank of the Jordan River believed to be the oldest continuously inhabited city in the world. In the time of Jesus, many of Israel's ruling and priestly classes lived there.

Jezreel Valley	Hebrew, meaning "God sows." A fertile valley southwest of the Sea of Galilee. In ancient times, this area had great strategic value since the Jezreel Valley provided the only east-west access between the Mediterranean coast and the Jordan Valley. It was also known as the Plain of Esdraelon
Joppa	Greek form of the Hebrew name, Jappa, meaning "beautiful." A splendid port town on the Mediterranean coast of Israel which is now incorporated within the modern city of Tel Aviv. It was situated in the territory that was originally allotted to the tribe of Dan [Joshua 19:46].
Judean Wilderness	A vast desert region that lies east of Jerusalem which descends in the direction of the Dead Sea. Because of its lack of water, the Judean Wilderness has been essentially uninhabited throughout history. It has very little vegetation and is marked by many natural terraces and deep ravines. An aquifer flows underground beneath the Judean Wilderness in a northeasterly direction into the Dead Sea.
kallah	Hebrew, meaning "totally." The name for the bride.
keffiyeh	Hebrew, meaning "sweat-cloth." (Greek: *soudarion*) A white cloth worn over the head hanging to the shoulders and held in place by a sweatband around the forehead. This cloth protected the head and neck from the sun.
kethōneth	Hebrew, meaning "tunic." A fairly tight-fitting undergarment, sometimes reaching only to the knee, but most often to the ankle.
ketubah	Hebrew, meaning "written thing," the written marriage contract. It was retained by the bride's father.

Kidron Valley	Hebrew, meaning 'turbid brook." The valley that separates Mount Moriah from Mount Olivet where a rainy season torrent flowed through the Valley in ancient times.
King's Highway	The eastern leg of the major trade route between Persia and Egypt which ran through Palestine. The King's Highway ran along the eastern edge of Perea on a north-south ridge known as the Sharra Highlands. Archeological evidence shows that the King's Highway was in use as far back as 3300 BC. The Israelites used the King's Highway, which they called, *Derekh Ha'Melech*, in advancing through Transjordan.
kittel	Hebrew, meaning "wedding garment." It was, typically, a robe or scarf given to each guest by the groom when they arrive at the wedding banquet. Everyone at the feast wearing identical wedding garments symbolized the union of the two families. [Note: today, the kittel is a white robe worn only by the groom; it no longer symbolizes the union of the families but rather the purity of the groom].
Kishon River (also spelled Qishon)	Hebrew, meaning "winding." A narrow, shallow river arising on the western slope of Mount Gilboa and winding its way northwest along the southern edge of the Jezreel Valley, passing just north of Mount Carmel, and emptying into the Mediterranean. It served as the border between Galilee and Samaria.
kohanim	Hebrew, meaning "priests."
kor	A unit of dry weight, equal to 935 liters.
Kuthim	Hebrew, meaning "idiots." The derogatory term used by Jews for the Samaritans.

Ladder of Tyre	A narrow passageway on the Via Maris, 7 miles south of Tyre, where the road between the mountains and sea was a series of steps cut in the white rock.
Lake Hula (also spelled Huleh)	Hebrew, meaning "transit." A small marshy lake in the Upper Jordan River at an elevation of about 230 feet above sea level. It is a gathering place for migratory birds but also a breeding ground for mosquitoes and malaria.
Leonites River	Greek, meaning "lion." A river which flows from the interior of Lebanon to the Mediterranean. The river flows swiftly during the rainy season, descends to sea level from about 3600 feet above sea level, over a distance of nearly 20 miles, from the base of Mount Lebanon where the river turns abruptly from the north. The river is known today as the Letani River.
ma'aleh	Hebrew, meaning "ascent." A sloped area on a river bank leading to a point for crossing the river.
ma'aser sheni	Hebrew, meaning 'second tithe.' An amount each man was required to bring with him to the celebration of Passover. It was either grain, wine or oil representing 1/10th of the produce of their land from the 1st, 2nd, 4th and 5th years of each 7-year cycle. It was to be consumed in Jerusalem and shared with the poor there. Those who did not have agricultural produce, had to bring the monetary equivalent
Machaerus	Hebrew, meaning "black fortress." Herod's palace overlooking the Dead Sea where there was also a prison. John the Baptist was beheaded there.
machloket	Hebrew, meaning "Torah debate."

Magdala	Hebrew, meaning 'tower." (Greek: Taricheae, "place of salted fish"). A town, also known as Magadan, located on the western shore of the Sea of Galilee in the ancient area known as Dalmanutha, a center of shipbuilding and fish processing for many centuries. Magdala was where they made the fish sauce known as garum, the principal export crop of Galilee.
Mahanaim	Hebrew, meaning "two camps." Once a city on the Jabbok River located where a host of angels came to comfort Jacob on his journey to meet his brother, Esau. It was later known as Jabesh-Gilead. By the first century, it was largely in ruins. There is some question about the precise location of Mahanaim. Most accept that it was 9 miles east of where the Jabbok enters the Jordan River valley.
Maktesh	Hebrew, meaning "hollow place." The market area in Jerusalem south of the Xystus Square where all the bazaars connected with the Temple were located.
mapeet	Hebrew, meaning "napkin." A small cloth towel used as a napkin.
mashal	Hebrew, meaning "wisdom saying."
matan	Hebrew, meaning "bride gifts." Gifts presented by the groom, with his father if he was still alive, to the prospective bride and her father in an attempt to win favor during marriage negotiations.
measure	a unit of liquid equal to 39 liters.
mechitzah	Hebrew, meaning "partition." The large opaque screen that prevented men and women from been seen by one another in the synagogue.

Megiddo	A very narrow canyon on the southeastern side of Mount Carmel. Controlling this canyon controlled the entire Via Maris trade route and land passage into Egypt from the north and east. This is the location of Armageddon, referred to in Revelation 16:16, where the end-times battle is to take place. In ancient times, there was a small city at Megiddo, but it was destroyed in 586 BC by the Babylonians; and it was never re-built.
mensarii	Latin, meaning "bankers." Since all temples throughout the Roman Empire maintained guarded treasuries, temples also served as banks. The Temple in Jerusalem operated a bank. The mensarii kept track of deposits and they loaned money for interest, but they did not pay interest on deposits. In those days, banks were not insured, so when a loan was made, with a depositor's approval, the bank and the depositor shared in the interest paid.
metaphor	Greek, meaning "to carry over." A literary device that contrasts some activity or situation with some other activity or situation for the purpose of illustrating a point.
metanoia	Greek, meaning "to turn around or go back."
midrash	Hebrew, meaning "to study." Rabbinic commentary intended to resolve problems in the interpretation of difficult passages of the text of the Hebrew Bible, using principles of hermeneutics and philosophy to align them with the religious and ethical values of the religious teachers of the time.
Midrashim	Hebrew, meaning "the commentaries." A collection of Rabbinic explanations and imaginative expansions on Biblical stores, particularly in the Torah, compiled between about 200 AD and 1200 AD.

mikvot	Hebrew, meaning "collections." Ritual immersion baths in Judaism for achieving ritual purity.
Mishnah	Hebrew, meaning "the review." A set of 63 volumes of commentary on Scripture compiled between about 536 BC and 220 AD.
miṭpaḥaṭh	Hebrew, meaning "shawl." A neck-cloth worn by women that covered their hair when they were in public.
mitzvah	Hebrew, meaning "commandment." A precept of Mosaic Law to be followed without condition.
mohar	Hebrew, meaning "bride price." The amount paid by the groom for his bride. The mohar was her "social security" in the event of her husband's death or their divorce. The mohar was normally converted into silver coins which she kept with her at all times.
Mount Carmel	Hebrew, meaning "God's vineyard." A 40-mile long mountain range on the Mediterranean coast, whose highest point is 1700 feet above sea level. It was on Mount Carmel that Elijah confronted the prophets of Baal. Later, the prophet Elisha lived on Mount Carmel.
Mount Eremos	Hebrew, meaning "wilderness." A small mountain overlooking both the Plain of Gennesaret and the Sea of Galilee. It is the traditional location of the Sermon on the Mount.
Mount Gerizim	Hebrew, meaning "apart from." A mountain near Shechem where the Samaritans built their version of the Temple.

Mount Hazor	Hebrew, meaning "grass." A tilted plateau, rising some 3400 feet above sea level, just south of Ephraim. It had excellent grazing land. It was here that Absalom had his brother Amnon killed avenging the rape of his sister, Tamar.
Mount Hermon	Hebrew, meaning "sacred." A 20-mile long mountain range just north of Israel in Syria and east of the Rift Valley trench. The highest point in the range is 9,200 ft. above sea level. The range provides a major source of snow melt water for Palestine.
Mount Lebanon	A mountain range in Lebanon running about 140 miles north-south. A number of peaks in nearly 10,000 feet in height; many are snow-covered most of the year. The Rift Valley trench separated the Mount Lebanon range from the Mount Hermon range.
Mount Moriah	One of three moderate-sized mountains, rising 2438 feet above sea level, on which the city of Jerusalem is built. The Temple was constructed on Mount Moriah; it is believed to be the site where Abraham was to offer his son Isaac in sacrifice.
Mount Olivet	One of three moderate-sized mountains, rising 2641 feet above sea level, on which the city of Jerusalem is built. The mount is always fresh and green even during the dry season. The southernmost slope, directly opposite the Water Gate, was sometimes called the Mount of Offense, believed to be where Solomon erected the 'high places" for the gods of his foreign wives.

Mount Tabor	Hebrew, meaning "pasture." A mountain located on the eastern end of the Jezreel Valley. It is shaped almost like a half-sphere, suddenly rising from the flat surroundings and reaching a height of 1,900 feet. It was from Mount Tabor that very bright beacons were lit to inform the northern villages of the beginning of Jewish holy days and of new months. It is the traditional site of the Transfiguration.
Mount Zion	One of three moderate-sized mountains, rising 2534 feet above sea level, on which the city of Jerusalem is built. David built his palace on Mount Zion; it was later replaced by King Herod's palace (which later became the Praetorium).
na'alayim	Hebrew, meaning "sandals." Footwear worn by all adults, except slaves. No footwear was worn in the house.
Nain (sometimes spelled Nein)	Hebrew, meaning "green pastures." A town located on the northwestern slope of the Hill of Moreh. The hill is between Mount Tabor and Mount Gilboa and it served as the site of first interments for many families in Lower Galilee. Jesus raised the dead son of a widow in Nain [Luke 7:11–17].
Nazareth	Hebrew, meaning "shoot" or "sprout." A village in Galilee occupying only about ten acres in the first century, extended mostly north-south on a hilltop about 1150 feet above sea level, near the valley where the trade route, the Via Maris, passed a few miles to the north. Throughout most of the first century, the population was not more than about 300 people.

Negev (also spelled Negeb)	Hebrew, meaning "dry land." A 4,700 sq.-mile rocky desert south of Judah with a few brown, dusty mountains interrupted by wadis and deep craters. The area does not have sand dunes typically associated with the Sahara or other deserts.
Nicanor Gate	The gate for entering the Court of Israel in the Temple. It had a pair of huge bronze doors that were so large that it required the united strength of 20 men to open and close them.
nisuin	Hebrew, meaning "the lifting up." The wedding feast, hosted by the groom's father, which joined the two families. The couple was already married at the erisin (betrothal).
Ophel	Hebrew, meaning "hill." A region in Jerusalem on the southern slope of Mount Moriah where the Temple priests resided when they were in the city on Temple duty.
Ordo	Originally, the Roman Empire's list of crimes, and their punishments. A Roman judge decided guilt or innocence, but the punishment was prescribed by the Ordo. Today, the term Roman Ordo refers to the book that provides information on daily celebrations and the readings at Mass.
ovna	Hebrew, meaning "birthing stone." At delivery, the midwife would catch the child and place the child on the birthing rock while the umbilical cord was severed. The expectant mother would have spent months polishing and getting the stone just right for her child. These ovnaiym (pl. of ovna) were family heirlooms, passed down from generation to generation.

Padan-aram	Hebrew, meaning "field of Aram." The area near Haran in upper Mesopotamia where Abraham and his father Terah settled after leaving Ur of the Chaldees, while enroute to Canaan [Gen 11:31].
paggim	Hebrew, meaning "green figs." The winter fig crop In December-January, dried in the sun, pressure cooked and formed into small round cakes, known as debelah. These were strung like beads in foot-long strings and packed in boxes for export.
parabolé	Greek, meaning "to place alongside," for comparison purposes.
Pella	Hebrew, meaning "marvel of God." A community about 20 miles south of the Sea of Galilee. For many centuries, Pella was a very prosperous city, named Pihilum, but by the first century it was little more than a small town.
Penuel	Hebrew, meaning "face of God." Once a city located where the Jabbok River flows into the Jordan. It was there that Jacob wrestled with God. In 924 BC, the Egyptian king, Shishak, completely destroyed the city of Penuel. After that, Penuel was never rebuilt and it remained just a pilgrimage site for people heading to Jerusalem.
Perea	Greek, meaning "beyond," referring to beyond the Jordan. Originally known as Gilead. The province east of the Jordan River extended from the Yarmouk River on the north to about one third the ways down the eastern shore of the Dead Sea and east to the Sharra Highlands. It was known to Jews as Judea-across-the - Jordan. The name, Perea, does not appear in the Bible, only the name Judea-across-the-Jordan.

Pharisees	Hebrew, meaning "separatists." A sect of Judaism that had its roots in the Babylonian Captivity period. With the destruction of the First Temple, the priestly class had no role, so a lay movement began that promoted regular gatherings for prayer and reflection on their scriptures. These gatherings were in houses in the Babylonian captivity area, which were called, beit-knesset, meaning "'house of assembly" (Greek: synagogue). After the building of the Second Temple, the synagogue experience continued in addition to worship at the Temple in Jerusalem. While most Jews could not regularly attend Temple services, they could meet at the synagogue for morning and evening prayers. In the time of Greek oppression in Israel, those who led the synagogues emerged, under the name, Pharisees, to actively resist the Sadducees who favored accommodating the Hellenization of Israel. In the first century, about 70% of the people attended synagogue but those who regarded themselves as Pharisees only numbered about 6000 [Josephus, Antiquities of the Jews, 17.42]. With the destruction of the Second Temple, the Pharisees were the only authoritative body left in Judaism. Pharisaic teachings and practices became the foundational, liturgical and ritualistic basis for modern Rabbinic Judaism.
pietas	Latin, meaning "loyalty." The profound responsibility each person had for the guidance and care of each member of their extended family. In the ancient Middle East, family came before all else.

Pools of Solomon	Three large rectangular reservoirs in the hill country 3 miles southwest of Bethlehem that collected water from local springs and rain runoff. They held nearly 75 million gallons. They were built by King Herod the Great to provide water, via aqueducts, to Jerusalem and his hill-top palace in the Judean Desert, called Herodium.
portoria	Latin, meaning "port duties." Roman import-export tax on everything one was bringing across a border between tetrarchies, other than the clothes one was wearing.
praetor	Latin, meaning "judge." An official appointed by Rome to hear legal disputes between Roman citizens and foreigners. In outlying areas of the Empire, such as ancient Israel, most judge appointees were unpaid, and many enriched themselves through bribes.
Praetorium	Latin, meaning "commander's tent." Originally, King Herod's palace in Jerusalem however, in 26 AD, when Pontius Pilate became prefect (governor) of Judea the Praetorium became Pilate's house when he was in Jerusalem
Ptolemais	Named after one of Alexander the Great's generals, Ptolemy. A city in Phoenicia that served as the Mediterranean port for Galilee. It was also known as Acre.
publicanus	Latin, meaning "public servant." (pl. publicani) [in Greek: telones] Professional who, every five years, bought a license, via auction, to collect taxes for Rome. They were at liberty to collect whatever fees they were able to.

qesasah	Hebrew, meaning "cutting off." A ceremony in which a person is expelled from the community. The people would gather beans into a large clay pot in the village center. Then they would smash the pot spilling the beans on the ground. They would vehemently stomp the beans into the ground and declare the exile "dead" – cut off from the community.
Quelle	German, meaning "source." A text of Jesus' sayings thought to be the source from which the evangelists (principally Matthew and Luke) worked. No remnants of such a text have ever been found.
Rabbah	Hebrew, meaning "great city." A city located in the Sharra Highlands on the eastern edge of Perea. The King's Highway passed through Rabbah. It was also known in Jesus' day as Philadelphia. Rabbah owed its location to the nearby Ain Ghazal ("Gazelle spring"), which is fed by snowmelt from Mount Hermon. There was perhaps no city whose strategic location did more to shape the history of the Middle East than Rabbah. It is today the city of Ammon, the capital of Jordan.
Rift Valley trench	The large trench that runs all the way from the Syrian Mountains through the Sea of Galilee, through the Dead Sea, all the way to the Gulf of Aqaba. It was formed by the Arabian section of the Asian Continental Shelf sliding against the African Continental Shelf, pulling the land apart along their line of contact and causing the collapse of the Rift Valley. There are places where the trench is nearly a half mile deep. The Jordan River flows along the Rift Valley trench.

Roman Reign of Terror	The period in Roman history, 90-96 A.D, when Emperor Domitian labeled Christianity an "outlawed superstition." Many thousands of Christians were executed by crucifixions, burnings, or being fed to the lions for sport, etc.
Royal Bridge	One of the architectural wonders of its day in Jerusalem. The bridge crossed the Tyropoeon Valley from Mount Zion to the porch area of the Temple. The construction of the bridge rivaled the building of the pyramids in Egypt.
Sadducees	A sect of Judaism consisting largely of the wealthy power brokers who controlled the Jewish court, the Sanhedrin. They drew their name from Zadok, the first High Priest of ancient Israel in the time of Solomon. The Sadducees accepted only the Torah (Law of Moses) and rejected the other Hebrew Scriptures as being "mere traditions" promoted by the Pharisees. They denied that there would be any bodily resurrection, because there was no mention of it in the Torah.
sadin	Hebrew, meaning "to accomplish." The finer linen under-dress worn by women under their tunic making their garments fully opaque.
Samaritans	Hebrew, meaning "guardians" (of the Torah). The Samaritans claim descent from the tribe of Ephraim and tribe of Manasseh (two sons of Joseph). However, their historic origin is in the Edict of Ezra in 457 BC. Ezra sought to "purify the community" by enforcing the dissolution of marriages between those who had returned from Babylon and those who had remained in Israel during the captivity period. Thousands of women, children and only a few men were "deported" from the Jerusalem area to the lands further north that had been apportioned to Ephraim and Manasseh after the Exodus. Great bitterness and hostility arose out of this action.

Sapporis	Greek, meaning "place of the birds." A grand city on a hill 938 feet above sea level, about 4 miles from Nazareth. In 4 BC, following an uprising, the Romans destroyed the city. Herod Antipas decided to rebuild Sapporis as his capital city, which he did, from 10 AD into the late 20's AD.
se'or	Hebrew, meaning "leaven." Also known by the Greek name, zume. A small portion of dough from the previous round of bread-making which was mixed with a small amount of freshly pressed grape juice and set aside for several days. The dough would gather microbes from the air which would feed on the sugar provided by the fruit juice to multiply many times over in the dough wad. This dough wad then served as the starter for the next round of dough preparation. It is sometimes incorrectly translated as "yeast."
Sea of Galilee	Originally known as the Sea of Kinneret in the Old Testament, also known as Lake of Gennesaret [Luke 5:1] and Sea of Tiberias. The "sea," which is actually a fresh-water lake, is about 14 miles north-south and 8 miles east-west. It is fairly shallow (typically 35 to 65 feet) with a maximum depth of only 141 feet. Because of its shallowness, the water is fairly warm, conducive to supporting a large number and variety of fish. Because of its position at the bottom of the Rift Valley trench, the Sea of Galilee is among the stormiest locations on earth for fishermen, because the trench captured storm clouds from the Mediterranean.
semukha	Hebrew, meaning "in contrast." Known in English as juxtaposition, a literary construct in which two things are presented in contrast to each other to make a point.

seven-stanza ballad	A literary construct common in the ancient world intended to increase the contrast between competing concepts or characters.
shadkhan	Hebrew, meaning "arranger" one who made marriage arrangements on behalf of a family.
Shalosh Regalim	The three Jewish festivals [Sukkot (Festival of Tabernacles), Passover and Shavuoth (Festival of Pentecost)] on which all able-bodied males over the age of 12 were required to pilgrimage to Jerusalem
Shechem	Hebrew, meaning "saddle." A city in Samaria named because of the shape of the land around it. It is located between Mt. Gerizim and Mt. Ebal. It was the place where Abraham first stopped on entering Palestine. It was there that God confirmed the first covenant He made with Abraham; and it was there that Jacob settled after his meeting with his brother, Esau, at Penuel. In Jesus' time, the city was known as Sychar. At Shechem (Sychar) is Jacob's Well.
shekar	Hebrew, meaning "old wine," more broadly: intoxicating.
Shekhinah	Hebrew, meaning "dwelling," more specifically, God's presence. Sometimes translated as the "glory of the Lord" as in Exodus 40:34 and Ezekiel 10:18.
Sheluchim	Hebrew, meaning "holy ones." The name given to the great prophets and ancestors.

Sheol	Hebrew, meaning "place of the dead." Also known by the Greek name, Hades. The description of Sheol varied with the text and the interpreter, but, in general, Sheol was the place to which all the dead went, both the righteous and the unrighteous. There they were separated into respective compartments; the righteous would perpetually dine with Abraham while the unrighteous would be excluded to spend eternity in total darkness. Sometimes, Sheol is mistakenly translated as "Hell."
Shephelah	Hebrew, meaning "lowlands." The valleys and foothills region between the Mediterranean coast and the central plateau area of Galilee, Samaria and Judea.
shiddukhin	Hebrew, meaning "mutual promise." The wedding arrangement / agreement made between families.
Shunem	Hebrew, meaning "second resting place." A town located on the southwest slope of the Hill of Moreh between Mount Tabor and Mount Gilboa. It served as the site of second interments for many families in Lower Galilee. The prophet Elisha raised the dead son of a widow in Shunem [2 Kings 4:8-37].
Sidon	Greek, meaning "fishery." The Phoenician capital city on the Mediterranean, which excelled in ship-building and glass production. The infamous Jezebel, who later would become Queen of Israel [1 Kings 16:31] was the daughter of the King of Sidon.
simlāh	Hebrew, meaning "mantle" or "cloak." The outer garment, loose fitting with fringes, often made of wool or flax.

Snir Stream	Hebrew, meaning "abrupt." A mountain stream arising in the Mount Lebanon range which joins the flow from the Dan Spring and the Banias River to form the Upper Jordan River. It is known today as the Hasbani.
soferim	Hebrew, meaning "lawyers." Also known as "scribes" and "scholars of the law." They were Jewish officials whose role was to serve as the interpreters and copyists of God's law.
synoptic	From the Greek word meaning "to be viewed together," referring to the Gospels of Matthew, Mark and Luke which include many of the same stories, often in a similar sequence and with generally similar wording.
talanton	Greek name for a measure of weight in gold. In the first century, one talanton ("talent") was 130 pounds of gold.
tallit	Hebrew, meaning "prayer shawl." A shawl worn over the head and shoulders by both men and women when praying.
Talmud	Hebrew, meaning "the instructions.' A set of rabbinic commentary, following the same 63 section structure of the Mishnah, compiled between about 200 BC and 500 AD.
Targumim	Hebrew, meaning "the explanations." Aramaic translation of Scriptures, reflecting biblical interpretations compiled between about 200 BC and 200 AD.
te'enim	Hebrew, meaning "figs." The main fig crop, harvested in August-September.
Tefilat HaDerekh	Hebrew, meaning "traveler's prayer." A prayer for safe travel recited before leaving home on a journey.

tefillin	Hebrew, meaning "to guard." Small black leather boxes, or phylacteries, containing scrolls of parchment inscribed with verses from the Torah, worn by all males, during weekday morning prayers, on their forehead and left arm.
tekhelet	A blue-purple dye which came from Eastern Mediterranean murex snails. Fishermen squeezed the snails to get a few drops of dye; It took thousands of snails to get enough to die one garment.
tekton	Greek, meaning "tradesman."
Temple Porch	(Sometimes called the Royal Porch). The porch area that ran all around the inside of the Temple wall, bounding the Court of the Gentiles. The porch was lined with marble pillars. The porch was the community meeting place where people sat on benches often "debating" for hours on end. The most popular area was known as Solomon's Porch (or the Portico of Solomon) which ran along the eastern wall of the Temple.
Temple Treasury	A set of thirteen large wooden boxes with trumpet-shaped bronze funnels located along the north and south walls of the Court of Women. The funnels guided the coins into the box and the sound these coins made against the metal would indicate how much people offered to the Temple.
Tenaim	Hebrew, meaning "agreements." The Groom's Promise. Before leaving the house of the bride's father, the groom would speak the Tenaim "I go to prepare a place for you in my father's house that where I am you also may be" [cf. John 14: 2-3].
tetrarchy	A political unit of the Roman Empire ruled by a king or prefect (governor).

threshing barn	A long building which was very wide on the western end; the sides and roof narrowed to produce a much smaller eastern end. This resulted in an overall funnel shape to the building. During the day, prevailing breezes were from the east. Following sunset, the breezes would shift to coming from the west into the west end of the threshing barn. The funnel shape of the building caused the air flow to accelerate in order to exit out the smaller eastern end of the building. The constant breeze in the building enabled separating the wheat from the chaff. The threshing barn was also the village meeting place for judgement by the elders as well as community decision-making.
Tiberias	The political and religious center of Galilee, founded in 20 AD on the west shore of the Sea of Galilee, by King Herod Antipas, to honor the Roman Emperor Tiberius. It was built on the ruins of the ancient Hebrew city of Rakkath. The city was a resort destination for the wealthy; the city had several hot spring health spas and a very large Roman amphitheater.
tirosh	Hebrew, meaning "new wine," more broadly: still fermenting or developing.
Todah (also spelled toda)	Hebrew, meaning "thanksgiving" a thanksgiving offering made in the Temple in Jerusalem, for such things as a good harvest or a childbirth.
toga	Latin, meaning "covering." An additional outer garment worn only by Roman citizens. A one-piece rather uncomfortable woolen garment draped loosely around the shoulders and down the body. The manner of wrapping of one's toga conveyed the citizen's social status. It was punishable by death for a non-Roman citizen to wear a toga.

triclinia	Latin, meaning "three couches." Formal indoor dining rooms in Roman homes, with couches along three sides.
tsedaqah	Hebrew, meaning "righteousness." A righteous person was one who kept mercy and justice in right balance.
tsedeq (also spelled tzedek)	Hebrew, meaning "righteous."
Tyre	Greek, meaning "strength." A city on the Mediterranean coast located on an island which enabled the Phoenicians to dominate the Eastern Mediterranean seaways. For centuries, Tyre could not be attacked by a land-based army. This so infuriated the Greek conqueror, Alexander the Great, who lacked his own navy, that he had his army spend seven months in 332 BC progressively piling rocks from the shoreline out to create a land bridge, or causeway, to the island. Today, the city is known as Sur.
Tyropoeon Valley	Hebrew, meaning "cheese mongers." The valley which separated Mount Zion from Mount Moriah thus passing through the center of Jerusalem. Over centuries, the Valley has been largely filled in with dirt and rubble in order to build upon it.
tzizit	Hebrew, meaning "tassels." Fringes attached to the corners of their outer garments. A tekhelet (or "blue" colored) thread was in each tassel. These were to serve as reminders to keep the Lord's commandments.

vastatio	Latin, meaning "retaliate a hundred-fold." The Roman practice of retaliating against "enemies of Rome" with extreme punishment, often including the execution of the offender's family, neighbors and even whole cites.
vernae	Latin, meaning ""home-born slaves." Members of a debt-slave's family who "belonged" to the Creditor. Upon their release, former debtors often had no means of support and did not wish to leave vernae behind. So, they frequently exercised their "right" [cf. Ex 21:1-6] to remain as a servant in the Creditor's household.
Via Maris	Latin, meaning "way to the sea." The western leg of the major trade route between Persia and Egypt which ran through Palestine. It passed through Galilee and on to the Mediterranean coast. On some maps, it's labeled as the Great Truck Road.
Vulgate	Latin, meaning "the common version." It is the Latin translation of Old and New Testament completed by St. Jerome in 382 AD. This quickly became the only interpretation in use by Christians for more than 1200 years.
wadi	Hebrew, meaning "seasonal stream." A stream, sometimes quite large, that flows only after snow melt off or a heavy rainfall.
Wadi Gharrar	Hebrew, meaning "sojourner." A wadi which intermittently flows into the Jordan River from the east near where John the Baptist ministered. It is fed by a spring known as the Aenon.
Wadi Qelt	Hebrew, meaning "shade." A wadi which intermittently flows into the Jordan River from the mountains around Jerusalem. The Jericho Road generally follows the path of the Wadi Qelt, a decent of about 1700 feet over 17 miles.

Wadi Ruqqad	Hebrew, meaning "lazy." A wadi arising in the Mount Hermon range and flowing south into the Yarmouk River. It forms the eastern edge of what is known today as the Golan Heights.
Water Gate	The gate in the southeastern wall of the city of Jerusalem which opened to the Jericho Road, Kidron Valley and Mount Olivet. It was the main gate in Jerusalem leading to the Temple area. It was in the square in front of this gate, in the year 458 BC, that the all the people gathered to hear Ezra the Scribe read to them the entire Torah and declared it the official Law of Moses. Hezekiah's Tunnel which brought water from the Gihon Spring into the Pool of Siloam passed under the Jerusalem wall near the Water Gate.
winnowing fan	A large pitchfork-shaped fan for scooping up wheat and chaff from the floor of a threshing barn for throwing the material into the breeze passing through the building. There was a large hole in the floor just ahead of the winnower. The heavier grain would fall through the hole into a grain bin below while the lighter chaff was carried by the breeze out the east end of the building where it was gathered into bundles for fuel. Men would take turns as winnower because throwing tons of material into the air in the course of a night's work was exhausting effort. This method of separating wheat from chaff in threshing barns was still in use into the early 20th century.
Xystus Square	Latin, meaning "smooth." The large public square, east of the Palace of the High Priest in Jerusalem, surrounded by a covered colonnade.

Yarkon River (also spelled Yarqon)	Hebrew, meaning "greenish." A meandering river arising in the Judean hills and flowing west into the Mediterranean Sea north of Joppa. Today, the river flows through the modern-day city of Tel Aviv.
Yarmouk River	Hebrew, meaning "cave land." It is the largest tributary of the Jordan River. Snow melt from the Mount Hermon range and several wadis combine to form a narrow and shallow river throughout most of its course, cutting a deep trench through the limestone as it flows west into the Jordan. Today, the Yarmouk forms the border between the Golan Heights of Israel and the country of Jordan.
Zarephath	Hebrew, meaning "smelting-shop." A small town on the Mediterranean coast, about half-way between Tyre and Sidon where the prophet Elijah fled from a drought and there he later raised from the dead the son of a widow. The town is near where the Leonites River flows into the Mediterranean.

Index of Parables

Common Name of Parable	Gospel References	Pages
Parable of the Attitude of a Servant	Luke 17:7-10	267-269
Parable of the Barren Fig Tree	Luke 13:6-9	210-213
Parable about Being like a Child	Matthew 18:1-5; Mark 9:33-37	229-232
Parable of Costs of Discipleship	Luke 14:25-33	226-229
Parable of the Feast	Matthew 22:1-14; Luke 14:15-24	309-318
Parable of the Fig Tree	Matthew 24:32-34; Mark 13:28-30; Luke 21:29-32	327-329
Parable of the Final Judgment	Matthew 25:31-46	347-349
Parable of the Fishing Net	Matthew 13:47-50	133-134
Parable of the Friend in Need	Luke 11:1-13	182-184
Parable of the Good Samaritan	Luke 10:25-37	173-176
Parable of the Growing Seed	Mark 4:26-29	128-129
Parable of the Head of Household	Matthew 13:51-52	134-135
Parable of the Invitations	Luke 14:7-14	221-225
Parable of the Joy of Finding	Matthew 13:44-46	132-133
Parable of the Lamp	Matthew 5:14-16; Mark 4:21-23; Luke 8:16-17	126-128
Parable of the Lender	Luke 7:36-50	106-110
Parable of the Lost Coin	Luke 15:8-10	239-241
Parable of the Lost Sheep	Matthew 18:12-14; Luke 15:1-7	234-239

Parable of the Mustard Seed	Matthew 13:31-32; Mark 4:30-32; Luke 13:18-19	217-219
Parable of the New vs. the Old	Matthew 9:10-17; Mark 2:15-22; Luke 5:29-39	74-80
Parable of the Persistent Widow	Luke 18:1-7	273-277
Parable of Pharisee and Tax Collector	Luke 18:9-14	277-281
Parable of the Prodigal Son	Luke 15:11-32	241-251
Parable of the Prudent and Wicked Servants	Matthew 24:45-51; Luke 12:42-48	201-206
Parable of the Rich Fool	Luke 12:13-22	192-194
Parable of Rich Man and Lazarus	Luke 16:19-31	257-263
Parable of the Shrewd Steward	Luke 16:1-8	256-257
Parable of the Sower	Matthew 13:1-23; Mark 4:1-20; Luke 8:4-15	111-121
Parable of the Talents	Matthew 25:14-30; Luke 19:11-28	333-344
Parable of the Ten Virgins	Matthew 25:1-13	329-333
Parable of the Two Foundations	Matthew 7:24-29; Luke 6:46-49	95-99
Parable of the Two Sons	Matthew 21:28-32	299-302
Parable of Unforgiving Servant	Matthew 18:21-35	163-166
Parable of the Vigilant Servants	Mark 13:33-37; Luke 12:35-41	197-201
Parable of The Weeds and the Wheat	Matthew 13:24-43	121-125
Parable of the Wicked Tenants	Matthew 21:33-46; Mark 12:1-12; Luke 20:9-19	302-309

| Parable of the Workers | Matthew 20:1-16 | 292-296 |
| Parable of the Yeast | Matthew 13:33; Luke 13:20-21 | 219-221 |

Index of Names & Subjects

Acts
 1:14, 92, 168, 272
 3:1-10, 288
 5:36-39, 271
 15:13-21, 168
 16:9-11, 32
Adam and Eve, 251, 362
adelphoi (see brothers)
Adoptionism, 147, 380
Adummim Pass, 189, 380
Age to Come, 94, 133
Agriculture, 45, 68, 85, 86, 111, 143, 187, 188
Ain Ghazal, 195, 201, 380, 395, 408
allegory, 3, 4, 117-120, 124
alma, 381
Al-Maghtas, 52, 53, 381
Altar of Burnt Offerings, 289, 290, 322, 346, 384, 387
am ha'aretz (see people of the land)
am ha'sefer (see people of the book)
anagnorisis, 147, 381
Annunciation, 7
antithesis, 295, 336, 362, 381
Antonia Fortress, 285, 286, 381
apostates, 118, 119, 296, 381
avodah (see prayer)

Banias River, 155, 156, 385, 413
bankers (*mensarii*), 337, 400
Beautiful Gate, 288, 289, 323, 382, 388
Beelzebub, 99-101, 382

Beisan, 26, 48, 49, 51, 89, 226, 382
berakhah (see blessing)
Bethabara, 47, 52, 55, 186, 189, 190, 382
Bethany, 37, 38, 89, 181, 182, 185, 186, 188, 264, 266, 267, 270, 272, 277, 281, 291, 382, 390
Bethel, 63, 64, 383
Bethesda, 100, 383
Bethphage, 63, 89, 267, 281, 383
Bethsaida, 55, 140-144, 159, 383
betrothal (*erusin*), 57, 239, 390, 404
betulah (see virgin)
betulim (see proof cloth)
Biq'ah Yitro (see Valley of Jethro)
Birah Ebhedh (see Castle of the Servant)
birthing stone (*ovna*), 97, 404
blessing (*berakhah*), 47, 171, 177, 241, 270, 291, 382
Bread of Life, 145, 146, 148
breath of life (*nephesh*), 102
bride gifts (*matan*), 56, 399
bride price (*mohar*), 56, 57, 239, 275, 401
brothers (*adelphoi*), 91, 92, 168, 169, 184, 272, 380
burnt-offering, 322-324, 384, 386

Caesarea, 149, 385
Caesarea Philippi, 23, 156, 157, 159, 160, 291, 348, 385

Cana, 55, 56, 58, 59, 66, 67
Capernaum, 23, 56, 58-61, 66, 56, 70-73, 78, 79, 85, 90, 91, 93, 95, 99-101, 135-137, 139, 141, 143-146, 148, 152, 156, 158, 160, 162, 165,168, 169, 171, 196, 229, 230, 236, 385, 392
Castle of the Servant (*Birah Ebhedh*), 196, 197, 199, 384
Catechism of the Catholic Church, 213, 214, 264, 265, 281, 339, 346, 362
cause-effect, 33, 325, 362
Cave of Machpelah, 104, 242, 385
Caves of Arbela, 70, 71, 90, 386
Cenacle, 350, 386
Chel, 288, 386
Chagigah (see festival offering)
chiasm, 16, 18, 19, 237-240, 250, 278, 387
1 Chronicles 21:1, 99
2 Chronicles
  22:1-9, 172
  25:18, 3
  30:24-26, 311
  35:7-18, 311
  35:20-27, 150
chuppah (see marriage chamber)
Chysorrhoas River, 209, 225, 387, 393
clothing, 46, 141, 322, 391, 396, 397, 401, 403, 409, 412-416

commandment (*mitzvah*), 78, 174, 401
communal meals, 45, 105, 203, 204
concept of time, 325, 326
1 Corinthians 15:7, 168
Court of the Gentiles, 287, 288, 311, 388, 414
Court of Israel, 289, 323, 387, 404
Court of Priests, 289, 290, 322, 323, 345, 384, 387
Court of Women, 288, 289, 323, 324, 388, 414
cutting-off ceremony (*qesasah*), 245, 246, 408

Damia (*A'dam*), 51, 187, 252, 388
Dan, 155, 156, 388, 396
Dan Spring, 155, 413
Daniel 12:2, 320
Darnel, 122, 388
David's Highway, 25, 149, 186, 190, 194
Day of Atonement (*Yom Kippur*), 36, 47, 72, 86, 209, 279, 290, 395
debtors, 12, 107-109, 256, 417
Decapolis, 129, 152, 156, 157, 187, 190, 206, 389, 391, 393
denarius, 12, 89, 247, 293, 389
Deuteronomy
  6:5, 321
  12:18, 107
  14:9, 82
  14:22-27, 84

Deuteronomy (con't)
  16:13-17, 171
  21:17, 241
  21:18-21, 249
  21:23, 103
  22:12, 46
  22:17, 330
  24:14-15, 107, 294
  26:5-11, 171
  32:4, 294
  33:17, 177, 270
  34:10, 230
Docetism, 147, 389
double burial (*ossilegium*) 103

earthquakes, 45, 110, 142, 209, 226, 308
Ecclesiastes 11:4, 115
eder-machaneh (see sheep-camp)
Ein Gedi, 54, 389
Ein Karem, 24, 389
Elders, 271, 297, 298, 309, 390, 394
En-gannim. 65, 172, 390
Encounter with the Woman in Tyre, 13-15, 152, 156
Encounter with Zacchaeus, 253-255
Ephraim, 62, 64, 65, 177, 269, 270, 272, 273, 277, 390, 402, 409
erusin (see betrothal)
Epicureanism, 191, 193
Essenes, 391
Essene Quarter, 350, 386, 391
Exaggeration, 22, 116, 219, 223, 238, 311, 335

Exodus
  13:17, 195
  21:1-6, 108, 417
  21:6, 107
  32:2-10, 204
expired or died (*va'yigvah*), 102
Ezekiel
  14:2-9, 3
  17:3-10, 3
  17:7, 305
  24:3-5, 3
  26:5, 82
  26:14, 82
  47:10, 82
Ezra, 62, 173, 175, 290, 354, 409, 418
ezrat nashim (see women's court)

fellowship dinners, 73, 74, 171, 172, 222, 223, 314
festival offering (*chagigah*), 322, 323, 386
First Sending, 8, 9

Gabbatha, 283, 391
Gadara in Decapolis, 190, 391
Gadara in Perea, 190, 191, 194, 266, 391
Galatians 3:28, 348
Galileearea, 162, 391
Gamala, 157, 158, 392
Garden of Gethsemane, 284, 392
Garis, 24, 48, 105, 110, 160, 392
garum, 59, 88, 125, 392, 399
Gehenna (see Hinnom Valley)

Genesis
- 2:7, 102
- 3:1, 337
- 3:1-13, 362
- 3:3, 337
- 4:23-24, 165
- 11:31, 405
- 12:1-8, 85
- 12:6-8, 64
- 12:7, 107
- 12:8, 177
- 12:8-9, 64
- 14:14, 155
- 18:6, 220, 390
- 22:2, 283
- 22:14, 283
- Ch. 24, 56
- 24:65, 47
- 27:1-40, 241
- 28:10-22, 63
- 29:29, 242
- 31:21, 225
- 31:38-41, 242
- 32:1-5, 242
- 32:2, 226
- 32:9-12, 242
- 32:22-32, 51
- 32:23, 232
- 32:24-32, 232
- 32:31, 232
- 33:1, 228
- 33:1-15, 242
- 33:16-20, 242
- 33:18, 64
- 34:1-31, 64
- 35:19-20, 104
- 38:15, 47
- 49:33, 103
- 50:7, 103

Gennath Gate, 178, 283, 392
Gennesaret, 23, 85, 93, 143, 144, 392, 401
Gerasa, 209, 217, 221, 225, 266, 387, 393
Gergesa, 129, 130, 134, 152, 158, 393
Gibeah, 177, 178, 228, 393
Gihon Spring, 282, 393, 418
Golan Heights, 129, 143, 157, 392, 418, 419
Gol'gotha, 179, 283, 392, 393
Gordon's Calvary, 284, 286
grace, 65, 120, 212-217, 265, 266, 313, 338, 339, 346
grave marker (*matzevah*) 104
Great Eschatological Feast, 94, 95, 199, 394
Great Sanhedrin, 61, 63, 100, 174, 266, 269, 271, 287, 297, 319, 383, 394, 409
Groom's Promise (*Tenaim*), 57

Habakkuk 1:14-15, 82
Hades (see Sheol)
Hallel, 323, 394
Hanukkah, 36, 42, 52, 102, 181, 184
Haran, 56, 242, 405
heretics *(minim), 358*
Herod (the Great), 21, 28, 34, 35, 43, 141, 149, 178, 189, 253, 283, 284, 285, 299, 341, 385, 407
Herod Agrippa I, 187
Herod Agrippa II, 318

Herod Antipas, 28, 59, 79, 110, 139, 141, 165, 187, 392, 410, 415
Herod Archelaus, 141, 283, 341-343
(Herod) Philip, 59, 141
he'tot (see ritual purity ceremony)
Hinnom Valley (*Gehenna*), 283, 285, 394
hirelings, 89, 158, 247, 293, 395
hittah (see wheat)
Holy of Holies, 72, 290, 395
Holy Place, 180, 290, 387, 395
honor challenge, 13-15, 17, 19, 61, 74, 111, 164, 202, 210, 212, 235, 236, 297, 315, 318, 319, 321

Hosea
  6:6, 77
  10:1, 305
  10:15, 64
hospitality, 48, 63, 108, 109, 130, 158, 171, 172, 220, 223, 224, 232, 235, 252, 255, 296, 311
Hulda Gates, 288, 290, 395

imagination, 5, 136, 251, 351, 352
Infancy Narratives
indentured servants, 32, 74, 107, 339
inheritance, 108, 192, 228, 241, 245, 246, 249, 307
Isaiah
  5:1-2, 305
  5:1-6, 3

Isaiah (con't)
  5:8, 131
  6:9-10, 117
  25:6-9, 94, 394
  27:2, 305
  28:24, 87
  28:24-28, 3
  30:29, 97
  32:20, 87
  42:6, 6, 180
  49:6, 21
  61:8, 294
  61:10, 247

Jabbok River, 27, 51, 187, 188, 195, 196, 201, 207, 208, 225, 232, 266, 380, 387, 395, 399, 405
Jeremiah
  5:17, 211,
  10:10, 174
  12:10, 305
  15:16, 16, 352
  17:13, 13, 179
  29:10-12 185
  31:14 104
Jericho, 25, 26, 51, 52, 86, 186-189, 194, 252, 253, 255, 266, 281, 320, 380, 382, 388, 395
Jewish burial practices, 102, 104
Jewish wedding customs, 56-58, 311, 315
Jezreel Valley (Plain of Esdraelon), 45, 48, 66, 86, 105, 110, 150, 161, 392, 396, 397, 403
Job
  1:6, 99

Job (con't)
1:10,	176
34:12,	294

John
1:6-8,	189
1:15,27,29,34,	189
1:28,	52, 55
1:29-33,	52
1:35-51,	55
1:43,	55
1:44,	55
1:46,	44
2:3,	58
2:12,	59
2:13,	35, 36, 61
2:14,	61, 288
2:20,	35, 37
3:1-2,	61
3:1-21,	298
3:15,	224
3:15-16,	333, 350
3:22,	61
4:3-4,	62
4:5,	64, 65
4:39,	65
4:43,	65
4:45,	66
4:46,	66
5:1,	100
5:2,	100
5:5,	101
5:16-18,	101
5:28-29,	265
6:1,	143
6:1-15,	143
6:4,	36, 143, 148
6:10,	143
6:15,	144
6:16-21,	144
6:17,	144
6:22-24,	145

John (con't)
6:22-66,	146
6:35,	145
6:38-40,	147
6:44,	313
6:52,54,60,	145
6:53,	147
6:66,	146
6:67,	146
6:68,	146
6:69,	146
7:1,	168, 184
7:3,	168
7:5,	92, 168
7:10,	168
7:30,	179
8:1,	179
8:6,	179
8:11,	180
8:12,	181
8:51,	265
9:1-41,	181
9:5,	180
9:39,	181
10:22,	42, 184
10:23,	288, 299
10:40,	186
11:3,	264
11:6,	264
11:17,	264
11:24,	264
11:25-26,	264
11:45-57,	181
11:46-48,	266
11:53,	266
11:54,	269
11:55,	35
12:1,	37, 270, 277
12:4-8,	277
12:9-10,	277
12:20,	290

John (con't)
  12:21, 143
  12:23-24, 291
  13:1, 351
  14:2-3, 57
  14:6, 58, 172
  14:22, 90
  18:28, 323
  19:13, 283
  19:16, 283
  19:17, 283
  21:1, 81
  21:7, 83
John the Baptist, 35, 37, 47, 52, 61, 74, 77, 78, 139, 165, 186, 189, 382, 389, 398, 417
Jonah 1:3, 149
Joppa (*Jappa*), 149, 396, 419
Joshua
  3:1-17, 51
  3:4-5, 85
  13:27, 81
  19:35, 110
  24:32, 64
Judean Wilderness, 53, 54, 389, 396
Judges
  8:17, 233
  9:7-15, 3
  14:14, 18, 3
  20:27, 63
Justification, 264, 265
juxtaposition (*semukha*), 295, 336, 362, 410

keriah (see tearing one's garment)
Kidron Valley, 283, 287, 290, 349, 350, 393, 394, 397, 418

1 Kings
  4:25, 211
  8:65, 311
  10:5, 287
  11:23, 103
  12:25, 64, 233
  17:7-16, 152
  18:16-45, 149
  19:19, 57
  20:35-43, 3
2 Kings
  4:8-37, 105, 149, 412
  9:22-28, 172
  14:9, 3
  15:29-30, 140
  16:7-9, 140
King's Highway, 23, 186, 188, 194, 195, 397
Kishon River, 65, 172, 397
kittel (see wedding garment),
kohanim (see priests)

Ladder of Tyre, 150, 398
Lake of Gennesaret, 80, 410
Lake Hula, 49, 398
land ownership, 131, 132
lawyers (*soferim*), 72, 173, 174, 413
leaven (*se'or*), 220, 221, 345, 410
Leonites River, 152, 153, 398, 419
Leviticus
  Chs. 11-15, 70
  11:19, 82
  19:9, 87
  19:18, 321
  23:5, 345
  23:27-28, 72
  23:40, 282

Leviticus (con't)
  24:10, 43
  24:10-23, 73
  25:23, 131
  25:29, 279
  25:35, 107
  25:43, 204
  27:30, 279
Light of the World, 127, 178-181, 290, 395
Luke, 32
Luke
  1:28, 213
  2:1-5, 35, 43
  2:4, 42
  2:22-38, 19
  2:22-40, 289
  2:46, 288
  2:52, 136
  3:1, 37
  3:19-20, 80
  3:21-23, 52
  3:23, 35, 42
  4:1, 53
  4:1-2, 53
  4:14, 66, 137
  4:16, 67, 138
  4:28-30, 67
  4:31, 68
  4:33, 70
  4:38-41, 70
  5:1, 70, 81
  5:2, 83
  5:12, 70
  5:18, 72
  5:21, 72
  5:23-25, 73
  5:27, 73
  5:29-39, 76
  6:1-2, 84
  6:3, 43

Luke (con't)
  6:6-11, 90
  6:12-16, 90
  6:20, 93
  6:46-49, 96
  7:1-10, 99
  7:11-17, 105
  7:28, 140
  7:36-50, 106
  7:49, 109
  7:50, 110
  8:1-3, 110
  8:2, 158
  8:4-15, 114
  8:16-17, 127
  8:19-21, 91
  8:22-23, 129
  8:22-25, 144
  8:26, 129
  8:26-39, 129
  8:30, 136
  8:37, 129
  8:41-56, 136
  9:1-6, 8, 139
  9:9, 139
  9:10, 140
  9:12-17, 143
  9:18-21, 159
  9:22, 159, 271
  9:28, 160
  9:28-36, 161
  9:31, 206
  9:35, 161
  9:36, 161
  9:37, 162
  9:51, 206
  9:51-52, 168
  9:52, 177
  9:53, 171
  10:1, 170
  10:9, 170

Luke (con't)
10:23-24,	352
10:24,	127
10:25-37,	16, 173
10:38,	181
11:1-13,	182
11:9-13,	237
11:15,	99
12:13-22,	192
12:22,	198
12:35-41,	197
12:36,	199
12:42,	203
12:42-48,	201
13:1,	209
13:2-3,	210
13:6-9,	210
13:18-19,	218
13:20-21,	219
14:7-14,	221
14:11,	280
14:15-24,	314
14:25,	225
14:25-33,	226
15:1-7,	234
15:8-10,	239
15:11,	241
15:11-32,	243
16:1-8,	10, 256
16:19-31,	258
17:7-10,	267
17:11,	177
18:1,	273
18:1-7,	273
18:9-14,	277
18:14,	223
18:15,	191
18:16,	191
18:22,	255
18:28,	269
18:31-33,	178

Luke (con't)
18:34,	178, 228
18:35,	185
18:45,	253
19:1,	253
19:2-3,	254
19:4,	254
19:11-28,	339
19:29-30,	281
19:41-42,	282
19:44,	282
19:45-46,	288, 291
19:46,	279
20:1,	288, 296, 298
20:7,	297
20:8,	297
20:9-19,	304
20:16,	308
20:19,	309
20:19-26,	318
20:27-40,	319
20:28,	319
20:33,	319
20:39-40,	320
20:41-44,	322
21:1,	324
21:1-2,	324
21:27,	326
21:29-32,	327
21:37.	179
22:8-12,	345
22:9,	345
22:14,	351
22:48-49,	272
23:23-24,	283
23:33,	282
23:48,	280

ma'aser sheni (see second tithe)
Machaerus, 139, 398

Magdala, 23, 45, 48, 59, 70,
　81, 85, 125, 126, 128,
　129, 135, 158-160, 166,
　217, 352, 386, 399
Mahanaim, 225, 226, 228,
　232, 266, 399
Maktesh (see Temple
　bazaars)
Malachi 3:1,　21
marriage chamber
　(*chuppah*), 57, 332,
　387
Mark, 30
Mark
　1:9,　　　　47
　1:9-11,　　 52
　1:12,　　　 53
　1:14,　　　 66, 137
　1:15,　　　 95, 293, 313
　1:16,　　　 70
　1:21,　　　 68
　1:23,　　　 70
　1:29-31,　　70
　1:39,　　　 70
　1:40,　　　 70
　2:3-7,　　　72
　2:9-12,　　 73
　2:14,　　　 59, 73
　2:15-22,　　76
　2:23-24,　　84
　3:1-6,　　　90
　3:7,　　　　90
　3:13-19,　　90
　3:21,　　　 91
　3:22,　　　 99
　4:1-20,　　 113
　4:21-23,　　127
　4:26-29,　　128
　4:30-32,　　218
　4:34,　　　 40

Mark (con't)
　4:35,　　　 129
　4:36,　　　 129
　4:37,　　　 129
　5:1-20,　　 129
　5:9,　　　　136
　5:21,　　　 135
　5:22-43,　　136
　6:1-6,　　　68, 137
　6:3,　　　　138, 168
　6:7-13,　　 8, 139
　6:13,　　　 139
　6:14-27,　　139
　6:17-19,　　79
　6:30,　　　 140
　6:32,　　　 140, 143
　6:34-44,　　143
　6:39,　　　 143
　6:45,　　　 144
　6:45-51,　　144
　6:46,　　　 144
　6:53-56,　　144
　7:24,　　　 148
　7:24-30,　　15
　7:31,　　　 152, 156
　7:32,　　　 157
　7:34,　　　 157
　8:1-10,　　 157
　8:10,　　　 158
　8:11-21,　　159
　8:22,　　　 159
　8:23, 26,　 141
　8:27-30,　　159
　8:33,　　　 160
　9:2,　　　　160
　9:2-10,　　 161
　9:9,　　　　161
　9:14,　　　 162
　9:31,　　　 162
　9:31-33,　　162
　9:33-37,　　229

Mark (con't)
10:1,	168, 186
10:13,	191
10:14,	191
10:21,	255
10:28,	269
10:31,	269
10:33-34,	178
10:46,	253
11:1,	281
11:11,	90. 291
11:12-14.	291
11:15-17,	288, 291
11:27,	288, 296, 298
11:33,	297
12:1-12,	303
12:2,	309
12:13-17,	318
12:18-27,	319
12:24,	320
12:28,	320
12:30-31,	321
12:32-33,	321
12:35,	322
12:41,	324
12:41-44,	288
12:42,	324
13:2,	325
13:26,	326
13:28,	211
13:28-30,	327
13:33-37,	198
13:34,	199
14:3-10,	181, 277
14:13,	345
14:17,	351
14:43-45,	272
15:14-15,	283
15:22,	283
16:9,	158

Mary, 7, 20, 21, 24, 33, 42, 43, 46, 47, 56, 58, 91, 92, 137, 138, 168, 212, 253, 272, 288, 289, 291
mashal (see wisdom saying)
matan (see bride gifts)
Matthew, 31
Matthew
1:3,	270
1:16,	42
1:19,	43
1:20,	42
2:1,	34
2:1-12,	34
2:16-18,	34
2:23,	137
3:2,	95, 293, 313
3:13,	47
3:13-17,	52
4:1,	53
4:12,	66, 137
4:13,	68
4:15,	56, 348
4:18,	70
4:19,	100
4:23,	70
5:1,	93
5:8,	254
5:14,	181
5:14-16,	126
5:27-28,	295
5:29-30,	22
7:21,	265
7:24-29,	96
7:29,	98
8:2,	70
8:5-13,	99
8:12,	205
8:14-15,	70
8:18,	129
8:24,	129

Matthew (con't)
- 8:28, 129
- 8:28-34, 129
- 8:34, 129
- 9:1, 135
- 9:2-3, 72
- 9:5-7, 73
- 9:9, 73
- 9:10-17, 75
- 9:18-26, 136
- 9:23, 103
- 10:1-4, 90
- 10:5-15, 139
- 11:11, 140
- 12:1-2, 84
- 12:9-14, 90
- 12:10, 90
- 12:14, 90
- 12:24, 99
- 13:1-23, 111
- 13:7, 129
- 13:9, 2
- 13:10, 4
- 13:31-32, 217
- 13:33, 219
- 13:34, 40
- 13:41-42, 205
- 13:44-46, 132
- 13:46, 132
- 13:47-48, 82
- 13:47-50, 133
- 13:51-52, 134
- 13:54-58, 68, 137
- 13:55, 168
- 13:56-57, 138
- 14:1-12, 79, 139
- 14:13, 140
- 14:15-21, 143
- 14:22-23, 144
- 14:34-36, 144
- 15:2, 176

Matthew (con't)
- 15:9, 176
- 15:21, 148
- 15:21-28, 13
- 15:22, 151
- 15:32-39, 157
- 15:39, 158
- 16:1-4, 159
- 16:13-16, 291
- 16:13-20, 159
- 16:21, 159
- 16:23, 160
- 16:24-28, 160
- 16:27, 265
- 17:1, 160
- 17:1-9, 161
- 17:14, 162
- 17:22-23, 162
- 17:23-26, 162
- 17:27, 163
- 18:1-5, 229
- 18:12-14, 235
- 18:21-35, 163
- 18:22, 164
- 19:1, 168, 186
- 19:2, 191
- 19:13, 191
- 19:14, 191
- 19:17, 265
- 19:21, 255
- 19:27, 269
- 19:30, 269
- 20:1-16, 292
- 20:16, 296
- 20:17-19, 178
- 20:29-30, 253
- 21:1, 281
- 21:12-13, 288, 291
- 21:17, 90
- 21:18-20, 291
- 21:23, 288, 296, 298

Matthew (con't)
21:24-25, 297
21:27, 297
21:28-32, 299
21:33-46, 302
21:44, 308
21:45, 309
21:45-46, 308
22:1-14, 310
22:15-22, 318
22:23-33, 319
22:24, 319
22:29, 319, 320
22:34, 320
22:37-39, 321
22:42-43, 322
23:5, 322
23:12, 223, 280
24:2, 325
24:30, 326
24:32, 211
24:32-34, 327
24:45, 203
24:45-51, 202
25:1-13, 331
25:14-30, 205, 333
25:31-46, 347
26:6-13, 277
26:18, 345
26:20, 351
26:47-50, 272
27:23-24, 283
27:33, 283
28:20, 139
matzevah (see grave marker),
Megiddo, 149, 150, 165, 400
menorah, 180
mensarii (see bankers0
metaphor, 4, 116, 117, 305, 338, 400

metanoia, 5
Middle Eastern storytelling, 1, 5-7, 9, 10, 16, 21, 39, 205, 253, 254, 295
midrash, 94, 236, 400
mikvot (see ritual baths)
minim (see heretics)
Mishnah, 94, 95, 174, 261, 279, 346, 401
mitzvah (see commandment)
mohar (see bride price)
Mount Carmel, 149, 194, 397, 400, 401
Mount Eremos, 93, 401
Mount Gerizim, 62, 401
Mount Hazor, 177, 270, 402
Mount Hermon, 155, 156, 195, 385, 387, 402, 408, 418, 419
Mount Lebanon, 153, 155, 156, 398, 402, 413
Mount Moriah, 282-285, 287, 393, 397, 402, 404, 416
Mount Olivet ("mount of olives"), 30, 38, 63, 89, 179, 181, 198, 267, 282-285, 287, 290-292, 324, 344, 346, 349, 382, 383, 392, 393, 397, 402, 418
Mount Tabor, 102, 161, 172, 206, 391, 403, 412
Mount Zion, 282, 283, 287, 394, 403, 409, 416
mustard (*chardal*), 218, 386

Nahum 2:2, 305
Nain, 102, 104, 105, 403

Nazareth, 7, 10, 24, 28, 35, 42-45, 47, 48, 56, 59, 60, 67, 68, 91, 92, 137, 139, 142, 171, 403, 410
Nehemiah 8:1-12, 290
nephesh (see breath of life)
Nicanor Gate, 289, 323, 357, 404
Nicodemus, 61, 298
nisuin (see wedding feast)
Numbers
   5:5-8, 205
   9:8, 230
   15:38-39, 46
   18:27, 279
   Ch. 19, 70
   20:17, 188
   21:22, 188
   22:2, 99
   23:24, 3
   Ch. 32, 187
   34:11, 81
   39:7, 279
Numerology, 12, 18, 101, 116, 164, 211, 262, 293, 316, 332, 335, 341, 357, 364

Ophel, 285, 404
Ordo, 205, 404
ossilegium (see double burial)
ovna (see birthing stone)

Padan-aram, 225, 242, 405
parable (definition), 2
Parable of the
   Attitude of a Servant, 267, 296
   Barren Fig Tree, 210, 339
   Being Like a Child, 229

Parable of the (con't)
   Costs of Discipleship, 226
   Feast, 278, 309, 348
   Fig Tree, 326, 327
   Final Judgment, 347
   Fishing Net, 130, 133, 312
   Friend in Need, 182
   Good Samaritan, 3, 16, 18, 65, 172, 173, 189, 237, 300, 301, 380
   Growing Seed, 128
   Head of Household, 130, 134
   Invitations, 221
   Joy of Finding, 130-132, 166
   Lamp, 126
   Lender, 74, 105, 106
   Lost Coin, 239, 240
   Lost Sheep, 234, 237, 239
   Mustard Seed, 217
   New vs. the Old, 74, 78
   Persistent Widow, 273
   Pharisee and Tax Collector, 277
   Prodigal Son, 241-243, 250, 251, 281, 305, 317
   Prudent and Wicked Servants, 196, 201, 348
   Rich Fool, 191, 192
   Rich Man and Lazarus, 257, 258, 320
   Shrewd Steward, 10, 255, 256, 301
   Sower, 4, 111, 116, 118, 123, 124
   Talents, 333, 339

Parable of the (con't)
  Ten Virgins, 329, 331
  Two Foundations, 95
  Two Sons, 298, 299
  Unforgiving Servant, 163
  Vigilant Servants, 196, 197, 201
  Weeds and the Wheat, 111, 121, 348
  Wicked Tenants, 302
  Workers, 292, 336
  Yeast, 219
Pass of Beth-Horon, 149
Pella, 50, 51, 405
Pentecost (*Shavuoth*), 4, 36, 47, 86, 87, 93, 129, 153, 287, 411
Penuel, 51, 64, 226, 232-234, 241, 242, 252, 281, 305, 405, 411
people of the book (*am ha'sefer*), 138, 213, 236, 381
people of the land (*am ha'aretz*), 236, 279, 381
Perea, 23, 28, 51, 141, 168-170, 186-188, 190, 207, 225, 266, 387, 388, 391, 393, 395, 397, 405, 408
1 Peter 2:23,   238
2 Peter
  1:4,   14, 324
  3:8-9,   326

Pharisees, 74-77, 79, 84, 85, 90, 99, 100, 158, 166, 179, 181, 223, 234-236, 238, 239, 249-251, 257, 259-263, 266, 272, 278-281, 308, 309, 318-320, 322, 381, 406, 409
Philadelphia in Perea (see *Rabbah*)
phylacteries (*tefillin*), 46, 322, 414
pietas, 91, 92, 194, 227, 246, 406
Pool of Siloam, 283, 350, 393, 418
Pools of Solomon, 283, 407
Pontius Pilate, 149, 209, 283, 323, 385, 407
port duties (*portoria*), 27, 407
Praetorium, 283, 391, 403, 407
prayer (*avodah*), 43, 77, 90, 144, 182, 183, 184, 185, 191, 213, 223, 237, 273-280, 322, 323, 345, 346, 350, 382, 394, 414
prayer shawl (*tallit*), 46, 291, 413
Present Age, 94, 133
Presentation, 19, 289
priests (*kohanim*), 3, 4, 18, 87, 131, 162, 173, 174, 178, 180, 266, 271, 277, 285, 290, 297, 298, 303, 305, 308, 309, 322, 323, 337, 346, 384, 391, 394, 395, 397, 404

proof cloth (*betulim*), 57, 330, 331, 332, 384
Ptolemais, 59, 150, 152, 392, 407
Psalm
  9:7, 294
  18:2. 97
  80:9,14,15, 305
  99:12, 294
  109:6, 99
  118:22-23, 307
  128:1, 21
publicanus (see tax collector)
Purim, 36, 73
pushback, 13, 14, 17, 19, 74, 77, 78, 80, 117, 202, 210, 235, 238, 250, 300, 302, 315, 318

qesasah (see cutting-off ceremony)
Quelle, 29, 75, 408

Rabbah (Philadelphia in Perea), 186, 188, 190, 194, 195, 196, 201, 207, 208, 380, 384, 408
Revelation
  12:7-12, 272
  12:10, 99
Rift Valley trench, 26, 49, 50, 51, 81, 86, 155, 156, 252, 388, 402, 408, 410
righteousness (*tsedaqah*), 5, 265, 277, 278, 293, 299, 302, 416
ritual baths (*mikvot*), 57, 285, 401
ritual purity, 17, 50, 70, 102, 104, 173, 174, 175, 176, 263, 401

ritual purity ceremony (*he'tot*), 104, 175
Roman Reign of Terror, 118, 296, 409
Roman Tax System, 27, 28, 59, 131, 392, 407
Romans
  9:4-5, 221
  10:12, 348
Royal Bridge, 287, 409

Sabbatical Year, 108
Sadducees, 61, 159, 166, 261, 263, 319, 320, 357, 394, 406, 409
Samaritans, 62, 63, 172, 262, 397, 401, 409
1 Samuel
  8:31, 177, 393
  11:1-12:31, 194
  23:29, 54
  24:1-2, 54
  30:12, 208
  31:10 49
  31:13, 226
2 Samuel
  6:19, 311
  12:1-5, 3
  14:5-20, 3
  13:14, 270
  13:21, 270
  13:23, 270
  13:28-29, 271
  18:9, 209
  19:1-9, 203
  21:14, 226
  22:3, 97
Sapporis, 28, 43, 47, 111, 138, 410
Sea of Galilee, 23, 25-27
Sea of Tiberias, 81, 410

second tithe (*ma'aser sheni*), 84, 87, 398
se'or (see leaven)
Septuagint, 355, 356
seven-stanza ballad, 278, 315, 411
Shalosh Regalim, 36, 411
Shavuoth (see Pentecost)
Shechem, 64, 242, 401, 411
sheep-camp (*eder-machaneh*), 270, 389
Sheluchim, 224, 230, 279, 411
Sheol (Hades), 257, 258, 260, 261, 412
Showbread, 180, 290, 395
Shunem, 102, 104, 105, 149, 412
Sidon, 13, 152, 412, 419
Sirach
  19:30, 247
  35:13-22, 275
  35:20, 276
Snir Stream, 155, 413
Song of the Vineyard, 305, 306
Sukkot, 36, 100, 173, 179, 411

tallit (see prayer shawl)
Talmud, 94, 363, 413
tearing one's garment (*keriah*), 103
Tefilat HaDerekh (see traveler's prayer)
tefillin (see phylacteries)
tassels (*tzizit*), 46, 322, 416
tax collector, 27, 28, 31, 162, 164, 166, 234, 253-255
Tel Aviv, 149, 396, 419
tekton, 28, 43, 414

Temple Bazaars (*Maktesh*), 287, 399,
Temple Porch, 286-288, 299, 311, 409, 414
Temple Treasury, 288, 324, 364, 414
Tenaim (see Groom's Promise)
threshing barn, 88, 89, 131, 274, 415, 418
Tiberias, 47, 90, 110, 111, 116, 121, 125, 128, 217, 415
1 Timothy 4:13, 99
2 Timothy 4:11, 32
trade routes, 22, 25, 86, 87
traveler's prayer (*Tefilat HaDerekh*), 47, 291, 413
tsedaqah (see righteousness)
Tyre, 13, 15, 148-152, 156, 398, 416, 419
Tyropoeon Valley, 283, 284, 297, 409, 416

Valley of Ajalon, 149
Valley of Jethro *(Biq'ah Yitro)*, 190, 384, 391

va'yigvah (see expired or died)
Via Maris, 23-25, 44, 48, 55, 56, 59, 392, 417
virgin (*betulah*), 57, 329-333, 381, 383, 384
Visitation, 389
Vulgate, 356, 417

Wadi Gharrar, 52, 61, 417
Wadi Qelt, 52, 189, 417

Wadi Ruqqad, 156, 157, 418
Water Gate, 287, 290, 350, 402, 418
wedding feast (*nisuin*), 57, 58, 199, 311, 312, 404
wedding garment (*kittel*), 58, 312, 313, 397
wheat (*hittah*), 12, 393
winnowing fan, 88, 418
Wisdom 3:1-3, 261
wisdom saying (*mashal*), 2, 399
woman caught in adultery, 358
women disciples, 110, 125, 158, 191, 231
women's court (*ezrat nashim*), 138, 391

Xystus Square, 287, 290, 350, 399, 418

Yarkon River, 149, 419
Yarmouk River, 26, 187, 405, 418, 419
yeast, 219, 220, 410
Yom Kippur (see Day of Atonement)

Zarephath, 152, 153, 419
Zechariah
   3:1-2, 99
   9:9. 281
   12:12-14, 138, 391

Walking the Parables of Jesus

Israel in the Time of Jesus

satellite photo from: NASA, *Visible Earth-Middle East*, 2001.
names and locations from: Israel Antiquities Authority, 2004.

Dcn Bob Evans
9/13/16

Walking the Parables of Jesus

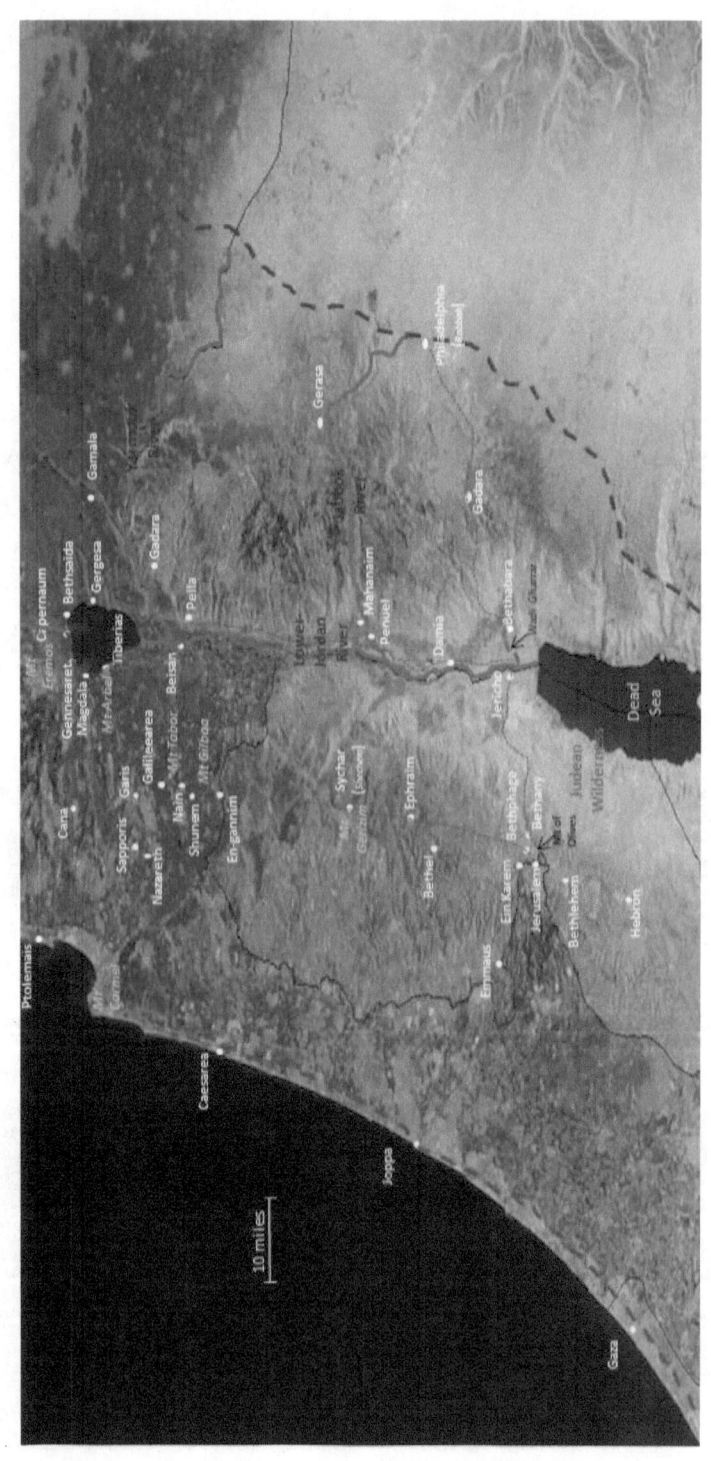

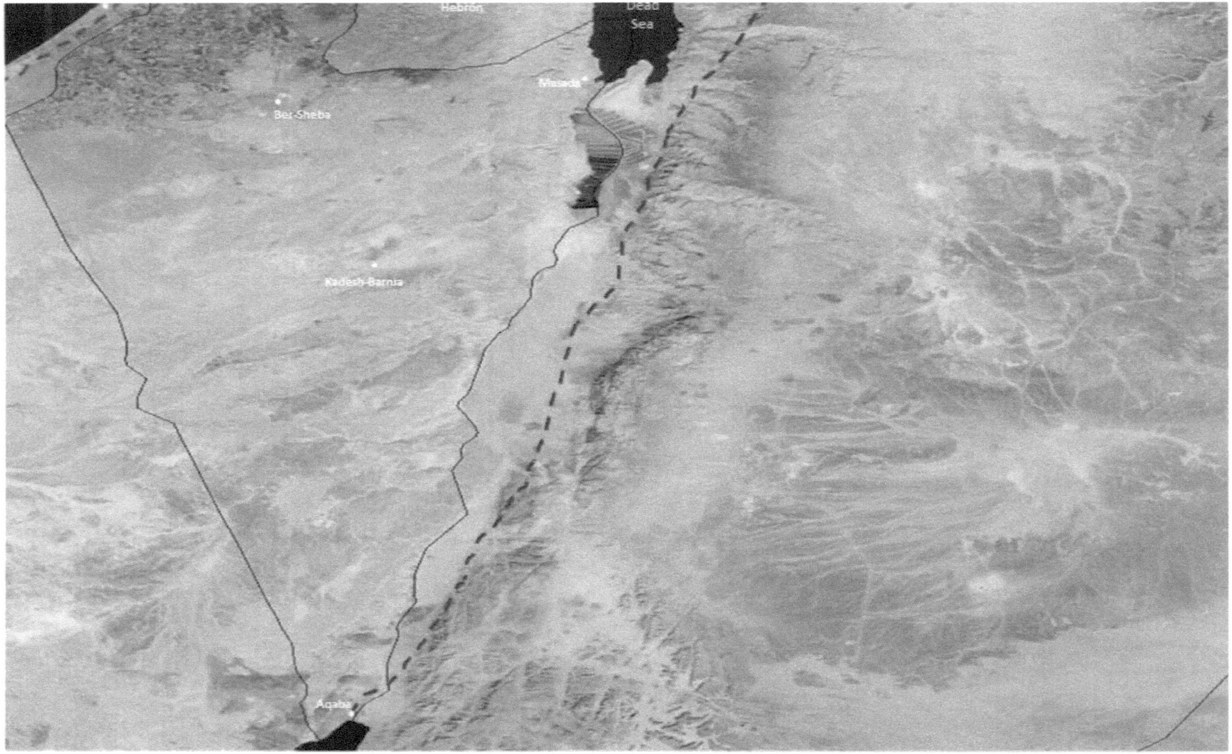

Israel in the Time of Jesus

satellite photo from: NASA, *Visible Earth-Middle East*, 2001.
names and locations from: Israel Antiquities Authority, 2004.

Dcn Bob Evans
9/13/16

www.ingramcontent.com/pod-product-compliance
Lightning Source LLC
Chambersburg PA
CBHW021148230426
43667CB00006B/298